THE MIRACULOUS FLYING HOUSE OF LORETO

The Miraculous Flying House of Loreto

SPREADING CATHOLICISM IN THE EARLY MODERN WORLD

Karin Vélez

PRINCETON UNIVERSITY PRESS
PRINCETON & OXFORD

Published by Princeton University Press
41 William Street, Princeton, New Jersey 08540
6 Oxford Street, Woodstock, Oxfordshire OX20 1TR

press.princeton.edu

LCCN 2018940059
ISBN 9780691174006

British Library Cataloging-in-Publication Data is available

Editorial: Fred Appel and Thalia Leaf
Production Editorial: Debbie Tegarden
Jacket/Cover Design: Amanda Weiss
Jacket Credit: Engraving of the flying house of Loreto, from Bartoli, *Historische Beschreibung des Heil. Hauses zu Loreto*, 1725. Courtesy of SLUB Dresden / Digital Collections / 3.A. 6718
Production: Jacquie Poirier
Publicity: Tayler Lord
Copyeditor: Kathleen Kageff

This book has been composed in Miller

Printed on acid-free paper. ∞

Printed in the United States of America

10 9 8 7 6 5 4 3 2 1

CONTENTS

LIST OF ILLUSTRATIONS & TABLES

Illustrations

Table

ACKNOWLEDGMENTS

THERE IS A DANGER for writers overly immersed in decades-long endeavors to see their topics writ large in all current events. In autumn 2017, as I was finishing this manuscript, Hurricane Maria blasted through the Atlantic causing much death and destruction. Responding to the disaster in his family's home island of Puerto Rico, popular composer Lin-Manuel Miranda released a fundraising song he called "Almost Like Praying." His chart-topping hit is based on "Maria," a number from the 1957 Broadway musical *West Side Story*. I was drawn to Miranda's "Maria" remake because it reminded me of my own drawn-out encounter with the star of this book, Mary of Loreto.

On the surface, Miranda's new lyrics have little to do with Maria/Mary: he makes a love song out of the names of all seventy-eight towns in Puerto Rico. But the effect is more than simply gathering the many villages that contributed to his formation. Chanted together, the words assume the power of a living prayer: the names are intoned variously in appreciation, entreaty, and even awe. The names in the following acknowledgments have likewise functioned "Almost Like Praying" for me. As was the case for Miranda, Mary is what indirectly precipitated the occasion to summon and to publicly recognize these particular people and places. I group their names below to loosely parallel the roles featured in my book chapters, to honor the diverse ways in which they have contributed to this work whose completion is its own small miracle.

The "First Authors" of this project are my teachers, founts of wisdom but also models of the kind of scholar I hope to become. Though some of them are not listed in the copious notes of this book, their questions and approaches have been foundational to my thinking. Most recently these mentors have included Jeanne Kilde, Jaine Strauss, and Jim Laine. In graduate school, where this took its first shape as a doctoral dissertation, I was fortunate to benefit from the sharp insights of Anthony Grafton, Kenneth Mills, William Chester Jordan, and Robert Darnton. William B. Taylor and Simon Ditchfield have also been kind and interested readers providing inspiration from graduate school forward. Before that, in the murky prehistory of my intellectual formation, Shanti Singham and Harry Payne planted seeds of French rebellion that have found their way from their undergraduate classrooms onto these pages. Still earlier, I was boosted on the shoulders of my grandparents who posthumously remain giants in my life. Henry Agostini, Ana Lydia Espada, Reverend Samuel José Vélez, and Gladys Vega encouraged all my writing and schooling endeavors. Their brave choices, fighting spirits, steadfast faith, and ambition also inspired their shy, overly curious granddaughter to dream big.

I have been fortunate to share the road with "Accidental Pilgrims" who have accompanied me through rough stages of the journey, offering encouragement and purpose in distant places and often continuing to provide this support when our paths diverged. This project would not exist in its current form had I not crossed paths with Shen Liu, Susan Hoang, Sang Mi Pak, Christina Esposito, Alicia Muñoz, Sushmita Hodges, Andrea Moerer, Aaron Bohr, S. J., and Lynn Hudson in Minnesota; Kimberly Juanita Brown and Ethan Hawkley in Boston; Danielle Kane and Christine Beaule in North Carolina; Katrina Olds, Caroline Sherman, Elizabeth Foster, and Sindhu Revuluri in New Jersey; Tami Miyashiro Visco, Heidi Natkin, Tanya Landsman, and Tara Sánchez in Williamstown; and Meena Kaur in New Hampshire and Tanzania.

Many "Holy House Builders" have aided this endeavor by sharing templates, suggesting structural modifications, providing space and time for layout, and constructing alongside me. I have run across them in groups first: at Macalester College, the Department of Religious Studies, the Humanities Faculty Colloquium, and several cohorts of intrepid senior undergraduate history majors; at the University of Minnesota, the University Honors Program 2016–17, the Institute for Advanced Study 2014–15 Fellows, the Atlantic History Working Group, the Missionaries and the Early Modern World workshop, the Center for Early Modern History, the Resilience and Sustainability Interdisciplinary Faculty Seminar, the Mediterranean Collaborative, the Religious Studies Program 2012 summer workshop, and the Theorizing Early Modern Studies Reading Groups; in Boston, the Urban Cultural History Workshop at the University of Massachusetts and the Boston Area French History group; in Seattle in 2014, the International Symposium on Jesuits in World History; in Galway, Ireland, in 2013, the International Symposium on Missions and Frontiers; and in Liverpool in 2010, the Rethinking the Iberian Atlantic conference. In Minnesota, two individuals stood out from this crowd of architects as groups onto themselves: I owe special thanks to Rivi Handler-Spitz and Katharine Gerbner for their solidarity, tireless reading of drafts, and dependably excellent feedback.

There are a number of scholars who generously offered their thoughts on the manuscript and its earlier incarnations without expecting any sort of public credit for it. Some of their suggestions resulted in major alterations and upgrades. These "Anonymous Renovators of Icons" have included my dynamite editorial team of Fred Appel, Thalia Leaf, Debbie Tegarden, and Kathleen Kageff, plus Princeton University Press's two anonymous reviewers; Luke Clossey, Andrew Redden, and the bold thinkers of the Institut für die Späte Altzeit; J. Michelle Molina, at Northwestern's 2009 roundtable on Jesuit research and beyond; and the regulars of the Forum for European Expansion and Global Identities conferences, who twice gave platform and redirection to chapters in progress. I am also grateful for the input and positive energy generated around this undertaking by my local colleagues Kirsten Fischer, Beth Severy-Hoven, Linda Sturtz, Chris Wells, Jennifer Gunn, Howard Louthan, J. B. Shank, Giancarlo Casale, Victoria Morse, Jeanne Grant, and Susie Steinbach. Distance notwithstanding, during this project I have benefitted from the acumen and humor of Kittiya Lee, Karen Melvin, Molly Greene, Kristen Block, Jane Murphy, Elizabeth McCahill, Daniela Bleichmar, Emily Michelson, Karoline Cook, Alexandra and Noble David Cook, Tania Munz, Mitra Sharafi, Ishita Pande, Liliana Leopardi, Katherine Wheeler, Carla Keyvanian, Javier Vélez, and closer at hand, Herta Pitman. Additionally, conversations with these generous scholars provided turning points for this work: Natalie Davis, Allan Greer, Laura Smoller, Alexandra Walsham, Robert Kendrick, Bernard Bailyn, Patrick Geary, Liam Brockey, Brandon Bayne, Virginia Reinburg, Thomas Tweed, Thomas Taylor, Jorge Cañizares-Esguerra, and Diana Walsh Pasulka.

At key junctures in the past decade, several institutions and patrons made this research count by allotting me generous funding and provision of space, time, or resources. Much gratitude goes to these "Counters, Namers, and Processers," including: the Woodrow Wilson Foundation for a 2014 Career Enhancement Fellowship; the Institute for Advanced Study at the University of Minnesota; Macalester College; the Northeastern University History Department; the Duke University Writing Program; Williams College for a 2006 Gaius Charles Bolin Fellowship; the Charlotte W. Newcombe Foundation for a 2005 Doctoral Dissertation Fellowship; the University of Toronto Centre for Reformation and Renaissance Studies; the Visiting Scholar program at the American Academy in Rome; the Conference on Latin American History for a 2003 Scobie Award for Preliminary PhD Research; the Instituto dos Arquivos Nacionais/Torre do Tombo for their 2003 Luso-American Development Fellowship for US Researchers; and Princeton University's Committee for Canadian Studies, Council on Regional Studies, Committee for Italian Studies, Program for

Latin American Studies, Shelby Cullom Davis Center, and History Department. To this list of institutions, I add the archivists, curators, and administrators who took extra time and interest to provide their expert assistance: Isabelle Contant, director of the Jesuit archives in St. Jérome, Québec, in 2005; Thomas Reddy, S.J., and José António Yoldi, S.J., at the Jesuit archives in Rome in 2004; Floriano Grimaldi, O.F.M., director of the archives at Loreto; Mauricio Valcanover, O.F.M., at the Convento de San José in Tarata, Bolivia, in 2001; Louis Blair, emeritus executive secretary of the Harry S. Truman Foundation; and Molly Magavern, the Williams College coordinator of the Mellon-Mays Fellowship. Also in this category, I am honored to thank these self-appointed benefactors who have been stalwart supporters of the entire process: Gayle Martino; Rebecca Schorin; Lucyna Bojanowska; Wilfredo and Sylvia Vélez; Henry Agostini and Wanda Lis Sanz; Mary and David Dennison; Ophelia and Macit Cobanoglu; and most recently, Sharon and Steve Roth. To close this section with those who possess the grit and attention to detail that make processers the stuff of legend, in the eleventh hour of this project, Dorothy Hoffman, Jeremy Roth, Samuel and Myrna Vélez earned my gratitude and utmost respect with how they tackled the enormous index.

Last and most importantly, it is a joy to credit the core of people who took a direct hit from my "Category Five, Hurricane Maria" work style and who still believed I could wring some beautiful refrain out of the havoc. They also met my overdramatic analogies with patient smiles, especially my fear that I was morphing into the worst possible distortion of my research subject, becoming a terrifying, perennially globe-trotting banshee carried away by Jesuits. Thanks in large part to these final individuals whose names have been my chorus and mantra, this did not happen. Instead, they have brought out the best of this project in me. For this reason I dedicate this book to my parents, Myrna Agostini and Samuel Vélez, who raised me to fly; to my husband, Jeremy Roth, and my son, Cedar, who gave me wonderful reason to land; and to my siblings, Lisanne, Darik, and Kevin, who in their families and professional lives continue to prove to me every day how people can make miracles real.

ABBREVIATIONS

ARSI	*Archivum Romanum Societatis Iesu*, Rome, Italy
ASJCF	*Archivum Societatis Iesu—Province du Canada Français*, St. Jérome, Québec, Canada
B. ANG	*Biblioteca Angelica*, Rome, Italy
BAV	*Biblioteca Apostolica Vaticana*, Vatican City
BNF	*Bibliothèque Nationale de France*, Paris, France
LAC	Library and Archives Canada, Ottawa, Ontario, Canada

PART I

First Landings

CHAPTER ONE

Introduction

Mysterious Anchorages

On 2 December 1295, a small, well-traveled house fell from the sky into the middle of a road leading to the town of Recanati, in Italy's Marche region.[1] There it sat, on a forested hilltop within sight of the Adriatic Sea, on property owned by a Recanatese woman named Laureta. When locals saw it, they went inside. There they found a beautiful dark painting of the Virgin Mary that they admired without knowing its origins. Their ignorance ended only when Mary herself appeared to identify the structure. She came in a vision to the little chapel's most frequent visitor, an unnamed hermit. "Go tell this to the people of Recanati, whose country I chose from among all the nations to locate my seat, . . . that this place is Holy, and terrible," she began.[2] Mary explained that the humble mud-brick structure was her own house, where she had been immaculately conceived, received the angel Gabriel's Annunciation, and raised the Christ Child. After her death, the apostles had used it as a small church, placing inside it an image of her carved by St. Luke himself.

Mary also spoke of her house's astonishing journey (figure 1.1.a). Angels had carried it away from Nazareth in 1291 to keep it out of the hands of Muslim invaders. It had landed three times along the way before coming to a final stop. First, it crossed the Mediterranean and was deposited on a hilltop near the town of Trsat, in a region that was then referred to by various names—Dalmatia, Illyria, Slavonia—but which corresponds today to

1. The following account of Loreto's origins is adapted from Girolamo Angelitta, *L'historia della Traslatione della Santa Casa della Madonna a Loreto* (1580).

2. "Narra questo al popolo di Racanati, il cui paese fra tutte le nationi ho eletto, per locar vi la sede mia . . . che 'l luogo è Santo, e terribile." Angelitta, *L'historia*, pp. 43–44.

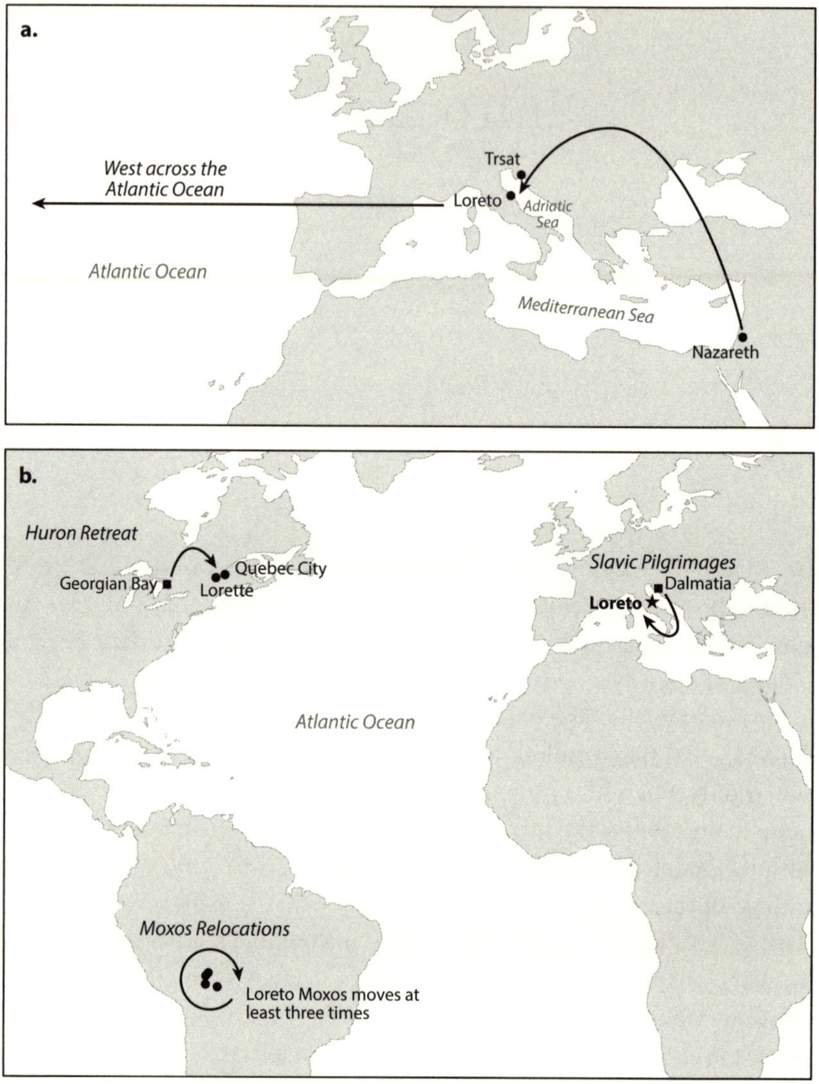

FIGURE 1.1. The flights of Loreto. Based on maps created by cartographer Gabriela Norton. a. Westward ho (1290–1550). b. Retreats, returns, and undertow (1550–1750).

the outskirts of the coastal city of Rijeka, Croatia. The house was in Trsat for three years, enough time for a respected prior, Alessandro, to receive his own explanatory vision from Mary, and enough time for a nobleman, Nicholas Frangipani, to build a small chapel around the structure. But Mary did not feel the people of Trsat properly venerated her, so she took off once more, flying over the Adriatic Sea in search of more loyal devotees. She descended in Italy in the forest near the town of Recanati on the eve of 10 December 1294. Though the house tarried for only eight months at this second layover, it came to be known as "Loreto" for the owner of the land, Laureta. Its subsequent moves were mere hops compared to its earlier travels. When two brothers quarreled over how to divide pilgrims' offerings to Mary, angels lifted her house to higher terrain. The structure's fourth and last flight was a shift still higher up the coastal ridge, a minor adjustment again intended to keep its early pilgrims safe from thieves.

These unexpected landings were described by the sixteenth-century historian Girolamo Angelitta as a miracle. Yet in the late 1500s when Angelitta wrote, his account was also read as a beautiful, peaceful allegory for the spread of Christianity to the rest of the world. Catholicism, like Italy's Holy House of Loreto, appeared to drop abruptly from the heavens into new lands, where it anchored itself with magical ease among new peoples. The analogy appealed to the energetic young missionary order of the Society of Jesus. In the 1600s, many Jesuits self-consciously cast themselves as the latest angels in the Holy House's travels, transporting the Loreto devotion across the Atlantic Ocean to the Americas. They named new frontier missions for Loreto (table 1.1). These sites stand as concrete, verifiable postscripts to the much older story about the surprising mobility of religious objects. But from the twenty-first-century vantage point, the more recent anchorages also surface as an extension of the original mystery. How did Catholicism fly, and land again? How did this religion move from its Mediterranean moorings out into the world?

Jesuit archives suggest an answer to these questions, though not necessarily the answer one might expect. Early Jesuit sources show that the movement of Loreto cannot be credited solely or even mostly to the Jesuits themselves. It was not a top-down endeavor. For starters, the Society of Jesus did not have any kind of official program to promote Loreto abroad. Their writings and approaches to the Italian devotion were scattered. The Jesuit letters that inform much of this book come from three disconnected seventeenth-century mission outposts named for Loreto: Lorette, built among the Huron in Québec, in eastern Canada; Loreto Moxos, established in the Amazon River basin between today's countries of Bolivia and Peru; and Loreto Conchó, erected farthest west, on a peninsula in Baja California.[3] Reports from these sites are supplemented with formal publications by the Jesuits and manuscript sources from Italy's Loreto shrine,

3. Most of these were collected in the Jesuit central archives in Rome, the *Archivum Romanum Societatis Iesu* (ARSI) and the Jesuit archives of the Québec province in Canada, the *Archivum Societatis Iesu-Province du Canada Français* (ASJCF).

Table 1.1: Selected Jesuit-Founded Loreto Sites in the Americas

Frontier Missions

Date	Name and Location	Jesuit Founders
1650s	Loreto of Guairá, Paraguay	Giuseppe Cataldini, Simone Mascetti
1674	Lorette-among-the-Huron, near Québec City, Canada, renamed *Jeune Lorette* (1697)	Pierre J.-M. Chaumonot
1682	Loreto Moxos, Peru/Bolivia	Cipriano Barace, Pedro Marbán, Antonio de Orellana, Joseph de Vega, Antonio Fernández, Manuel Carillo
1697	Loreto Conchó, Baja California	Juan Maria Salvatierra, Francisco María Piccolo

Holy House Replica Chapels

Date	Name and Location	Jesuit Founders
1674	Lorette-among-the-Huron, near Québec City, Canada	Pierre J.-M. Chaumonot
1679	Colegio de Tepotzotlán, Mexico	Juan Bautista Zappa
1680	Colegio de San Gregorio, Mexico City	Juan Maria Salvatierra
169?	Colegio de Guadalajara, Mexico	Juan Maria Salvatierra
1697	Loreto Conchó, Baja California	Juan Maria Salvatierra, Francisco María Piccolo

the Vatican Secret Archives, Franciscan missionary collections in Bolivia, the French national libraries in Paris, the Portuguese national archives of the Torre do Tombo in Lisbon, and Spain's Archives of the Indies in Sevilla. Taken together, these founts reveal that Jesuit activity surrounding Loreto was tangential to the plans of the original Italian sanctuary and even to the initiatives of the Jesuit order itself.

Even before the Argentine Jesuit Cardinal Jorge Mario Bergoglio became Pope Francis, scholarship lionized Jesuits as the ultimate professional missionary organization at the heart of the early modern Catholic Church.[4] Seen in broader global company of diffusers of Loreto, however,

4. Works like Luke Clossey's *Salvation and Globalization in the Early Jesuit Missions* and Liam Brockey's *Journey to the East* have emphasized the strong links in the Jesuit worldwide network and have underscored Jesuit successes in proselytizing in far-flung regions. In Western civilization and introductory history courses, the Jesuits continue to be trundled out as prime examples of the Catholic Church's refashioning of itself in the wake of the Protestant Reformation.

the Jesuits who carried this Italian devotion abroad do not stand out for primacy or elite leadership. Ordinary Catholics were already transporting Loreto abroad, and some Jesuits individually opted to join them in doing so. Jesuits, laymen, and converts alike were engaging in the same processes and stumbles around moving Loreto. In this sense, the history of Loreto is truly a history of Jesuits in—and upstaged by—the world. Modern privileging of Jesuit professionalism and internal dynamics has obscured the improvisation that Jesuits in the field shared with the laity.

This book endeavors to show the myriad human hands behind the Holy House's emergence on the Italian and global scene. Movers ranged beyond French, Spanish, Portuguese, and central European Jesuits to include Monquí pilgrims from Baja California, Moxos house builders in Bolivia, Huron female mission leaders in Canada, Inka procession organizers in Peru, Slavic migrants in the Adriatic basin, and German atlas makers, among others featured here (figure 1.1.b). These disparate groups had parallel experiences as unofficial authors, inadvertent pilgrims, unlicensed architects, unacknowledged artists, and unsolicited cataloguers. As the adjectives suggest, the experiences of these individuals who got bundled into the history of Loreto turn Loreto's founding parable on its head. Their participation does not reveal clean, purposeful landings. Instead, their diverse interpretations point to disorder, decentralization, and independent enactments of belief that spilled across boundaries of nation, empire, church, and period.

This is not the sort of accounting that is usually made of the Catholic Church in the seventeenth century. But it is in this very real individual chaos that one can discern the *how* behind the spread of Christianity. It should be noted that this proposed human mechanism of transport differs in magnitude from the Loreto sanctuary's updated twentieth-century explanation of its most famous miracle. Since the 1900s, the Catholic Church has modulated its authorized version of the arrival of Loreto's Holy House by acknowledging human agency, but it has done this so literally that it has prompted criticism. Giuseppe Santarelli, the director of the Congregazione Universale della Santa Casa, espouses the sanctuary's position and the Catholic Church's party line: He reports that a family of Byzantine nobles called "Angeli" were the actual movers of the Holy House in the late 1200s, and they were miscoded in Loreto's archives as "angels."[5]

5. Santarelli, *Loreto*, pp. 13–15. Art historian Ronald Lightbown argues persuasively that the documents on which this conclusion is based (the *Chartalarium Culisanense*) are forgeries (Lightbown, *Carlo Crivelli*, p. 43). But the argument of this book owes a large debt to Santarelli and another Franciscan historian of Loreto, Floriano Grimaldi. Santarelli

While Santarelli attaches one group of high-ranking devout to one isolated movement of one revered Catholic object, this book delves into the multiple anchorages and re-anchorages of Loreto to argue that many groups of self-appointed, mixed-rank, often peripheral amateurs carried Catholicism in general to new peoples. In order to root their personal and occasionally unorthodox devotions in new ground, these Catholics reached across cultures and deliberately wrote themselves into the glittering official script of Catholic movement. Their actions offer an alternative understanding of what drives globalization: spontaneous mass participation, not institutions, political mandates, or impersonal forces. "World Christianity" thus ceases to fit the mold of a prepackaged export and becomes the sum total of thousands of insider reformulations.

How to Read This Book, and How to Read a Miracle

The purpose of this study is not to pick apart a magnificent example of a miracle, but rather to test other strategies that today's historians can contribute to the understanding of a genuinely strange event. The next chapter critically revisits the approaches that historians have traditionally brought to bear to illuminate Catholic miracles. These deconstructive approaches do tell much about Loreto's first landings, but they also show some places where historians need to stretch or supplement their classic methods to find new answers. Chapter 2 closes by explaining the alternative approach taken in this book: instead of paring down, this history endeavors to reconstruct and consider the accumulated whole.

As outlined in chapter 2, the methodology for this project is culled self-consciously but directly from its subject matter. The way this history is being written in 2017 resembles the way Loreto's mythohistory was itself formed centuries ago. While this may seem an obvious consequence of an experiment of reconstruction, it bears repeating that the purpose here is

---

catalogued, compiled, and republished much of the corpus of writings relating to the Virgin of Loreto and has also drawn attention to the oral tradition preceding and coinciding with Loreto's textual history. Grimaldi, a director of the archives of the *Santa Casa*, published the most thorough regional history of the sanctuary, describing Loreto's local beginnings in the Marche. Both men hint at a multiplicity of Catholic participants involved in historicizing Lauretan devotion. I take up their hint vigorously and extend my search for agents across the Atlantic. Santarelli's most complete interpretation of Loreto's origins can be found in: Santarelli, *La traslazione della Santa Casa di Loreto*; also, Santarelli, *Indicazioni documentali inedite*. Grimaldi's exhaustively researched local account of Loreto is: Grimaldi, *Devozione e Committenza nelle Marche*.

not to blindly reproduce Loreto's past or Loreto's sources, but rather to answer the question: How, and why, could a miracle like Loreto be persuasive to people? Because of how it was made, told, and refashioned. Methodology is part of the answer to the mysterious endurance of miracles, which is why there is a full chapter devoted to making it transparent.

In order to understand how Loreto moves people, and how it was moved by people, the remaining chapters follow the mythohistorical mold. They highlight accretion and emphasize the interconnections between the original and its aftermaths. The chapters are structured to repeatedly demonstrate this process of overlay, from the moment of first encounter to final anchorages. Each chapter opens with an "Anchoring Ideal," a compelling and carefully constructed early narrative of arrival such as the one that opened this chapter: a mysterious house lands. The attractive elegance of these sanitized ideals is presented first to accentuate the contrast between them and the "Actual History" that follows.

The "Actual" chapter sections survey variant experiences among Catholics as they found their own ways to reflect and articulate the ideal. These people's messy and collaborative attempts to apply the essence of Catholic miracles reverberate back on the ideal. Miracles like Loreto's landing had staying power partly because of the earnest efforts of these people to connect with old ideas, yet their innovations and criticisms also produced change. For historians, the dissonance between people's gritty experiences and the initial motivating mystery is essential; it indicates the intrusion of reality into an ever-growing, jointly reimagined narrative.

To demonstrate how the real and the ideal interact, each chapter closes with an in-depth consideration of a "New Expression" of Catholicism, a more radical example of a lived practice being taken up and negotiated by new people. This last snapshot of a fresh inflection of devotion is offered in the same spirit as the three Jesuit missions that appeared early in this chapter, appended to the famous Italian Holy House. Which one is the true Loreto, the older Italian site or the more recent offshoots that continue to carry forward its name? By setting them both alongside each other, this book insists that both make the truth, in combination.

Following Part I, the work is divided into two main parts to reflect the exceptional journeys and pairings that mark Loreto's mythohistory. Part II, "Approaching Loreto," describes the multiple *journeys* of authors and pilgrims to and from Loreto. Part III, "Leaving Loreto," focuses on the *pairings* (and uncouplings) of objects associated with Loreto, including the Holy House, the image of Mary, and the name Loreto. The third essential component of the Loreto corpus, the *lived experience* of a multiplicity of people, is highlighted throughout both central parts of the book, most especially in the "New Expression" concluding sections of all chapters. In this way, the three dimensions foregrounded in Loreto's founding narrative—movement, additions, and real situations—are used to reconstruct a full picture of the power of miracles, rather than to pick the miracle apart (Part IV).

This brings us back to the initial miracle of Loreto, and the central question looming behind this study: How did *Catholic devotion* spread? The miracle of Loreto preserves in amber a response verified by other archives. Beneath Loreto's persistently captivating narrative of mysterious Christian arrival, there are hundreds of thousands of individually orchestrated and negotiated Catholic landings, some gathered here. These landings have been paradoxically obscured and enshrined in the historical record of Catholicism. They are presented here as a hypothesis: Vast and *voluntary* participation was key to Catholicism's movement and survival. Real, repeated self-enlistment, viewed by today's more skeptical audiences as miraculously unlikely, *did* contribute profoundly to the global diffusion of religion.

CHAPTER TWO

Deconstructing a Miracle

Habits of Historical Deconstruction

Since the miraculous flying house first surfaced, people have applied historical methods to better understand it. But these attempts have fallen short at explaining three hallmarks of the Loreto devotion: its movement (journeys), its grafting onto new venerated objects (pairings), and its lasting appeal (due in part to people's continued real, lived experiences). These aspects have carried over into our own times. In the mid-twentieth century, the Virgin of Loreto hitchhiked on a rocket: a medallion of her was carried to the moon.[1] Five centuries after her Italian landing, this local incarnation of Mary was breaking atmospheric bounds, still imparting the same message: Christianity (and humans) were on the move.

Instead of addressing real movement, most scholars writing about the flying house of Loreto have been sidetracked by how magnificently it represents the category of miracle. They have brought to bear the analytical apparatuses from their respective disciplines that are usually mustered for the special situation of confronting the impossible. Researchers have tended to focus narrowly on six distinct elements of the Loreto devotion's past: the objects at its center; the political agendas surrounding it; the possibility of divine presence; the intrusion of the paranormal; the opportunity it provides to empathize with past peoples; or the particular time and place where it emerged. These facets are each summarized here because, in combination, they do provide much information about Loreto. However, taken separately, these habitual methodologies are limited: they

1. As the patron saint of "aeronauts" she was taken on a medallion in 1969 on the Apollo lunar module. Bulgarelli, "Holy House of Loreto," p. 88.

do not adequately address mobility, accumulation, or endurance, nor do they treat seriously their sources' sweeping claims to report reality. This chapter finishes by presenting an alternative reconstructive approach that does address these components. This book puts the proposed methodology to the test on the miracle of Loreto.

The first half of this chapter includes basic background and descriptions of key features of Loreto's devotion, as indicated by the subheadings. But the bulk of the chapter is directed primarily to readers who are interested in the methodological scaffolding that holds up miracles and histories alike. What are the possible avenues that have been explored by those keen to crack past mysteries like Loreto's flying house? How do particular choices of focus constrain understanding? And of most interest to this project: How do the ways that people describe an event contribute to that event's staying power? These are questions broached and answered in the following surveys of both deconstructive methods and reconstructive counterapproaches.

OBJECTS

What are the physical objects that make up Loreto, and why are they holy? Particularly since the twentieth century, archaeologists and art historians have placed Loreto's material core in the limelight. Thanks to the efforts of these specialists, the visible centerpieces of Loreto's miracle have been carefully examined, classified, and functionally analyzed. The two objects in question, a very old house and a Marian icon, come across as deceptively plain at first viewing and require some unpacking.

The *Santa Casa*, Mary's Holy House as experienced in Loreto, is a thirty-one-foot-long by thirteen-foot-wide edifice with three entrance doors, one window, and no roof. In the thirteenth century it consisted of only three low walls of sandstone, a material not common in the Loreto area, where there are no sandstone quarries.[2] At some point before the fourteenth century, a fourth wall was added where the altar is still placed. The three original walls were then raised in height with local bricks that were once frescoed with scenes of Mary's life. Archaeological excavations carried out from 1962 to 1965 showed that the *Santa Casa*

2. The missing fourth wall, according to Catholic tradition, was provided by the grotto that Mary's house leaned up against in Nazareth. The rareness of the stone has been much disputed: for an eloquent early example of skepticism, see the account of the French Protestant Maximilien Mission, *Nouveau voyage d'Italie fait en 1688* (1691). Misson's doubts about Loreto's stones are remarked on by E. Chevalier, "Le pèlerin de Lorette," p. 216.

has no foundations and rests on top of a stone-paved road.[3] Between the fourteenth and seventeenth centuries, the sacred object of the *Santa Casa* was increasingly surrounded by concentric walls and ceiling of marble and stone, enclosed "rather in the manner of a Russian doll."[4]

Nestled at the heart of this sanctuary complex, placed above the altar inside the *Santa Casa*, a black, wooden statue of Mary stands about three feet tall. She holds the baby Jesus in one arm. This latest face of the Madonna of Loreto inherited the niche from a sixteenth-century statue and an even more ancient icon.[5] While Loreto's founding myth makes it seem that the image and house arrived on Italy's coast together one December evening in 1294, actually, the icon seems to have preceded the Holy House. Papal documents list Loreto as a country chapel in the early 1300s, but it was already distinguished by a miracle-working painting of Mary.[6] We know that by 1315 the Madonna was already being recognized by wealthy locals or pilgrims who left donations because in that year, a group of Ghibellines were put on trial in Recanati for breaking into Loreto's church to steal jewels hanging from the church's icon.[7]

These descriptions are interesting, but what was it that drew pilgrims to these objects? What made them meaningful?[8] Historians have focused on the Holy House, in particular, as being a unique combination of two categories: reliquary and relic. This duality amplified its sacred nature.

3. Alfieri, "Il sacello della Santa Casa"; *La Basilica della Santa Casa di Loreto* (Grimaldi, ed.); Santarelli, *Loreto*, pp. 6–13.

4. Boyer, *Cult of the Virgin*, p. 83.

5. Changes to the Madonna's image are the subject of chapter 6 of this study. The current statue of Lebanese cedar wood was designed in 1921 by Enrique Quattrini and Leopoldo Celani to replace the earlier statue, burnt in a fire.

6. The first papal document referring to Loreto does not allude to any *Santa Casa*. Signed by Pope John XXII in Avignon, this 1320 assignment of a benefice simply describes Loreto as a "ruralis ecclesia," a country church. Even before this, in 1310, Carl Ludwig von Schendem, a German Carmelite monk, left the first written reference to the Madonna of Loreto; he reported that he knelt before her image and vowed to found a Carmelite convent, but he mentioned only the icon. Earlier ecclesiastical documents have been noted: one from 1193–94 that was "destroyed" but spoke of a church of Mary "in fundo Loreti" that was granted by the bishopric of Numana (near Ancona) to the monastery of Fonte Avellana; and another from 1285 certifying a land claim by the ex-bishops of Recanati "in fundo Laureti." *La Madonna di Loreto nelle Marche*, p. 12; Lightbown, *Carlo Crivelli*, p. 42.

7. Lightbown, *Carlo Crivelli*, p. 39.

8. The ordinariness of the Holy House and Marian image call to mind Patrick Geary's observation on the potentially problematic unmarked nature of relics: "As a physical object, divorced from a specific milieu, a relic is entirely without significance. . . . Unlike a book or illustration, a relic cannot itself transmit [culturally induced] perception from one community to another, even if these communities share identical cultural and religious values." Geary, *Furta Sacra*, pp. 5–6.

Reliquaries are vessels, usually portable, that are designed to protect or showcase a piece of the sacred. They derive their importance from the holy article they harbor. The *Santa Casa* shielded a miracle-working image of Mary. But the *Santa Casa*'s contact with Mary also placed it within the enduringly popular Catholic category of relic. Relics are objects construed to have miraculous powers because they are concrete physical remnants of a saint who walked on the earth. They are usually bones, but they can also be images of holy people or items that they touched during their lifetimes.[9]

As a relic of Mary, the *Santa Casa* is unusual. The Virgin Mary presents a special case among Catholic holy figures. According to medieval Catholic tradition, Mary is the only person to have ascended to Heaven entire when she died, leaving behind no body or skeleton. Because of this, physical remnants of her are relatively rare and include breast milk or clothes that came in contact with her body.[10] Perhaps to compensate for this scarcity of actual bones, there are a large number of relics associated with Mary that are icons, two-dimensional, reputedly ancient paintings of her such as the original image venerated at Loreto. Part of the *Santa Casa*'s claim to fame was that it did not merely function like an icon. It did not just represent Mary; it had literally been inhabited by her. In his sixteenth-century history of Loreto's origins, Angelitta accentuated this extraordinary dimension of the Holy House. He wrote: "in this great, Holy and terrible place, the living Christ, God, & man, along with his Mother, and disciples had eaten, drank, slept, prayed."[11] In this respect, the *Santa*

9. On the power of relics as images that did *not* require activation or consecration to be effective: Freedberg, *Power of Images*, pp. 92, 97.

10. Mary's milk, in powder or liquid form, was a cornerstone relic in European shrines including Walsingham, Chartres, Genoa, Padua, Rome, Venice, Avignon, Paris, and Naples. Some of its sources were caves with white walls along the route of Mary's flight from Herod. These sites like the Milk Grotto of Bethlehem drew non-Christian pilgrims as well. In the absence of other corporeal remains, Mary's clothes were also seen as powerful relics. Chartres had Mary's tunic, supposedly donated by King Charles II the Bald in the year 870. One of the sites that claimed Mary's slippers was Notre Dame de Soissons, a Benedictine monastery for women in northern France. Mary's veils were venerated in Prague as early as the fourteenth century. On the pre-Christian Greek origins of the *Virgo Lactans* devotion: Ryan, "Persuasive Power of a Mother's Breast," pp. 61, 63. On milk grottos: Sered, "Rachel's Tomb and the Milk Grotto of the Virgin Mary." On Muslim pilgrims there: Cuffel, "'Henceforward All Generations Will Call Me Blessed.'" On Mary's tunic at Chartres: Cassagnes-Brouquet, *Vierges Noires*, p. 79. On Mary's slippers: A. Clark, "Guardians of the Sacred." On Mary's veils: Sronek, "Veil of the Virgin Mary."

11. "In questo luogo grande, Santo, e terribile, Christo vivente, Iddio, & huomo como la Madre, e Discepoli hauui mangiato, bevuto, dormito, fatto oratione." Angelitta, *L'historia*, p. 16.

Casa was an impressively original relic connected to Mary as well as to other Catholic notables, including Christ and his disciples.

The *Santa Casa* was also an extraordinarily spectacular reliquary. Seventeenth-century sermons compared the *Santa Casa* to two other giants among reliquaries, the Ark of the Covenant and the Holy Sepulcher.[12] The biblical reliquary of all reliquaries, the Ark of the Covenant, is referred to in Exodus 25:10–22. It is the sacred wooden chest, gilded in gold, that held the tablets of the law given to Moses by God. The ark is a reliquary in the sense that it protects its relics, the tablets, highlighting their sacred value with its richness but also separating human observers from the divine object within. The Holy Sepulcher is an even more apt comparison for the *Santa Casa* because it is an "empty" reliquary: for a brief moment, this tomb held Christ's body. That instant was enough for it to retain some of Christ's spirit, even without his bones or clothes.

The *Santa Casa*, though not a tomb, had likewise served as a temporary "house" for Mary and Christ, the divine incarnated on earth.[13] Unlike churches, which are often described as figurative "houses" of God and which also contain relics, the *Santa Casa* was purportedly the real deal, the *actual* house of Christ and Mary.[14] But here, the *Santa Casa* capitalized on its church-like dimensions to be as much of a standout among reliquaries as it was among relics. Most reliquaries securely encase their relics.[15] Yet in the case of the *Santa Casa*, visitors can walk inside as if entering a church, and stand a few feet away from its otherwise unenclosed icon. From the moment of its public identification with Mary's house in

12. Tosi, *I Tre Voli della Santa Casa* (1655), pp. 812, 814. The Ark of the Covenant was also represented on the sixteenth-century doors of Loreto's basilica, as if to accentuate the similarities between the two reliquaries. Giannatiempo López, "Antonio Calcagni," p. 241. For comparisons between the *Santa Casa* and the Holy Sepulcher in sermons: Giuseppe Maria, *Predica in Lode della Santa Casa* (1670), pp. 15–17.

13. It has been noted that the *Santa Casa* also loosely resembles a martyrium, or a place where a martyr's remains were kept. But though it shares the commemorative focus of a martyrium, the *Santa Casa* does not seem to have emphasized holy sacrifice to the same degree as the Holy Sepulcher, the Basilica of St. Peter, or the Church of St. Catherine on Mt. Sinai. Bulgarelli, "Holy House of Loreto," p. 81.

14. Natalie Zemon Davis notes that this "holy house" motif is not unique to Catholicism: in Islam, the Kaaba in Mecca—a reliquary of sorts, sheltering the sacred stone of the Hajar el Aswad—is referred to as a holy "house" in translations by Leo Africanus (1485–1554), Moroccan traveler and writer. Personal communication, 18 February 2005.

15. Dierkens, "Du bon (et du mauvais) usage."

the fourteenth century, this church-reliquary offered audiences uncommon intimacy and opportunity to link with the holy figure at its center.[16]

These categorizations help to illuminate the objects' potency, but in and of themselves, they do not explain how the Holy House and Madonna of Loreto landed or moved onward again. Art historian Jennifer Roberts has recently called for studies of objects that reckon better with movement. Writing of the eighteenth and nineteenth centuries, Roberts reminds us that prior to our age of Internet, in order "to disseminate, circulate, or otherwise transmit an image . . . a picture (a physical thing) had to be floated, rolled, or dragged across the earth. The process took muscle and it took time. . . . Every moving picture . . . was subject to the inconvenience of 'having to pass through the world.'"[17]

Roberts calls attention to the complexities of physical transit of a single artifact, but another crucial aspect of such movement is multiplication. The corpse of St. Francis Xavier is a Catholic relic that illustrates both Roberts's point about objects being dragged and the additional dynamic of replication. Like the objects featured at Loreto's shrine, Xavier's body was both moved and copied. Pieces of this Jesuit missionary were scattered throughout the world after his death in China in 1552, with some of his bones ending up in Goa and Rome; additionally, wooden simulacra of his dead body were painstakingly transported as far as South America and Arizona.[18]

16. Another site that offered pilgrims this intimacy of contact was Rome's *Scala Sancta* (the stairs of Pontius Pilate's palace in Jerusalem that Jesus climbed on the Friday before he was crucified). Pilgrims could climb the same twenty-eight steps where Christ had purportedly set foot, though these stairs were eventually encased in protective wood. Interestingly, the stairs, like the Holy House, were replicated around Europe in Italy, France, Germany, the Czech Republic, and even Canada. Triff, "Rhetoric and Romanitas," p. 76; Witcombe, "Sixtus V and the Scala Santa."

17. Roberts, *Transporting Visions*, p. 1.

18. Xavier's corpse was scattered piecemeal across the globe after it was exhumed in 1553. With regard to Asia, Xavier's posthumous travels have been represented as the Catholic bridging of East and West or even a way to chart the Goan diaspora. In South America, there are at least two wooden sculptures of Xavier's corpse in the Church of San Pedro in Lima and the Church of San Miguel in Santiago de Chile. In North America, there are also at least two extant wooden statues that represent Xavier reclining in death: one at the mission of San Xavier el Bac on the Tohono O'odham reservation south of Tucson, Arizona, and another at the mission of Magdalena del Kino just south of the Mexico-US border. The Bac mission's statue was commissioned in 1759 to emulate a Xavier statue in Veracruz, Mexico, and the Magdalena del Kino mission's statue seems to be a reappropriated statue of the dead Christ. The South America and Arizona sites are associated with the Jesuits, who took special pride in Xavier as one of their own. On the Xavier statue at Magdalena: Griffith, *Beliefs and Holy Places*, pp. xiv, 33–34, 45, 49. On the sculpture at Bac: Donohue,

For Loreto's two sacred centerpieces, there are as yet no comprehensive analyses describing how the house and icon passed through the world à la Xavier, valued in the original and in hard copy. Part of the mystery surrounding Loreto is that its two central relics did move and anchor onto an Italian hilltop, but then they physically traveled further via proliferation in the seventeenth century and beyond. How, and why? These open questions require additional research strategies.

POLITICAL AGENDA

A second popular strategy for grappling with Catholic miracles is to approach them as matters of political manipulation. For instance, in his 2001 article "Of Miracles and Special Effects," theorist Hent De Vries places miracles and technological special effects in the same category. He advocates for a "politics of the miracle" to highlight the technicity and "human fabrication" surrounding many miracles.[19] The temptation is indeed great to look for human wizards behind the scrim, and to emphasize their goals and impact.

Historian Craig Harline adopted this angle in his 2003 study *Miracles at the Jesus Oak*. Harline wrote that what most interested him about a miraculous oak dedicated to Jesus in the woods of the Spanish Netherlands was the "sometimes subtle, sometimes bombastic arguing about defining and controlling and proclaiming and seeking miracles."[20] Consequently, his book features people who make miracles work for them: tailors who try to divert pilgrims to their own chapel; church officials who refuse to validate as a miracle a woman who believes she has been healed; and towns that fight over controlling the miracle-working oak. Historian Katherine Ludwig Jansen has likewise demonstrated that it was not only high clergy who had political agendas they advanced by way of miracles. Commoners among the Catholic laity also actively contributed to the production of

---

"Unlucky Jesuit Mission of Bac," p. 135; for a photograph: Umberger, "Bac on the Border." On the South America sculptures: Bailey, "Iconography of Jesuit Saints," p. 473 (Lima) and p. 479n30 (Santiago de Chile). On Xavier's corpse in the Catholic world: Brockey, "Cruelest Honor"; Pinch, "Corpse and Cult of Francis Xavier." On Xavier and the Goan diaspora: Fernandes, "Tomb Raider," p. 18.

19. De Vries, "Of Miracles and Special Effects," pp. 42, 48. De Vries invokes Jacques Derrida's "Faith and Knowledge" (in *La Religion*, 1966) to call on scholars to focus on the "mediation and mediazation without and outside of which no religion would be able to manifest or reveal itself in the first place" (p. 51).

20. Harline, *Miracles at the Jesus Oak*, pp. 6–7.

religious meaning. Writing of Mary Magdalen in the Middle Ages, Jansen highlights "creative consumers," untrained, occasionally illiterate devotees who selectively emphasized particular details they heard in sermons about Mary Magdalen in order to satisfy their own "needs and desires."[21]

In the case of the Loreto sanctuary, there are many studies that bring out the politics surrounding the sanctuary during its early years and later centuries. The most prominent of these works feature priests and literate clerics who influenced Loreto's history.[22] This study endeavors to follow Harline's and Jansen's broader attunement to the functionality of religion across social divides. It draws attention to nonpriestly contributors who impacted the miracle genre as well.

Yet there are at least three limitations to analyzing the case of Loreto with an eye only for the strategic motivations of these varied participants. First, linking miracle accounts to particular human patrons inaccurately creates the impression that Loreto's resonance was limited to the lifetimes of those generative individuals. Second, stressing those patrons' Machiavellian management skills minimizes the possibility of their having experienced sincere religious feeling or any emotion that transcended calculated function. Third and most problematically, overemphasizing politics can result in interpretations that favor human authors as the sole formulators of miracles at the expense of other causes. The Jesus oak gets lost beneath human machination.

DIVINE PRESENCE (MYSTERY)

There is a competing, inverse third approach that downplays human input to elevate, instead, a potential supernatural source for miracles: the divine. Interestingly, one of the proponents of this third interpretive strategy is none other than the *Oxford English Dictionary*. This well-respected source declares a "miracle" to be a matter of faith, not academic inquiry. According to the *Oxford English Dictionary*, a phenomenon like the landing of Loreto's Holy House is a "surprising and welcome event that is *not explicable* by natural or scientific laws and is therefore considered to be

21. Jansen, *Making of the Magdalen*, pp. 336, 285.

22. Most recently, see Lightbown, *Carlo Crivelli*; Hamilton, "Ottomans, the Humanists and the Holy House of Loreto." But the premier political history of Loreto dates to 1906, when Ulysse Chevalier famously contended that the legend of the *Santa Casa* was not based on fact, but was the strategic product of human imagination (*Notre-Dame de Lorette*).

a work of divine agency."[23] By definition, then, a miracle cannot be explained in real-world terms and must be ascribed to otherworldly causes.

One way that some Catholics have applied that definition has been to leave miracle accounts unanalyzed as a mark of devotion. For example, the Jesuit James Martin recently criticized the American icon Thomas Jefferson for literally "scissor[ing] out the miracles . . . the uncomfortable parts" from the Christian scriptures to create his own rational version of Jesus. Martin suggests that Jefferson fundamentally misunderstood the nature of miracles. A miracle is a permanent "mystery," Martin argues, "something not to be solved, but to be pondered."[24] The *Oxford English Dictionary* and the Jesuit Martin coincide in their assessment that miracles are useful primarily for symbolic or spiritual contemplation. Miracles do reverberate powerfully when interpreted this way, as suggested by the allegorical reading of the Holy House's arrival that opened this chapter.

Moving beyond allegory, however, some historians have lately determined to acknowledge that nonhuman forces may be at play in reported cases of the miraculous. They argue that when sources apportion responsibility for mysterious events to gods, spirits, fairies, or the like, historians should handle these claims just as they do for any other active agent or natural force suggested by the record: they should investigate whether the hypothetical circumstance may, indeed, have contributed. In their 2016–17 series of essays "The Unbelieved and Historians," these researchers contend that irrespective of a scholar's own religious beliefs, when analyzing supernatural occurrences, "we might usefully . . . remember that we are dealing with nonhuman actors, whom we do not know well."[25] Divine forces should be held in the realm of real possibility when interrogating improbable occurrences, subject to the same rigorous evaluation and proof as proposed factors like military leadership or the weather.

Such open-mindedness is admirable, but when "the unbelieved" or "mysterious" by whatever name are taken to be the dominant (or even partial) cause for a miraculous event, it has the shock potential to outshine every other cause. Certifying divine presence can stymie any further investigation into what actually transpired. In the ensuing consideration of Loreto's flying house, practical questions of how and why are therefore deemed as central as contemplating or recognizing the divine.

23. *Oxford English Dictionary*, www.oed.com, accessed online 26 February 2015; emphasis added.

24. J. Martin, *Jesus: A Pilgrimage*, pp. 4–5.

25. Clossey et al., "Unbelieved and Historians, Part II," p. 5; also: R. Clark et al., "Unbelieved and Historians, Part III," and Clossey et al., "Unbelieved and Historians, Part I."

THE PARANORMAL

A fourth inroad for scholars investigating otherworldly flight has gained popularity more recently: paranormal studies. Those who take this approach share the impulse of the researchers in the previous section to take the mysterious seriously. Yet they differ in their quarry and their apparatus of interrogation. Appropriately, a scholar of the Spanish Inquisition, Gustav Henningsen, best exemplifies a paranormal-attuned methodology. He revisits how seventeenth-century official interrogators questioned witches' flight in order to make his case that we should not "ignore, or *explain away*, what does not match our present scientific knowledge."[26] Henningsen's exploration of flying witches leads him to consider telepathy, out-of-body experiences, collective dreaming, and other such possible motors of otherworldly flight, all neglected and illuminating aspects of "a psychological reality, a human cyberspace that defies all imaginations."[27]

No paranormal specialists have yet tackled the flying house of Loreto, though they have been drawn to another roughly contemporary Italian Catholic luminary of levitation: the seventeenth-century saint Joseph of Cupertino, famed during his lifetime for public episodes of flying. Yale historian Carlos Eire wrote a fiery appeal to fellow intellectuals not to dismiss Cupertino's flights as fantasy, but to reckon with them.[28] Philosopher Michael Grosso responded by bringing parapsychology to bear; he compiled a compelling and thorough array of evidence surrounding Cupertino's flights to demonstrate the "historical reality of Joseph's levitations."[29] Noteworthy here is how levitation, recategorized as paranormal, is discussed as a particular brand of reality.

This avenue for analysis could prove fruitful for making sense of the miracle of Loreto. While it is not the one pursued here, this study has drawn inspiration from how Jeffrey Kripal, prominent scholar of the paranormal, parses phenomena that appear impossible. Kripal emphasizes that seemingly unreal occurrences like a flying house "are not simply

26. Henningsen, "Witches' Flying," p. 71.

27. Ibid., p. 72.

28. Eire, "Good, the Bad, and the Airborne," p. 323. Eire is not a Jesuit, but one of his colleagues interestingly tracks how Eire's own Catholic spirituality has informed his openness to the supernatural: Rittgers, " 'He Flew.' "

29. Grosso, *Man Who Could Fly*, p. 89; see, too, Grosso's thorough online compilation of documentary evidence of St. Joseph's flights: "Evidence of St. Joseph of Copertino's Levitations."

physical events. They are also *meaning events*."[30] As such, while they manifest materially, there is also a narrative component to their realness. It is the combination of these two dimensions, a real, confounding event plus accompanying narration, that allows the impossible to continue to provoke "terror and bedazzlement."[31] Both narration and the physical realities surrounding Loreto will be presented together in this book to accentuate what Kripal captures so well: the enduring charisma of the improbable.

EMPATHY

A fifth and by far most popular methodology of historians in reckoning with miracles is to take them as opportunities to exercise empathy with people of bygone eras. This is the way the preferred interpretation runs: In the thirteenth century, back in the distant past (the more distant, the better), *some* people believed that the Holy House of Loreto was authentic, and perhaps by looking at their reasoning, we can come to understand who they were, as distinct from us. For instance, the art historian Ronald Lightbown's assessment of the endurance of the Holy House of Loreto hinges on sympathizing with "the increased anxiety . . . [of] priests who had long served at the shrine" who wanted "to prevent the demolition of the old, humble chapel."[32] It can be useful to acknowledge what is alien about the thinking of those priests of yore. The dissonance between our perspectives and theirs might lead to more accurate reconstruction of the past, a foreign land that often requires extra energy to understand.[33]

Interestingly, in empathetic interpretations, it ends up not mattering that an event such as a house's mysterious landing may have in fact occurred. What matters most is to retrieve long-gone mindsets: some people back then *thought* (or needed to think) that a house appeared.[34] This kind of analysis creates a distance between twenty-first-century individuals and our predecessors that can ironically curtail the very empathy that was the original goal. Distinguishing too sharply between us today and Catholics

30. Kripal, *Authors of the Impossible*, p. 25.

31. Ibid., p. 9.

32. Lightbown, *Carlo Crivelli*, p. 44.

33. Darnton, *Great Cat Massacre*, pp. 3–7.

34. Michael Saler elucidates this consequence of the empathetic approach in his survey of groups of twentieth-century fans of Harry Potter, *Lord of the Rings*, and other fantasy novels. According to Saler, the fantasies that motivate these people matter not because they are based on essential truth, but because they influenced these people's decisions. Saler, *As If*.

yesterday feeds a modern hubris that isolates our time, now, as exceptional. The novelty and accelerations of technology can make us forget that we are not the first to confront the loose cannons of shrinking worlds and global participation. Loreto's history can and should be explored with an eye to issues that still matter now as they did then: migration, diaspora, violence, Jesuit leadership, and even open authorship also troubled seventeenth- and thirteenth-century denizens. Instead of intellectually separating past worldviews from present, it can be constructive to stretch our applications of empathy, to devote as much compassion to today's *mentalités* as we do to yesterday's. By extending empathetic analysis, we might perceive previously unnoticed repetitions across eras.

For example, yesterday as today, harboring old traditions did not necessarily denote knee-jerk conservatism. Historian Diana Walsh Pasulka illustrates this for our times by including both rupture (the watershed of the 1960s Second Vatican Council) and reappearances in her 2015 study of Catholic purgatory, *Heaven Can Wait*. Pasulka demonstrates that the resurfacing of old notions of purgatory might indicate internal criticism, updating for current audiences, or even basic defense of safe space to contemplate the dead. She invites empathy for overlooked subsections of contemporary Catholics who have contributed to the doctrine of purgatory: creative fiction writers behind the video game *Dante's Inferno* and the movie *Sixth Sense*, Internet apostolates, and collectors of stories of ghostly visits from beyond the grave.[35] These Catholics of our own twenty-first century counter Catholic mainstream culture to invoke older church traditions. According to Pasulka, they do so in part to justify "that their curiosity and desire to know about the otherworld is sanctioned."[36] As Pasulka has done for purgatory, this overview of Loreto narratives strives to align yesterday and today with a sympathetic eye for where and why recurrences with tradition surface.

MOMENT (CONTINGENCY)

The sixth, and final, habitual approach historians prefer to bring to miracles is to fix events precisely to a specific time and place. To foreground the advantages of this predilection first, in the case of Loreto's elusive Holy House and Madonna statue, historians have found answers to the burning

35. Pasulka, *Heaven Can Wait*, pp. 148 (diversity), 18 (pop culture), 144 (Internet), 154 (supernatural stories).

36. Ibid., p. 147.

question of when these objects actually "arrived" in Italy. The calculations have not been simple. There is a troubling gap between 1295, the officially accepted date of landing at Loreto, and other extant references to the Holy House.[37] It is not until the late 1300s, a full century postlanding, that it crops up in construction records: Angel Rinaldi (1383–1412), a bishop of Recanati, is credited with the belated building of the first church designed to encircle and protect the *Santa Casa*.[38] Nearly another century passed before the Holy House itself was made known in writing. In 1472, Pietro Tolomei published the first account to describe the journey of Mary's house from Nazareth to Loreto. The specific landing date of 1295 did not surface until fifty years later still, in the early sixteenth-century works of Girolamo Angelitta. But in spite of these tardy, after-the-fact mentions, at least one early image suggests that the oral tradition surrounding Loreto's church *did* emerge close to when Angelitta claimed, in the 1290s or early 1300s. There is a 1325 miniature by an illuminator of manuscripts in Paris, Jean Pucelle, who depicted the Virgin of Loreto standing in a house carried by angels.[39]

These chronological computations are informative and are part of a long tradition of making sense of Christian history in particular. Pulitzer Prize–winning journalist Jon Meacham is one who has lately applied this tactic to his quest for the historical Jesus. He reported on how scholars have fixed Christ's birth and the creation of an accompanying narrative to specific years and locations.[40] But such historicizing fails to speak to how and why the stories of Christ or Loreto's Holy House persisted beyond their points of origin. These analyses have pinned fluid, evocative

37. Lightbown, *Carlo Crivelli*, p. 42. Lightbown is so unsettled by the chronological disjuncture that he suggests that the *Santa Casa* actually "arrived" *not* in 1295, but in 1396, a date comfortably closer to its first mention in print. But the Catholic Church currently stands by Angelitta's 1290s dates as the precise moments of the *Santa Casa*'s arrival in Italy. The church astutely adds that while the building itself was present from that point forward, the "discovery" of its actually being Mary's house happened far more gradually. Their official position is outlined in: Santarelli, *Loreto*, pp. 1–16.

38. Santarelli, *Tradizione*, pp. 14–15.

39. Santarelli, *Loreto*, pp. 14 (fig. 8), 19. Pucelle's miniature is the earliest known representation of the translation of the Holy House. Pucelle headed a workshop of artists in Paris in the 1320s and 1330s.

40. Meacham, "Birth of Jesus"; also, "Who Killed Jesus?" Meacham has helped to popularize the historical search for Jesus with his focus on how the story of Christ's nativity was constructed after Christ's lifetime and informed by Greco-Roman mythology. But Albert Schweitzer and more recently Bart Ehrman predate and showcase Meacham's methodology of critical readings of the Bible as a historical source. Ehrman, *Forged: Writing in the Name of God* (2012); Schweitzer, *Quest of the Historical Jesus* (1911).

Christian myths to discrete moments instead of addressing them as progressive compositions refined by dialogue across many centuries and regions.[41]

Two scholars who have successfully approached their subject as a cumulative, ever-unfolding narrative are Alex Golub and Jon Peterson. They track how the Austronesian concept of "mana" was pulled away from its origins in Melanesia, transported by anthropologists and "quasi-anthropologists" including Carl Jung, Mircea Eliade, and Joseph Campbell, impounded by fantasy and science fiction writers, and eventually ended up being used by role players as a unit of spell power in the online game of *World of Warcraft*, its most common usage today.[42] Instead of lamenting this as a decline of a once fixed and multifaceted concept, Golub and Peterson urge intellectuals to become attuned to the "more complicated dialogue of voices . . . in a globalized world of cultural production, in which 'their' concepts have circulated widely."[43]

Nonetheless, Golub and Peterson, like Meacham, follow traditional chronology, tracking their targets from a point of origin up to present day, marking key moments of development on a timeline. To be fair, in the case of miracles, the limits of this classic method of dating and locating are as much due to the subject matter as to the discipline of history. An analogy serves to illustrate: Miracles resemble butterflies. An entomologist might take a dead butterfly specimen and pin it to a board for study. It is difficult, with the butterfly thus pinned, to determine how it flies in life. If movement is part of the essence of the butterfly that we wish to understand, we need a new strategy that will allow us to assess its living motion, to chart how it fluctuates its form, defies strict category, and crosses boundaries of time and space. In the remainder of this work, a reconstructive approach is tested as a way to do better justice to Loreto, as a means to study this miracle in flight, alive and out in the world. Such an approach requires setting aside fixed chronology.

41. One inadvertent result of fixing chronology in this way can be to create nostalgia for a bygone era, a period that falsely appears to have done better justice to intricacy. For instance, in her in-depth study of Mary Magdalen in the medieval period, historian Katherine Jansen concludes: "In applying the principle of historicity to the cult of the saints, we have no doubt gained in historical accuracy. . . . But the gains should not obscure the losses. We must not forget that it is our own age that officially memorializes Saint Mary Magdalen as [merely] a disciple; it was the 'Dark Ages' that honored her as a preacher and apostle of apostles." Jansen, *Making of the Magdalen*, p. 336.

42. Golub and Peterson, "How Mana Left the Pacific."

43. Ibid., pp. 336–67.

Limits of Deconstruction: Incompleteness and Religious Reality

All the focuses above help to make sense of Loreto, but the Achilles' heel that holds most of them back is partial analysis. Rather than address the whole complexity of miracles, when intellectuals hone in on select aspects, they effectively deconstruct, or peel away, some essential layers in order to privilege others. An emphasis on objects might obscure the mechanisms of movement; stressing politics alone can shut out nonhuman causes; highlighting divine mystery or paranormal phenomena diminishes other contributing factors; practicing empathy to one time period might distance us from relevance to today; fixing chronology fails to reckon with the persistence of miracles. Taken singly, these focuses do not fully capture what actually occurred in the past with the flying house of Loreto.

The question of what really happened is central to all historical investigations on miracles and religion itself, even when it is not voiced directly.[44] It is so vital for historians that each of the six areas surveyed above subconsciously answers it through its focal point. What do historians feel that they can comfortably demonstrate is *real*? Objects, political agendas, mystery (divine presence), paranormal phenomena, the mindsets of former peoples (empathy), and particular moments in the past that can be densely contextualized. This book adds yet another trackable reality to that list: mobility. But each of these demonstrable, partial answers stops short of validating miracle accounts' entire claim to reality. Each still leaves an uncomfortable open question about "whether the [scholarly] interpretation . . . concern[s] events that happened and actors that existed, or not."[45]

Did the Holy House of Loreto really fly? Yes, if flight is taken in the sense of mysterious movement. It moved in many ways and at many times, leaving substantial physical and narrative detritus in its wake. To prove this, however, one must cluster the many approaches historians have habitually favored piecemeal. More importantly, one must also appreciate

44. It is not my goal here to psychoanalyze academics or the discipline of history about why the question "What is real?" is not explicitly voiced in most studies of miracles, but some scholars have produced helpful overviews and theories about how intellectuals approach (and fail to approach) miracles. See Harline, *Miracles at the Jesus Oak*, p. 3; Clossey et al., "Unbelieved and Historians, Part I"; Watkins, *History and the Supernatural*, pp. 203, 208, 211 on medieval churchmen's reactions to miracles, reactions that resemble those of modern intellectuals; Pasulka, *Heaven Can Wait*, pp. 5–6 (abstraction and symbolic interpretation), 166 (real-world effects), 173 (realism); Henningsen, "Witches' Flying."

45. Schilbrack, "Religion, Models of, and Reality," p. 447.

miracles and religion not as categories of belief but as historical records of reality.

Anthropologist Clifford Geertz famously conceded that both scholarly and indigenous narratives about religion were "fictions" but clarified that this was only "in the sense that they are 'something made,' 'something fashioned'—the original meaning of *fictio*—not that they are false, unfactual, or merely 'as if' thought experiments."[46] To Geertz, religion in every culture was not simply an idealized, human-made model *for* reality, but also and most importantly a model *of* reality, grounded in people's lived experiences and conditions.[47] For this study, miracle-infused religious accounts of Loreto's past have been read with an eye for the reality that attracted Geertz. They have been scoured not just in search of objects, politics, divine mystery, the paranormal, empathy, moment, or even mobility, but to find the actual human events, the instances of realness that undergird all these.

An Alternate Reconstructive Approach: Chronicling Mythohistory

What does a *re*construction of Loreto's past look like, and how exactly does it attempt a fuller, reality-based picture? First, in contrast to the deconstructive histories discussed previously, this work merges two categories that are generally treated separately: history and myth. Second, while this study aspires to be more comprehensive than others on Loreto, it does not compile all previous work on the subject in one place or presume to apply all the above habitual approaches at once. Instead, it selectively targets three aspects of the grand narrative of Loreto that seem key to determining the authenticity of its flight: journeys, pairings, and lived experience. How these aspects were chosen is explained further below.

To begin with, it may seem counterintuitive to foreground myth in a work of history. A 2005 updated definition of myth describes it as "a credible, dramatic, socially constructed re-presentation of perceived realities that people accept as permanent, fixed knowledge of reality, while

46. Geertz, *Interpretation of Cultures*, p. 15.

47. Schilbrack, "Religion, Models of, and Reality," pp. 430, 445–46. Geertz's insistence that religion serves as a "model *of*" reality has brought him criticism. Nancy Frankenberry and Hans Penner argue that Geertz is proposing a theory of "truth" (*Language, Truth and Religious Belief*). But Schilbrack disagrees, saying that Geertz's attention to *conditioned* reality is distinct from any idea of essential truth.

forgetting (if they ever were aware of it) its tentative, imaginative, created and perhaps fictional qualities."[48] Myth still tends to be associated with invention in contrast to history that is linked to reality. But some researchers have lately reasserted the connection between myth and history in situations where mythological narratives, culled from vibrant oral traditions, are the primary surviving evidence of people's pasts.[49]

These historians have been able to reconstruct the past from myths by honing in on details that appear to preserve events of significance. Gary Urton, for example, has followed mythical threads across many different oral and written narratives to track how meanings endured (and were repeated) for the Inka across time and space. To make sense of his subject matter of Inka religious accounts, he has added levels of interpretation instead of stripping them away.[50] Carolyn Dean has also used reconstructive methods in her thorough analysis of Inka attitudes toward stone as sacred. Dean says of her source material, "[Stones] had histories that were passed down through generations of worshippers. . . . Whether we call [these] stories myths, legends, fables, tales, or oral histories, they recorded the meanings of, and so made meaningful, certain rocks."[51]

With all its iterations and reiterations, the miracle of Loreto's flying house resembles Inka myths and histories of stones. It can likewise be illuminated by being read as history, with repeated meanings being interpreted as reverberations from a past event. For many Catholics engaging with Loreto, as for many Inka, myth-tinged narratives were linked to concrete moments in their own lives; some of these moments are featured in the closing "New Expression" sections of chapters to follow. Loreto's flights were not retold simply because they were manifestos of the spectacular or affirmations of cultural unity. They retained value because they were also *history:* beneath the flashes of mystery, they also chronicled smaller

48. Dan Nimmo and James Combs as quoted by Coupe, *Kenneth Burke on Myth*, p. 6. This definition is not so different from Roland Barthes's classic interpretation of myth as functional and directly opposed to history. In his foundational *Mythologies*, Barthes limited the purpose and effects of myth to persuading people of the importance of their culture. Viewing myth this way does not necessarily limit its impact. Most famously, Joseph Campbell popularized allegorical, universalizing readings of myth in his comparative analysis of world mythology. Campbell and Moyers, *Power of Myth*.

49. Wonderly, *Oneida Iroquois Folklore, Myth and History*. This category does not just include historians of indigenous peoples; see, for instance, Payne, *Where Myth and History Meet* (2001).

50. Urton, *History of a Myth*; also, Urton, *Inca Myths*, pp. 28–29, 33.

51. Dean, *Culture of Stone*, p. 26.

incidents that *really happened*, not just once to a prominent legendary individual, but *many* times to *many* people over long periods.[52]

To underscore the necessity of both mythological and historical strategies for deciphering miracles, the cumulative record of Loreto's past will be referred to in this book as "mythohistory."[53] The combination label is a reminder that the founding corpus of Loreto is neither strict mythology nor standard history. It is not just a symbolic code to be deciphered, but rather a rolling record of individual realities, a live phenomenon still observable in perennial flight.

How can so many hidden individual realities be retrieved? This book attempts to find them by focusing on what is most disorienting to modern readers in the records of Loreto. In his seminal interpretation of cat massacres in Paris in the 1730s, Robert Darnton encourages historians to follow anthropologists by beginning with what is most difficult to understand.[54] This is an advantage for scholars bent on reconstruction rather than deconstruction: it prioritizes details in Loreto's records that are most often ballasted because they are unfamiliar or perplexing.

There are three recurring elements that seem most confusing in Loreto's mythohistory (in addition to the unexplained and repeated landings already noted above). These three aspects of the preserved record do not seem to advance religious, political, or cultural agendas, yet they were retained as surely as the objects of house and icon at the devotion's center. Here they are taken as clues to genuine patterns in Loreto's past. The aspects retained in Loreto's founding narrative are: first, a precisely defined journey (a movement); second, the pairing of its two central relics (an addition); and third, the shared particularities of lived experiences (real situations) as opposed to imagined stories. Each of these aspects of Loreto's origin narrative is considered briefly below because they are repeated in different forms across Loreto's burgeoning mythohistory. At core and

52. This is a dynamic that historian Carl Watkins also observes in medieval English records: he emphasizes that chroniclers conserved particularities that may seem jarringly out of place but served to commemorate authentic events. Watkins, *History and the Supernatural*, pp. 15–16.

53. I do not use "mythohistory" here in the same sense as historian Michael Thomas Carroll, who recently mustered the term in his fascinating *Popular Modernity in America: Experience, Technology, Mythohistory*. Carroll's "myth" prefix calls attention to the "ideological and cultural construction of the subject" (p. xii). By contrast, I do not stress the fabricated aspect of myth but look instead at its preservative qualities: narratives of myth can and do absorb nonconstructed truths of "real" events and experiences.

54. "By picking at the document where it is most opaque, we may be able to unravel an alien system of meaning." Darnton, *Great Cat Massacre*, p. 5.

in its many layers, the Loreto miracle suggests that movement, additions, and real situations are central to the spread of religion.[55] A reconstructive methodology focused on these aspects uncovers a dimension of Catholicism that has been overlooked: the communal formulation of its miracles.

JOURNEYS

First of all, strange journeys—movements—were doggedly preserved in Loreto's mythohistory. The Loreto sanctuary insisted on a curious foreign provenance for its relics: Dalmatia. Technically, the *Santa Casa* and Marian icon came from Nazareth in the Holy Land.[56] According to a tradition shaped largely by Italians, however, it tarried first on the opposite Adriatic shore. This odd local interruption was never edited out of Loreto's origin accounts.

Other medieval relics had mythohistories that involved elaborate multistop journeys, but these did not give so much attention to intermediary stops. For example, in Russia in the summer of 1383, the icon of the Virgin of Tikhvin appeared four times in and around the forests near Novgorod before it finally took root and indicated the place for a future monastery to be built enshrining it.[57] The Tikhvin Madonna's four previous locations were not deemed important enough to name. Nor were the two short-lived stops of Loreto's relics in the vicinity of Recanati, prior to their entrenchment at Loreto. But Loreto's mythohistorians retained and emphasized its relics' hiatus at Trsat.

There are two potential conclusions to infer from this. First, the detail may memorialize an actual trail of provenance back to Dalmatia. This possibility is explored in chapters 3 and 8. Second, the particularity may have been retained in order to authenticate a component of Loreto's mythohistory that was deemed particularly miraculous: its journey. The Madonna

55. These three aspects roughly correspond to three of the categories described by Thomas Tweed as being cornerstones of religion: (1) moving across space (journeys); (2) moving across time (pairings of objects that endure); and (3) moving in the moment (lived experience). Tweed also has a category of moving into the cosmos that is not separated out in this analysis of Loreto. Tweed, *Crossing and Dwelling*.

56. Much has been made of Mary's house being in Nazareth before it embarked for Loreto in the 1290s. On St. Louis hearing mass in the *Santa Casa* in Nazareth in 1253: Begg, *Cult of the Black Virgin*, p. 242. On pilgrim reports that Mary's house was viewed in Nazareth as late as 1289: Santarelli, *Tradizione*, p. 14. On archaeological excavations in Nazareth (1955–60): Santarelli, *Loreto*, pp. 6–8.

57. Lidov, "Miracle-Working Icons," p. 54.

of Loreto's specific Dalmatian roots gave her a veneer of movement that was provocatively real and memorable, not metaphorical.

Back in the fourteenth century, when Loreto's mythohistory was first being formulated, people were evidently privileging movement, in the form of a concrete, verifiable journey, as central to religion and to expansion. Today's religious studies scholars and evolutionary biologists concur and bring corroborating theories to bear, seven centuries late. In his theoretical tour-de-force *Crossing and Dwelling*, Thomas Tweed defines "crossings," or traversals across geographical and cosmological space, as foundational to many world religions.[58] He also notes the connection between "dwellings," homes conceptually central to religious belief systems, and crossings: for instance, Cuban Catholics in Miami carried their concepts of spiritual homeland to Florida. They enacted celebrations to the Cuban Madonna of Charity there, linking themselves back to their home island. Tweed would not be surprised to see dwellings cross, and crossings dwell, in the mythohistory of Loreto.

Interestingly, neither would the biologist Alan De Queiroz, who uses the words "miracle" and "miraculous" no less than seventeen times to explain his scientific findings about the transoceanic journeys of monkeys and other animals. As is the case with the Holy House of Loreto, the mechanisms of monkeys' movement across sea and time seem inconceivable, "fundamentally unpredictable . . . improbable, rare, [and] mysterious."[59] But De Queiroz concludes that in a *long* "history acted out over many millions of years," these events "are [common] outcomes of a game of almost unimaginably large numbers," a game in which "the miraculous . . . become[s] the expected."[60] Movement is bound to happen over time: a monkey or a structure might be washed up on a different shore, with or without human intervention. In a human context, such landings signify deeply and incite wonder about the means of transit.

Tweed and De Queiroz are introduced here after descriptions of Loreto's mythohistory to demonstrate that our recent century does not have a monopoly on theorizing and exalting movement. Historical periodizations have contributed to the notion that zipping around the globe is unique to today. The relative ease of global transport from the twentieth century forward has turned the experience of movement mainstream.[61]

58. Tweed, *Crossing and Dwelling*, pp. 79, 123.

59. De Queiroz, *Monkey's Voyage*, pp. 299–300.

60. Ibid., pp. 299–300, 304.

61. Tweed notes that today "we can distinguish biped and quadruped religion, galleon and steamship religion, railroad and airplane religion. We can even talk about motorcycle

Historians have also made the pitch for the 1500s and 1600s, the heyday of Loreto's expansion, as an era of intensified mobility that presaged our modern refinement of mass transit: Natalie Zemon Davis's *Trickster Travels: A Sixteenth-Century Muslim between Worlds* (2007) and Linda Colley's *The Ordeal of Elisabeth Marsh: A Woman in World History* (2008) draw attention to how individuals trekked across the planet even without airplanes. But the mythohistory of Loreto was stressing movement before these watersheds on the conventional timeline. This analysis of Loreto's global spread features a wide spectrum of Catholics who moved to varying degrees, beginning in the late 1200s and ranging into the 1760s. Their actual travels suggest that the importance of journeying has been passed like a baton between times, peoples, and religions through miracle narratives like Loreto's. The flying house encodes and celebrates genuine movement.

PAIRINGS

Second, odd pairings or additions are accentuated in Loreto's origin narrative. Loreto's aggregated mythohistory presents the Mother of God as leaping the sea with travel ballast: a house in tow. From the inception of Christianity, it was common for Catholic sites in Europe to amass multiple relics. In most cases, however, there was no effort made to link the unrelated objects together into a single metanarrative. More often, a church's holdings resembled a cluttered Renaissance *wunderkammer* of disconnected novelties. The Church of the Madonna of San Luca in Bologna was a case in point. By 1505, their inventory included the head of St. Petronio, the heads of St. Dominic and St. Floriano, the hand of Santa Cecilia, the heads of St. Isidore and St. Proculus, a ribbon worn by the Virgin, a spine from the Crown of Thorns, and the head of St. Anne.[62]

But Loreto's relics were teamed up in narrative, and moreover, they were teamed *in transit*. For the Virgin Mary in particular, this was not commonplace. Madonnas tended to fly solo. Like other Catholic relics, Marian icons were occasionally found to have independently transported themselves from one location to another. It was a long-standing and cherished Catholic belief that relics had a latent power to self-propel.[63] These earthly vestiges of the saints were understood to be inherently restless,

---

religion." But he also acknowledges that "the movement of people . . . is not new, and is not confined to the modern west." Tweed, *Crossing and Dwelling*, pp. 125, 124.

62. Webb, *Patrons and Defenders*, p. 230.

63. On the self-propelled nature of medieval relics: Geary, *Furta Sacra*, pp. 33, 109.

so much so that when one arrived—by whatever means—there was frequently concern over whether it would stay. Some Marian objects, like the statue of the Virgin of Polignan in France, were chained down to prevent them from flying off again.[64] This roving impulse among Madonnas seems to have precluded their ready partnering with other sacred objects.

Why, then, did Loreto's Marian icon and Holy House get joined in transit? As with Loreto's Dalmatian journey, two interpretations seem plausible to explain the retention of this detail: first, that it happened, that the house genuinely did first get noticed because of the presence of an early image; or second, that over time, people continued to feel strongly that this pairing made Loreto more believable and somehow more authentic. In the ensuing chapters, new anchorages for Loreto are shown to have lost the specific attributions of Dalmatia and a house-and-icon team, but they nonetheless preserved the spirit behind them. At the Jesuit frontier missions named for Loreto, the long journeys of origin that were remembered were bona fide overseas voyages, and Marian icons were paired with real homes and churches. Later specificities of pairing seem to be practical records of true experience, additions from life rather than mere symbols.

Taking accretions seriously as measures of reality is an approach advocated by a leading scholar of religion, Robert Orsi. In his discussion of apparitions of Mary, Orsi criticizes scholars for reducing these dramatic eruptions of "radical presence or realness" into the human sphere. According to Orsi, historians have tended to inadequately describe apparitions either only by their social function or by their resistance to modernity. But he also sympathizes with the peculiar challenge of making sense of encounters that are eventually buried under "too many candles, too many statues and images . . . too much desire and need, too many souvenir stores hawking too many things . . . too much intimacy, exposure and vulnerability"—in short, too many pairings.[65] Orsi calls these moments of miraculous encounter "abundant history" because they seem to almost necessitate abundance in order for us to make sense of them, in any time period. He proposes that what is required for understanding is not to dig through all the excess to find a real moment before all the overlay, but also to *add* to the accretions, "to write abundantly about events that are not safely cordoned off in the past, but whose routes extend into the present, into the writing of history itself."[66]

64. Cassagnes-Brouquet, *Vierges Noires*, p. 56; Vélez, "Urban Driftwood," p. 62.
65. Orsi, "Abundant History," pp. 12, 14.
66. Ibid., p. 16.

Orsi espouses a sweeping degree of "abundance," a receptivity to embellishment that has inspired the reconstructive approach followed here but that is also reminiscent of some of Loreto's own early mythohistorians. The abundant first chronicles of Loreto reveal a Catholicism that is powerfully accretive: it is always in flux and reinvention, never frozen or static. While such an optimistic picture of Catholic devotion cannot sum up the entire history of the Catholic Church, with its many internal hierarchies and associations with imperial power, it nonetheless offers an important window for understanding how Catholicism may have proliferated via addition.

In a literal sense, many of the Catholic communities in transit who figure in Loreto's epic travels survived because they accepted and integrated new populations. For example, Jesuit mission settlements were often patchworks of refugees; for the Huron and the Moxos populations who joined those communities, migration made additions necessary. This inclusivity counters recent studies of diaspora that have focused on migrating populations' preservative or exclusionary self-bounding.[67] Instead of fixating on a single nation or social class and what they did to hold together as a discrete entity, this more comprehensive record of the many different groups associated with Loreto reveals openness. Italian, French, Spanish, Portuguese, Slav, Jesuit, Huron, Moxos, Monquí, and Inka communities all invited other people in. Addition was a crucial mechanism for spreading devotion.

LIVED EXPERIENCES

Third, a key feature preserved in Loreto's mythohistory is lived experience. Real events somehow became encoded in the founding narrative of this Italian Madonna. There is a difference of degree in this observation as well: It is not just a handful of celebrity, rare occurrences that got bundled into the mythohistory, but many, varied experiences that included those of the nonelite. Historians have shown renewed interest lately in retrieving

67. For instance, Daviken Studnicki-Gizbert's *Nation upon the Ocean Sea* describes how Portuguese merchants conserved their shared culture and sense of home when they were overseas. Engseng Ho considers how genealogy was used to delineate boundaries between others and the Hadrami diasporic community of Yemen in *The Graves of Tarim*. Thomas Tweed also calls attention to the boundary-enforcing dimensions of diaspora in his study on exiled Cuban Catholics that highlights how for these Catholics far from home, religion "draws boundaries around *us* and *them*; it constructs collective identity and, concomitantly, imagines degrees of social distance." Tweed, *Crossing and Dwelling*, p. 111.

how the "unlearned" laity helped formulate Catholic doctrine and practice.[68] For instance, William Pinch highlights how the Paravas, poor fishermen in Goa on the western coast of India, volunteered crucial testimony for the Europe-based canonization procedures for Francis Xavier in the seventeenth century.[69] This book likewise transcends regional studies of Catholicism to showcase ordinary people's wide-scale involvement across the globe, putting their contributions alongside those of better-known Catholics.

Obviously, with such a degree of participation, there are disagreements in the record. Reconstruction of Loreto's past involves reckoning with the cumulative amassing of *all* these occasionally contradictory formulations and reformulations. The end goal is not to mark where one articulation eclipsed another. The aim is instead to create a holistic picture of the many moments in the past when variations were tolerated and included. This can require some detective work to find sources related to Loreto's mythohistory that are not considered part of the official canon.

For instance, in the late 1400s, an unlinked poem, letter, biography, and travel account each differ about whether the Madonna of Loreto landed in Italy with or without a hitchhiking house. The Mantuan poet Fra Battista Spagnuoli casually presented the "without" version. He excised the *Santa Casa* entirely from his 1481 poem "Parthenice," describing the solitary migration of a Marian icon from Nazareth to Dalmatia to Loreto.[70] Spagnuoli's contemporary, Francisco Suriano (1450–c. 1528), was less subtle about expressing his opinion on the matter. He had twice served as superior general to the Franciscans in the Holy Land, where he had also worked as a papal legate. Suriano had been to Nazareth. On that authority, he wrote that Italy's Holy House of Loreto could not possibly be Mary's house transported.[71] Around the same time, in 1485, the humanist G. B. Petrucci begged to differ with Suriano and Spagnuoli's versions. Petrucci

68. Watkins, *History and the Supernatural*, p. 4; also, Pasulka, *Heaven Can Wait*, p. 148.

69. Pinch, "Corpse and Cult of Francis Xavier."

70. Lightbown, *Carlo Crivelli*, p. 43. Lightbown sees this thread of the Lauretan Virgin moving as an icon, *without* her house, as being repeated throughout the fifteenth century, including in an account about Loreto written by the Neapolitan Loise de Rosa (1385–1475) and in a speech given by Bonfini in Recanati in 1478. Spagnuoli's decision may have been an attempt to update the Loreto narrative to keep abreast of the taste of humanist readers. Alison Frazier describes fifteenth-century humanist writers who similarly edited saints' lives to keep them current for their audiences: Frazier, *Possible Lives*.

71. "The true Holy House [was] carved out of the rock of the hillside of Nazareth," he argued, "and [is] therefore of its nature immovable." Suriano as paraphrased by Hamilton, "Ottomans, the Humanists and the Holy House of Loreto," p. 4.

noted Loreto in his *Vita* of St. Giacomo della Marca. There, he included the tag-along *Santa Casa* and the four-stop journey, but he omitted the angels who were fast becoming central to the tale as the relics' mythic transport.[72] Just one year later, the travel account of Frenchman Georges Lengherand voiced still another perspective. Lengherand wrote of Mary and the *Santa Casa* traveling in tandem, but he reported an extra stop to their Loreto-bound itinerary. He had them land in Greece as well.[73]

The existence of these late-1400s variants suggests that there were multiple oral traditions surrounding the Madonna of Loreto. The devotion's later chroniclers evidently had choices to sort through when they defined her relic complex. Although some of these variants ended up on the cutting-room floor, they are retrieved here as crucial pieces in the puzzle of what allows a mythohistory to flourish: not conformity, but some allowance for diversity of opinion.

That said, historian Carl Watkins urges scholars not to overstate the space Catholicism has allowed for varying opinions. He cautions: "We need to avoid being dazzled by the diversity that we have discovered. . . . Meanings might indeed proliferate. . . . [But] cores of shared thought and action gave medieval Christianity its power."[74] Concurring with Watkins, this book strives to associate the diverse laity with "cores of shared thought" as much as with fringe revisionism. Catholicism's core still tends to be presented mostly as the brainchild of high church administrators. But here, the actions of individuals, often untrained laymen, are shown to contribute to central Catholic principles as influentially and as often as they contradict them. Impulses among laymen to repeat or emphasize the shared core are explored in depth here, as in chapter 7's overview of the Litany of Loreto.

Limits of Reconstruction: Chronology, Zoning, and Violence

In order to reconstruct and understand the miraculous flying house of Loreto, this work forwards the most baffling but definitive characteristics of Loreto's mythohistory: journeys, pairings, and lived experience. But this methodology does have some limitations as well that need to be flagged before proceeding. The first weakness is chronology. Since Loreto's

72. Petrucci as paraphrased by Santarelli, *Tradizione*, p. 17.

73. [Lengherand], *Voyage de Georges Lengherand*, p. 75.

74. Watkins, *History and the Supernatural*, p. 12.

mythohistory preceded modern academic segregations, it defiantly spans historians' temporal divides. Secondly, and for the same reason, the mythohistory bridges frontier and metropole, two zones that are traditionally contrasted instead of being grouped together. Finally, the mythohistory minimizes violence as a mechanism for the diffusion of Christianity.

One might expect a historian to distance herself from the mythohistory for these reasons, to honor today's predilections to emphasize chronology, zoning, and violence instead of echoing what appear to be outdated attitudes. But the project of this book is reconstruction, not deconstruction. The three elements are therefore not discussed below simply as limitations to be corrected. Instead they are incorporated thoughtfully into the methodology to stand as additional evidence for comprehending why the miraculous Holy House of Loreto still flies. The intent of such reconstruction is not to blindly replicate the problems of Loreto's mythohistory, but to knowingly call attention to all the parts of the whole that have given it lasting power, including those that sit less comfortably with current disciplinary preferences.

Of the three limits faced by historians reconstructing Loreto, the first is arguably the most grievous: disrespect for chronology. Historians are trained to avoid anachronism and worry rightly about inaccurately imposing later motives or realities on earlier peoples. To avoid this, they tend to treat time periods discretely and to proceed from the oldest ones forward to present day. For example, Katherine Ludwig Jansen's first chapter of *The Making of the Magdalen* begins with Mary Magdalen's earliest recorded moments; her epilogue is set centuries later, addressing Tridentine reformers who altered the Magdalen's story. She subtitles these bookend sections "From History to Legend" and "From Legend to History," indicating her chronological trajectory from a point of origin in established reality (history) through fictional embellishments (legend) and back to a reaffirmation of a history that emerged at a particular fixed moment in time.[75] But this reconstruction of Loreto flips Jansen's order, starting in this chapter by moving from legend to mythohistory, and concluding with a chapter that takes the reader from mythohistory back to the legend of where Loreto began. The book ends with the thirteenth century by way of the seventeenth century rather than proceeding in order.

75. Jansen, *Making of the Magdalen*, pp. 18–46 (chapter 1: "'In Memory of Her': From History to Legend"), pp. 333–36 (epilogue: "'In Memory of Her': From Legend to History").

Why upset periodization? This is not done to artistically replicate the chronological disorder of Loreto's mythohistory. There is a tried-and-true historical methodology being applied here: to take *later* experiences, well documented in the seventeenth century, to help deduce what happened in the less chronicled thirteenth century at the moment of Loreto's genesis. The practice of backward projection has been used with some success by other historians and anthropologists who are faced with lack of early source material. Inga Clendinnen attributes the technique to archaeologists and refers to it as "upstreaming." In her work on the Maya of the sixteenth-century Yucatán, she is able to refer to later documents such as the eighteenth-century *Book of Chilam Balam of Chumayel* to tentatively recreate some of the worldview of the earlier Maya who are her focus.[76]

In this book, however, it is not just the lack of sources that drives this approach, but an interest in retrieving experiences that were shared across eras. Loreto's mythohistory suggests that Catholics in the thirteenth century had future audiences in mind; those future audiences in turn built consciously on foundations established in the thirteenth century. This awareness between times is evident in thoughtful repetition. Later devotees of Loreto chose to repeat and accentuate certain parts of the mythohistory. This repetition simultaneously served to honor ancestors and to speak to future viewers about what still mattered. As described above, scholars like Diana Walsh Pasulka, Alex Golub, and Jon Peterson have productively mustered such repetitions (and the ruptures these illuminate). Their work attests to how conversations like the ones surrounding Loreto can run forward and backward through time and should be presented in all their achronological fullness.

A second disciplinary point of contention a historian might bring to this reconstruction of Loreto's mythohistory is the uncomfortable broadening of geographical frame. The wide dispersal of the miracle of Loreto ended up aligning far-flung regions with more central sites. To study both fringe and hub at once contradicts the geographic specialization favored by intellectuals today. For instance, religious studies scholar James Laine describes a religious "mood" of public, organic performativity that he tacitly associates with zones of cultural encounter.[77] As discussed at length in

76. Clendinnen, *Ambivalent Conquests*, pp. 132–33. For another excellent example of how *The Book of Chilam Balam* has been mustered to understand indigenous Christianity predating the time of its composition: Carrasco, "Borderlands and 'Biblical Hurricane,'" pp. 362–63.

77. Laine's examples for the kind of religious practice that he calls "mood," drawn from an article by E. Valentine Daniel, are associated with new frontiers (the United States)

chapter 5 below, in the case of Loreto, the mood that Laine describes is evident in frontier Jesuit missions, but it is also visible in Italy's sanctuary to the Madonna of Loreto, in major European cities, and in that central zone that historians love to contrast with the periphery. Loreto's mythohistory thus somewhat preposterously traces out a "megazone" that cuts across frontier and metropole, national, cultural, and imperial divides, and even time periods. Within this enormous zone, behaviors observed in Europe are also discernible in the sparsely populated margins of overseas empires among non-European populations, and vice versa. These shared behaviors have been tagged in Loreto's mythohistory as good Catholic behaviors, signs of successful religious expansion.

This study takes the unbounded geographic component of mythohistory seriously, not as Catholic propaganda or a symbolic claim, but as a historical trace of life experiences that *did* get transmitted across borders, that *were* in fact shared between people of disparate regions, and that *were* read by some who were involved as denoting Catholicism. But in contrast to some early accounts that articulate Loreto's mythohistory, the megazone sketched out in this book is not intended to designate an unambiguous sphere of Catholic presence or to circumscribe the outer reaches of Catholic influence. Indeed, it is best described in sharp contrast to this, as a "jumbling" in which Catholics were present.

Clifford Geertz used the word "jumbling" when characterizing the movement of religions in today's ultimate megazone of the entire planet, adding adjectives like "piecemeal, headlong, fitful . . . unorganized." He observed that religions now inhabit "a world where more and more people and the selves they have inherited are . . . out of context: thrown in among others in ambiguous, irregular, poly-faith settlements."[78] Geertz suggested that this is a recent development, but Loreto's mythohistory demonstrates that it is not.[79] A goal of this project has been to do justice to the chaotic

as opposed to old traditional spheres (India). Laine argues: "I would submit, then, that what Daniel calls religion, this Christian thing, is in fact that style of religion produced by cultural change and cross-cultural encounter." Historians continue to primarily associate transformative cross-cultural encounters with first contact zones on imperial frontiers rather than with "Old World" centers in Europe and Asia. Laine, "Mind and Mood in the Study of Religion," p. 242; Daniel, "Arrogation of Being."

78. Geertz, "Shifting Aims," p. 12.

79. Ibid., pp. 11–12. Geertz himself credits an early twentieth-century intellectual, Alphonse de Lamartine, with the "jumbling" characterization, which suggests that the mobility of religions is not so recent a development. While I extend this "jumbling" notion as far back as the thirteenth century, I do agree with Geertz that there are particular scales and realities of migration today that differ from mobility in the past.

jumble in the megazone, not to retroactively assign order to it. To that end, shared behaviors are presented here not as definitive markers of Catholic faith but as possible turning points when Catholicism might (and often did) find new footholds.

This book contends that within the megazone, one can readily discern repeated *communal* expressions of Catholicism. Communal as mustered here does not mean community or "communitas" in the sense intended by anthropologist Victor Turner. Turner famously characterized rituals as establishing intense feelings of comradeship across social, hierarchical, and cultural lines. Because of this undifferentiated bonding or "communitas," Turner viewed ritual participants as willingly cooperating to reinvigorate or even innovate societal values.[80] It can be tempting to view the joint construction of Loreto's mythohistory as a massive ritual generating communitas.[81] Indeed, some have argued that "myth is the script of ritual and arises alongside it."[82] To such myth ritualists, the mythohistory discussed here could be read as Victor Turner's vision on steroids: within the megazone's liminal bounds, Catholics of all cultures, ranks, and genders celebrated their common encounters with the miraculous and cooperatively edited Catholic doctrine as needed.[83]

But this is not at all what the historical record shows. The megazone of Loreto's diffusion as described here was too big to produce this sort of self-conscious or idyllic participant community. Many of those involved in the making of Loreto's mythohistory were unaware of each other. Others were all too aware of existent imbalances of power between them and could not experience their joint participation in a unifying way.[84] In this book, *communal* is therefore used to qualify activity in the megazone and to contrast with *communitas*. "Communal" does not denote ritual glue. Here, it serves

80. Olvaeson, "Collective Effervescence and Communitas," pp. 93, 104, 107.

81. Turner himself might have agreed: he saw all ritual as religious, intended to "celebrate or commemorate transcendent powers." Turner and Turner, "Religious Celebrations," p. 201.

82. The classicist Jane Harrison and biblical scholar Samuel Hooke are two early "myth-ritualists" who connected myth and ritual in this way. Segal, "Myth-Ritualist Theory of Religion," p. 175.

83. This may sound like a distorted idealization of Victor Turner's intent, but actually, Turner himself was a convert to Catholicism, and his elaborations of "communitas," particularly later in his life, seem to harbor a hopefulness for precisely this unifying power in religious (particularly Catholic?) ritual. On Turner's Catholicism: Deflem, "Ritual, Anti-structure and Religion," pp. 18–19.

84. Darlene Juschka showcases this dynamic in the parallel, geography-stretching case of medieval pilgrimage. Juschka, "Whose Turn Is It to Cook."

simply to indicate the involvement of many people, in varied ways and with untidy, if measurable, effects.

This dynamic of diverse forms of participation, some of it *not* of the bonding variety, leads to the third and most important caveat for those intent on reconstructing mythohistory in order to understand Loreto. Holistic as it appears to be, there is a missing piece in the picture: violence. This is not to say that violence is not present in the historical record. For those attuned to its contours, it is painfully evident in the very founding narrative of Loreto and in much that is chronicled here. But violence is relegated to the background and dramatically overshadowed by the flying house. One way that it gets subsumed is that thinking with a megazone can serve to erase imperial, national, and local divides that normally stand as crucial reminders of political bloodshed and division. Another way violence is sidelined is that narratives surrounding Loreto have tended to prioritize the shared and resilient, à la Victor Turner. As noted at the beginning of this chapter, the mythohistory of Loreto has an antiseptic veneer that has been taken by some, including many seventeenth-century Jesuits, as an indicator of miraculously peaceful diffusion. Loreto's reconstructed past is *not* an account of how the Catholic Church advanced by means of armies and military conflicts.

The combative side of Christian expansion (Protestant and Catholic) retains a strong grip on the American popular imagination owing to terrorism and wars in the Middle East.[85] Current events have provoked a resurgence of interest in some chapters of Catholic history such as the Crusades, the Conquest, and the Inquisition, moments when Catholics brutally enforced and pushed their faith on others and on their own.[86] This study does not purport to substitute for such thematic histories of political domination, but it does aim to temper the persistent stereotype that Catholicism in particular pressed outward mostly by sword and stake.[87]

85. There has been a proliferation of studies on Protestant Christianity in particular with regard to recent political events. See: Herbert, *Faith-Based War*; Longman, *Christianity and Genocide in Rwanda*; Baker, *Gospel According to the Klan*; Doyle, *Fighting Like the Devil for the Sake of God*; Juster, *Sacred Violence in Early America*. Also, these latest compendia of comparative violence across world religions give valuable context to Christianity: *Oxford Handbook of Religion and Violence*; Jonathan Fine, *Political Violence in Judaism, Christianity and Islam*.

86. For instance, see recent revisitations of these moments of Catholic notoriety including: Fancy, *Mercenary Mediterranean*; Claster, *Sacred Violence*; Altman, *Contesting Conquest*; and *Judging Faith, Punishing Sin*.

87. There are still too few accessible and sophisticated histories that showcase alternative, nonmilitaristic forms of Catholic diffusion. Stuart Schwartz has won awards for

Aggressive imposition alone cannot explain the reach and hold of Catholic devotion in the early modern period. This reconstruction of Loreto's spread uncovers concurrent, counterpoint sensibilities to violence: journeys of wandering, not military occupation; accretions, not weedings; and experiences that bridged instead of dividing. These three components so prominent in Loreto's mythohistory were as essential as warfare in the global diffusion of Catholicism. Their popularity transcended era and region. In the work that follows they are given full measure, not to replace but to critically supplement the reality of violence.

---

beginning to fill the void with *All Can Be Saved.* Schwartz considers how hundreds of people around the world who were arrested by various Iberian Inquisition courts managed to sustain a refrain of tolerance toward other religions. Still, his counternarrative of broad-minded early modern Catholics feels stifled by the Inquisition's dominance.

PART II

Approaching Loreto

FIGURE 3.1. Silver seal of Cardinal Gallo (c. 1580s), owned by the Museo-Pinacoteca della Santa Casa di Loreto. Photo: Caldari Giovanelli from *Le Arti Nelle Marche* (Milan, 1992), reproduced by permission of the Delegazione Pontificia per il Santuario della Santa Casa di Loreto.

CHAPTER THREE

First Authors

THE MYTHOHISTORY OF LORETO was fixed in ink and cast in metal in the late sixteenth century, leaving a dominant visual imprint that today's visitors must still reckon with as they approach the old sanctuary. Two small objects serve to illustrate how Loreto's complicated origins were compressed into a single brand: an official shrine seal and a papal medal. The seal shows the Madonna of Loreto and her house paired in flight, carried by angels (figure 3.1).[1] This deceptively simple image was stamped repeatedly on all official civil and religious documents pertaining to Loreto throughout the 1600s. It eventually became the standard representation of the Lauretan devotion in Europe.[2] Presented in marvelous isolation, the duo of Mary and her *Santa Casa* give the impression of quiet, magical mobility.

The effect of this carefully selected imagery is evident when the adopted seal is set alongside a commemorative medal cast around the same moment, in 1586. Numismatics specialist Daniele Diotavelli describes this medal as also depicting the Virgin Mary holding the baby Jesus, sitting atop the *Santa Casa,* held aloft by angels. But the medal encloses the scene with bastions, referring to the actual 1580s extension of Loreto's defensive walls to completely encircle the pilgrimage site. The obverse side shows the face of Loreto's most celebrated patron, Pope Sixtus V, who had just elevated Loreto to the status of city when it had previously been subject to

1. Giovannelli, "Il Cardinale Antonio Maria Gallo," p. 90.

2. In particular, paintings and carved models associated with Loreto came to display Mary perched on the roof of her moving house. Boyer, *Cult of the Virgin,* pp. 80–81; *La Madonna di Loreto nelle Marche,* figures 65–90 for twenty-eight examples mostly dating from the seventeenth and eighteenth centuries, the focus period of this book.

its urban neighbors, Recanati and Macerata.[3] Since the early 1500s, Pope Sixtus V's predecessors had begun to use Loreto as the papacy's active seaside fortress, part of a string of coastal defenses against the incursion of Ottoman Turks. At certain points in the sixteenth century, more soldiers trundled through the sanctuary than pilgrims.[4]

Considering the official shrine seal and the celebratory medal side by side, the seal notably excises human faces and fortifications from the picture. Some of Loreto's first sixteenth-century histories strained to follow the official shrine seal's dramatic omission of the site's highly militarized reality. But the seal gradually stamped out most alternative representations. It was the perfect emblem for the casual expansion that came to mark early modern Catholicism: Mary and her house flew. This was a new kind of domination, not by sword, but by movement. The subtle pitch resembles twentieth-century news reports about the convenience store Wal-Mart: disturbingly innocuous, all it had to do was to arrive in a new neighborhood and open its doors, and local competition would be displaced.[5] The gritty details of the process of landing are edited out.

As noted in chapter 1, accounts of Loreto and Catholic expansion are dominated by this sort of polished product, with a marketing agenda so clear that it outshines reality.[6] This chapter critically reexamines Loreto's historical "brand" by putting faces back in the picture, looking at some of the first authors of Loreto's origin story. It opens with the architects of Loreto's shrine seal, Cardinal Antonio Maria Gallo and Cardinal Rutilio Benzoni. Moving down the ranks and back in time, there are two earlier sixteenth-century chroniclers who laid the groundwork for the high clergy's selective mythohistory: a shrine governor, Pietro di Giorgio Tolomei, and a local secretary, Girolamo Angelitta. Like Virgin and house, and

3. Diotavelli, "Medaglie e sigilli."

4. A hint of the disruption caused by the surges of military presence comes from neighboring Macerata. In 1566, Macerata was turned into an emergency base for four thousand infantry and cavalry. All these soldiers were headed toward Loreto and Italy's eastern coast, to reinforce the Papal States' defenses. Lightbown, *Carlo Crivelli*, p. 47; Hamilton, "Ottomans, the Humanists and the Holy House of Loreto," p. 11; Spence, *Memory Palace of Matteo Ricci*, pp. 29–30.

5. The Wal-Mart analogy stems from historian William B. Taylor's insightful comment that the growth of Marian devotion in the early modern Spanish empire has been exaggerated to resemble "Wal-Mart style" takeovers. Taylor, "Two Shrines of the Cristo Renovado," p. 947.

6. On the complexity and effectiveness of Catholic propaganda from this time period: Soergel, *Wondrous in His Saints*; Levy, *Propaganda and the Jesuit Baroque*.

seal and medal, these men are first introduced in pairs and then grouped in larger company because, sometimes unbeknownst to each other, they worked in tandem to reconstruct Loreto's past. Their overlaps and contradictions illuminate the often inadvertently collaborative project of building official shrine history. The cardinals and shrine administrators set the stage for the chapter's ensuing consideration of two seventeenth-century Jesuit shrine chroniclers, the lesser-known Raphael Riera and the higher-ranked Oratio Torsellino. Those men point, in turn, to their contemporaries across the Adriatic Sea, Nikolà Frankopan and fellow Slavic Catholics who also contributed to Loreto's emerging narrative.

Before turning to these writers, it is important to sidestep our own blinding and oversimplified twenty-first-century emblem of Catholic authorship. Blockbuster stories like *The Da Vinci Code* (2003/2006) have invited audiences to think of the makers of religious history as conspirators with subversive agendas.[7] They prompt us to look for a priest or two secretly plotting to manipulate people. The subjects of this chapter were practicing Catholic men with influence and with a unified message redolent with symbolism. But beyond this, they do not look much like the scheming antagonists stamped on our psyches by popular media. These sixteenth- and seventeenth-century creators diverged most pointedly from today's conspiracy theories because of their lack of organization. This chapter does not show a hierarchical chain of command hiring people to broadcast one set triumphalist script, but instead reveals multiple authors independently taken with the same story and borrowing from each other's renditions.

What did these first composers of Loreto's past have in common? Here again, they confound modern expectations. First, they were remarkably close to the shrine that they validated. Their presence as eyewitnesses or visitors added credibility to their reportage. Simon Ditchfield has noted

7. Dan Brown's best-selling novel *The Da Vinci Code* was translated into forty-four languages and sold over eighty million copies worldwide before being turned into a widely viewed movie. It is one of the best known of a fiction genre of conspiracy theory that casts secretive fringe groups such as Freemasons and Illuminati as villains. In the Catholic corner of this burgeoning genre, the plotters include *Opus Dei* featured in *The Da Vinci Code* and, often, the Jesuits; these generally male, elite Catholic networks hide truths about Christian history in order to find profit or treasure like the Holy Grail. On the profound cultural impact of Catholic conspiracy fiction like *The Da Vinci Code*: Newhaiser, Farias, and Tausch, "Functional Nature of Conspiracy Beliefs," p. 1007; Hjarvard, "Mediazation of Religion," p. 11. On the Jesuit conspiracy genre: Pavone, *Wily Jesuits*; Worcester, "Anti-Jesuit Polemic."

that every diocese in Tridentine Italy had its "local Baronio" engaged in that famous cardinal's project to preserve the particular, acting in the capacity of on-site devotional advocate.[8] Many of the self-appointed historians described here fit that profile. Their personal interest and their expertise stemmed from their real proximity to the action. Second, the early authors discussed below wrote with a keen awareness of the corpus that preceded them and continued to flourish around them. They did not set out to invent, but to bolster. They published and recorded about Loreto not to contribute originality, but to add comprehensiveness and depth to an already existing entry in the metaphorical, ever-expanding encyclopedia of Catholic understanding.

Anchoring Ideal: An Official Shrine Seal Produced by Many

The two most politically powerful articulators of Loreto's origins are best introduced through their common ground with fellow authors: their proximity to the scene of the action, and their flair for embellishment. Both men were also appointed to their posts as Cardinals by the same patron, Pope Sixtus V (1585–90).[9] Sixtus V was not the first pope to back Loreto, but during his five-year reign, he supported projects to artistically and defensively restructure the pilgrimage site, most notably by calling forward two energetic reformers, Antonio Maria Gallo and Rutilio Benzoni.[10]

8. Cardinal Cesare Baronio (1538–1607) transformed Europe's crowded scene of Catholic saints by undertaking a massive project to research and validate each of them, resulting in the twelve-volume *Annales Ecclesiastici*, a canon of Catholic holiness updated for the sixteenth century. Simon Ditchfield considers the local repercussions of Baronio's initiative in *Liturgy, Sanctity and History in Tridentine Italy*, p. 327.

9. Pope Sixtus V (Felice Peretti) was born in Montalto, Italy, to a Dalmatian family who had fled to Italy to avoid Turkish invasion in the mid-1400s. It is tempting to credit his Dalmatian background with causing him to take such interest in the Loreto shrine when he became pope. He brought Loreto to international attention by funding art and defensive walls there and by contributing to churches that were being dedicated to Loreto in other cities including Macerata. *Le Arti nelle Marche al Tempo di Sisto V*; Valone, "Women on the Quirinal Hill," p. 136n36.

10. Other popes who patronized Loreto included Popes Gregory XI (1370–8), Nicholas V (1447–55), Pius II (1458–64), Paul II (1464–71), Innocent VIII (1484–92), and Julius II (1503–13), who credited the Madonna of Loreto with saving his life in the siege of Mirandola. On Gregory XI, Nicholas V, and Pius II: Santarelli, *Loreto*, pp. 17, 20. On Pius II and Paul II: Lightbown, *Carlo Crivelli*, pp. 40, 42, 47. On Innocent VIII: Hamilton, "Ottomans,

TWO CARDINALS: GALLO AND BENZONI

Pope Sixtus V named Cardinal Antonio Maria Gallo to the newly created post of Protector of the Loreto Sanctuary in 1586. Gallo was a young thirty-three at the time. Born in Osimo, just northwest of Loreto, his quick rise up the ecclesiastical ranks eventually led him back home again: he started as Bishop of Perugia, became Cardinal and Protector of Loreto, and finally was named bishop of his own hometown of Osimo. Even from his final seat in Osimo, Cardinal Gallo continued to administer to the Loreto shrine until his death in 1620.[11] His initiatives at Loreto included starting construction of a new sacristy at Loreto to store the burgeoning collection of votive offerings from pilgrims.[12] Gallo also ramped up security dramatically by creating two new corps of foot troops and cavalry, installing a new aqueduct to preempt siege tactics that might cut off the city's water supply, and reconvening the Order of Lauretan Knights.[13] These knights used the vantage point of Loreto's hilltop—the highest in the region, heightened further by new fortifications—to scan the sea for Turkish war ships.

Gallo was accompanied by another high-ranking cleric, the bishop of the newly clustered diocese of Recanati-Loreto: Rutilio Benzoni. Benzoni moved away from his native Rome to reside at his provincial post of Loreto for twenty-six years, from his 1586 appointment until his death in 1613. He was eagerly hands-on with his programs at Loreto. Benzoni not only organized Loreto's first seminary for aspiring priests; he also precisely laid out the course of study for its students. Similarly, he did not merely supervise the flurry of artistic renovation; he also personally selected or approved the iconography to be portrayed in every aspect of Loreto's basilica, from sacristy to bronze doors to cupola.[14] Cardinal Benzoni, along with

---

the Humanists and the Holy House of Loreto," p. 11. On Julius II: Ranucci and Tenenti, *Sei Riproduzioni della Santa Casa di Loreto in Italia*, p. 36.

11. Caldari Giovannelli, "Il Cardinale Antonio Maria Gallo," p. 85.

12. Curzi, "La committenza Gallo," p. 94.

13. The Order of Lauretan Knights was established by Pope Paul III in 1545 to guard Loreto's basilica against sea attacks from the Ottoman Turks. It was briefly abolished by Pope Gregory XIII (1572–85) after the 1571 Battle of Lepanto, a naval defeat for the Ottomans at the hands of the "Holy League" of Spain, Venice, and the papacy. Loreto's Knights reassembled in 1586 in response to a fresh onslaught of Turkish coastal raids. Their numbers hovered between 200 and 330 (a peak reached in 1656). Caldari Giovannelli, "Il Cardinale Antonio Maria Gallo," p. 90; Diotavelli, "Medaglie e sigilli."

14. Grimaldi, "Il Vescovo Rutilio Benzoni."

Cardinal Gallo, was also responsible for choosing and adopting Loreto's official shrine seal.

Why did such high-ranking men take an interest in this coastal shrine? Before them, it was mostly known only in the immediate region, overshadowed by the large neighboring Adriatic seaport of Ancona.[15] If it was just Cardinal Gallo of Osimo who had invested his energy here, one could answer the question by arguing that it was simply close neighbors of the shrine who took a self-serving interest in promoting their nearest claim-to-fame. But the existence of a dynamic *pair* of cardinals challenges that premise. Cardinal Benzoni of Rome was participating as earnestly as his colleague from Osimo. His parallel actions help situate these two cardinals as part of a wider transformation of Catholic Church authority. Late sixteenth-century bishops cleaved to a new administrative ideal that transcended personal origins and small hometown loyalties. Fired up by the episcopal reforms of the Council of Trent (1545–63), these leading bureaucrats often lived in or frequented the cities to which they had been assigned; they actively participated and invested in restorations throughout their region; and they catalyzed local religious devotions by publicizing them farther afield.[16] Gallo and Benzoni were part of this Counter-Reformation trend.

The interventions of Cardinals Gallo and Benzoni at Loreto show a deliberate wresting of this site from its coastal anchorage, and a fresh impulse to share it with the broader world. From the vantage point of these men, being important locally was no longer enough. Loreto's story had to be disseminated more widely, not just for the profit of the shrine center or for the career advancement of the church officials involved, but for the good of the Catholic Church itself. Gallo and Benzoni chose to broadcast the specific parts of Loreto's past that seemed advantageous to a church wracked with growing pains and challenged by emerging Protestants. In Loreto, they found a site that tangibly demonstrated that Catholicism could fly, and fly far.

15. Ancona was the largest city of the Marche region in the fifteenth century. It had alliances and treaties with the Dalmatian coastal cities of Ragusa, Zara, Segna, and Scutari. Lightbown, *Carlo Crivelli*, p. 28.

16. Olds, "How to Be a Counter-Reformation Bishop"; Ditchfield, "'Of Dancing Cardinals and Mestizo Madonnas.'"

TWO SHRINE ADMINISTRATORS: TOLOMEI AND ANGELITTA

Miracles kept people interested in the Catholic Church.[17] But what inspired Cardinals Gallo and Benzoni to emphasize miraculous flight were two earlier chroniclers of Loreto who had painstakingly demonstrated that there was truth behind the movement of Mary and her house. Like the paired cardinals, the two chroniclers who verified this had lived at or near Loreto, and one had been officially entrusted with shrine management. Pietro di Giorgio Tolomei was the first to produce a printed history of Loreto's shrine origins, published in Latin in 1472.[18] He was one of the first governors of the Loreto shrine, presiding over it from 1454 until his death in 1473. This was a prosperous period in which Loreto basked in the attention of Pope Paul II and Niccolò dell'Aste, bishop of the neighboring city of Recanati, who chose to build his apostolic palace and raise a new basilica at Loreto.[19] Governor Tolomei was from the neighboring village of Teramo, which explains his favored nickname, "Il Teramano," the man from Teramo. Tolomei's title and his connections to the countryside beyond the shrine brought him immediate readership and publicity. Vicenzo Casale, the papal governor of Bologna, arranged for Tolomei's text to be translated into Italian, Slavonic, Greek, Spanish, French, German, and even Arabic so that it could be made available to the full spectrum of Loreto's pilgrims.[20] These translations, in abbreviated format, were eventually posted as explanatory displays for visitors to the Lauretan sanctuary.[21]

Sixty years after Tolomei produced his grounding account, another printed history emerged to enrich Loreto's mythohistory. Girolamo

17. "The enduring appeal of the miraculous throughout the Early Modern period and beyond cannot be overstated." Ditchfield, *Liturgy, Sanctity and History in Tridentine Italy*, p. 129.

18. Tolomei, "Translatio," pp. 104–7.

19. Lightbown gives the opening date of Tolomei's governorship as either 1450 or 1454 and notes that he was already working for the shrine in 1437. Lightbown, *Carlo Crivelli*, pp. 42–43; Santarelli, *Tradizione*, pp. 10–11.

20. Hamilton, "Ottomans, the Humanists and the Holy House of Loreto," p. 5.

21. Well into the 1600s, pilgrims to Loreto reported the shrine's history with language so close to that of Tolomei's 1472 "Translatio" that it seems likely that they copied directly from his account. Tolomei's history might have been circulated in print at the pilgrimage site, but today one abbreviated paragraph of it hangs prominently on display, carved in six different languages on stone tablets placed throughout the basilica. I assume that these modern placards replaced older ones.

Angelitta wrote his *Lauretanae Virginis Historia* in Latin around 1531.[22] He was working next door to Loreto as a secretary of the city government at Recanati, a post he held from 1509 until 1561.[23] While he compiled his history, Loreto's *Santa Casa* was being sheathed in marble by artists set to work by Pope Julius II. Angelitta's *Historia* circulated more widely than stone embossments at the shrine. Plaques of the account of his predecessor, Tolomei, were encountered primarily by pilgrims arriving at Loreto. But Angelitta's work quickly reached readers outside the shrine. This was partly due to the author's self-promotion. Before his work even reached the press, Angelitta presented a manuscript copy of it to Pope Clement VII when the pope passed through Loreto.[24] The book's popularity surged even after Angelitta's death, especially at the end of the sixteenth century. It saw new editions in Italian and French translation in 1580, 1590, 1596, and again in 1600.[25]

Tolomei's and Angelitta's histories were both widely read and translated. Clearly, the shrine of Loreto had started to go public even before the cardinals Gallo and Benzoni got to it and gave it a brand in the late 1500s. But the juxtaposition of Tolomei and Angelitta's earlier accounts with the stamp used by cardinals shows an additional dynamic to how Loreto was being diffused. While the later cardinals pared away details to focus on one strong symbolic message of forward motion, Tolomei and Angelitta gathered all the details available to them to track past motion. During the Reformation period, high-ranking Catholic officials like the aforementioned cardinals often acted as strict editors.[26] But Tolomei and Angelitta moved in lower circles where they were not being urged to prune. They dug deeply into the existing archives to compose their accounts, exhaustively compiling all earlier knowledge.

Tolomei's history demonstrates his thorough research, though it was elegantly succinct. After specifying the identity of Loreto's *Santa Casa*, he fixed the starts and stops of the relic's journey: Nazareth, Dalmatia, the forest near Recanati, and finally Loreto. Because Tolomei was the first to

22. Santarelli, *Tradizione*, p. 19.

23. Ibid., p. 24; Lightbown, *Carlo Crivelli*, p. 42.

24. Hamilton, "Ottomans, the Humanists and the Holy House of Loreto," p. 17.

25. Brizay, "Pèlerins et pèlerinages," p. 211n11. The version of Angelitta consulted for this book is the 1580 edition, translated into the Italian vernacular and published in Loreto's neighboring city of Macerata. One copy of this edition can be found in Rome's Biblioteca Angelica, sewn into the back of another work on Loreto, *Compendio di alcune cose notabile successe in Loreto* (Ancona, 1582).

26. On the sixteenth- and seventeenth-century purging of "excesses" by the "cerebral center" of the Catholic Church and elites: Hsia, *World of Catholic Renewal*, p. 200.

print these details, some modern scholars have insinuated that they are his sole invention.[27] But he was not pulling the story from the air, nor was his version as original as its printed novelty has made it seem. In the fifteenth century, the Loreto shrine already had a trove of Latin manuscripts chronicling the devotion's earliest days. Giacomo Ricci, a priest from Brescia, visited Loreto in 1467—six years before Tolomei's publication—and consulted these papers.[28] Ricci's 1468 report of what he saw still exists in manuscript form. He wrote about Loreto's origins and named as his source some old, mostly illegible, and already-decomposing manuscripts that he was allowed to view there.

Ricci's manuscript gives the same core narrative as Tolomei's: Mary's house, already turned into a church by the apostles and containing an image of Mary carved by St. Luke, was moved from Nazareth by angels after a war with the infidels; it was transported to Illyria (Dalmatia); it was not honored sufficiently there, so the angels moved it again to territory near Recanati; it shifted twice more within these environs before stopping on the property of a woman called Loreta. The consistency between Ricci's reconstruction and Tolomei's slightly later version suggests that both men drew from the same Lauretan archival fount.[29]

Tolomei also buttressed his rendition of events with another source of information. He mustered extensive oral testimony, demonstrating that the culture of orality still carried weight in the sixteenth century for confirming Catholic devotions. Tolomei told of three witnesses whom he had heard tell with his own ears: a local Augustinian hermit, Fra Paolo, saw lights in the sky on the feast day of the Nativity; Paolo di Rinalduccio (deceased c. 1448) reported that his grandfather's grandfather personally saw angels carrying the house; and Francesco Priore explained that his great-grandfather visited the house when it was still in the forest near Recanati, before its final move to Loreto.[30] Such verbal depositions from

27. Lightbown problematically deflects this common charge from Tolomei to the whole "credulous" genre of priests: "[Tolomei] has been accused of deliberately falsifying [Loreto's] history, but in reality seems to have been only kindly, devout and credulous. . . . Certainly some scholars have attributed the creation of the legend of the Holy House, or at any rate the increased anxiety to diffuse it more widely, to a desire among priests, like Teramano [Tolomei], who had long served at the shrine, to prevent the demolition of the old, humble chapel, sanctified by the faith of generations in its miracles." Lightbown, *Carlo Crivelli*, pp. 42, 44.

28. Ibid., p. 41. Giacomo Ricci's manuscript has recently been published in parts in *Virginis Mariae Loretae Historia*, pp. 35–39, 106–7. It is considered to be the earliest written account that connects Mary's Nazarene house with Loreto.

29. Santarelli, *Tradizione*, pp. 10–11.

30. Ibid; also, Lightbown, *Carlo Crivelli*, p. 40.

witnesses were not only collected as evidence in the sphere of religion.[31] They were also gathered to settle legal disputes in medieval Europe.[32] Tolomei's choice of evidence for his founding history of Loreto demonstrates that orality and textuality remained interdependent in the 1500s. Spoken words still held great weight.

Oral proof continued to persuade a few decades later when Angelitta wrote his shrine history. Interestingly, Angelitta chose to retain Tolomei's verbal depositions and every last bit of verification proffered by him. He also added extensively to three types of relic substantiation that were only briefly mentioned by Tolomei: miracles, a trip to the source of the *Santa Casa*, and chronology. First, Angelitta's work included a list of current, recent miracles associated with the Madonna of Loreto as if to demonstrate her continuing potency. Miracles remained accepted as the ultimate measure of sacred validity after the Council of Trent and well into the seventeenth century.[33]

Second, Angelitta filled in the picture of a trip that took place at an unspecified moment sometime in Loreto's shrouded first decades, long before Angelitta's watch. Tolomei had noted this corroborating journey. But Angelitta fleshed out the detail: sixteen men "of reputation, full of faith and integrity," were sent by Recanati's city council to retrace the house's steps as reported by Mary.[34] They went first to Trsat, where they heard talk of the house's former presence there. They proceeded to complete a full pilgrimage to the Holy Land. In Nazareth, they found and inspected an abandoned foundation taken to belong to the house of Mary. The foundation had measurements that matched those of the structure in Loreto. Once again, this sort of trip to ascertain the truth of relics has been remarked on as a trademark of medieval Catholicism.[35] Angelitta's later sixteenth-century inclusion and *enhancement* of the journey of the skeptical Recanatese shows that early modern Catholics still appreciated this

31. Even under church auspices, oral testimony served multiple purposes. It could bolster a shrine history or corroborate sainthood, but it could also prove that one was a heretic. See, for instance, the stream of witnesses interviewed for the 1584 Inquisition trial of the miller Menocchio in the Italian village of Montereale: Ginzburg, *Cheese and the Worms*, pp. 3–7.

32. Geary, "Oblivion between Orality and Textuality," p. 116.

33. For instance, Françoise Crémoux looks at 750 miracle texts collected by the Hieronymites of the Guadalupe shrine between 1510 and 1599, amassed to demonstrate the strength of the Virgin of Guadalupe. Crémoux, "Réalité et représentation," pp. 221–30.

34. The men are not named; the fullest extant account of their travels can be found in Angelitta, *L'historia*, pp. 45–48.

35. Geary, *Furta Sacra*, p. 54.

kind of firsthand confirmation. His aside also gave residents of his home city of Recanati a key role in the history of the shrine next door that they considered to be their own.

Angelitta's third and most elaborate addition to the saga of Loreto's origins was chronology. He was the first to publish and assign the precise date of the eve of 10 December 1294 to the arrival of the *Santa Casa* in Italy.[36] Angelitta associated each movement of the *Santa Casa* with an exact calendar date: 9 May 1291 for the house's first translation from Nazareth to Trsat, Dalmatia; 10 December 1294 for its landing in the woods of Recanati; August 1295 for its shift along the coast to the hill owned by two brothers; and 2 December 1295 for its final move on top of the road between Recanati and the sea. These dates were not chosen arbitrarily.[37] They correspond with the fall of Acre to the Mamluks of Egypt in 1291, an event that marked the defeat of Western crusaders in the Holy Land. In 1291, the last crusaders retreated, perhaps with armfuls of whatever Christian relics they could save from the Muslim occupying forces.[38] This thirteenth-century routing of Christians resulted in a movement, both actual and exaggerated, of "holy places [coming] to reside in the West."[39] With his fleshed-out chronology, Angelitta evoked the smoke and rubble of Acre. He suggested earthly motives for Mary's flight, as she was herself routed from the Holy Land.

The power of the shrine seal of Loreto that opened this chapter did not derive purely from the cardinals who adopted it. It stemmed also from these earlier shrine affiliates, Tolomei and Angelitta, who unknowingly

36. Santarelli, *Tradizione*, p. 24.

37. Lightbown suggests that the dates *are* arbitrary, stating that Angelitta compiled them "either from conjecture or from tradition elaborated by a plentiful use of imagination. . . . Angelitta [is] not a very dependable authority." He gives no good reason for this assertion, other than being troubled by Angelitta's exactitude. Lightbown, *Carlo Crivelli*, p. 42.

38. Morris, *Sepulchre of Christ and the Medieval West*, p. 294. This flight from the Mamluks suggested by Angelitta parallels the actual movement of immigrants between Dalmatia and the Marches after the fall of Constantinople to the Ottoman Turks in 1453. In chapter 8 below, I argue that this more recent wave of Ottoman-escaping refugees contributed essentially to the shape of Loreto's mythohistory.

39. Ibid. Angelitta appears to have chosen the year of departure more for that symbolism than for accuracy. The port of Acre surrendered to the Mamluks on 28 May 1291; Angelitta set the Holy House scrambling from the scene an excessively safe three weeks before this. Historian Bernard Hamilton notes with amusement that he jumped the gun slightly (perhaps deliberately?) with his reckoning: "We may reflect that it is fortunate that this vote of divine no-confidence was unknown to the crusader garrison of Acre which at that time was still fighting spiritedly against the Mamluk army." Hamilton, "Ottomans, the Humanists and the Holy House of Loreto," p. 17.

contributed to the shrine's later expansionist brand by carefully chronicling a house and statue in motion. More interestingly, in spite of cardinals fixing the historical imprint of Loreto into an official stamp in the 1580s, authors continued to contribute to Loreto's origin story. Episcopal branding did not freeze Loreto in time; it simply set parameters for data that continued to roll in. New, independently gathered proof was now supposed to indicate the movement that made Loreto distinctive.

Many of the later contributors had far less authorization than the first writers described above. They were not employed directly by the shrine nor charged with supervising it. But one can recognize shades of Tolomei and Angelitta, and Gallo and Benzoni, in the next sets of authors described below. The Jesuits Raphael Riera and Oratio Torsellino, and Slavic Catholics like Nikolà Frankopan, were also neighbors of, temporary residents of, or visitors to Loreto. They wrote of what they saw with their own eyes and heard with their own ears. Like Tolomei and Angelitta, they presented accumulated evidence, building on rather than deconstructing earlier renditions. Like Gallo and Benzoni, each of them highlighted the journeying of the Catholic objects at the core of Loreto's pilgrimage site. Their output stands as a crucial reminder that the history of Loreto was not determined exclusively or primarily by high-ranking church authorities, nor by insiders who detachedly engineered one singularly clever message for output. Instead, the shrine's origins were still being cobbled together piecemeal during the sixteenth century and beyond, with many hands underwriting and overwriting the cardinals' seal.

Actual Eyewitnesses: Two Jesuits at Loreto, Riera and Torsellino

Raphael Riera (1528–82) published a Latin history of Loreto, *Historiae Almae Domus Lauretanae Liber Singularis*, in 1565.[40] He was the first historian of Loreto who was not a native of Loreto's Marche region. At the time of his writing, though, he had lived in Loreto for a full decade. Riera had moved there from the Jesuit college of Palermo. He was dispatched to Loreto to join the freshly established Jesuit Collegio dei Penitentieri and ended up spending the rest of his life there.

40. Sommervogel, *Bibliothèque de la Compagnie de Jésus*, tom. 7, p. 1843; Santarelli, *Tradizione*, p. 19. A copy of Riera's *Historiae* can be found in Martorelli, *Teatro Istorico*, vol. 1, pp. 1–150. Riera also published a list of miracles associated with Loreto: Riera, *De' miracoli della B. V. M. di Loreto* (1573).

It was a heady moment for Jesuits at Loreto. The Society of Jesus had been recognized by Pope Paul III only twenty years earlier, in 1540, and its members were eager to prove themselves. The founder of the order, Ignatius Loyola, had been inspired by a pilgrimage to Loreto and encouraged all aspiring Jesuits to visit the sanctuary.[41] But Riera came to Loreto as part of a separate initiative more sustainable than pilgrimage. The Society of Jesus was formally invited there in 1554 by the governor of Loreto, Gaspare de' Dotti, and the latest Protector of the *Santa Casa* of Loreto, Cardinal Rodolfo Pio Leonelli di Carpi.[42] Cardinal Carpi was an early patron of the Jesuits, but beyond this, he specifically requested Jesuits because of their international membership. The Italian shrine was badly in need of multilingual confessors.[43] Pilgrims were arriving from increasingly distant corners of Europe wanting to confess to a priest in their own language. Confession was a crucial part of pilgrimage and of Catholic life in general.[44] It was the first step on the road to penance, a central rite of Catholic worship. During confession, the faithful would enumerate their transgressions privately to a trained priest. The priest would respond by assigning prayers or tasks to perform in order to atone for sins. On 3 December 1554, five Jesuit priests and nine students and lay brothers reported to Loreto to answer Dotti and Carpi's call to create a branch of official confessors for the shrine. Between them, the Jesuit arrivals spoke Italian, Latin, Spanish, German, French, and Flemish.[45]

So Raphael Riera came to Loreto primed to lend a sympathetic ear to pilgrims from his native region of Catalonia and, more broadly, from Spain. He joined an extremely diverse and overworked shrine staff. In addition to his Jesuit colleagues hailing from all over Europe, there was a small army of secular priests serving the diocese of Recanati-Loreto. There were also Capuchin Friars Minor, another young order bringing

41. Tacchi Venturi, *Storia della Compagnia di Gesù in Italia*, vol. 2, pp. 29–30, 36.

42. Santarelli, "Gli Ordini Religiosi al servizio della Santa Casa."

43. This was not a problem unique to Loreto or the 1500s. One eighteenth-century Italian pilgrim, Nicolà Albani, left a patchy trail of confessions in his travels across Europe because he could not find confessors who understood his dialect. Julia, "Curiosité, dévotion et *politica peregrinesca*," p. 299.

44. Of the seven Catholic sacraments, two—penance, and the partaking of the Eucharist in mass—were the most regular and repeated experience for Catholic devout, especially during the Counter-Reformation period. The other sacraments (baptism, confirmation, marriage or ordination, and extreme unction) were rites of passage that affected Catholics once in a lifetime. Burgess, "'Longing to Be Prayed For,'" p. 49; De Boer, *Conquest of the Soul*, pp. 43–83; Myers, *"Poor, Sinning Folk."*

45. Santarelli, "Gli Ordini Religiosi al servizio della Santa Casa."

their energy to Loreto by express invitation.[46] Finally, there were crowds upon crowds of pilgrims.

Riera was bowled over by the bustling atmosphere of Loreto. His excitement at being on the scene seeped into his 1565 *Historiae*. It reads as less of a history and more of a breathless, live news report. Thus, Riera contributed two new strains to Loreto's mythohistorical corpus. First, he described large numbers of Slavic pilgrims visiting the Loreto sanctuary and begging the Madonna to return to them.[47] These Slavic contributions to Loreto's origin narrative are discussed further below.

Second, Riera told of miracles at Loreto that he had witnessed directly. For instance, soon after his arrival, "heavenly flames" were seen flashing around the hill of Loreto and even inside the basilica. Riera wrote that one day in 1555, in full daylight and in the middle of a sermon given by one of his Jesuit colleagues, fire appeared over the Holy House and hovered overhead long enough for everyone to see. Riera was so awestruck that he fell to the ground and felt spiritually refreshed for days afterward.[48] According to Riera, Loreto's miracles were unfolding *today*, in real time. The vivid primacy of his writing was seized on by later Jesuit writers who privileged recent miracles at Loreto over its murky origins.

Raphael Riera was only the first in a parade of early modern Jesuits who took avid interest in the shrine. It was not only Jesuits who were writing about Loreto, but they are the focus here because of the choice of some of their later members to portage the devotion overseas, a choice that is

46. Ibid. Jesuits and Capuchins replaced the Carmelites, the first religious order to be invited to Loreto by a shrine administrator in 1488. The Carmelites left Loreto after a rocky decade of service interrupted by frequent outbursts of plague. Arriving in 1554, the Jesuits had a three-year head start on the Capuchins but still felt the competition keenly. Capuchins had split off from the older Franciscan order in 1525 in a reform movement originating right in Loreto's backyard, in the Marches of Italy. Unlike the Jesuits, the Capuchins came to the Loreto shrine as locals. Over time, Jesuits stuck to their duties as confessors while Capuchins branched into all the other priestly services offered to pilgrims, supporting the secular clergy. Nowadays, Franciscans still officiate at the shrine. Regni, *Loreto e i cappuccini*.

47. Santarelli, *Tradizione*, pp. 59–63. The Jesuit Torsellino included this report in his history of Loreto in 1598, and it continued to be repeated in later centuries in works such as Cesare Renzoli's *La Santa Casa illustrata e Difesa* (Macerata, 1697). Catholics often requested that images return to them: Geary, *Furta Sacra*; Christian, *Apparitions in Late Medieval and Renaissance Spain*; Christian, *Local Religion in Sixteenth-Century Spain*.

48. Oratio Torsellino repeated Riera's account of these miracles almost in full in his history discussed further below. Perhaps this is because Riera was a fellow Jesuit. Torsellino prefaced his paraphrasing with this declaration of his source's credibility: "Raphaell Riera is a learned and godlie Priest of the Societie of Iesus [who was] by chance . . . present among the multitude." Torsellino, *History of our B. Lady of Loreto*, pp. 261–62.

part of the puzzle this study endeavors to solve.[49] To give but a partial list of some of the better-known Jesuits who published accounts of Loreto, Gaspar Loarte, Louis Richeôme, Pietro Valerio Martorelli, Wilhelm Gumppenberg, and Francisco Florencia all wrote about the *Santa Casa* before 1800. Also in their number, there was a prominent Jesuit chronicler who turned out to be the most popular Lauretan historian of all, though he differed markedly from his ebullient colleague Riera.

The Roman Jesuit Oratio Torsellino (1544–99) was one of the most eminent intellectuals in Italy in the late sixteenth century. The contrast between his educational pedigree and the humbler track of Raphael Riera reveals an internal tension within the early Society of Jesus resulting from its welcoming the sons of Europe's elite, but also beginning to recruit more broadly.[50] Torsellino was a recognized pedagogue, having taught at the Jesuit seminary in Rome and at the Jesuit college in Florence. He was also a prolific writer, churning out Latin grammars and instruction manuals, prayer books, a life of St. Francis Xavier, a commentary on Cicero, and even a ten-volume universal history.[51] Torsellino's five-volume *Lauretanae Historiae* (Rome, 1598) was one of his last projects. He researched the topic exhaustively for almost ten years. Like Tolomei, he gave weight to trusted oral accounts: Torsellino began his investigation by exchanging correspondence with colleagues who personally remembered miracles associated with the Madonna of Loreto.[52] Like Angelitta, he sought to verify the Holy House's journey: Torsellino even hiked through the woods of Recanati with his elder colleague, Riera, to see for himself the impression the Holy House had left at one of its earlier stops.[53] From his colleague

49. Members of the Capuchin branch of the Franciscan order also published copiously about Loreto, where they were posted alongside the Jesuits in the sixteenth century. Regni, *Loreto e i cappuccini*.

50. Alden, *Making of an Elite Enterprise*; Zupanov, "Aristocratic Analogies."

51. Sommervogel, *Bibliothèque de la Compagnie de Jésus*, tom. 8, pp. 138–41. Torsellino's universal history, *Historiarum ab origine mundi usque ad annum* (Rome, 1598, reprinted in 1658, 1676, and 1714), brought him the most fame posthumously when—after centuries of circulation and use at Jesuit schools—it was banned by the Parlements of Paris (1761) and Rouen (1762) for being dangerous to the Catholic faith.

52. One of these 1594 letters reads like a list of responses to questions from Torsellino. Jacobus Borghi sent him two comparatively low-key miracle stories in which the Virgin of Loreto enticed a wayward child into returning to church, and then saved a local woman from a burning house. ARSI Ital. 161 (Borghi to Torsellino, 30 December 1594), fols. 208–12.

53. From Torsellino's description in the late 1500s, this earlier site was already deteriorated, poorly marked and little preserved. Torsellino, *History of our B. Lady of Loreto*, pp. 50–51. This is the 1608 English translation of Torsellino's 1598 *Lauretanae Historiae*.

Riera, he also adopted the methodology of on-site immersion. Torsellino visited the sanctuary and resided there on and off throughout the 1590s while he looked through the archives, lecturing and preaching to the Jesuits at Loreto on the side.[54]

Torsellino lived at the pilgrimage site well after the 1550s honeymoon period of Jesuit arrival that had set Riera expounding on Loreto's glory. In fact, Torsellino got pulled into administrative infighting at the Jesuits' recently opened school for Slavs at Loreto, the Collegio Illirico. He was apparently "so scandalized at the disorder of this college that he wanted to write to the Pope [about it]."[55] During his time at Loreto, Torsellino was also distracted by his own interests elsewhere. He wrote frequently to his friend Claudio Acquaviva (1543–1615), who happened to be superior general of the Society of Jesus.[56] These letters say little about his findings on the *Santa Casa*. Torsellino wrote to Acquaviva more often about his frustrating efforts to found a Jesuit college at Pesaro, on the Adriatic coast north of Loreto.[57]

When Torsellino did bring up his Lauretan research with the superior general, it was to stress how trying it had been. In his preface to *Lauretanae Historiae*, he wrote: "I pray God as the worke hath beene difficult and painfull, so it may be profitable."[58] Among other headaches it caused him, Torsellino complained that "the indiligence of our forefathers in committing

54. In 1592, for instance, he led mass ten times inside the *Santa Casa* as part of a vow he had taken with a Jesuit colleague. ARSI Ital. 160 (Torsellino to Acquaviva, 7 May 1592), fol. 276.

55. "É restato tanto scandelizato del mal ordine di questo coll.o che voleva scriverne al Papa." ARSI Ital. 161 (1592 *Memoriale interna alle cose del Collegio Illirico*), fol. 145v. The incident that upset Torsellino involved a dispute over who had authority at the Collegio Illirico, an external visitor sent by the Roman headquarters of the Society of Jesus, or the problematic rector of the college whom the Roman visitor was investigating. The college's students had complained to Rome about the rector's management and were refusing to obey him.

56. Claudio Acquaviva, born to a wealthy Italian family, was the fifth superior general of the Society of Jesus from 1581 to 1615. He was the youngest to assume that post (appointed at age thirty-seven) and has the reputation of being one of the best leaders of the order. During his three-decade generalate, the Jesuit order more than doubled in size, reaching thirteen thousand members. Cantù, "Il Generalato di Claudio Acquaviva."

57. Torsellino's enthusiasm over Pesaro led him to write to Acquaviva several times a week, as in this series of letters in the summer of 1592: ARSI Ital. 160 (Torsellino to Acquaviva, 28 May 1592), fol. 297; ARSI Ital. 161 (Torsellino to Acquaviva, 18 June 1592), fol. 12; ARSI Ital. 161 (Torsellino to Rector of Loreto, c. 1592), fol. 14; ARSI Ital. 161 (Torsellino to Acquaviva, 21 June 1592), fols. 21–22v.

58. Torsellino, *History of our B. Lady of Loreto*, p. xxix.

[events] to writing, hath diminished a good parte of this History." But he also expressed wonder at the mystery of the *Santa Casa*, a wonder that might have sustained him in completing the voluminous project. He wrote that "first truly the very beginnings of this sacred Chappell are so admirable and so unusuall that they may seeme almost incredible."[59] Overall, though, in contrast to Riera, Torsellino's tone suggests that he finished the arduous research out of duty, perhaps at the request of his patron, Cardinal Pietro Aldobrandini (1571–1621), an avowed devotee of Loreto and supporter of the Jesuits.[60]

Regardless of Torsellino's frustrations with the task, his history confounds most expectations one brings to the product of a sixteenth-century Jesuit literary giant. First, Torsellino is remarkably understated about celebrating his own society's involvement with Loreto. For instance, in June 1585, only a few years before Torsellino began his research, Loreto's Jesuit college of confessors had welcomed visitors from far-off Japan.[61] These high-profile Japanese guests were new Catholic converts escorted in their European travels by the Jesuit missionaries who had introduced them to Christianity. Their arrival drew crowds from all over the Marches.[62] Though Torsellino's history brought the Loreto shrine from its origins to the present day, he made no mention at all of that recent event. Torsellino omitted an example that would have reflected positively on the Jesuits *and* the Loreto shrine, identifying the two as beacons of worldwide Catholicism.

But Torsellino's account is surprisingly free of rhetoric of global expansion. Though Cardinal Antonio Maria Gallo bestowed his approbation on the book in 1598, Torsellino's work does not put forward that cardinal's

59. Ibid., p. xxx. Torsellino's aside about how the Holy House's origins seemed "incredible" call to mind how twenty-first-century Jesuits approach miracles as a category that is not meant to be clarified in human terms, but that is best left as mysterious (see chapter 2 above).

60. Ibid., pp. xxv–xxvi. Torsellino dedicated his history of Loreto to Aldobrandini, who in addition to being a cardinal was also the nephew of Pope Clement VIII.

61. For a fascinating historically based reimagining of a Japanese perspective on traveling westward and encountering Catholicism: Endo, *Samurai*.

62. Francesco Mercato (1541–1603), Jesuit rector of Loreto, and Alessandro Leni, one of the Jesuit escorts of the Japanese, both wrote about the dramatic reception of the Japanese embassy to Loreto. See ARSI Ital. 159, tom. 2 (Mercato to Acquaviva, 16 June 1585), fols. 47–48v; ARSI Ital. 159, tom. 2 (Mercato to Bobadilla, 19 June 1585), fols. 64–65v; ARSI Ital. 159, tom. 2 (Leni to Ariosto, 13 June 1585), fols. 36–37v; ARSI Ital. 159, tom. 2 (Leni to Acquaviva, 13 June 1585), fols. 55–57. Also: ARSI Ital. 159, tom. 2 (Voglia to Acquaviva, 14 June 1585), fols. 43–44.

telltale stamp of Loreto as an emblem of Catholic outreach to the *world*.[63] For instance, his last chapter, provocatively entitled "The Celebrity and Majesty of the House of Loreto," sets out to describe the "incredible confluence of strangers" at Loreto.[64] In addition to the local "Picentians" and Italians, he listed pilgrims from across the Alps and the sea: "Sclauonians, French and [F]lemings . . . Spaniards, Portugals, Polonians [and] Germanes."[65] This list of Europeans is varied and impressive, but in a global frame, it comes across as provincial. Torsellino does not step off toward the continents of Asia and the Americas where the Jesuits had such vested and growing interest. Torsellino had himself written a biography of Francis Xavier, Jesuit missionary to India and Japan. But it was evidently not part of Torsellino's project to use his history to show Loreto's seepage into every global nook and cranny.

Yet thanks in part to his book, Loreto did start to seep out into that wider world. This was partly due to Torsellino's target audience, his fellow Jesuits. Torsellino explained his choice to use Latin instead of Italian to write about Loreto as a way to give his work a reach as wide as the Roman empire and Christian religion.[66] Latin still functioned as a lingua franca in the sixteenth century among Jesuits and educated elites. The book reached them in its first fifty years of release: Torsellino's Latin compilation was reprinted eight times. By the mid-1700s, Jesuits had further translated the *Lauretanae Historiae* into German, English, Czech, Spanish, Italian, and Tagalog.[67] Along with Ignatius of Loyola's *Spiritual Exercises*, Torsellino's account of Loreto ranks as one of the Jesuits' most translated publications.[68] The *Lauretanae Historiae* was widely distributed in Jesuit circles throughout the 1600s. Even missionaries posted far afield who had never visited Loreto were familiar with Italy's roaming

63. For Gallo's standard approbation, see Torsellino, *History of our B. Lady of Loreto*, p. i.

64. Ibid., book 5, chapter 28, pp. 532, 538.

65. Ibid., pp. 532–33.

66. On Latin: ibid., p. xxiii; on the Christian religion: ibid., p. xxv. The 1608 English Catholic translator of Torsellino's *Historiae* (identified only as "T. P.") is far more direct about "the desire of the Author and Translatour of this worke [to make known that the] most mercifull Mother of Loreto . . . hast made thy most dear & most beloved house to follow the religion & honour of the Christian name from Country to country, & from place, to place, to incline the hartes of sinners to repentance." Ibid., pp. ii–iii.

67. Sommervogel, *Bibliothèque de la Compagnie de Jésus*, tom. 8, pp. 138–41. Torsellino's work was reprinted in Rome in 1598, 1600, 1612, 1614, 1615, and 1621; in Venice in 1615; and in Prague in 1630.

68. Burke, "Jesuits and the Art of Translation," p. 28.

Santa Casa and Madonna thanks to Torsellino. His work firmly grounded the moving house in the consciousness of early modern Jesuits.

Exactly what did Torsellino convey to his globe-trotting readership about Loreto? Interestingly, he chose to evoke local experience rather than advocate outward expansion. His work resembles the papal medal described at the start of this chapter more than it does the cardinals' official shrine seal. Instead of using Loreto's past to make a case for the export of Catholicism, Torsellino devoted the most space in his work to two issues that still colored the Marian sanctuary's present: war and miracles.

Torsellino's history ends with a description of seasonal celebrations at Loreto. For those who could not make it to the shrine to see for themselves, Torsellino told of annual crowds of residents of the Marche in procession.[69] More pointedly, he remarked on the presence of armed military engaged in maneuvers and displays around Loreto. "Likewise at all times of the yeare," he reported, "bands of souldiours and Troupes of Horsmen going to the war, come to Loreto, and when they haue receiued the holy Mysteries, they honour the B. Virgin with sporting-shewes in warlike fashion."[70] Torsellino devoted many pages to the soldiers around Loreto, and the resulting picture diverges from the idyllic image on the Loreto shrine seal that emerged in the same decade as Torsellino's volumes and that made no reference to armies. By contrast, this Jesuit eyewitness was clearly struck by the number of armed fighters on the Adriatic coast. He devoted six chapters to the threat of Turkish attack, with gripping titles such as "Divers assaults of the Turks are repulsed by miracle."[71] The run-ins with Turkish forces and corsairs that Torsellino described had a recency that eclipsed the mysterious Holy House landing in the distant past: most of the battles with Ottoman Turks had occurred within the last few

69. "For there is no Citty, no Towne, no Village, nor no Streete of the Territory of Picene, which doth not yearly in troupes and multitudes, visit the B. Virgin of Loreto." Torsellino, *History of our B. Lady of Loreto*, p. 533.

70. Ibid., p. 538. The French army gets special mention from Torsellino in book 3, chapter 23, "The French Army doth honour the sacred House" (pp. 288–90). That chapter refers to the 1557–58 French military expedition into the Marches when François de Lorraine (1519–63), Duke of Guise, was sent to aid Pope Paul IV in reconquering Naples from the Spanish army.

71. See, for instance, Torsellino's book 1, chapter 25 ("Pope Calistus III fortifies House vs. Turks & puts them to flight"); book 2, chapter 4 ("Army of Turkes put to flight by miracle"); book 2, chapter 19 ("Divers assaults of the Turks are repulsed by miracle"); book 3, chapter 18 ("A haffa of the Turks cured by Loreto and brings gifts"); book 4, chapter 28 ("Many are delivered from the servitude of the Turkes"); and book 4, chapter 21 ("The help of the B. Virgin of Loreto in the Victory gotten of the Turks by sea").

decades, within memory of Torsellino's living contemporaries. Current events therefore seemed to justify Torsellino's side comment that perhaps the Holy House had left Dalmatia in previous centuries in order "to relieve Italy, the fortresse of Christian Religion with the present helpe."[72]

However, Torsellino's six chapters on Turks and handful of descriptions of soldiers are outnumbered by his obsessive collection of miracles. Like Riera, Torsellino reported the miracles, interviews, and events he personally heard around the sanctuary. Like Angelitta and Tolomei, he drew heavily on previous accounts of these miracles, referencing earlier histories often and occasionally quoting them verbatim.[73] If Tolomei and Angelitta's histories resembled snowballs, absorbing all prior records in their path, Torsellino's was an all-encompassing avalanche of nearly six hundred pages, the bulk of these concerning the miraculous. Twenty-eight chapters of his first book are devoted to simply describing Loreto's most celebrated miracle, the translation of the *Santa Casa* and Marian image from Nazareth to Italy. Of the remaining one hundred and twenty chapters, half of them—fifty-nine—are given over to reporting more recent miracles attributed to Loreto's Madonna.[74] The manner in which Torsellino chose and presented these encounters with the Madonna of Loreto contributed to his work's enduring appeal. It is worth looking at some of these miracles closely, as they were Torsellino's main preoccupation. One set of miracles in particular also captures and emblematizes fellow contributors to Loreto's mythohistory and affords a rare opportunity to see how sixteenth-century authors may have viewed each other, not as competitors but as collaborators in a joint project to validate a holy site.

New Expression: Nikolà Frankopan and the Miracle of the Slavs

The unwitting stars of a subset of Torsellino's Lauretan miracles are several Dalmatian or Slavic priests. According to the shrine archives and histories consulted by Torsellino, back in the distant 1290s, the Virgin Mary had abruptly left the thin strip of Dalmatian shore on the other side of the

72. Ibid., p. 28.

73. Torsellino devoted a full chapter to Tolomei's history (book 1, chapter 28: "History of Loreto by Tereman the Governor"). He also repeated Angelitta's chronology.

74. The other half tell of rich donations, construction projects, indulgences, jubilee celebrations, and other public recognition (mostly papal and Italian) of Loreto's greatness.

Adriatic, to seek greener pastures in Italy.[75] Dalmatia had lost the relics of Holy House and Madonna statue that pilgrims trekked to Loreto to see. Perhaps to make up for the tragic pathos of these abandoned Dalmatian Catholics, Torsellino chose to glorify some of their priests. But he did not merely put eloquent and heroic words into the mouths of Catholic clergy from the other side of the Adriatic. The Dalmatians Torsellino chose to depict as priests were not technically priests. They were community leaders, ordained metaphorically by traumatic life experiences. Torsellino chose to highlight and literally promote these fellow creators of Loreto's mythohistory in order to accentuate their spiritual exemplarity.

For instance, in describing one of Loreto's more gruesome miracles, Torsellino cast "a Dalmatian Priest [who] commeth to Loreto, carrying up, with his hand, his bowells pulled out of his bellie."[76] This sorry anecdote explained a popular early attraction for pilgrims to Loreto, preserved intestines (later replaced by wooden ones) hung on the sanctuary wall.[77] These were the remnants of a hapless Christian enslaved and disemboweled by Turks.[78] Usually when writers featured this miracle in their books about Loreto, they assigned the intestines to an anonymous Christian sailor.[79] But Torsellino made a Dalmatian priest of him. He quoted the devout Dalmatian's brave words to the Turks: "You are deceiued. . . . My bowells indeed you may take from me, but Christ and Marie you cannot

75. Today this strip of coastline constitutes part of the country of Croatia. In the sixteenth century, it was called "Dalmatia," and it encompassed the narrow lowlands between the sea and the Dinaric Alps. It was occasionally still referred to as the western frontier of "Illyria," the name for the ancient Roman province in that area. Italians also referred to these neighbors across the sea as "schiavoni," or "Slavs." That label denoted Albanian- and Croatian-speaking Catholics who aligned themselves with the pope in Rome, in contrast to Serbian-speakers farther inland who practiced Eastern Orthodox Christianity.

76. This is Torsellino's title for chapter 18 of book 2. Torsellino, *History of our B. Lady of Loreto*, p. 181.

77. Torsellino did not approve of this display. He was glad that it was eventually replaced by a commemorative painting because when faced with intestines, real or wooden, "the rude people, which came to the Church of Loreto, busied their mindes [with the] spectacle . . . & reuerenced the mother of God with lesse care, then they ought to have donne." Ibid., p. 183.

78. On the very real threat of this sort of capture by Turkish corsairs in the Adriatic, consider these two incidents alone: in 1510, more than one hundred villagers were captured in a raid on the Italian coastal city of Otranto; around the same time, on the other side of the Adriatic, an entire village was abducted near Persato, Dalmatia. R. C. Davis, "Counting European Slaves on the Barbary Coast," pp. 91–92.

79. See, for instance, Bralion, *L'Histoire de Nostre Dame de Laurette*, p. 128.

take from me."[80] Again, by calling attention to a violent backdrop of captivity, Torsellino differentiated his history from the seal chosen by Loreto's cardinals. While the cardinals focused exclusively on Mary and her house paired in peaceful flight, this Jesuit author focused instead on some miracles of Loreto that were clearly products of a zone of war.

Standing alongside the disemboweled Dalmatian in the pages of Torsellino's history was "Nicolas Frangipane," the most memorable Dalmatian and one of the most dramatic figures in the entire compilation. Torsellino did not officially give Nicolas Frangipane the laurels of priesthood, but he might as well have. The Roman Jesuit used him as a mouthpiece to deliver a sort of funeral oration, emotional, empathetic, and geared to console. First he set the scene: back in the thirteenth century, when the *Santa Casa* disappeared from its first landing spot in Trsat, the Dalmatians searched for it everywhere, weeping.[81] "Finally being ouercome with wearisomenes . . . they went swarming to Frangipane . . . [to ask] of him aduise and helpe," Torsellino narrated.

> And though he him selfe did need comfort, as wounded with the common griefe, & more sorrowfull then was fitting for his part; notwithstanding he ouercame himself, and dissembling his sorrow, aswaged the lamentation of the people with his authoritie and wisdome: *In very deed* (quoth he) *so it is, that you have receaued so greate a losse . . . that no teares, no sighes, no wayling, is able to extinguish your griefe of mind. But now truely you seeme to complaine without cause seeing Almightie God hath graunted you the vse of the heauenly gift without prescribing any time, & therfore there is no reason, why you should grieue that it is required againe, when he would haue it so, that gaue it; but rather should giue God thanks for granting you the vse of so great and so fruitfull a pledge for certaine yeares, and should recompence the present discommoditie, with memorie of the former commodities.* And he promised them to do his best endeuour, in some sort to supply the great losse, which they had receiued by the departure of the heauenly gift.[82]

Torsellino continued with lengthy praise of Frangipane's leadership. Frangipane proceeded to build a new church at his own expense, "as a

80. Torsellino, *History of our B. Lady of Loreto*, p. 182.

81. Torsellino's descriptions of this moment emphasize Slavic tears and weeping. For more on the Jesuit obsession with tears: Vélez, "'Do Not Suppose That Those Tears Proceed from Weakness.'"

82. Torsellino, *History of our B. Lady of Loreto*, pp. 30–31. Emphasis added.

solace to [the Dalmatians] for their grieuous losse."[83] Because of his efforts to rebuild, his acceptance of God's will, and his faith that the Madonna had not abandoned them, Torsellino concluded that "the B. Virgin [did not] suffer [his] wordes to be in vaine: for afterward sundry miracles were wrought in that place . . . and her helpe [was] not wanting to the Sclavonians."[84] The Dalmatian noble was a flashpoint for miracles that verified Mary's power. Frangipane was affected by the originating miracle of the Holy House's arrival in Dalmatia. When that miracle passed onward, and his community lost the sacred objects that grounded their devotion, he started over. This ability to begin anew brought new miracles to the forsaken Dalmatians.

Who was Nicolas Frangipane? As with many components of Torsellino's history, this man was not a narrative invention, but a modified truth. He was presented as an instructive example to all Catholics about how to cope with loss, but at the same time, he was based on a real person and real peoples on the other side of the sea. His presence in Torsellino's magisterial account of Loreto's past is tacit acknowledgment of the role of Slavic Catholics as coauthors, contributors who were helping to establish Loreto's important place in the Catholic world.

Frangipane was the Italian spelling for "Frankopan," a prominent family of Catholics who spanned the Adriatic with their Catholic devotional practices and who were among the earliest devotees to the Madonna of Loreto. The Frankopans came from the island of Krk, the largest island in the Adriatic Sea. They rose to power there at the end of the twelfth century and spread to the mainland. By the mid-1500s, the Frankopans controlled most of the Dalmatian coastline and nearly half of the Kingdom of Croatia.[85] But even before they exploded out of Krk, this family was vigorously engaging with the church. They welcomed into their island fiefdom some of the first Franciscans to settle in the region.[86] They also invited clergy to Krk who could give mass in Glagolitic, or old church Slavonic, a language associated with the early church.[87] Ivan Frankopan, one of the fifteenth-century princes, had a rare Glagolitic church manuscript from the eleventh

83. Ibid., p. 31.

84. Ibid., p. 32.

85. On the centrality of the Frankopan (Frankapan/Frangipani) family in Croatian political history and on their ties to Italy: J. A. Fine, *When Ethnicity Did Not Matter in the Balkans*, pp. 149, 168, 567.

86. "Frankopan Family, Princes of Krk."

87. The Frankopans apparently used Glagolitic for business as well, and in two odd cases in 1372 and 1452, for agreements with Paulicians, a Manichean heretical sect. Stefanic, "Two Frankopan Glagolitic Charters."

century in his possession. When he died in 1486, the prized parchment was split into pieces and given to friends as a relic; it was thought to be a part of a Bible written in the ancient Croatian language by St. Jerome.[88]

By happy coincidence, there were a number of early Frankopans who bore the name "Nikolà." Prince Nikolà I of Krk, the "Nicolas Frangipane" of Lauretan legend, was one of the first Frankopans to settle in Trsat in the late 1200s.[89] This Nikolà is mentioned by name in many of the Loreto histories above. He purportedly built the first church to the Madonna of Loreto when she passed through Dalmatia. But closer to Torsellino's own time, in the 1450s, a Frankopan father and son, both called Nikolà, briefly reigned over the whole coastal region of Dalmatia as co-bans and made an extravagant donation to Loreto.[90] As this book aims to show, there can be much in a shared name, especially when it is oft-repeated.[91] "Nikolà Frankopan" was a name that was recognized in the sixteenth-century Adriatic sphere, in Dalmatia and the Marche alike. By Torsellino's time, the name connoted wealthy Slavic nobles, past and present, who were deeply Catholic and who linked the Croatian and Italian shores by making traceable connections between Marian shrines.

For there was another shrine at the spot where Loreto's Holy House had first tarried, a location that had been visited by Italians in search of Loreto's roots, on verifying journeys that were recapped by Angelitta, Riera, and Torsellino. The placement of the pilgrimage site of Trsat sharply evokes Loreto. Like many Mediterranean sacred shrines, Trsat stands on high ground overlooking the sea. One approaches it via an impressive staircase of five hundred steps commissioned by a military captain, Petar Krusic, in the mid-1500s, around the time that Cardinals Gallo and Benzoni were

88. Vucinich. "Review," pp. 205–6.

89. "Pope Visits Our Lady of Trsat."

90. Torsellino notes a "Nicholas Frangipane" in his appended list of rich donors, "The Donaries of Princes & Noblemen." I assume that this was one of these intermediary Nikolàses. Torsellino based his 1598 table on previous shrine records of donations from wealthy pilgrims. Curiously, the earlier Frankopan nobles—from the mythohistorical Nikolà I to the Martin who initiated construction of the fifteenth-century Trsat complex—are not recorded as visitors in the Loreto shrine's rosters. The first pilgrim with the last name "Frankopan" to be noted in Loreto was "Bernadino Frangipane" from Senj (Segno), Croatia, who came to Loreto in January 1497, to fulfill a vow. Grimaldi, *Pellegrini*, p. 269.

91. For instance, coincidentally shared names sometimes resulted in claims of overseas kinship, as was the case for the Florentine Pazzi family and the Lithuanian noble family of the Pacas in the seventeenth century. The similarity between their names led both families to develop a trans-Baltic legend of Italian origins for the (unrelated) Pacas family, with the Pacas family eventually sharing patronage with the Florentine Pazzi family toward St. Mary Magdalene de'Pazzi. Baniulyte, "Italian Intrigue in the Baltic."

creating Loreto's seal. By that time, Trsat was also a popular local pilgrimage destination and was acknowledged outside of the Balkan peninsula as a thriving Marian sanctuary.

Which site came first? The mythohistory of the Holy House, notably emanating from Loreto and not Trsat, nonetheless named Trsat as the older sacred ground, the place where the Holy House had first rested. Loreto's Italian governor Tolomei was the first to put it in print in 1472 that the Holy House had stopped near the town of "Tersatto" beside the river "Fiume," sites that loosely correspond to today's suburb of Trsat in the port city of Rijeka, Croatia, alongside the Rijecina River.[92] About fifty years later, in 1520, Tolomei's Latin work was translated into the Croatian language under the title "The declaration of the Church of Santa Maria of Loreto," a title that suggests that Italy had something new and significant to announce to the opposite shore.[93] It was only after this tardy emergence of the Italian governor's work in the Croatian language that Slavic writers, too, began to remark on a connection between Loreto and their already booming shrine of Trsat. The first printed mentions of the Holy House of Loreto from Slavic writers appear a full century after Tolomei, in the 1600s.[94] Bartol Kasic's *Istoria Loretana* (Rome, 1617) and Franjo Glavinic's *Historia Tersettana* (Udine, 1648) both repeated Tolomei's version of events: the Holy House was at Trsat before it arrived in Loreto.[95] Notably, Kasic and Glavinic also drew on the work of another Italian—Angelitta's 1531 *Lauretanae Virginis*—when they assigned thirteenth-century dates to the Holy House's landings at Trsat and Loreto.

So it seems that Italian authors at Loreto provided the basis for the *Santa Casa*'s appearance in Trsat's history. The possibility remains that there was a shared Dalmatian-Marchegian oral tradition known to the Italian governor, Tolomei, when he wrote his 1472 history. But regardless, a strangeness remains: Trsat existed independently prior to all these printed histories, with the Italians at Loreto choosing belatedly to hook it into their own emerging tradition.

92. Tolomei, "Translatio," pp. 104–7.

93. The Croatian title for the declaration was "Izgovorenie od carkve od Svete Marie de Lorite." Grimaldi, *Pellegrini*, p. 268.

94. Slightly preceding them, and worth mention here though it is not a history, there was a 1582 map of the Holy House of Loreto's journey, the project of a Slav. Natale Bonifatio, a mapmaker and engraver from the Croatian town of Sebenico (Sibenik) who was working in Rome, etched this map and included the Holy House's stop in Dalmatia. Beans, "Note from the Tall Tree Library."

95. Orešković, "La dévotion à la *Santa Casa*," pp. 73–88.

The shrine of Trsat accepted Loreto's Holy House as a late grafting onto its own historical origins. Trsat first emerged as a local pilgrimage site around the same time as Loreto did, in the fourteenth century.[96] Again counter to projections of Loreto's first historians, early Catholic devotion at Trsat was *not* centered on the empty foundations of the Holy House.[97] The shrine of Trsat developed around an old Byzantine-style icon of the Virgin Mary.[98] Trsat's tradition explaining their miracle-working image reveals an interface between shores that is even more peculiar than the Jesuit-favored story of Dalmatia's loss of the *Santa Casa*. According to Trsat's official shrine history, Pope Urban V met pilgrims from Trsat in Loreto in 1367 and presented them with an icon of the Madonna.[99] This is an elegant inversion of Loreto's mythohistorical trajectory for Mary. While her *Santa Casa* flew from Trsat to Loreto, this Marian image moved from Loreto back to Trsat.

The message here is conflicted. Though it is not made explicit, Pope Urban V's gift to Trsat comes off as a consolation prize, bestowed in exchange for Italy's acquiring the *Santa Casa*. Even though it is chronologically implausible that Italy would have acknowledged Dalmatia's loss so early, such is the implication of the account.[100] There is also the question of the identity of the recipient pilgrims. According to some variants of

96. Pope Martin V (1417–31) left the earliest papal documents that refer to Trsat, granting indulgences to pilgrims. Trsat stands alongside Marija Bistrica (near Zagreb) as one of Croatia's oldest Marian Catholic shrines. Pavicic and Batarelo, "Management and Marketing of Religious Sites," pp. 55–56.

97. Torsellino reported in the 1590s that all that there was at Trsat to refer to Loreto's Holy House was a small plaque explaining that the relic had once been there. Torsellino, *History of our B. Lady of Loreto*, p. 49.

98. The Madonna of Trsat is depicted half-length against a gold background with her head tilted to the left; she is clad in a blue headdress and a red dress. She holds the baby Jesus who is empty-handed and dressed in rose. It is not clear whether the icon displayed in Trsat was based on the original Lucan icon of the Madonna of Loreto. However, the icon of the Madonna of Trsat is painted as white-skinned and blonde and does not belong to the group of black Madonnas, like the later statue of the Virgin of Loreto discussed in chapter 6 below. Also unlike the Virgin of Loreto, the Madonna of Trsat is not pictorially connected with the *Santa Casa* of mythohistory. For an image of the Madonna of Trsat: "Mary's Trsat."

99. For the official updated version of Trsat's shrine history in English: "Trsat and Our Lady Sanctuary."

100. Such is also the account distributed by the Catholic Church today: "Pope Visits Our Lady of Trsat," p. 1. In the 1360s, however, Loreto was only just establishing the identity of its major relics. As mentioned in chapter 2, surviving references to Loreto in the 1300s are focused on an image of the Madonna, not on the Holy House that linked the Italian site to Dalmatia. Also as noted above, the first papal acknowledgment of pilgrims coming to Loreto was in 1375 when Pope Gregory XI offered them an indulgence; Loreto's

Trsat's oral tradition, the pope offered the icon in response to a specific request by none other than the noble Dalmatian family of Frankopans, of Nikolà fame.[101]

The Frankopans had honed in on the seaside outpost of Trsat in the 1300s, establishing it as a family seat before their ascent to power. Over the next two centuries, they imported Franciscans to minister to the needs of their family and to oversee their private church.[102] As their fortunes grew the Frankopans fortified the entire town, turning Trsat into a hilltop fortress. They were a militant crew, in good company with the soldiers marching through the pages of Torsellino's history. Eight of the Frankopan men went on to be *bans* or viceroys of Croatia, supervising the region under the military auspices of Hungary.[103] In addition to being Catholic, the Frankopans built their reputation on fighting prowess. The combination later struck their countryman the Jesuit Juraj Habdelic as distinctly Slavic. "Slovenian and Croatian gentry care more about good horses and useful weapons, with which they can defend the Christian religion and their country, than about clothes and adornment," he wrote.[104] It was not an insult, but a statement of how they stood by Christianity, sword in hand.

The sword was necessary for survival in the hotly contested zone of Dalmatia.[105] Three military powers converged there in the 1400s. To the west, the Ottoman Turks advanced straight into the Balkan peninsula.

---

first shrine record explicitly referencing Slavic pilgrims dates to 1436. Evidence therefore points to linkages between shores occurring later than the 1367 icon exchange in Trsat's mythohistory.

101. Oliver, *Croatia*, p. 97.

102. The first family church of the Frankopans at Trsat was dedicated to Mary, and associated with Martin Frankopan (d. 1479). Oliver, "Croatia Traveler."

103. These included: Ivan Frankopan (d. 1393); Nikolà Frankopan (d. 1432); his son, also Nikolà Frankopan, who served as co-Ban from 1456 to 1458; Stjepan Frankopan (d. 1481); Kristof Frankopan (d. 1527); Fran Frankopan, who served as co-Ban from 1567 to 1573; Nikolà Frankopan of Trsat, ban from 1617 to 1622; and Fran Krsto (d. 1671). Also, one Frankopan noblewoman, Katarina, married a ban of Croatia, Nikolà ubic Zrinski (1543). The Croatian names of the Frankopans are used here. They are also commonly referred to by their Hungarian names (János, Miklós, István, Kristóf, Fran) and English names (John, Nicholas, Stephen, Christopher, Francis), and their last name appears with the spelling variant *Frankapan*; in Hungarian as *Frangepán*; and in Italian as *Frangipani*. J. A. Fine, *When Ethnicity Did Not Matter in the Balkans*, p. 567.

104. Juraj Habdelic as quoted by McWilliam, "Baroque in Croatia," p. 712.

105. In point of fact, there were other options for survival. Consider the deft religious and imperial maneuvering described by Skendi, "Crypto-Christianity in the Balkan Area under the Ottomans."

Taking up arms for Christianity, to the east, the Venetian navy patrolled the Adriatic Sea; to the north, Hungary dominated the Illyrian interior by force of arms.[106] This was the backdrop for one last Nikolà Frankopan, a contemporary of Torsellino's who was still a child when the Jesuit began researching his account of Loreto.

This Nikolà Frankopan was ban of Croatia from 1617 to 1622, three decades after Torsellino's shrine history was published. He began his career inauspiciously as a military captain at Senj attempting to reign in unruly Uskok pirates to keep them from interfering with Italian shipping.[107] He rose in the ranks. While ban of Croatia, he resided often at Trsat, the Marian sanctuary and his family's outpost. Under this Nikolà's guardianship, projects were initiated to renovate and embellish the pilgrimage site, and the first Croatian-authored histories of the Dalmatian devotion appeared.

The oldest namesake of this Nikolà Frankopan had supposedly hosted Loreto's *Santa Casa* and lost it. The next two Nikolàs in his lineage had acknowledged the Italian site with largesse. But this last Nikolà looked to his own side of the Adriatic. He built it up with a local pride reminiscent of one of his countrymen, the well-known humanist and Catholic layman Marko Marulic (1450–1524) of Split. Marulic passionately researched the ancient Roman ruins in Croatia. He also wrote *De institutione bene vivendi* (Venice, 1506), a book in Latin that defended Catholicism and was so well-loved by Jesuits on the opposite shore that one of them, St. Francis Xavier, carried the book with him all the way to India. Marulic is remembered for these pro-Italian masterpieces.[108] Yet in 1501, he also wrote "Judith," an epic poem in Croatian encouraging his countrymen to be strong in their faith as they fought off the Turks.[109] And alongside that, rarely mentioned, is Marulic's short polemical treatise "Against Those Who Contend that Blessed Jerome was an Italian."[110] Illyrians had long believed

106. I focus here on the conflagrations leading up to the early modern period, but it is worth noting that between the late sixth century and the fifteenth century, Dalmatia was annexed more than thirty times to a staggering variety of conquerors including the Byzantines, Avars, Greeks, Holy Roman Empire, Serbians, Croatians, Magyars, Mongols, Normans, Sicilians, Venetians, and Neapolitans.

107. From 1611 to 1613 while Captain at Senj, Nikolà Frankopan tried to keep the Uskoks from attacking Christian ships and failed. The Uskoks have themselves been described as "hardy . . . Christian refugees"—corresponding surprisingly to the themes of this book. Rothenberg, "Venice and the Uskoks of Senj," pp. 148 (Uskoks), 153 (Frankopan). For more on the Uskoks' activities around Rijeka: Bracewell, *Uskoks of Senj.*

108. Kadic, "St. Francis Xavier and Marko Marulic."

109. Ibid., p. 16.

110. Petrovich, "Croatian Humanists," pp. 626, 631, 637.

that St. Jerome was theirs, born in Stridon in the region of Istria. Marulic refused to let the Italians claim the saint. It was time for Catholicism to stay in Dalmatia.

But someone forgot to give pilgrims the memo. Behind Torsellino's celebration of Nikolà Frankopan's ancestors were less high-ranking Slavic Catholics who had been observed at the Loreto shrine within Torsellino's own lifetime. As noted previously, Raphael Riera, Torsellino's Jesuit contemporary, published the first printed reference to Slavs at Loreto in 1565, recounting their public show of weeping and demanding the house's return.[111] Riera wrote that he had seen these lamenting pilgrims with his own eyes while he worked as a confessor at Loreto. He reported that at Loreto in his time, in the 1550s, the numbers of pilgrims from Dalmatia swelled. He noticed *crowds* of them at Loreto.

Riera's observations correspond to shrine and civic records. Before 1500, there are only a few scattered reports of pilgrims to Loreto hailing from the area of Trsat.[112] It was not until the mid-sixteenth century that Loreto's priests made note of mass pilgrimage by Slavs.[113] This intensification was spurred by developments on both sides of the Adriatic Sea. Affiliates of the Loreto sanctuary were publicizing the Dalmatian provenance of Loreto's relics as they consolidated a history of the devotion. Meanwhile, Catholics at Trsat were starting to point to Loreto to enhance their own Marian shrine. Each shore referenced and built on the claims of the other, creating a "brilliant, concentrated web" of ocean-spanning culture worthy of Braudel's Mediterranean.[114] Of course, as the Frankopan military fame

111. On Riera and the Slavs: Santarelli, *Tradizione*, pp. 59–63. On Slavic pilgrims actually weeping at Loreto: Vélez, "'Do Not Suppose That Those Tears Proceed from Weakness.'"

112. The earliest Lauretan archival documents to indicate Slavic pilgrims are two 1436 manuscripts that identify pilgrims from Fiume (Rijeka) and Segna (Senj), Croatia. Across the Adriatic, the state archives of Zara name seven "schiavoni" who set out for Loreto before 1500: Theoddorus de Prandino (1403–41); Simon Damiani (1440–76); Joannes de Calcina (1439–91); Marin Maronam (1474–1514); Karotus Vitale (1451–63); Tomas Stancic (1448–91) from Serebenico; and Andrija Fajeta (1441–86) from Arbe. Grimaldi, *Pellegrini*, pp. 266–69.

113. Ibid., p. 269.

114. Braudel, *Mediterranean and the Mediterranean World in the Age of Philip II*, p. 131. I quote Braudel slightly out of context to evoke his famous sense of seaboards sharing culture and religion. Actually, Braudel speaks of the Adriatic here with a heavy colonial valence, as a "sphere of triumphant Italian culture" in which Venice dominated the Balkans. But later historians such as Floriano Grimaldi have applied Braudel's most positive valences to Loreto's mythohistory; Grimaldi concludes that the Loreto devotion demonstrates that Slavs and Italians "all belong to the same [Adriatic] community and cohabit in the same [maritime] territory." Grimaldi, *Pellegrini*, pp. 11–12.

suggests, this trace of Catholic shared patterns emerged in the midst of battlefields that were also caught in the Jesuit Torsellino's comprehensive net, when he dredged deep for information about Loreto's origins.[115]

What is remarkable is not that Torsellino chose to include some of the grit, but that he lifted out of it a Christian hero who tastefully complemented the flying house and Virgin on Loreto's seal. Torsellino crystallized all Slavic Catholics into one larger-than-life mythical ancient personage, Nicolas Frangipane. He commended this past Dalmatian spiritual leader not for his family's battle prowess, but for his respect for Loreto. Unaware of the Nikolà Frankopan growing up in his own era, Torsellino's portrait was also nonetheless surprisingly accurate about what his contemporary would do: release Loreto and focus on his own shore.

It may seem a stretch to designate the myriad Nikolà Frankopans and their company as living "authors" of Loreto's mythohistory, instead of presenting them as fictional characters appropriated by later chroniclers of the shrine. Unlike Angelitta and Tolomei or Riera and Torsellino, these Slavic Catholics did not explicitly pick up pens or publish books to preserve Loreto's past. But they belong nonetheless in the company of these first historians because of their substantial additions to Loreto's mythohistory, as acknowledged in print and broadcast by seventeenth-century writers like Torsellino. Their additions were incorporated into the official narrative partly because they could be mustered to support the sixteenth-century Italian cardinals' initiative to showcase Catholicism on the move. There was no better demonstration than the Slavs themselves for proving that "the House of Nazareth *was* transported out of Sclavonie into Italy," and that its convoluted mythohistorical journey had followed a real route.[116]

There is also no better demonstration than the Slavs of the unplanned collaboration that underpins shrine mythohistories. It was not literary giants and church authorities alone who formed the corpus describing Loreto's origins. Much like today's popular *Star Wars* franchise, the credit for

115. Eric Dursteler praises the trend "to perceive a more integrated, complex, and multi-faceted early modern Mediterranean," but he also warns that "caution must be exercised. . . . As Ugo Tucci recently warned, the tendency to depict the Mediterranean as 'a sort of universal hug' brings with it certain risks. There is a danger that the 'black legend' of Mediterranean battlefields will be replaced with an equally imbalanced depiction of Mediterranean bazaars that ignores the sea's long history of antagonism, division, miscomprehension, exploitation and violence. This is a history we are very familiar with, and which should not be ignored." Dursteler, "On Bazaars and Battlefields," pp. 433–34.

116. Torsellino, *History of our B. Lady of Loreto*, p. 33. Emphasis added.

its shape and power cannot be solely ascribed to one screenwriter, George Lucas. Actors, directors, producers, and a legion of fans continue to add to the already crowded *Star Wars* universe through updated movies, blogs, fan fiction, junior novelizations, adult science fiction books, action figures, and cartoon spin-offs, to name just a few outgrowths of the original that keep an army of copyright lawyers gainfully employed.[117] Who is responsible for phenomena like *Star Wars* and Loreto's flying Holy House? Not just writers, men of high position, contracted staff, and spiritual leaders, but indeed everyone who is amused and touched by the burgeoning enormity of a narrative that has gone epic.

This chapter has presented and tagged a variety of contributors as the "first authors" of Loreto's history. Their diversity requires a rethinking of the category of "authors" and "authorized," to be more accurate about whom we credit for composing a mythohistory. Clearly it cannot be a single scribe seated at a desk in isolation, conjuring a story out of thin air and delivering its only pristine, uncluttered version. Early accounts of Loreto demonstrate instead that authors, and those authorized to chronicle Loreto, would be better envisioned as a fast-growing group of eyewitnesses, researchers, and above all, collaborators. Their ranks include the elite and powerful, such as Cardinals Gallo and Benzoni; the Loreto shrine governor Tolomei; the hypereducated Roman Jesuit Torsellino; and multiple noble Nikolàs of the Frankopan family. But they also include less wealthy and more ordinary Catholics such as Angelitta, the secretary of Recanati; the Jesuit Riera, one of many confessors at work at Loreto; and masses of Slavic pilgrims who journeyed to Loreto in the mid-1500s. Barriers of position, wealth, and religious credentials are broken by their joint project: All were acting to underline or add parts of Loreto's history, and all felt themselves qualified to do so. Many quoted each other, consciously or unknowingly. Their products were as diverse as their backgrounds: concise visual emblems, multivolume compendia, printed declarations translated into multiple languages, and even nods of acknowledgement from a distant shore. In this list the printed word appears much like the Catholic

117. One of the most unusual participatory offshoots of *Star Wars* is the direct self-identification of fans with *Star Wars* categories. In the April 2001 census of the United Kingdom, 390,000 individuals across England and Wales entered their religion into the census as "Jedi," the faith of the knights in the *Star Wars* movies. *Star Wars* also continues to inspire conversations across centuries on everything from space defense systems to returning to a Republic style of government. "Census Returns of the Jedi"; Shefrin, "*Lord of the Rings*, *Star Wars*, and Participatory Fandom"; Charles, "Remembering and Restoring the Republic," pp. 292, 298; Rushing, "Ronald Reagan's 'Star Wars' Address."

Church authorities whose stamps and medals opened the chapter. Like cardinals, printed books had clout, but they did not hold a monopoly on generating the past, nor did they exist independently of the many other sources that informed them. Because of this interdependent dynamic, the company of authors crafting Loreto could therefore continue to grow in style as well as number.

CHAPTER FOUR

Accidental Pilgrims

THERE WAS NO better place to be touched by, and to actually touch, Loreto's sacred past than Loreto itself. The earliest written descriptions of Loreto star pilgrim after pilgrim making the trek to Loreto to experience it for themselves. Here we will follow their footsteps to the sanctuary. But before embarking, it should be noted that there was a proper way to go on pilgrimage in the seventeenth century. Unlike tourism, pilgrimage did not simply involve traveling to see a famous place to satisfy one's curiosity about it. It was a ritual of spiritual cleansing. To this end, a pilgrim was expected to prepare his or her soul before and throughout the journey. Fortunately for us, Loreto was so prominent a pilgrimage site that it was featured in one of the top-selling how-to guides for pilgrimage in early modern Europe. The French Jesuit Louis Richeôme first published his *Pilgrim of Loreto* or *Le Pelerin de Lorete* (Bordeaux: S. Milanges) in 1604.[1] Richeôme had himself made a pilgrimage to Loreto as a Jesuit novice. Like his predecessors and fellow Jesuits Raphael Riera and Oratio Torsellino, Richeôme had seen the Holy House and Madonna of Loreto with his own eyes. But his book of instructions to pilgrims could not have been more different from his colleagues' firsthand reports.

While Riera and Torsellino highlighted external and publicly visible aspects of Loreto, Richeôme's version of Lauretan pilgrimage reads instead as a paean to interiority.[2] Over the course of nearly one thousand pages,

1. It was popular enough to go through several editions: it was republished in Latin in Cologne (1612, 1621) and Paris (1628, English translation 1626). J. C. Smith, *Sensuous Worship*, p. 213n95.

2. In this sense it resembles the genre of *Zardino de Oration*, meditation guides that urge garden visitors to retire privately to ponder and pray after they experience the place.

the Jesuit describes how to mentally prepare for a pilgrimage to Loreto, how to steel one's mind against temptations on the road, and what to think and do while at the shrine. The book is written from the point of view of a fictional pilgrim, Lazare, who is on a journey of spiritual initiation that ends in his return home and his death.[3] Speaking through Lazare, Richeôme resembles an official guide rather than a pilgrim.[4] His voice is directive, helping audiences to manage their spiritual emotion properly. In the conclusion to his book, Richeôme advises the reader on exactly what to ponder on one's journey home from Loreto: not the material remnants of the miraculous flying Holy House at Loreto, but the life of Christ. The Jesuit's generalized afterthoughts for pilgrimage are not tied to the physical shrine center of Loreto but could apply to *any* holy site, imagined or real. Richeôme's book is thus frequently interpreted as representing a turning point for European pilgrimages, a moment when literal visits to specific shrines were being replaced by purely interior journeys one could experience from the comfort of an armchair.[5]

Richeôme's description of an idealized trip to the *Santa Casa* cuts against the lived experience of the majority of its seventeenth-century visitors. But Richeôme's manual was not a distinct, competing trajectory of Catholic devotion that encouraged mind over matter, nor was it written to replace a thoughtful Catholic's road trip with meditation. This Jesuit author's book was produced from within, and for, the stream of real pilgrims walking to Loreto. Its contrast with that stream highlights an essential tension between what pilgrimage was supposed to be, and what was actually happening en route to Loreto.

This chapter describes how some Catholic pilgrims tried to reconcile the Jesuit official advice of mental self-discipline with their first intense

---

Louis Richeôme specialized in writing this sort of guide to contemplating images. See, for instance, his *Tableaux sacrez des figures mystiques du tres Auguste Sacrament et Sacrifice de l'Eucharistie* (Paris, 1607). Knaap, "Meditation, Ministry, and Visual Rhetoric," p. 161.

3. Gomez-Géraud, "Entre chemin d'aventure."

4. At Catholic sites such as the Sacred Mountain of Varallo in Italy, or the Holy Sepulcher in Jerusalem, pilgrims were often accompanied by Franciscan guides rather than being allowed to roam aimlessly. These guides explicated Christian symbolism for visitors. Freedberg, *Power of Images*, pp. 116, 120.

5. Fabre, "'Ils iront en pèlerinage,'" pp. 181–82n54; Burkardt, "Voyage de dévotion," p. 522.

encounters with the Madonna of Loreto. The pilgrims' stories that follow involve both contemplative quests for spiritual improvement and transformative run-ins with the material manifestations of Catholicism. Yet they flip the order recommended by Richeôme of contemplation first and real world next. Often in the 1600s, Catholics began their pilgrimages with an unmediated direct encounter with the outside world, only after turning inward to self-examination.

The first pilgrims considered here are the Jesuits who loom large behind the good-pilgrimage rubrics of this time period. For Jesuits, too, there were at least four ways in which pilgrimages put real-world encounters before contemplation. Jesuits undertook pilgrimages as deliberate tests of physical fortitude; as visible indications of their group membership; as chances to meet Mary and the saints face to face; and as ways to literally touch what they had been trained to imagine. So while Jesuit letters describing their pilgrimages to Loreto echo their colleague Richeôme's idealism, they also reveal the difficulty of upholding his standard.

Next in this chapter, the Jesuit template for pilgrimage is tested against the reported experiences of two non-Jesuit travelers to Loreto, Nicolà Albani and Pierre Chaumonot. These men's accounts demonstrate that the expectations of the Jesuits were not unique to their society, but were shared by many of their contemporaries. Albani and Chaumonot's roundabout paths to Loreto additionally showcase a dimension to pilgrimage that was not addressed by Richeôme: lack of intention. Coincidence also colors the experience of a Huron convert to Catholicism, Ignace Tsaouenhohoui, who journeyed from the mission of Sainte-Marie to Québec City in the early 1650s. Considered last in this chapter, Tsaouenhohoui's odyssey strangely resembles Albani's and Chaumonot's approaches to Loreto.

Inadvertent pilgrims like these were not following Jesuit scripts. To the contrary, their real, borderline miraculous brushes with the Virgin Mary were triggering productive reflection among Catholics about the process and meaning of sacred journeys. Their experiences stretched the definition of pilgrimage from Richeôme's internalized model and from the Jesuits' four-part externalization. For these Catholics, pilgrimage consisted of accidental detours, not purposeful training; gritty company, not elite membership; desperate, rather than simply hopeful, outreach to the divine; and touch first, not last.

Anchoring Ideal: Jesuit Instructions and Expectations of Pilgrimage

Catholic pilgrimage was far older than the Jesuits.[6] But Jesuit perceptions of pilgrimage are especially informative of wider seventeenth-century European attitudes toward the practice. This is not just because of the primacy of some of their published works about pilgrimage, such as Richeôme's manual. It is also because of the centrality of pilgrimage in the formation of their order. The founder of the Society of Jesus, the Basque former soldier St. Ignatius of Loyola (1491–1556), attributed his career change and spiritual transformation to pilgrimage.[7] Ignatius's own life encapsulates how pilgrimage became, first and foremost, a planned test of spiritual potential for Jesuits who wished to emulate their founder.

After recovering from a serious battle wound, Ignatius resolved to make a pilgrimage to the Marian shrine of Montserrat in Catalonia in 1522. There he pledged to give up his sword and serve the Virgin Mary. He then spent nearly two years journeying to Jerusalem and the Holy Land as a pilgrim. Ignatius founded the Society of Jesus in part out of a desire to return to Jerusalem as a pilgrim.[8] When dictating his autobiography, Ignatius recalled that when he saw Jerusalem, he "felt great consolation. . . . He always felt this same devotion on his visits to the holy places."[9] Back in Europe, Loreto was one such holy place that reminded Ignatius of the Holy Land. Loreto's Holy House especially resonated for him as a sacred structure where Mary had once lived. From Rome, where he spent his last decades, Ignatius avidly encouraged Jesuit pilgrimage to the nearby sanctuary.[10]

6. It also remained popular well beyond the Jesuits' first century and for longer than is generally noted. Shalev, "Death of Pilgrimage?"; Birch, *Pilgrimage to Rome in the Middle Ages*.

7. On Ignatius's frequent references to himself as "the pilgrim" in his writings: O'Malley, *First Jesuits*, p. 271; Olin, "Idea of Pilgrimage in the Experience of Ignatius Loyola"; Tylenda, "Introduction," p. 8.

8. The legendary founding moment of the Society of Jesus was when Ignatius Loyola and a group of his followers in Paris met at Montmartre on 15 August 1534 and vowed "to make a pilgrimage to Jerusalem—[and] if this were not possible, they would put themselves at the disposal of the pope." Official recognition of the Society of Jesus came later with the papal bull *Regimini militantis*, issued by Pope Paul III on 27 September 1540. McCoog, *Society of Jesus in Ireland, Scotland, and England*, p. 14.

9. Loyola, "Autobiography," pp. 86–87.

10. Ignatius himself also approved the dispatch of the first Jesuit confessors to Loreto in 1554, with the Jesuit *Collegio Penitentieri* (college of confessors) formally established there in 1561, shortly after his death. Tacchi Venturi, *Storia della Compagnia di Gesù in*

The first Jesuits heeded his recommendation and seem to have made the multiday trip between Rome and Loreto frequently.[11] Two of the society's most well-known missionaries, Alexander Rhodes (1591–1660) and Matteo Ricci (1552–1610), made the pilgrimage. Both Rhodes and Ricci visited Loreto before embarking on their missionary endeavors, as if it were a dry run for the emotional challenges and travel hardships of their distant postings. Rhodes went to help reconcile himself to his assignment to serve in China and Vietnam.[12] Ricci had been born in the shadow of the Loreto sanctuary, in the city of Macerata, and his visit there on the eve of his departure to China seems almost a farewell to home.[13] Both missionaries later wrote that their time in Loreto sustained them in their distant posts.

Pilgrimage to Loreto was gradually institutionalized in the first decades of the order. It became one of the pillars of Jesuit practical training, along with service at a hospital, teaching Catholic doctrine to students, and hearing confession.[14] Novices were instructed to undertake the pilgrimage in traditional ascetic style, walking and begging their way from Rome to Loreto.[15] As the headquarters for the Society of Jesus, Rome housed a growing number of Jesuit seminaries, or colleges. Students spilled out from these toward the coastal sanctuary, rehearsing the physical discomfort and life of poverty that they were about to undertake as itinerant preachers in the Society of Jesus.

Walking to Loreto's Holy House was almost an audition for the aspiring Jesuit, measuring up his stamina and conviction. Jerome Nadal (1507–80), one of the first ten Jesuits and a key figure in shaping Jesuit educational policy, used the word "test" when he wrote of two hopeful young Calabrian applicants to the society. Nadal wrote that "the first test that they made was to make a pilgrimage to Loreto; they came back from there and

---

Italia, vol. 2, p. 30; ARSI Rom. 122, tom. 1, fol. 6; also: Santarelli, "Gli Ordini Religiosi al servizio della Santa Casa."

11. Ignatius's executive assistant, Juan de Polanco, made the pilgrimage in 1555 along with fellow Jesuits Luis Gonçalves de Câmara, Diego Guzmán, and Gaspar de Loarte. They went to offer prayers to the Madonna of Loreto for the recovery of the ailing Pope Marcellus II (1501–55), who lived to fill the shoes of papal office for only twenty-two days. Fabre, "'Ils iront en pèlerinage,'" p. 173.

12. Ibid., pp. 174, 178.

13. Spence, *Memory Palace of Matteo Ricci*, p. 259.

14. O'Malley, *First Jesuits*, p. 362.

15. Ibid., p. 271; Tacchi Venturi, *Storia della Compagnia di Gesù in Italia*, vol. 2, pp. 29–30, 36.

behave in a most edifying manner."[16] But not all would-be Jesuits passed the test so easily. In fact, the Jesuit founder, Ignatius of Loyola himself, had worried that some novices on pilgrimage might go to extremes and make themselves sick in trying to prove themselves, while others might be led far astray on the road.[17]

Jesuit novices were not supposed to get too caught up with pilgrimage. They were not lone, stricken wanderers beseeching God: they were simply *practicing* that behavior for their own spiritual growth, and for the benefit of the order. The latter became a second major externalizing dimension of pilgrimage for the Jesuits: to represent their society well. Especially in the first century of the Society of Jesus, novice pilgrims traveling under the protection of the society were made conscious that they were the public face of the new order, and should therefore be exemplary pilgrims. Ignatius Loyola set this forth exhaustively in a 1548 letter of patent for a Flemish novice, Antonio Vincko:

> Having been in our house for some time to the edification of all, [Vincko] leaves with the pious intention of going on a pilgrimage to Our Lady of Loreto, begging, without money and dressed in the clothing of the poor for greater mortification and greater merit, according to the practice of members of our Company who, by various tests, like this one of pilgrimage, and of serving at hospitals and other tests still, live in a general manner to acquire the experience of virtue and spiritual profit of those who desire to enter our Company.[18]

The Society of Jesus introduced itself to the world through pilgrims like Vincko.

The Society of Jesus also denied crucial letters of patent to those they felt were unworthy. "If you judge him to be incorrigible," wrote a superior in Rome to the Jesuit provincial of Sicily about one Juan Ignacio in 1555, "send him back or send him on a pilgrimage to Loreto, without viaticum and without a letter . . . so that no one will receive him in any part as a member of this Company."[19] By the seventeenth century, the road be-

16. Nadal to Gonçalves de Câmara, 21 November 1555, as quoted by Fabre, "'Ils iront en pèlerinage,'" p. 171. On Nadal: Bangert and McCoog, *Jerome Nadal, S.J., 1507–1580*.

17. Fabre, "'Ils iront en pèlerinage,'" pp. 168–70. For the story of one Jesuit-schooled "professional pilgrim," Jacques Agnès, who embodied Ignatius's fears of straying when he was apprehended in Caen, France, in 1748 for begging and suspected murder: Julia, "Aveux de pèlerins," pp. 452–53.

18. Loyola as quoted by Fabre, "'Ils iront en pèlerinage,'" p. 172.

19. Letter from Rome to Jerome Domenech, 11 January 1555, as quoted by Fabre, "'Ils iront en pèlerinage,'" p. 170.

tween Rome and Loreto had become a showcase of Jesuit idealized group identity.

On this road, Jesuits could demonstrate and publicly reenact one part of their founder's life. Often seeking out Ignatius was as important, to prospective Jesuits, as looking for Mary.[20] In the first century after his death, Jesuits built up pilgrimage sites around Rome that were associated with *Saint* Ignatius Loyola, freshly canonized in 1622. Loreto appears at the outer fringes of this seventeenth-century pilgrimage circuit of "Roma Ignaziana."[21] Along with Ignatius's tomb and the La Storta chapel outside Rome's city walls where Ignatius had experienced a vision, the Marian shrine on the Adriatic was a place where Jesuits could go to retrace the footsteps of their society's founder. Novices were steeped in the story of Ignatius Loyola's stirring to action in front of the Virgin of Montserrat. They prayed in front of Ignatius's favorite image of the Madonna della Strada displayed in the Church of the Gesù in Rome.[22] The example of Ignatius made it seem possible to Jesuit novices that they, too, might have that rare and coveted experience of a connection with the Holy Mother.[23]

The trip to Loreto was not just a rite of passage and public performance of Jesuit identity, then, but a crack at holy *experience*. This is the third goal evident in Jesuit seventeenth-century pilgrimages: to personally bond with the divine. It is important to note the element of serendipity in this sort of contact expected of young Jesuits at the Loreto shrine.[24] While the exercise of pilgrimage could be planned in advance and even mandated, transformative encounters with the Virgin of Loreto and Jesuit saints were not available on order. Nor did they synchronize neatly with Jesuit membership if and when they did occur. For Pierre Chaumonot, one of the pilgrims considered further below, a spiritual connection with Mary

20. A twentieth-century Catholic splendidly expresses the urgency of the quest for Ignatius, though he is not a Jesuit: Hansen, "Saint Ignatius of Loyola, the Pilgrim," p. 112.

21. Levy, "'A Noble Medley and Concert of Materials and Artifice,'" p. 59.

22. The Madonna della Strada and the Madonna of Loreto are singled out as the two advocations of Mary most popular, historically, with the men of the Jesuit Order. "Devoción a María."

23. Claudio Acquaviva, fifth superior general of the society, sent out a circular letter to all members in 1586 stressing the importance of the Virgin Mary to their lives and work; Acquaviva's letter had an impact as far as China, where it touched Matteo Ricci. Spence, *Memory Palace of Matteo Ricci*, p. 242.

24. Special thanks to Dr. Laura Smoller for the idea of "serendipity" among the Jesuits, taken from her comment on my paper, "Jesuits, Miracles and the Image of the Madonna of Loreto on the Spanish-American Frontier, 1680–1720." American Historical Association Panel Session 162: "Knowledge and Belief in the Spanish Atlantic." Washington, DC, 5 January 2008.

actually preceded his Jesuit laurels. Chaumonot was moved to become a Jesuit in part because of an early visit to the Loreto shrine when he was a runaway.

Even if Chaumonot had been a full-fledged Jesuit when he first engaged with the Madonna of Loreto, which he was not, there was precious little guidance in Jesuit pilgrimage manuals like Richeôme's for the actual moment of raw encounter. Exactly how was a Jesuit or average pilgrim supposed to recognize or react to a sign from Mary? As novices knew, the Jesuit founder Ignatius had himself seen apparitions of Mary and Christ. But reports of his visions offered little clue for comportment beyond stating that "these things [that Ignatius] saw strengthened him [in his faith] then and always."[25]

Jesuit experts muddied even that clarity by casting the net wide in their reports of saintly reactions to the divine. The esteemed Jesuit hagiographers Jean Bollandus (1596–1665), Heribert Rosweyde (1569–1629), and their assistants sifted through thousands of reports of supernatural events in order to compile their multivolume *Acta Sanctorum*, or *Lives of the Saints*. They weeded out accounts that they saw as inauthentic or unsubstantiated. Bollandus was confident enough to assert that he had excised from his collection every event that one might suspect was invented.[26] That said, consider the Bollandists' rendition of how St. Agnes of Montepulciano (1268–1317) encountered Christ and the Virgin Mary.

According to the *Acta Sanctorum*, St. Agnes had prayed to actually see the baby Jesus during her lifetime. Her prayers were answered when Christ appeared to her in this form. After a joyous interval spent with the Holy Infant, Mary herself arrived to retrieve her son. But St. Agnes refused to let go of Jesus. Mary grabbed her child, and St. Agnes proceeded to engage in a violent tug-of-war with the Holy Mother. Of course Mary won, but St. Agnes triumphantly came away with a crucifix that she had ripped from the young Christ's neck before he was taken from her.[27] This anec-

25. These visions happened at Manresa: "Often and for a long time, while at prayer, [Ignatius] saw with interior eyes the humanity of Christ. The form that appeared to him was like a white body, neither very large nor very small, but he did not see any distinction of members. . . . He has also seen Our Lady in a similar form, without distinguishing parts." Loyola, "Autobiography," p. 80.

26. "I say then, first, that there are in this work no lives which any one may have the slightest suspicion of being entirely imaginary, as they are always based on the testimony of some Martyrology, or other unassailable authority." Bollandus as quoted by Collis, "Preface of the *Acta Sanctorum*," p. 302.

27. *Acta sanctorum*, Aprilis II, p. 797, as summarized by Klapisch-Zuber, "Holy Dolls," p. 325.

dote about St. Agnes has many symbolic implications about the Dominican nun's piety that far outweigh the literal details. Perhaps this is why Jesuit hagiographers retained it in full. But approach it for the moment as if you were an ordinary Catholic pilgrim hoping, like St. Agnes, to see baby Jesus in this world. Approach it like a young Chaumonot, Albani, or Tsaouenhohoui, searching for models for how to negotiate or comprehend a visit from the Virgin Mary.

St. Agnes had touched the Christ child and was left with a crucifix as a reminder of the life-changing encounter. One might come away from this Jesuit Bollandist narrative thinking that physical touch and material mementos were a surefire way to engage with the holy. Touch was the fourth and last tacit directive emerging from seventeenth-century Jesuit pilgrimages, during which novices were sanctioned in using their physical senses to manifest the divine. Once again, the founder of the Society of Jesus, Ignatius, pointed Jesuits to this behavior figuratively as well as literally. Like Richeôme, Ignatius insisted that mental preparation was necessary, in advance, to be ready to carry something away from a vision of holy figures like Mary.

Ignatius led the Jesuits to Mary via *The Spiritual Exercises*. This four-week program of contemplation composed by Ignatius himself was revisited often by Jesuits over the course of their training and afterward. The practice and repetition of it was one of the cornerstones of Jesuit formation.[28] Novice, lay brother, or priest, each Jesuit was led through the meditation and also directed others through the process scores of times in their lives. It was their most familiar road map to spiritual improvement, and it offered a clear directive: Begin with Mary.

The Spiritual Exercises is a catalyst for introspection and imagination. A practitioner begins and ends the month of reflection by turning inward, examining his or her conscience. It is the middle that is pivotal, however. At the second week, Ignatius suggests that one shift focus to God by using all the senses—smell, sight, sound, touch, taste—to envision one's way through Christ's life. Conjuring this sort of vivid "mental representation" of all the places visited by Christ incites empathy and intense reflection about Christ's sacrifice and teachings.[29] Follow the exercitant to this turning point for a moment. After a lengthy review of personal struggles, it is the first day of the second week. The first contemplation recommended is the Incarnation of

28. Ganss, *Spiritual Exercises*, pp. 1–14.

29. For aspiring Jesuits with vivid imaginations, this sort of rehearsal could lead to vivid and sensorily rich conjuring. See, for example, Ruiz De Montoya, *Spiritual Conquest* (1639), pp. 200–201.

Christ. Ignatius, filtered through text and the spiritual director guiding the exercises, urges the exercitant to picture where it all started:

> [Make] a mental representation of the place. It will be here [that one strives] to see the great extent of the surface of the earth, inhabited by so many different peoples, and especially to see the house and room of our Lady in the city of Nazareth in the province of Galilee.[30]

The path to Christ and God begins in this small, quiet space, inside the house of Mary. It is a space Jesuit minds disciplined themselves to imagine countless times.

It is also a space they could actually *experience* at Loreto. Ignatius's multifaceted approach, introspective yet rooted in real pilgrimage, helps to make sense of the popularity of Richeôme's guide to Loreto. *The Spiritual Exercises* was not intended to replace or overshadow Catholic journeys, but to help evoke or process them. For Jesuits in the 1600s, pilgrimage brought the earthly and heavenly into sharp interplay. A trip to Loreto began as a kind of entrance examination to test one's mettle; it continued as a way to publicly announce one's membership in the Society of Jesus; it had the potential to lead further, to a personal meeting with Mary; and that last hoped-for meeting could be instilled or magnified through touching a relic like the Holy House.

Interestingly, the pilgrims to whom we now turn lived a neat reversal of what Jesuit training strove to artificially construct by sending novices to Loreto. Albani, Chaumonot, and Tsaouenhohoui did not find Mary through the carefully orchestrated steps of Jesuit training. They all reported life-changing encounters with Mary that happened without any of the practices of *The Spiritual Exercises*, and with very little prior preparation. First, these men did not choose tests of character as part of their training, but they unintentionally stumbled into them. Second, the Catholic groups in which they found solidarity were not elite or restricted like the Society of Jesus. Third, their encounters with the divine were not optional or helpful to them in terms of advancing a spiritual career, but they were matters of life and death. Finally, it was touch, not a trained imagination, that was their key portal to the divine. Yet by reading their experiences alongside and after those of the Jesuits, one can discern how chance journeys like theirs undergird, rather than undercut, the official apparatus of pilgrimage. What these men encountered was the very goal and aspiration at the heart of Richeôme's guide, Ignatius's *Spiritual Exercises*, and

30. Loyola, *Spiritual Exercises*, p. 49.

the Bollandists' exhaustive collection of saints' lives. All those Jesuit tomes presented as hopeful aids for pilgrims also stood as tributes to haphazard pilgrims who found their way to Loreto regardless.

Actual Encounters: Albani's and Chaumonot's Detours to Loreto

Many pilgrims seemed to stumble upon Loreto almost accidentally in its first centuries as a shrine. Unlike the hyperfocused Jesuit novices trailing Ignatius, these pilgrims were journeying elsewhere. Loreto was in their way, situated at the crossroads between the two far more prestigious pilgrimage destinations of the Holy Land and Rome. To the east, Loreto fronted the Mediterranean and was an easy walk from Porto Recanati and Ancona, ports of embarcation for pilgrims headed to Jerusalem. Overland, to the west, Loreto was only a week's distance by foot from Rome, with its numerous Christian sites and ancient monuments.[31] The Roman papacy seemed bent on deflecting some of the pilgrims from Jerusalem toward their own western seat. As early as the thirteenth century, Pope Innocent III was pouring money into building projects in the March of Ancona and liberally awarding indulgences to pilgrims there.[32] Loreto seemed to benefit directly from Rome's attention and gravitational pull, acting as a convenient stopover for long-distance travelers to Rome who arrived from the north via Venice, France, and Germany.[33]

The Italian pilgrim Nicolà Albani was among those who unexpectedly detoured to Loreto in the early eighteenth century. He left his hometown of Melfi in southern Italy to make his way to Spain, to the famous shrine of Santiago de Compostela in Galicia. This shrine to St. James the Greater in northwestern Spain was better known across Europe than Loreto. Santiago de Compostela had dominated European pilgrimage circuits since the twelfth century.[34] It was also more difficult to reach for the Italian Albani and thus more prestigious—spiritually and generally—for him to achieve.

31. In 1743, it took the pilgrim Nicola Albani only six days to walk from Rome to Loreto: he left Rome on 4 July and arrived in Loreto by 10 July. Julia, "Curiosité, dévotion et *politica peregrinesca*," p. 286n192.

32. As pilgrimages to the Holy Land declined owing to danger, Rome became a more viable alternative for pilgrims. Birch, *Pilgrimage to Rome in the Middle Ages*, pp. 191, 195.

33. On pilgrims detouring to Loreto from Venice: Gonneau, "Les pérégrinations de Vasilij Grigorovic Barskij, 1723–1747," p. 220. On pilgrims from Germany: Duhamelle, "Les pèlerins de passage à l'hospice zum Heiligen Kreuz de Nuremberg au XVIIIe siècle," p. 44.

34. *Pilgrim's Guide to Santiago de Compostela: A Critical Edition*; Ruiz, *From Heaven to Earth*.

It took him two years to make the round trip. Early in his journey, before sailing for Spain from the port of Naples, Albani detoured out of curiosity to see Rome. From Rome, Loreto was not far, so he added the side trip as an afterthought. Already, with this diversion, Albani was "very far . . . from the advice to the Loreto pilgrim given by the Jesuit Louis Richeôme, when he recommended that one should keep himself 'from being curious in the face of vain and useless things.' "[35]

But in other ways, Albani's journey to Loreto involved a sincerity and success that confounded some Jesuit pilgrims-in-training. According to Albani, he sidetracked to Loreto because he felt directly touched by Mary. When he got there, it was his turn to touch: he was so moved by his contact with the Holy House that he strove to commemorate the momentous encounter, in ways both figurative and concrete. In 1743, Albani published an extensive travel account of his entire spiritual odyssey to Compostela and back, entitled *Veridica Historia* ("True History").[36] In it he devoted several passionate pages, diagrams, and watercolors to Loreto.[37] Albani's Lauretan reflections have little in common with the Jesuit Richeôme's *Pilgrim of Loreto*, but they do resemble the work of another Jesuit, Pierre Chaumonot. Chaumonot wrote about Loreto half a century before Albani. He mentioned the site in an autobiography he wrote toward the end of his life, in the late 1680s, after he had joined the Society of Jesus.[38] But when he recalled how he first came to Loreto shrine in 1623, Chaumonot emphasized that he was not a scrupulously primed Jesuit novice, but a twelve-year-old runaway. His approach to Loreto made even Albani's casual detour sound meticulously planned.

35. Julia, "Curiosité, dévotion et *politica peregrinesca*," p. 261.

36. The full title of Albani's two-volume publication was: *Veridica Historia o' sia Viaggio da Napoli a S. Giacomo di Galizia fatto dal Sig.r Nicola Albani. Nativo della Città di Melfi Dove dà Notizia delle Città, Terre, Casali, Castelli e quanti luoghi che nel detto Viaggio vi sono, com'anche tutto le Meraviglie, e Curiosità che in essi si vedono, con far noto ancora le disgrazie a lui successe nel detto Viaggio, e che miracolosamente sia stato liberato* (Naples, 1743).

37. Twenty-one of these plates have been reproduced in color in a recent Spanish translation of Albani's original manuscript: Albani, *Viaje de Nápoles*.

38. Chaumonot finished his autobiography in 1688, five years before he died. The original manuscript has been lost, and the earliest extant copy of it is an abbreviated version that appears in the Archives du Séminaire du Québec, Lettres R, numéro 4, "Lettre circulaire contenant un abrégé de la vie et de la mort du père Chaumonot, décédé au collège de Québec le 21 février 1693." A more complete copy of the 1688 original is *La Vie du R. P. Pierre Joseph Marie Chaumonot de la Compagnie de Jesus, Missionaire dans la Nouvelle France, Ecrite par lui-même a l'ordre de son Supérieur*. J. M. Shea, ed. New York: Presse Cramoisy, 1858. The edition cited hereafter as "Chaumonot, *Autobiography*" is the 2002 English translation of the 1858 Shea publication.

Chaumonot was born into a modest family in the village of Sainte-Colombe in rural France, son of a vintager and the second of five children. His childhood resembled that of a "juvenile delinquent."[39] Because he was such a troublemaker, Chaumonot's father sent him to live with his uncle, a priest in the nearby town of Châtillon-sur-Seine, so that he could improve himself through education. But Chaumonot was a reluctant student. He preferred to study music instead of Latin. To this end, he stole money from his uncle and ran away with a friend, to pursue music training with the Oratorians in Beaune, a city to the south. His money ran out, and he wrote to his mother asking for more, but his father intercepted the letter. Chaumonot *père* demanded that his wayward son come home at once to make amends, but this spurred the boy to flee farther still. Chaumonot resolved to go see Rome. Alone for the most part, and on foot, he begged his way to Italy, where he, like Albani, found himself in the shadow of the Loreto shrine.[40]

In their first foray into Loreto, neither Chaumonot nor Albani was accompanied by Jesuits, novice or otherwise; nor did they carry the letters of patent that attested to their official membership in, or protection by, an established Catholic group. They kept grittier company. For Albani, that company consisted of forgers. Albani paid them to forge the requisite documents that identified him as a pilgrim.[41] Burgeoning numbers of pilgrims had led to extra paperwork. So many strangers were passing through European urban centers begging for charity that locals had trouble distinguishing between who was a genuine pilgrim and who was a vagabond. Cities such as Piedmont, situated in the middle of the overland pilgrimage route between northern Europe and Rome, began to require all strangers to show a document declaring their name, nationality, and goal of trip.[42]

39. This is the assessment of Steve Catlin, publisher of the 2002 English translation of Chaumonot's 1688 confessional autobiography, as it appears on the back cover of Chaumonot, *Autobiography*.

40. Chaumonot, *Autobiography*, pp. 7–13.

41. Albani reported paying an Italian for false pilgrimage patents, including one in Portuguese to gain him entrance to the confrerie of St. Francis, and another in Latin to use with the Dominicans. He complained of having to get new passports at many of the cities where he stopped because each was good for only one pilgrim destination, and when he got there it was promptly signed and collected. He was occasionally also asked to produce certificates of confession from pilgrimage sites where he claimed to have been, in order to prove that he was a pilgrim and thus eligible for charity. Julia, "Curiosité, dévotion et *politica peregrinesca*," pp. 308, 273.

42. In Piedmont, anxiety over the amount of begging and wandering intensified and culminated in their senate's legislation of an additional passport in 1772. Landi, "Législations sur les pèlerinages," p. 465.

Pilgrims could expect this sort of regulation everywhere in Europe by the seventeenth century. Travelers were required to produce letters of patent and, if pilgrims, to wear traditional dress that would identify them as such. Those who were not fortunate enough to qualify for letters of patent from Catholic authorities kept local document forgers in business.

Like Albani, Chaumonot too had joined a southward-wending stream of vagabonds who little resembled the Jesuit novices tidily rehearsing pilgrimage to Loreto. Drawn by the possibilities of the booming cultural and political center of Rome, many French men and women left their homes to refashion themselves or find spiritual consolation in Italy at the turn of the sixteenth century.[43] Sheer numbers of French drifters gave rise to a picaresque subculture where the ordeals of life on the road were taken as a rite of passage or a script of personal transformation.[44] Many whom Chaumonot encountered on the road braved the hunger, cold, and disease to search for apprenticeships. Jacques Callot (1592–1635), famed engraver from Lorraine, memorialized in miniature much of what he saw on his adventurous flight to Italy as a sixteen-year-old in search of artistic training.[45] Some of his works, such as *The Fair at Impruneta* (1620) and *Two Pilgrims* (1622), attest to the reality that one of the biggest groups to be found on early modern roads—perhaps second only to soldiers—was pilgrims.

The cadre of poor drifters dominated the scene at sanctuaries like Loreto to such a degree that one eighteenth-century French dictionary defined "pilgrimage" as "a mixed-up journey of devotion" undertaken by "beggars who, out of superstition, idleness or debauchery, go to Our Lady of Loreto, or Santiago de Compostela in Galicia, begging for alms all the way."[46] Chaumonot's retelling of his childhood gives the sense that he was quite comfortable among such "false pilgrims."[47] At this early juncture in his life, Chaumonot was as undirected as they were. Loreto afforded fine company for confusion.

43. Evidence of French women on the road frequently centers on those who did not survive, such as one 1593 report of a female cadaver discovered in a field by the road between the cities of Modena and Reggio. Her papers were found nearby stating that she was en route to Loreto to honor a vow. Artioli, "Le long de la via Emilia," p. 20.

44. Writing a century later than Chaumonot about his own experience as a runaway, French essayist Jean-Jacques Rousseau helped make this tradition of transience famous. Rousseau, "Les Confessions" (1782–89).

45. Bruwaert, *Vie de Jacques Callot*.

46. "Voyage de dévotion mal entendue . . . des gueux qui, par superstition, par oisiveté ou par libertinage, vont se rendre à Notre-Dame de Lorette, ou à S. Jacques de Compostelle en Galice, en demandant l'aumône sur la route." Diderot and D'Alembert, "Pèlerinage," pp. 282–83.

47. Julia, "Compostelle, Lorette, Rome," p. 242.

Even so, Chaumonot, like some of the self-professed pilgrims in his countryman Callot's engravings, did begin to set himself apart from this larger group of itinerants. Chaumonot's account of his travels shows that regardless of his actual purpose and destination, the one tried-and-true protection he had against some of the dangers he faced was to "cry pilgrim." When he was caught sleeping on strangers' lands, when he had to forge or borrow papers for entering a city, when he needed to beg for food or shelter at a hostel, the people he met were consistently kinder if he said he was a pilgrim. So this was the persona he assumed during his travels. It did not always work: he was nearly compelled to serve in the French army at one point in spite of his insistence that he had higher spiritual goals to attend. But for the most part the ploy was effective, especially when he breached the language barrier and gave the illusion of fine Catholic education by announcing his identity in Latin. In one village in Italy, he shouted "Nos sumus pauperes peregrini" ("We are poor pilgrims") to calm some irate villagers who discovered him and his companions sleeping in their haystack.[48] Chaumonot's early experience with pilgrims and with Latin was partly self-defense.[49] In his early roving, Chaumonot came to see his schoolboy Latin—with its implicit link back to the church—as his ticket to respect.[50]

It would be a mistake, however, to dismiss Chaumonot and his fellow errants on the pilgrimage trail as calculating survivors. Though they were more randomly drawn to Europe's shrines, these wanderers rehearsed pilgrimage with the same hope as Jesuit aspirants, and with added desperation. They, too, walked to Loreto suffering trials, in search of a better life. Fallen on hard times, French and Italian runaways like Chaumonot sought out the Virgin Mary for assistance. This was not dissimulation. In 1606, a magistrate in Padua questioned Orsola, a sixteen-year-old girl from Treviso who had been abandoned by a female companion while the two were en route to Loreto. Left entirely alone, Orsola was arrested for soliciting money outside the church so that she could make her own way to

48. Chaumonot, *Autobiography*, p. 10 (army) and p. 11 (haystack).

49. Chaumonot was not the only one to use the tags of "pilgrim" and Latin to project authenticity and status on the road. Russian traveler Vasilij Grigorovic Barskij broke into Latin to win himself a seat at the dinner table of the Capuchins at Loreto in the 1720s. Gonneau, "Les pérégrinations de Vasilij Grigorovic Barskij, 1723–1747," pp. 232–33.

50. Good Latin garnered respect because it was rare in the ranks of pilgrims. It differentiated Chaumonot from the more common lot of uneducated youths arrested around Loreto in the early 1600s for disturbing the peace and for not appearing to be in earnest in their pilgrim ventures. For the stories of some of those arrested: Landi, "Législations sur les pèlerinages," pp. 460–61.

the shrine. The magistrate asked her: "Why are you begging in this town, why not stay at home, why do you want to follow someone who has left you here, especially when you have nothing to do in Loreto?" Orsola answered: "I have been wanting to visit the Holy Mother of Grace, that's why I took to the road with that woman."[51] Her sincerity was evident in her words as well as in her continued efforts to get herself, somehow, to Loreto.

Wandering and vagrancy were not always as aimless as they appeared. For Orsola, Chaumonot, and even Albani, travel could be genuinely redirected and validated by the familiar ritual pattern of Catholic pilgrimage. Returning to Albani, this moment of validation as a pilgrim struck him unexpectedly during an overnight in the woods on the outskirts of Loreto. In the forest outside of the small settlement of Cività Castellana, he had just put out his fire to go to sleep when four assassins staked camp within earshot, loudly discussing their crime. Albani was terrified. He prayed fervently to the nearby Madonna of Loreto. When the murderers left in the morning without finding him, Albani took his safety as a miracle.[52] His visit to the Loreto shrine abruptly changed from one of devout curiosity to one of thanksgiving. Albani's account of his approach to Loreto vividly illustrates a hope he shared with Jesuit novices and pilgrims who had studied Richeôme's manual: that Mary could be found near her sanctuaries, and that she would personally answer pilgrims' prayers.[53]

Albani was thus able to distinguish himself from the broader mass of vagabonds, assassins, and drifters he passed in his travels not simply by forging papers and having pious intentions. He felt intensely authentic as a pilgrim because the Madonna of Loreto had heard and responded to his prayers. The same turned out to be true for Chaumonot. After weeks of walking, begging, and sleeping outdoors, Chaumonot arrived at the Loreto sanctuary in appalling condition. He recalled thinking:

51. 1606 court records of Padua as quoted by ibid., pp. 457–78.

52. Albani painted a watercolor commemorating this miracle that he labeled descriptively: "Quatro Assassini che giunti a Lui vicino, e stando tutte la Notte, e al far del Giorno se n'andorno senz accorgersi, che il detto à canto si era stato." / "Four assassins who were near to him, and were there all night, and at daybreak left without knowing, that the aforementioned had been right next to them." Julia, "Curiosité, dévotion et *politica peregrinesca*," plate 4 and p. 248n45.

53. One survey of Hieronymite codices from the sixteenth century shows that pilgrims who came from Spain and Portugal to visit the Marian sanctuary of Guadalupe dominated the Guadalupe miracle accounts. This suggests that local pilgrims were more keen to report or experience miracles than long-distance pilgrims. Crémoux, "Réalité et représentation," pp. 221–30.

> From head to toe, everything about me was disgusting. I was barefoot, having thrown away my shoes that were so broken up that they were hurting me. My shirt was rotting and my torn clothes were full of lice. Even my head, that I no longer combed, was full of such disgusting excretions that puss and worms produced a terrible stink. . . . [I wondered,] What will become of me? Who can put up with my smell and dirt?[54]

In this pathetic state, he stumbled into the Holy House of Loreto where he prayed to the Virgin Mary for help. When he exited the Holy House, a young man approached him and asked him what was wrong with his hair. He cleaned Chaumonot's head and bandaged it. It may seem like a small moment, but it contained an earnest desperation much like Albani's in the forest, hiding from assassins. Both men felt that their health and well-being were in peril. It was this immediate and urgent need that led them to call on the Madonna of Loreto. The need came first, and the proximity of the Madonna—and her nearly instantaneous answer to prayer—felt fortuitous. Neither man had been on the road to specifically petition this incarnation of Mary, yet both were led to do so by extenuating circumstances.

Both men also expressed the centrality of the Virgin of Loreto's intervention in their lives by instinctively making vows on site. Vows were an essential feature of pilgrimage, serving as visible tags that a pilgrim's journey was not mere tourism, but "the very antithesis of casual travel."[55] A vow began as an unspoken, unmediated pact between a person and a saint or Madonna. It was often a bargain plea for a miracle. Sometimes it came in advance of divine favor: a person could vow to make a pilgrimage in hope that the saint would reciprocate and help him.[56] Often, though, a vow came in reaction to a life-changing event, as it did for Albani and Chaumonot. In that case, the beneficiary would pledge to somehow publicly acknowledge the holy figure who had intervened on his behalf. So while a vow began as an internal promise agreed on between a pilgrim and a saintly intercessor, it had an essential performative, external dimension. Eventually, one's private gratitude was to be made visible as human action, the more dramatic, the better. For instance, in January 1579, several hundred residents of the city of Tours in France vowed to embark on a

54. Chaumonot, *Autobiography*, pp. 11–12.

55. Maniura, *Pilgrimage to Images in the Fifteenth Century*, p. 105.

56. Ibid., p. 113. In the sixteenth-century confraternity register of miracles for Poland's Marian shrine of Czestochowa, 74 of 255 records concerned people who had vowed to undertake a pilgrimage to the shrine.

pilgrimage out of gratitude to a local saint when they survived an earthquake in January 1579. They processed to the shrine en masse and dressed in penitential white robes.[57]

Nicolà Albani got carried away with his vow. When he eluded death at the hands of assassins in the woods of Cività Castellana, he had been moved to pledge something highly significant to the Madonna of Loreto. He impulsively promised permanent chastity in return for his life. As the excitement of cheating death wore off, however, he regretted the extremity of his promise.[58] It was a serious matter to break a contract with the divine.[59] Compilations of miracles at pilgrimage sites like Czestochowa in Poland were rife with examples of harsh penalties for those who reneged on vows.[60] Albani ended up requesting professional help to avoid such consequences. When he finally arrived at his end destination, the sanctuary of Santiago de Compostela, he confessed to a priest that he had made a vow to the Madonna of Loreto that he did not intend to keep. He repented for it and felt reprieved and formally released of it.[61]

Chaumonot displayed a similar ambivalence toward vows in his youth. He did not promise chastity to the Madonna of Loreto, nor a life of service. At the time, he vowed simply to honor her appropriately when his life circumstances improved. The young Chaumonot purposefully left his part of the deal open-ended. This is also how he first approached the membership vows of the Society of Jesus.[62] Chaumonot wrote candidly in

57. Galpern, *Religions of the People in Sixteenth-Century Champagne*, p. 184.

58. Albani was not the only pilgrim to regret a rash and extravagant vow. In 1542, Spanish sailors on an expedition to California were caught in a storm. They vowed to make a pilgrimage to the Virgin of Guadalupe's shrine in Spain "stark naked" if she would spare their lives. They lived, but Spain's Guadalupe sanctuary lacks a report of the promised spectacle of nudity. Bouvier, *Women and the Conquest of California*, p. 15.

59. On the increasingly contractual nature of agreements with God in the seventeenth century, whereby God was not only witness but also a party to human bargains: Vallance, *Revolutionary England and the National Covenant*, p. 82.

60. In one case, a Hungarian woman made a vow in order that her stillborn child might survive. The child lived for a few months, but when she was slow to deliver on her vow, it promptly died. Maniura, *Pilgrimage to Images in the Fifteenth Century*, p. 105.

61. Julia, "Curiosité, dévotion et *politica peregrinesca*," p. 306.

62. For Jesuits, there were four official vows to be taken: poverty, chastity, and obedience (commitments Jesuits shared with other religious orders such as the Franciscans), and a fourth vow unique to the Jesuits, concerning acceptance of mission directives. These vows were intentionally staggered to chart a member's trajectory of spiritual development. To join the order, Chaumonot would not have had to take vows until after two years of his novitiate. At that time, before making his "first vows" of poverty, chastity, and obedience, he would be led once more through *The Spiritual Exercises* to reflect on whether he felt that being a Jesuit was his true calling. These vows would be repeated after several years

his autobiography that when he finally decided to enter a religious order at the age of twenty-one, he chose the Jesuits over other orders largely because Jesuit entrance vows were not irrevocable.[63] He was as cautious and hesitant a novice as he was a pilgrim. Chaumonot's early diffidence toward promising anything concrete to either the Madonna of Loreto or the Society of Jesus makes his later fervor about vows all the more telling.

Before turning to Chaumonot's making good on his promise, there is a fourth and last aspect of his encounter and that of Albani that stands out: the importance of touch. Writing from the vantage point of age seventy-seven, decades after the childhood encounter, Chaumonot still recalled in painful detail his wretchedness and humiliation when he arrived at the Marian pilgrimage site. He remembered both the experiences of touching and being touched. Chaumonot wrote of entering the small Holy House of Loreto to pray and touch its walls. He also told of being healed by the touch of human hands when he exited the sacred relic.

Touch was also the part of Albani's visit to Loreto that made the deepest impression on him. He kissed the ancient walls on the interior of the structure's marble encasement several times.[64] In his two-year travels to many pilgrimage sites, this was the closest that Albani got to a relic. He touched or kissed many statues: in Rome, the face of the statue of St. Peter in the Church of St. Peter in Chains, and the statue of St. Peter in St. Peter's Basilica; and in Montserrat, the statue of the Virgin. At his final destination, Santiago de Compostela, he even stood in a long line to hand over his pilgrim's hat, robe, and staff. His garments were touched to the statue of St. James and returned to him, and then he was allowed to touch the statue.[65] All those moments of contact resonated for Albani, but none captured his imagination as much as laying his hands on the actual wall where Christ and Mary had also leaned. It was the Jesuit

---

of service. Jesuits who were professed, or fully trained as priests, then had the option of taking the fourth vow. Over the course of their lives, most Jesuits did not progress past three vows; the fourth was seen as the capstone of a Jesuit career. O'Malley, *First Jesuits*, pp. 345–49.

63. "I did not hesitate to ask the Doctor whom I was serving 'who are the Jesuits?' He answered that there were good ones and bad ones, that they accepted only people of high birth and intelligence, that their order was no more austere than others, and that they could leave even after vows. These last bits of information that he gave me did not discourage me—I could decide to join them for a while. Hence, you can see that I was not yet quite ready for God's Kingdom because I was already looking back before having put my hand on the plough." Chaumonot, *Autobiography*, p. 14.

64. Julia, "Curiosité, dévotion et *politica peregrinesca*," p. 248.

65. Ibid., p. 304.

Spiritual Exercises made tangible, a hands-on experience that helped him imagine himself close to the Holy Family. A local preacher, Luigi Lazzari, summed up the charged atmosphere surrounding the Holy House in a 1669 sermon. He enthused: "[Christ (and Mary)] lived here within, prayed here, slept here, ate here, thought here, worked here. . . . Christ touched the *Santa Casa* infinite times."[66] How exceptional for the common man to be given the chance to touch where Christ and Mary had touched, too.

As Albani's experience at other shrines showed, most Catholic relics were protected and hidden by elaborate reliquaries. But at Loreto, the original inside walls of the relic were bared to the sight, touch, and kisses of pilgrims.[67] This produced an atmosphere that was not solitary or conducive to silent contemplation. When Albani crawled around the Holy House three times, on his knees, before entering, he did so in the company of many. A French Protestant visitor, Maximilien Misson, wryly described the behavior of crowds he saw there in 1688:

> Picture forty or fifty people, men, women and little children, all of them on their knees crawling around the Holy House in one direction, encountering the same number of people coming from the other direction. Each one has their rosary and murmurs their paternosters: however, they all want to get in close to the wall, as much to shorten their path as to be as near as possible to this Holy Place, which results in them crashing into each other frequently, causing more than a little embarrassment.[68]

Once again, however, it would be an error to belittle the potency of pilgrims' brief direct contact with the Holy House of Loreto because of the clamoring shared company. Albani was so affected by the chance to lay his hands on this object that it colored the rest of his visit to Loreto. After visiting the Holy House, Albani bought two keepsakes associated with that

66. Lazzari, *Dodici Sermoni sopra la S. Casa di Loreto*, pp. 110, 69.

67. Touching the walls of the Holy House was remarked on in at least six principal guidebooks published by Frenchmen who visited Loreto from 1691 to 1790. The walls of the *Santa Casa* are remarkably intact today considering this continued practice and the volume of visitors over the centuries. On the protective function of reliquaries: Dierkens, "Du bon (et du mauvais) usage." On the guidebooks: E. Chevalier, "Le pèlerin de Lorette."

68. Misson as quoted by Brizay, "Pèlerins et pèlerinages," p. 209. Misson was a Protestant jurist who is best known for his widely read account *Nouveau voyage d'Italie fait en 1688* (La Haye, 1691), chronicling his travels in Italy. For more on his visit to Loreto: E. Chevalier, "Le pèlerin de Lorette."

relic.[69] It is important to note that Albani had plentiful choice when he decided to buy these souvenirs. Pilgrims sought out holy sites partly to provision themselves with physical fragments of the sacred.[70] Like other sanctuaries, Loreto met pilgrims' demand for merchandise with enthusiasm, boasting an exceptionally comprehensive array of goods, from cheap to expensive.[71] These included the customary paper prayer cards, lead statues, pilgrim badges, rosaries, holy water, ribbons, flowers, certificates of pilgrimage, and indulgences believed to be efficacious regardless of the shrine that sold them.[72] At Loreto, there were so many of these common and reproducible objects available for sale that it provoked some criticism for excess.[73] But at another sanctuary to Mary, Monserrate in Catalonia, Albani had chosen precisely this category of generic souvenir, departing satisfied with some standard-pattern crucifixes that he bought from local hermits.[74]

At Loreto, however, Albani chose otherwise, actively seeking out merchandise that had not only been in contact with Loreto's famed Holy House, but that distinctly evoked it. By the early 1600s, the Loreto sanctuary offered uniquely identifying merchandise tied to the Holy House, the object that lingered in the memory of many long after their recollection

69. Albani added to these an "authenticated veil of the Virgin," a tiny piece of black cloth attached to a paper image of the Virgin of Loreto harbored inside the Holy House. This cloth was also a product related to direct contact: it had been cut from an actual veil used to cover the statue of the Lauretan Madonna on Good Friday. Julia, "Curiosité, dévotion et *politica peregrinesca*," pp. 307–8.

70. One profiteering French pilgrim, Denis Vesraquin, resold his sacred purchases in the late 1700s. He bought souvenirs wholesale from the shrine of Notre-Dame de La Délivrande in order to sell them again. But most pilgrims did not find that the rampant consumerism at shrines sullied the spiritual benefits afforded by souvenirs. Julia, "Aveux de pèlerins," pp. 447–48; Kaufman, *Consuming Visions*, p. 55.

71. The range in quality troubled some people, occasioning a lawsuit in 1603. Giovanni Baglioni, an Italian painter, had visited Loreto and brought back a lead image of the Madonna of Loreto for his colleague, Orazio Gentileschi. But Gentileschi was angered that the image Baglioni bought was not silver. He wrote an insulting letter to Baglioni about it that escalated into libel charges. Langdon, *Caravaggio: A Life*, pp. 264, 272.

72. Indulgences were an especially important draw for Loreto pilgrims: the Duchess of Tuscany returned from a 1600s trip to Loreto with an indulgence from Pope Paul V. BNF Lorraine 270, fols. 171–80; Provost, "L'image du pèlerin," pp. 274, 283. On pilgrim badges and other merchandising: Freedberg, *Power of Images*, p. 120; Koldeweij, "Lifting the Veil on Pilgrim Badges."

73. The French Catholic pilgrim Abbé Jérôme Richard wrote a critique of Loreto's souvenirs in his *Description historique et critique de l'Italie* (Dijon, 1766). E. Chevalier, "Le pèlerin de Lorette," p. 219.

74. Julia, "Curiosité, dévotion et *politica peregrinesca*," pp. 307–8.

of the Madonna statue faded.[75] First, Albani purchased three envelopes of dust scraped from the walls of the Holy House on Good Friday, an auspicious holy day in Easter Week. These were supposed to protect the bearer from contagion.[76] By association and act of being touched to the primary relic, common objects like dust assumed some of the holy aura of the shrine center where they were procured.[77] Such items did not have the awe-inspiring power of the main relic, but they were seen as more potent than a casual memento.[78]

Second, Albani came away with a Lauretan article also recently innovated in the seventeenth century: a blueprint of the Holy House.[79] It was the product most peculiar to Loreto by far, and one of the best sellers owing to its abundance and cheapness. The earliest form of this broadsheet surfaced as part of the Loreto sanctuary's celebration of Pope Urban VIII's jubilee year of 1625. It was a set of engravings of the floor plan, layout, and wall-by-wall views of the *Santa Casa*, with details explained in Latin (see ahead to figure 5.1).[80] In later years, details were also printed in vernacular languages including French, Italian, and German. Albani reprinted these floor plans in his *Veridica Historia*. His predecessor, the French pilgrim Pierre Chaumonot, did more than reprint the floor plans; he commemorated his encounter with the Madonna of Loreto by putting these plans to use, actually building a replica of the Holy House in Canada.

Chaumonot wrote that his building of a Lauretan Holy House in Québec nearly forty years after encountering Loreto was in response to the

75. Another early modern pilgrimage site that felt the need to particularize their souvenirs was Ely, in England. Vendors in Ely sold silk necklaces (and eventually cloth kerchiefs) called "St. Etheldreda's chains." These recalled the distinctive manner of death of St. Etheldreda (640–79), who expired from a tumor on her neck. Nilson, "Medieval Experience at the Shrine," p. 115.

76. Julia, "Curiosité, dévotion et *politica peregrinesca*," pp. 307–8.

77. Because sacred dust was not exclusive to Loreto's Holy House, Albani's packets were labeled. Dust gathered in the Holy Land floated about Europe; dust from the walls of the Holy Sepulcher in Jerusalem also circulated in metal ampullae. Morris, *Sepulchre of Christ and the Medieval West*, pp. 227–29; Freedberg, *Power of Images*, pp. 129–30.

78. On the possible use of badges and other shrine souvenirs as secondary relics with "amuletic function": Freedberg, *Power of Images*, pp. 124–30.

79. By the time of Albani's visit, Holy House broadsheets were so prevalent that it is not clear whether Albani procured his at the Loreto shrine, or whether he simply picked them up later and elsewhere. But when he published his travel account, *Veridica Historia*, in Naples in 1743, it had five pages of the series. These prints are reproduced in Julia, "Curiosité, dévotion et *politica peregrinesca*," plates 5–9.

80. Ranucci and Tenenti, *Sei Riproduzioni della Santa Casa di Loreto in Italia*, p. 153.

Madonna of Loreto's intercession and his first amorphous vow. As a child gone astray, stumbling into the great Italian shrine, his vow had no shape; but over the course of his life, as he became a Jesuit and worked as a missionary overseas, the vow took form and manifested itself physically as a Holy House replica.[81] Building a replica to fulfill a vow is not as unusual as it sounds. Copies of Loreto's relic are considered in the next chapter, but here, it is Chaumonot's choice that is of interest. He had a wide range of ways in which he could honor the Madonna of Loreto. Much like Albani's selection of shrine mementos, Chaumonot's decision to focus on the Holy House was significant. It showed how much that relic had touched him.

Chaumonot's choice of location is also telling. Nearly four thousand miles from the Loreto sanctuary, in eastern Canada, new Catholics were in motion in ways that he recognized from his own early adventures on the pilgrimage trail. Like he and Albani, these individuals approached holy sites desperately and without advance planning, via epic detours. They, too, made their journeys to certify their membership in a mixed company that was neither exclusive nor polished. The company these latest pilgrims kept included refugees and enemies of war as well as Jesuits. Some, like Chaumonot and Albani, felt the miraculous intervention of Mary. They expressed this holy connection not through vows or buying souvenirs, but by physical movement: as St. Ignatius of Loyola had done, they journeyed repeatedly back toward where they had felt her presence. Finally, these converts also touched first and imagined after, reversing the trajectory laid out by the Jesuit Richeôme. Like Chaumonot and Albani, they came to appreciate the Virgin of Loreto only after they had seen, touched, and personally experienced her trappings and something of her journey. Perhaps these new Catholics would not have called themselves pilgrims. Still, the parallel patterns of spiritual growth were evident enough for one veteran pilgrim, the now-Jesuit Pierre Chaumonot, to recognize them as such. Consider some of the similarities that he perceived between his own circuitous path toward faith, and one Huron convert in particular: Ignace Tsaouenhohoui.

81. On the progressive sharpening of his vow, Chaumonot noted that before leaving Europe, he and his friend Poncet "decided, once it became possible, to build a chapel in Canada called Notre Dame de Lorette"; later, when writing about the chapel's construction, he repeated that he had intended to build a Holy House "ever since [he] left Europe." Chaumonot, *Autobiography*, pp. 24, 42–43.

New Expression: A Huron Ignace on the Way to Lorette

The first glimpse of Ignace Tsaouenhohoui in Jesuit records shows him hidden in a tree trunk. He concealed himself there for two days in autumn of 1651 to break away from Iroquois warriors who had captured him in combat at Long-Sault and taken him to their stronghold at Onondaga.[82] When his Iroquois captors set out to attack communities in the St. Lawrence River Valley near Québec City, they unwisely brought him along, allowing him an opportunity to escape. Tsaouenhohoui fled through the forest for sixteen days until he made it to the French settlement of Trois-Rivières, where he divulged important military intelligence about new groups of warriors assembling against the French.[83] One historian, Guy Laflèche, had trouble categorizing Tsaouenhohoui: "[He] did not seem to play any political role, and was not counted among the leaders [of the Christian Huron] until three years before his death."[84] Yet from the moment of his dramatic arrival in the written archive, Tsaouenhohoui—like his overseas contemporaries Albani and Chaumonot—was an unlikely beacon of Christianity, and a surprising Catholic spirit-in-formation. All the battlefield conflagrations and chaos that he suffered seemed to be leading him toward not just the French, but Christianity. For instance, he was captured by the Iroquois in the battle of Long-Sault, one of the conflicts that followed the dissolution of the Jesuit mission of Sainte-Marie.[85] But when Ignace finally escaped from his captors, he did not return to his home region by Lake Huron. He ran eastward instead, trailing the retreating Christian Huron mission community of Sainte-Marie, which strongly suggests that he had personal or familial ties to that community.

Where, exactly, was this nascent pilgrim headed? According to the Jesuit Richeôme, good pilgrims should travel intentionally toward a particular shrine or sacred ground. Originally, Tsaouenhohoui was from the town of Arhetsi, near Georgian Bay and Lake Huron, in the Huron heartland where missionaries established their outreach to the Huron.[86] As his

82. Laflèche, *Les saints martyrs canadiens*, p. 385.

83. "On the 7th Tsanhohy, an escaped Huron, arrived; he brought tidings of a new Army of 600 men and reported that he had met Father Menar who was going up with the Outaëk." *Jesuit Relations* (Thwaites, ed.), vol. 45, p. 53.

84. Laflèche, *Les saints martyrs canadiens*, p. 385.

85. For exhaustive accounts of the Huron retreat and ongoing series of battles afflicting this Huron population: Trigger, *Children of Aataentsic*, pp. 763, 767, 820–25.

86. Reuben Gold Thwaites as quoted by Trigger, *Children of Aataentsic*, p. 856n6. The town is identified as one of the "mission towns of mixed population" in Huronia in the

travels took him far afield from Arhetsi, four Christian destinations stand out in his life: the Jesuit mission of Sainte-Marie; the small city of Québec, which he approached twice; the Notre Dame de Foye mission; and after his death, the mission of Lorette. This high number of temporary moorings calls to mind the multiple stops of the Holy House of Loreto on its thirteenth-century flight from Nazareth.

For Tsaouenhohoui, the first landing was Sainte-Marie. The mission of Sainte-Marie among the Huron (Wendat) had started well for the Jesuits and converts involved. In 1639, the Jesuit Jérôme Lalemant (1593–1673) had supervised a handful of young French laborers, soldiers, and Jesuits in the building of Sainte-Marie, envisioned as the first permanent base of Jesuit operations in a region where they had already established missionary presence.[87] By the mid-1640s, at the height of Jesuit activity in the area, the fortified village housed twenty-seven Jesuits, thirty-nine French workmen, and occasional ranks of French soldiers.[88] The Jesuits had deliberately positioned this new headquarters close to the Huron town of Quieunonascaran, where the Jesuits' predecessors in Canada, the Catholic Recollet missionaries, had made their base twenty years earlier. The Jesuits had hoped to find already baptized Huron at Quieunonascaran who would gravitate toward Sainte-Marie.[89] While this did not happen, Sainte-Marie did draw a considerable number of Huron from the outlying area who were curious to talk with the Jesuits. Ignace Tsaouenhohoui may have been among these initial visitors.

Sainte-Marie had extensive guest quarters for visiting Huron, longhouses built in traditional style so that they would feel at home. Some stayed overnight, others for months, and after a time, a small number even stayed permanently. Like their Jesuit brethren in the Moxos heartland in South America, the Jesuits in Canada attempted to segregate the Huron

---

1630s and 1640s: Fenton, "Problems Arising from the Historic Northeastern Position of the Iroquois," fig. 12n25.

87. The Jesuits had already set up missionary residence in two large Huron towns, Ossossané and Teanaostaiaé. On the staff of missionaries and skilled French laborers (*donnés*) working at French Jesuit outposts: Trigger, *Children of Aataentsic*, pp. 666–68, 702.

88. In 1644 twenty-two French soldiers wintered there as they made their way back to Québec; in 1649, six soldiers were dispatched to Sainte-Marie to help defend the site against the Iroquois. On the early days of Sainte-Marie: Hayes, *Wilderness Mission*.

89. In the 1620s, the Recollets had managed to convert Auoindaon, an eminent resident of Quieunonascaran, to Catholicism; he was gone by the time the Jesuits arrived. On Auoindaon: Trigger, *Children of Aataentsic*, pp. 391, 433, 474–75. On the Recollets: Trigger, *Children of Aataentsic*, pp. 298, 374, 385–92; Axtell, "Art of Reduction."

into groups for easier instruction. Catholic Huron were invited to reside in longhouses inside the town walls of Loreto. Those who had not yet converted could also stay in a guest longhouse, but outside the palisade.[90] The separation sent a clear message to the Huron about one of the benefits of converting: Catholicism would allow them social access and proximity to the French. These varied, close residential arrangements gave young Huron like Tsaouenhohoui exposure to the French that was not uniformly positive. Within months of the Jesuits opening their doors to the Huron at Sainte-Marie, there was an outbreak of smallpox that decimated the community. The epidemic divided the remaining Huron into two camps, one that supported the Jesuits and accepted baptism, and another that actively opposed them.[91]

Tsaouenhohoui may have been a smallpox survivor who chose to cast his lot with the Jesuits during or after his illness. In the Jesuit records, he is referenced most often by a Christian name, "Ignace," indicating that he was baptized. He will henceforth be referred to by that name here. It was not common for Jesuits to bestow the name of St. Ignatius, the founder of their society, on the newly converted. They tended to save that name either for adult converts of remarkable worthiness, or for those who were on the brink of death and thus in extreme need of divine intervention.[92] It is unclear which situation applied to Ignace.

But if he was indeed residing near or inside the Sainte-Marie mission in the late 1640s, Ignace would have seen it swell with even more casualties and refugees, both Jesuit and Huron.[93] In autumn of 1648,

90. May 2005 visit to the reconstructed site and archaeological museum of Sainte-Marie among the Hurons, Huronia Historical Parks, Midland, Ontario, Canada. On the effects of the segregation: Trigger, *Children of Aataentsic*, p. 672.

91. Lalemant, "Of the Persecutions Excited against Us [1640]," pp. 90–91. Among the acts taken to drive out the Jesuits, one of the French *donnés*, Jacques Douart, was murdered outside the palisade in 1648. Historian Bruce Trigger argues that this factionalism centered on the Jesuit presence ended up making the Huron more vulnerable to Iroquois attack, thus sealing their defeat and dispersal. But the Iroquois were undergoing similar rifts to different effect. Trigger, *Children of Aataentsic*, pp. 746–50; Richter, "Iroquois vs. Iroquois."

92. For example, in Canada in 1675, the Jesuits wrote of a baby "Ignace" who was on the brink of death; they described consoling his native mother who had come to pray to the Virgin Mary and offer a porcelain necklace in hopes that Mary would intervene to save her son. The baby died. *Relations Inédites de la Nouvelle-France*, p. 215.

93. To give just one illustration of mortality rates precipitating flight, nearly all the Catholic Huron warriors of Ossossané were killed in a single attack. Ossossané was the oldest Jesuit mission to the Huron, and its warriors included some of the Jesuits' most loyal converts. There were also five Jesuit casualties or martyrdoms from this single concentrated period of warfare, 1648–49. These deaths included Antoine Daniel (1648), Noël

the Iroquois, traditional enemies of the Huron, had ramped up their attacks on Huron using new weaponry they had acquired from their Dutch and English allies. The French had refused to similarly arm their allies, the Huron, creating an unevenness that had immediate impact on their people.[94] For instance, in one single attack among the many that unfolded in 1648, when the Iroquois destroyed the Huron mission town of St. Louis with gunfire, five hundred Huron (mostly women and children) ran to Sainte-Marie to seek protection.[95] The situation finally led the Jesuit superior of the mission, Paul Ragueneau, to decide to dramatically abandon the mission of Sainte-Marie.[96] The survivors spent a miserable winter sheltered on the nearby Gahoendoe Island that could not sustain the large and ever-growing population of refugees. This drove a core group of Sainte-Marie survivors, including three hundred Huron, seventeen Jesuits and lay brothers, and forty-three *donnés*, to make a desperate journey of eight hundred miles to seek shelter to the east, under the protection of the French military at Québec City.[97]

The arduous trip makes the Jesuit novices' two-week practice walk between Rome and Loreto pale by comparison. Here was real need, fear, and prayer. Still, we do not find the budding pilgrim Ignace in this group. Not everyone wanted to leave Gahoendoe Island or was able to undertake the long trek. Given his capture, it seems that Ignace was among those left behind to continue to hold the Huron-French line against the Iroquois. When he did finally set forth to Québec, extracting himself from Iroquois hands, he followed his fleeing comrades alone and spontaneously. He must have known the destination of the large Sainte-Marie contingent of Catholic refugees, because he surfaced in Québec less than a year after they had stumbled in during July 1650.

Chabanel (1649), Charles Garnier (1649), and the most famous pair, Jean de Brébeuf (1649) and Gabriel Lalemant (1649). They were captured in the company of hundreds of Catholic Huron warriors, who were also killed and who were, ostensibly, the primary target of the Iroquois. Trigger, *Children of Aataentsic*, p. 766.

94. Carpenter, "Making War More Lethal"; Snow, "Iroquois-Huron Warfare."

95. The Hurons were not only running to Sainte-Marie. They also sought shelter at Tionnontaté, another large town in the area. Trigger, *Children of Aataentsic*, pp. 763, 767, 820–25.

96. They burned it down to avoid its desecration by the Iroquois. Ragueneau, "Of the Capture of the Villages of the Mission of St. Ignace, in the Month of March of the Year 1649," p. 112.

97. ASJCF Fonds Joseph Chaumonot BO-258-01, "Destruction de la Huronie [1649–50]," pp. 505–23.

Québec City trumped the Marian sanctuary of Loreto in the 1650s for sheer numbers of petitioners who arrived outside its walls praying for safety and deliverance. While the differences between Québec and a pilgrimage destination are obvious, this is the astonishing similarity that makes comparison fruitful: Catholics detoured there, in large numbers, actively soliciting help. The Huron of Sainte-Marie arrived at an urban center already overburdened with refugees from the Iroquois wars, most relegated to the outskirts of Québec's walled city because they were Indians. The Sillery mission, the Jesuit enclave to the south of the city, was stretched to capacity with Algonquin, Montagnais, and Abenaki, many of them newly arrived and also seeking French military protection.[98] Although the Sillery Jesuits offered to harbor the newcomers, the Jesuits of Sainte-Marie demanded special treatment for their Huron protégés. Through personal connections, they managed to find homes for several of the extended Huron families inside the city walls, placing them with upstanding French Catholics of Québec and with the Ursulines and the Hospitalière nuns.[99] This left about two hundred Huron in Jesuit care.[100] They found space for them directly in the shadow of Fort St. Louis, inside Québec's Upper Town next to the Ursuline convent. There, the Huron built longhouses where they passed the winter, and the Jesuits spent eight thousand livres feeding and clothing them.[101]

Anticipating more Huron arrivals from Gahoendoe Island and the war-torn Georgian Bay, the Jesuits petitioned one of their wealthy benefactresses in Québec, Eléonore de Grandmaison, who sold them a cleared section of land on the Ile d'Orléans, an island in the St. Lawrence River

98. The Sillery mission has generally been assessed as a Jesuit failure, but there was clearly more afoot there in the 1600s than that pronouncement allows. For an interesting study on how Jesuit efforts at Sillery appealed more to Montagnais men than women: Devens, "Separate Confrontations." For the standard argument on Sillery: Ronda, "Sillery Experiment."

99. The Jesuits expressed concern that the Huron would not get along with the Algonquins at Sillery, as in the past the Huron had fought with the Algonquin. In Québec, they found three Frenchmen who agreed to feed and house an extended family each; the Hospitalières took charge of the sick; and the Ursulines welcomed the clan of the oldest Catholic Huron in the group, Pierre Ondakion. Trigger, *Children of Aataentsic*, p. 802.

100. Some of the Huron had also left the group before reaching Québec. They decided to stay at Trois-Rivières, a thriving French and Indian settlement on the banks of the St. Lawrence River in between Montréal and Québec. Trois-Rivières included a French fortress established in 1634 and several Algonquian and Montagnais settlements. Robie, "Kiotsaeton's Three Rivers Address."

101. Trigger, *Children of Aataentsic*, p. 802.

within sight of the city.[102] In early spring of 1651, the Jesuits moved thirty Huron families onto this island where they hoped the Huron could sustain themselves with their traditional practices of hunting and agriculture. Out of nostalgia or hopefulness, they again named the new Huron settlement "Sainte-Marie." The Jesuits and Huron promptly erected cabins, a residence for the Jesuits, and a chapel there. However, in a move characteristic of the state of war in Canada, the Jesuits also helped the Huron to put up a defensive fort, just as they had on Gahoendoe Island.[103]

This is where Ignace was housed when he arrived in the area in late 1651. Perhaps his brother and sister were among the families allotted space there.[104] Years previously, when the exhausted French runaway Chaumonot arrived in Loreto, he had found a moment of rest and care within the sanctuary. Ignace likewise found brief respite in the mission life of Sainte-Marie on the Ile d'Orléans, for five years. During this time he appears to have married another Huron Catholic convert, Marie Ouendraka, with whom he had two children.[105] But in May 1656, the Iroquois found the Huron and struck again.

A Mohawk war party from Trois Rivières hid outside the town at Ile d'Orléans while the Huron attended church.[106] When the Huron stepped beyond the fortification to work in the fields, the Mohawk captured seventy-one of them, mostly women and young children. They loaded them onto forty canoes and brazenly sailed by Québec City in full daylight, forcing the

102. Gérin, *La Seigneurie de Sillery et les Hurons de Lorette*, p. 96.

103. Trigger, *Children of Aataentsic*, p. 803; F. Martin, "Précis historique sur la mission Huronne," p. 317.

104. Certainly by the 1670s, Ignace and his sister and brother had been reunited and had all opted to cast their lot with the Jesuits around Québec. After Ignace's death, his sister was separately hailed by the Jesuits as "one of our best Christians." Ignace's brother also outlived him and was a respected member of the Catholic Huron mission community. On Ignace's sister: "Chapter II: Of the Mission of Saint François Xavier at Onneiout," *Jesuit Relations* (Thwaites, ed.), vol. 55, p. 53. On Ignace's brother: "Chapter IV: Of the Huron Mission," *Jesuit Relations* (Thwaites, ed.), vol. 53, p. 119.

105. His twenty-year marriage to Marie Ouendraka is described in his eulogy, "The Account of the Most Christian Death of Ignace Saouhenhohi," *Jesuit Relations* (Thwaites, ed.), vol. 53, pp. 96–122. The Jesuits commented as well on the devotion of Marie and Ignace's surviving children, whose prayers they deemed were a significant factor in helping Marie recover from a long illness in 1676. It appears that their children's earnest Catholic prayers may have stemmed in part from Marie Ouendraka's iron discipline. On prayers: "Huron Mission," *Jesuit Relations* (Thwaites, ed.), vol. 60, pp. 56–65. On discipline: "Chapter V: The Constancy of Marie Oendraka in her Afflictions, and her Zeal in Allowing No Sin in Her Family," *Jesuit Relations* (Thwaites, ed.), vol. 55, pp. 30–31.

106. The Mohawk were one of the five nations of the Iroquois confederacy along with the Oneida, Onondaga, Cayuga, and Seneca.

Huron captives to sing as they passed, to mock the French.[107] Sainte-Marie's loss of most of their women was followed by two equally dramatic losses of men. In 1658, angered by the continued raids of the Iroquois, twenty-three young Huron men formed a war party. Against the wishes of the French, who were attempting to make peace with the Iroquois, they set out from Québec to attack the Iroquois, to little effect and much death.[108] Two years later, forty more Huron warriors assembled in Québec led by the Catholic convert Annaotaha. This time they joined forces with the French under the command of Adam Dollard des Ormeaux. They set out to attack the Onondaga, a branch of the Iroquois confederacy. But as the Jesuit historian Félix Martin aptly labeled it, the battle was a "disastrous affair."[109] The joint French, Huron, and Algonquin party was intercepted near Montréal by other Iroquois, a band of Mohawk and Oneida. While the Québec troops were deciding what to do, some of the enemy Mohawk approached the Huron in the group. It turned out that many of these "Mohawk" were actually formerly Huron, captives from Georgian Bay who had since been adopted by their captors. They encouraged their Huron relatives and acquaintances to leave the French. Some of them did, and some of them didn't; but in the ensuing chaos, all but four Huron and seven Frenchmen deserted, were killed, or were captured.[110] Between 1656 and 1660, in a span of only four years, the Huron of Sainte-Marie had lost half their number under the so-called protection of the French and the Jesuits. It must have felt something of a miracle that when the dust settled, Ignace Tsaouenhohoui, his wife, Marie Ouendraka, and their two children were still standing.

Those who were left scattered to the winds after these attacks, fissuring the shrinking community along tribal lines.[111] Many of them naturally put their trust elsewhere than the French, in fact settling with the Iroquois

107. F. Martin, "Précis historique sur la mission Huronne," p. 317; Trigger, *Children of Aataentsic*, pp. 809–10. Trigger notes that when the captives arrived to Trois-Rivières, the Jesuits posted there met with them to console them but did not intervene to rescue them, perhaps feeling that they did not wield enough local power to negotiate for their release.

108. Trigger, *Children of Aataentsic*, p. 816. Trigger suggests that the French refused to arm the Huron because of renegade expeditions such as this one.

109. F. Martin, "Précis historique sur la mission Huronne," p. 317.

110. Trigger, *Children of Aataentsic*, p. 816.

111. Leon Gérin sees the fissure as happening along clan lines instead of tribal ones. He notes that the Huron who joined the Mohawk were of the Bear clan. Though the eight Huron clans were clearly a factor in the Huron decision, I have chosen to use Trigger's political designations, as these seemed to unite Huron across clan lines. Trigger, *Children of Aataentsic*, pp. 816, 54–59 (on Huron clans); Gérin, *La Seigneurie de Sillery et les Hurons de Lorette*, pp. 96–97.

who had already absorbed much of their number by force. The Arendarhonon Huron joined the Onondaga; the Attignawantan Huron resettled with the Mohawk. But Ignace and his family were among the barely one hundred Huron converts of Sainte-Marie who chose to stay with the French. In June 1656, shortly after the Mohawk attack on the Ile d'Orléans, these Huron left the clearly unsafe island and returned "uninvited" to Québec City.[112]

Ignace emerged as the leader of this de facto group of survivors; he led them back inside the safety of French walls. Some French settlers who sympathized with the Huron situation gave land to him directly.[113] Following the customs of Huron tribal leaders, Ignace divided the land evenly between all the remaining families. In 1658, the former governor of New France, Louis D'Aillebout, donated further to their support, establishing a fortified camp for them inside the city and allotting more land for them to cultivate south of the city.[114] The Huron lived there for almost a decade, under the unformalized leadership of Ignace and some of the Jesuits who had accompanied them since Sainte-Marie I.

Why did Ignace choose to stay with the French?[115] Pierre Chaumonot, the Jesuit former pilgrim and contemporary of Ignace, confidently cited the Huron's devotion to Catholicism as his motivation. Yet this loyalty to a new faith appears to have particularly manifested itself and solidified in him *after* he cast his lot with the French a second time, during his third anchorage near Québec, at Notre Dame de Foye.

The Huron mission town name of Notre Dame de Foye was a refreshing departure from the nostalgic Sainte-Marie, and it signaled a fresh beginning for the Huron and the Jesuits. The name derived from a statue of Notre Dame de Foye that had been sent to them by Jesuits in Belgium.[116] After the French had finally made peace with the Iroquois in 1667, the

112. Trigger, *Children of Aataentsic*, pp. 810–11.

113. Gros-Louis and Gros-Louis, *La Chapelle Huronne de Lorette*, p. 241; Latourelle, *Compagnon des Martyrs canadiens*, p. 194.

114. D'Aillebout had been governor from 1648 to 1651, at the time of the Huron's first arrival in Québec. Trigger, *Children of Aataentsic*, p. 815; F. Martin, "Précis historique sur la mission Huronne," p. 317.

115. His wife, Marie Ouendraka, also opted to stay with the French. Her devotion is discussed further in chapter 6, under "*New Expression*: Marys and Maries Out in the World." Like Ignace, she was described as "a very virtuous Christian woman" by the Jesuits for her steadfastness to Catholicism during a long illness. "Huron Mission," *Jesuit Relations* (Thwaites, ed.), vol. 60, pp. 57–58.

116. Notre Dame de Foye of Dinant was an advocation of the Virgin Mary originating in Belgium, as distinct from the better-known French medieval saint, Sainte Foy. F. Martin, "Précis historique sur la mission Huronne," p. 318.

Jesuit Chaumonot managed to procure lands for the Sainte-Marie Huron outside of Québec, on the edge of the *seigneurie* of Sillery. The Huron helped to build their new mission town while temporarily residing in Beauport, north of Québec. In 1668, led by Ignace Tsaouenhohoui, the Huron resettled there under Chaumonot's guardianship. There, for the last three years of his life, Ignace was recognized officially as the political leader of the group of converts. During that interval he also had two more children with Marie but lost his first two children, one of them a daughter whom he mourned until the moment of his death.[117] When he died in 1670, he was recognized for both his exemplary Catholicism and his openness to the French. The doors of his house were apparently always open to French settlers stopping in Notre Dame de Foye to warm themselves before church. Perhaps for this reason, the Bishop of Québec insisted that Ignace's body be brought back to the city for a formal burial mass.[118]

Ignace's influence extended beyond the grave to another budding community. Chaumonot was deeply touched by Ignace's serendipitous, convoluted journey, and by its resemblance to his own trauma-healing approach to the Madonna of Loreto.[119] So the Jesuit chose to fulfill his vow at the end of his own life by building a replica of the Holy House of Loreto among this specific community of Huron, with the direct aid of Ignace's widow, Marie Ouendraka. Chaumonot planned the construction project to coincide with another move for the Catholic Huron. In 1673, deforestation and the expansion of Québec City required the Huron to relocate from Notre Dame de Foye to a new site that Chaumonot christened "Notre Dame de Lorette," in anticipation of the sacred house he planned to erect at its center.[120] The details of this replica are discussed in the next chapter, but here, what is relevant is the Huron engagement with Chaumonot's imported relic. As much as Jesuit teachings, what allowed the Huron to comprehend the Holy House was their own experience as Christian refugees.

117. "He often invoked his daughter, who had died two years before with the reputation of sanctity, saying to her: 'Gaouendité, my daughter, remember that thou didst promise me, at the time of thy death, that thou wouldst come and succor me at mine. That time is now at hand; do not forget thy poor father.'" "Account of the Most Christian Death," *Jesuit Relations* (Thwaites, ed.), vol. 53, pp. 103–4.

118. Ibid., p. 109.

119. It was not just the Jesuit Chaumonot, but also other French settlers who were horrified by the slaughter of the Huron and who responded to the trauma with "survivor's guilt" by reaching out to the Huron. Blum, *Ghost Brothers*, pp. 30–31.

120. Trigger, *Children of Aataentsic*, p. 818.

Part of the refugee experience for these remaining Huron involved membership in the wider Catholic community. They had gambled that choosing to live with other Catholics might allow them to survive. These Huron converts, like aspiring Jesuit novices on their way to Loreto, tried out their Catholic membership over the course of their journeys. Just as it did for pilgrims in Europe, membership in the Catholic seventeenth-century sphere involved being open to a broad cross-section of novel populations. Like Chaumonot surrounded by vagabonds, and Albani surrounded by pilgrims on their knees circumscribing the Holy House, these Huron deliberately joined a wider stream to see where it would take them. As noted above, it brought them in contact with the French of Québec City, with the bishop himself taking interest in Ignace's Christian burial. But in the winter of 1673, it also brought them in touch with the Madonna of Loreto introduced by the Jesuits, and with the Iroquois enemies they had fought so fiercely.

Huron stretching to be open to a new face of Mary, and a new influx of enemies, is evident from the first moments of construction of Notre Dame de Lorette. Because the Lorette mission settlement was new, family residences had to be raised at the same time as the Holy House replica. While the replica was being finished, Chaumonot asked if anyone in the community would be willing to give up half of their cabin to be used for church services. Ignace's widow, Marie, and her brother, François Athoricher, were the first to respond. They generously offered up their entire cabin to serve as a temporary chapel for ten months, moving their own family to a rudimentary shelter in the meantime.[121] In the same year, in an even more impressive display of compassion, the Huron of Lorette accepted more than fifty Iroquois into their new mission settlement. These former enemies had become refugees themselves. But in their 1673 annual report, the Jesuits were amazed that "our Hurons, themselves poor, have shown [such charity] to clothe, house, feed and even adopt" these Iroquois, an act "all the more pure and heroic, as they have received so much bad treatment from that nation."[122]

This community that had nearly dwindled away after decades of rifts with the Iroquois actually *grew*, now, because of Huron Catholic hospitality. By 1676, according to Jesuit tallies, there were three hundred Catholics in Notre Dame de Lorette, a full third of them Catholic Iroquois searching,

121. *Relations Inédites de la Nouvelle-France*, pp. 306–7.
122. Ibid., pp. 296–97.

as the Huron had, for asylum.[123] Taking these simultaneous acts as parallel, the Huron opening of their doors to the Jesuits' Mary and to the Iroquois reflects a remarkable empathy drawn from their own life experience. These Huron had survived because they had been taken in so many times, by the French settlers of Québec and by fellow Indians in other mission towns. Now they had the chance to return the favor, and to give Mary and their former enemies shelter from the cold.

Beyond these reasons, Huron and Iroquois cultural practice had recently swung toward tolerating the replenishment of their home populations with captives.[124] But this functional, familiar custom does not diminish the Christian dimension to Huron actions, reflected in their new and clear understanding of the small sacred space that the Jesuits were placing at the center of their community. The Jesuit Martin Bouvart noted that the Huron had barely arrived in their new village of Lorette in 1674 when they made a vow to St. Anne, the mother of Mary, and offered her a wampum belt that they hung inside the new Holy House replica and chapel.[125] These adopted Catholic gestures of vow and address to St. Anne, a venerated figure, suggest Huron investment in their new village as a *Catholic* site as well as a Huron space. Bouvart described the presentation the Huron made to St. Anne. He wrote that when they displayed the wampum belt, they "asked the mother of the mother of God, that [given that] she had formerly taken care to give her daughter a house in Nazareth, [she might turn] to making a similar one in the New World."[126] The Huron prayed for a Lauretan replica of their own, as a visible acknowledgment that they, too, were now part of St. Anne and Mary's Catholic world. Entering a Holy House of Loreto meant being part of a new and powerful company that included Jesuits, Iroquois, and French.

Looming above this human company, however, was the divine. As with Chaumonot, Albani, the Jesuit novices, and many pilgrims en route to

123. LAC Collection Félix Martin (1611–1776), MG18-H27, "De la Mission des Hurons de N. D. de Lorette en 1676," fol. 53.

124. On the changes to Huron and Iroquois warfare in the seventeenth century, and the impact on both peoples, see: Carpenter, "Making War More Lethal"; Richter, "War and Culture"; Blick, "Iroquois Practice of Genocidal Warfare (1534–1787)."

125. On Huron choice to indigenize Catholicism by using wampum belts in Catholic rituals: Vélez, "'Sign That We Are Related to You.'"

126. "Ils demandaient à cette mère de la mère de Dieu, que comme elle avait eu autrefois le soin de pourvoir sa fille d'une maison à Nazareth, elle s'employât à présent pour lui en faire avoir une semblable dans un nouveau monde." ASJCF no. 324 (1675 *Rélation du Père Martin Bouvart, S.J.*: "De la Chapelle de Notre Dame de Lorette en Canada), fols. 6–7.

Loreto, the Huron did not stay on that track simply for human camaraderie. They made a serious vow to the mother of Mary. Many felt that their very survival was due not just to French Catholic charity, but to their own Catholic prayers being answered. The wandering Ignace had articulated this sense of being touched and protected by the Catholic God and saints even before the mission of Lorette and its Holy House replica were constructed. Ignace left behind his own words, refracted through the Jesuit Chaumonot's extensive eulogy in his honor.[127] While Chaumonot's predecessor the Jesuit Oratio Torsellino had imagined a speech from the Slavic Catholic Nikolà Frankopan about the loss of Loreto (chapter 3 above), Chaumonot was afforded the opportunity to record snatches of remembered speech that he heard in real time. Ignace breaks through the conventional memorializing prose of a standard eulogy when Chaumonot recorded this encounter between the dying man and his wife, Marie Ouendraka:

> [As Ignace] always answered me that he had no apprehension [of death], his wife, fearing that he had some sentiment of presumption, said to him, "Ignace, take heed lest there be some vanity in saying, 'I do not fear death.'" To which he replied: *"Put a few questions to those who have seen me in the country of the Iroquois,—in the midst of the torments, and on the point of being burned over a slow fire,—and thou shalt know from them whether I have ever shown the least weakness in the face of all the cruelties that were exercised on my body. Now if I did not fear death then,—although I was not so well instructed in the future life, and had not the help of a Father and of the Sacraments of the Church,—why should I fear to die now, when I see myself so powerfully sustained, and when God has given me a firm hope of soon seeing again, as Saints in Heaven, my children who died a short time ago?"*[128]

Toward the end of his life, Ignace—like the aging Chaumonot—remembered earlier trauma. He reminded his wife and the Jesuit at his bedside of his captivity among the Iroquois, which in retrospect was a turning point for him on a path toward Christianity. According to Ignace, he now had a new consolation to help him confront suffering: Catholicism. The fact that Chaumonot recorded this tangential conversation in such detail in his account of Ignace's death suggests that the Jesuit recognized

127. Chaumonot is identified as the author of Ignace's eulogy by Laflèche, *Les saints martyrs canadiens*, pp. 232–33.

128. "Account of the Most Christian Death," *Jesuit Relations* (Thwaites, ed.), vol. 53, pp. 102–3. Emphasis added.

and perhaps also remembered what it was like to face death when wandering and in peril, versus when firmly grounded in the Catholic faith.[129]

Without being raised on the European pilgrimage circuits, and with no prior familiarity with the Madonna of Loreto and her famous relic, these Huron Catholics approached Chaumonot's Holy House much as he had, years ago back in Italy. They underwent circuitous detours, new mixed company, divine connection, and finally also the last organic dimension of pilgrimage that had influenced Chaumonot: touch. The Huron of Lorette noted that touching and experiencing the Holy House replica helped them to imagine. A Jesuit observer noted: "They call it in their language *Marie etiondata*, the apartment of Mary, because it was there that, according to belief, Mary had her bed, and where it is certain that she often dressed and cared for her holy infant."[130]

As a tribute to the tactile and visual power of the Holy House for the Huron, they chose to keep a small physical copy of it when they were forced to move once more. In 1697, four decades after Ignace's first approach to Québec City, the Huron were relocated again, one final time, to a site called Jeune Lorette. The move was partly due to the popularity of the Holy House replica among French settlers of Québec. The replica became a pilgrimage site for those in the city, who could conveniently walk five miles upriver to reach it, and who came hoping for miracles. Competition arose between the new mission's small congregation of one hundred fifty and the French who outnumbered them. When the Huron left for Jeune Lorette, they took with them a significant piece of the original little house of Mary: a small wooden sculpture of the Holy House.[131] As with the pilgrim Albani faced with many choices in the vendor stands around Loreto, the Huron chose not to portage an image of Mary or a different adornment from the site they were leaving. They carried with them a sculpture evocative of Mary's sacred house. The Huron had touched, and been touched by,

129. On the occasional affinity between Jesuits and indigenous converts at traumatic moments prior to death: Vélez, "'Do Not Suppose That Those Tears Proceed From Weakness.'"

130. "Nos Sauvages, pour honorer un si saint lieu dans sa representation, n'entrent qu'après avoir communié dans le retranchement [du *camino santo*]. . . . Ils le nomment en leur langue *Marie etiondata, l'appartement de Marie*, parce que c'était là où, à ce que l'on croit, la Sainte Vierge avait son lit, et où il est assuré qu'elle a souvent habillé et chauffé son divin enfant." "Mission des Hurons a Notre-Dame de Foye et a Notre Dame de Lorette," pp. 317–18.

131. Vélez, "Des Noms En Litige: Les Hurons de la Jeune-Lorette," pp. 134–43 in "Les voyages outre-mer d'un nom."

shared houses. This physical experience was intrinsic to their engagement with Catholicism.[132]

Extreme situations of holy encounter such as those of Huron refugees, and to a lesser degree, the frightened Albani and the runaway Chaumonot, stretch our understanding of pilgrimage. They stand in counterpoint to the Jesuit practice of pilgrimage as crystallized in Richeôme's manual and as represented by Jesuit novices. But they do not contradict them. Instead, they raise the question: Which was the working model for pilgrimage, the printed manual, or the real experience of being lost and found on the road? Jesuits like Chaumonot variously deemed both of these authentic expressions of Catholic faith. Indeed, accidental pilgrims brought an intensity of need to the rite of passage that transformed the ideal, making it seem possible and not just hypothetical. Beneath and alongside seventeenth-century pilgrimage rubrics are delinquents and refugees who suffered while traveling, found their way into spiritual support groups, called out to the divine, and genuinely felt that they touched it and were touched by it. There would be no Loreto and no fictional Lazares without scores of real Albanis, Chaumonots, and Ignaces.

132. On the centrality of "dwellings" or concepts of the home to religion in general: Tweed, *Crossing and Dwelling*, pp. 81 (on the impermanence of homes), 103 (on religion as "housework" and "homemaking"). For how home making and the Holy House of Loreto worked for the newly Catholicized Huron of Lorette specifically: Vélez, "A North American Case Study: The Mission of Lorette," pp. 158–61 in "Catholic Missions to the Americas."

PART III

Leaving Loreto

CHAPTER FIVE

Holy House Builders

THE FAMOUS FRENCH ESSAYIST Michel de Montaigne reported a peculiar subgenre of miracle when he visited the Holy House of Loreto in 1581: a warning. He recalled:

> People are forbidden to scrape off any piece of the wall [of the *Santa Casa*]; and if it were allowed for them to take any of it, the wall would be gone before three days. This place is full of infinite miracles, for which I refer to books; but there are several very recent ones that tell of the misfortune befalling those who took some part of the building, even with the permission of the Pope; [there is] one small patch of brick which was removed during the Council of Trent and was taken there.[1]

To late sixteenth-century visitors, the physical evidence of thieves and the recency of their "misfortune" emanated like an alarm klaxon from the Loreto sanctuary: *Do not remove stones from the Holy House of Loreto. Better people than you have tried and nearly died.*[2] It recalls today's security guards in the ruins of Rome's overcrowded Forum, tiredly blowing

1. "Il est défendu au peuple de rien esgratigner de ce mur; et s'il estoit permis d'en emporter, il n'y en auroit pas pour trois jours. Ce lieu est plein d'infinis miracles, de quoy je me rapporte aux livres; mais il y en a plusieurs et forts recens de ce qui est mesadvenu à ceux qui par devotion avoient emporté quelque chose de ce bastiment, voire par la permission du Pape; et un petit lopin de brique qui en avoit esté osté lors du Concile de Trente y a esté rapporté." Montaigne, *Journal de voyage* (1580–81), p. 140.

2. Regardless of warning, some pilgrims persisted in tearing pieces from Loreto's Holy House. In 1758, an Augustinian monk named Marcarius took a stone from the original *Santa Casa* wall and carried it to Vienna. The pilfered stone was set into the wall of a *Santa Casa* replica that had been built in Vienna in 1627 at the behest of Eleonora Gonzaga, to serve as a chapel inside the Hapsburg family church of St. Augustine. Stannek, "Al cospetto della Vergine," p. 236.

whistles to ward off the memento-grasping hands of tourists. Montaigne likely encountered the Trent story in several forms. It was engraved in a stone plaque posted at the sanctuary and circulated in print and by word of mouth.[3]

Like pilgrimage instruction manuals and official shrine seals, at first glance, the account sounds suspiciously top-down. It reads as if it was thoughtfully crafted by upper management in order to protect Loreto's relic from the many untrained and overzealous pilgrims arriving at the sanctuary; indeed, it even stars a high-ranking Catholic official important enough to procure papal blessing and attend the Council of Trent. Furthermore, the account emerged at a time when the desire for relics had reached a fever pitch.[4] By the turn of the sixteenth century, relics were a fixture of every cathedral and royal treasury, on regular display to remind Catholics of the presence of the divine.[5] Collecting was fueled by controversy with Protestants that charged relics with additional significance as markers of Catholicism. Not even a vigorous trade in bones from Cologne and Rome's catacombs could supply enough of them to meet demand. Some relic-hungry Catholics resorted to tearing off body parts of recently deceased candidates for sainthood such as the Jesuit Francis Xavier.[6] But it was not just human bodies that were in very real danger of

3. A commemorative plaque was put up in the Loreto church to mark the miracle. This account of events appears in print surprisingly soon after the actual event as a chapter in Angelitta's *L'historia* (1580): "Miracolo d'una Pietra de la S. Casa di Loreto" (pp. 82–87). The story is also repeated in book 4, chapters 3 and 4 of Torsellino's *History of our B. Lady of Loreto* ([1598]/1608), pp. 337–50.

4. This was not an entirely new phenomenon in Europe. To note only three of many medieval examples of relic frenzy: in the mid-1400s in Rome, guards had to be posted in the chambers of the recently deceased holy woman Francesca Romana (1384–1440, canonized in 1608) to keep her admirers from walking off with pieces of her corpse or her clothes. Stones were a more unusual genre of relic, but not unheard of: one cathedral in Ancona, San Ciriaco, kept as relics the stones said to have been thrown at St. Stephen. Also, in the late twelfth century, Florence housed collections of stones believed to be pieces of the Holy Sepulcher, taken from its walls in Jerusalem. On Francesca Romana: Tour of Tor de' Specchi Monastery, Rome, Italy, 9 March 2004. On San Ciriaco: Lightbown, *Carlo Crivelli*, p. 38. On Florence and the sepulcher stones: Morris, *Sepulchre of Christ and the Medieval West*, p. 227.

5. On the centrality of relics to Catholicism from the earliest days of Christianity: Brown, *Cult of the Saints*.

6. In 1554 in Goa, a Portuguese woman bit the toe off the corpse of the recently deceased Xavier in an "act of profound, if somewhat gruesome, piety." A few decades later, the Jesuits in Rome requested and received the detached lower right arm of Xavier's body. The upper part of his right arm was then divided in three and sent to Jesuit colleges at Macao, Cochin, and Malacca. Xavier's internal organs were also exported as relics. Wright, *God's Soldiers*, pp. 3, 5. On this same fate befalling bodies of martyrs in the seventeenth century:

being ripped apart by overenthusiastic relic hunters. When Montaigne's rumored church official seized his stone in the late 1500s, the Holy House of Loreto seemed poised to meet a fate akin to Xavier's: wide dispersal at the hands of crowds of well-meaning devout.

Given this atmosphere, it makes sense that the Loreto sanctuary curators publicized and amplified this warning miracle as a form of crowd control. But the miracle was not a disembodied fabrication contrived to rein in the masses.[7] It was a true story about a real bishop, Gaspar do Casal. Although Catholic bishops of the Reformation period remain emblematic of elite church authority and restrictive controls, Bishop Casal is captured in Montaigne's journal and Loreto's annals engaged in the same grasping as pilgrims and commoners.[8] His participation demonstrates the far reach of a mood, evidenced among seventeenth-century Catholics of all backgrounds, to experience religion in hard copy.

In the twenty-first century, we distinguish between virtual reality—imagined worlds often recreated vividly on computer screens—and hard copies, paper printouts, or three-dimensional physical objects that can be held in hand. Three hundred years ago Catholics were also familiar with these modes. For instance, with the help of *The Spiritual Exercises* of Ignatius Loyola, Jesuits trained their minds in virtual reality, intensely imagining biblical scenes. At the same time, they sought out hard copies, making pilgrimages to the Holy House of Loreto where they could literally touch the walls of Mary's abode. Bishop Casal's failed attempt to take a stone from the Holy House indicates the importance of portable touchstones for Catholicism.[9] It is best understood alongside other quests for the tactile among pilgrims, including one unique to Loreto: making copies of the Holy House for personal use. These private replicas were a sanctioned alternative to dismantling Loreto's relic. The bishop's experience

---

Gregory, *Salvation at Stake*, pp. 298–307. On bones as a commodity: Johnson, "Holy Fabrications"; Ditchfield, "Martyrs on the Move," esp. p. 289.

7. Famed historian John Elliot warns against scholars' tendency to "overestimate the passivity of seventeenth-century societies and to exaggerate the capacity of those in authority to manipulate those societies for their own ideological ends." Elliot, "Concerto Barroco," p. 28.

8. Some accounts do not name the bishop; there is a possibility that it was not Gaspar do Casal, but his predecessor, Bishop João Soares, who should be connected to this miracle (see n24 below). Recent historiography supports reconceptualizing this golden age of the episcopacy as a time of innovation and local negotiation, much of which happened outside of official church processes of canonization or relic authentication. On how the Bishop of Jaén, Cardinal Baltasar Moscoso y Sandoval, stepped in to authenticate an already vibrant local devotion in mid-seventeenth century Arjona, Spain: Olds, *Forging the Past*.

9. Plate, "Stones"; Vélez, "Stones and Bones," pp. 16–17.

thus paradoxically stood as both a caution to let the sacred building be, and an invitation to erect sacred buildings in new form. It was a shared mood for hard copy, rather than the elite mind of a few administrators, that allowed the Holy House of Loreto to move out into the world.

Religious scholars tend to separate mind and mood and arrange them hierarchically, though they acknowledge their interdependence. James Laine notes that these terms show "a cleavage between *styles* of religious life that have yet to be classified."[10] Nonetheless the categories have been invoked and even assigned to particular practitioners of religion. In his work on the subject, Laine observes that generally "for the reformer, mind trumps mood."[11] This suggests that we may be predisposed to associate the reform-minded Bishop Casal and Jesuit missionaries with the self-conscious products of mind: doctrine, constructed text, ideology, intellectualism, pedagogy. Pilgrims and new Catholic converts, on the other hand, are more commonly associated with organic displays of mood: choreographed ritual, popular or lived religion, and creativity.[12] Thomas Tweed masterfully flips this dichotomy in his *Crossing and Dwelling: A Theory of Religion*. His case study of Cuban Catholic immigrants at a 1993 festival of Our Lady of Charity in Miami reveals enough mind entangled in his Catholic subjects' mood to redefine religion. To Tweed, religion is about movement, spatial practice, active bridging, and "confluences of organic-cultural flows that intensify joy and confront suffering by drawing on human and superhuman forces to make homes and cross boundaries."[13] There is both mind and mood in that definition, but it is the mood of the Cubans who Tweed observed that led him to be mindful of dwellings and crossings. Tweed's entry point of mood beautifully fits the pilferers of stones and copyists of the Holy House featured below. Through Tweed's definition, they can be understood as having felt profoundly enough to recreate a symbolic dwelling magnificently suited for crossing borders, spiritual or literal. But they are not presented here as exemplars of Religion with a capital R. Instead, their actions serve to demonstrate how Catholic mood (and mind) could lead to concrete movement. Italy's *Santa*

10. Laine, "Mind and Mood in the Study of Religion," p. 239. Laine builds on the terms "mind" and "mood" as they were mustered by anthropologist E. Valentine Daniel, who in turn built the vocabulary from philosopher Charles Sanders Peirce's work about the Firstness (icon), Secondness (index), and Thirdness (symbol) of experience. Daniel, "Arrogation of Being."

11. Laine, "Mind and Mood in the Study of Religion," p. 242.

12. Ibid., pp. 239–49.

13. Tweed, *Crossing and Dwelling*, p. 54.

Casa, solidly anchored in place and weighted down under marble encasements, was physically hauled off its hill not as a clear-cut result of strategy, but because of many individuals' "taken-for-granted values," or mood.[14]

The object on the move, the *Santa Casa*, did not land in the same form in which it departed. Its transfers changed its meaning.[15] After considering Bishop Casal's interrupted theft and its repercussions, this chapter surveys multiple iterations of the Holy House of Loreto that were built from blueprints distributed at the Loreto shrine in the seventeenth and early eighteenth centuries. It closes by honing in on the replicas of the Jesuits, especially a diverse string of Holy Houses left by one Jesuit, Juan Maria Salvatierra, across Mexico. Individually and as a group, holy house builders in Europe and on the American frontiers wavered between creating accurate, rooted copies that were thoughtfully integrated into their new surroundings, and making imperfect, drifting copies that were unmodified and intrusive to their new settings. This variety suggests that what mattered most in spreading the Loreto devotion was felt intent (mood), not following instructions (mind).

Anchoring Ideal: A Bishop and a Blueprint

Gaspar do Casal displayed intent when he approached Loreto. The bishop wanted a piece of Loreto's great relic for himself.[16] While on his way to the meetings of the Council of Trent (1545–63), he dispatched a servant to fetch a stone of the Holy House to take back home to Portugal with him. He wanted to place it in the foundation of a new church that he was dedicating to the Madonna of Loreto. The bishop had even formally procured the pope's permission to do so. But though he intended to put it to pious use, as soon as the piece of the *Santa Casa* arrived in his possession, the bishop fell ill. He realized that the stone was the cause. Fearing he would die if he did not return it to Loreto at once, he personally carried the stone back to Loreto. The bishop's processional display of penitence was so grand that it drew thousands of observers who spread the news.

14. Laine, "Mind and Mood in the Study of Religion," p. 242.

15. Ditchfield posits that the multivalency of Catholic symbols makes them inherently pull toward the universal: "the capacities of saints to be simultaneously bearers of more than one meaning or embodiments of more than a single identity should remind us that devotion to saints and sacred space in general could never be exclusively 'local.'" Ditchfield, "Tridentine Worship and the Cult of Saints," p. 222.

16. Casal was acting Bishop of Leiria when he attended the Council of Trent. He was reassigned to Coimbra in 1579. Paiva, "Bishops and Politics."

Witnesses called the event a miracle, for both the bishop and the walls of the Holy House survived by grace of God.[17]

Like the origin story of the arrival of Loreto's Holy House, this miracle account shrouds its multiple human creators. Loreto's shrine administrators used the story of this bishop to manage pilgrims' behavior, but they did not invent him. Gaspar do Casal was a real and independent agent, first author, and pilgrim. At Loreto, he was known for three actions: he took a stone; he fell ill, interpreting his sickness as divine chastisement for his actions; and he then felt driven to undo the perceived offense by publicly returning the stone.

Bishop Casal's first and second actions were not remarkable, though they were replete with the mood to touch (and own) the holy. As someone both high-ranking and devout, he possessed double credentials for moving Loreto's famed relic, in part or whole. Royalty and saints were known to have transported some of Europe's most prestigious relics to new locations.[18] Why shouldn't a bishop carry a bit of Loreto home to increase the devotion's fame? Nor did rank dictate all; Casal was pious. There were many histories of relics that had been transferred by deeply spiritual anonymous hermits or travelers.[19] Likewise, even when Casal fell ill, there was precedent to help him make sense of his ailment, anecdotes that he would have been steeped in as an educated church administrator. Some Catholic relics had been seen to dig in their heels and cause harm when people tried to move them to places they did not want to go.[20] Miracles of relics choosing to stay put were so common in Europe at this time that it was natural for Casal to think that the Holy House of Loreto wanted to stay in Italy, intact.

It is the bishop's third action that surprises. Instead of surreptitiously sending his servant back to Loreto with the problematic stone, Gaspar do Casal chose to personally return it to the Holy House, making his deeds

17. Angelitta, *L'historia*, pp. 82–87.

18. Monasteries in southern France frequently connected their relics to Charlemagne. Remensnyder, "Topographies of Memory."

19. For instance, the original image of the Madonna of St. Luke in Bologna was reportedly brought by a Greek pilgrim, Teocle Kmuya, who found it in the Church of Divine Wisdom in Constantinople and then carried it to Bologna via Rome in 1160. Gharib, *Le Icone Mariane*, pp. 178–83.

20. In Catalonia in the ninth century, when the Bishop of Manresa tried to move the statue of the Madonna of Montserrat to his local cathedral, it would not budge. The Madonna of Czestochowa demonstrated similar obstinacy in Poland in the 1430s: when robbers tried to steal her image from the monastery chapel, they were miraculously immobilized. Begg, *Cult of the Black Virgin*, pp. 248–49 (Czestochowa), 256–57 (Montserrat).

into a public commentary and corrective. This shows exceptional self-consciousness, ambition, and what Laine refers to as *mind.* Casal lived at the dawn of an era of bishops as prized exemplars. High-ranking secular church leaders made up a significant one-sixth of the saints canonized in the century after his death. Bishops were catapulted to saintly prominence in part by the reforms of the Council of Trent that Casal himself attended.[21] He publicly fit himself into this mold with his penitential procession to Loreto, modeling appropriate behavior for fellow Catholic devout.

The twenty-fifth session of the Council of Trent in 1563 had focused on relics such as Loreto's Holy House. At that session, possibly attended by Casal, the importance of relics to the church was affirmed while the regulations for authenticating them were tightened.[22] Institutional interest in promoting local relics was never greater than it was in the aftermath of the Council of Trent—so long as attention was paid to authenticity in the face of Protestant skepticism.[23] Casal's return of the stone was effective in this regard. It boosted the validity of Loreto's Holy House without derailing the bishop from his original wish to spread the Lauretan devotion beyond Italy. Casal returned to Coimbra and erected his church to the Madonna of Loreto as planned, minus a Holy House stone.[24]

21. These "saintly bishops" included: Carlo Borromeo (1538–1610), Archbishop of Milan; Gregorio Barraigo (1625–97), Bishop of Venice; François de Sales (1567–1622), Bishop of Geneva; Michele Ghislieri (1504–72), or Pope Pius V; Toribio of Mogrobejo (1538–1606), Archbishop of Lima, Peru. Hsia, *World of Catholic Renewal*, pp. 127–29.

22. Johnson, "Holy Fabrications," pp. 275–77.

23. Ditchfield, "Tridentine Worship and the Cult of Saints"; Frazier, *Possible Lives*. Interestingly, the most searing critique of the Holy House came not from a Protestant, but from a Catholic, Pier Paolo Vergerio, whose seventy-five-page *De Idolo Lauretano* (1554) prompted other Catholics to rank him alongside the "heretics" Calvin and Luther for disparaging the authenticity of Loreto's relic. A century after Vergerio's polemic, authors were still publishing point-by-point refutations of it such as: "Scritura di Autore Anonimo sopra la verita del miracoloso trasporto della S. Casa," pp. 17–51; Martorelli, *Teatro Istorico della Santa Casa*, vol. 2, pp. 165–88.

24. It seems likely that Bishop Casal would have been able to procure secondary relics from the Loreto sanctuary to provision his new church dedicated to Loreto in Coimbra. At Loreto's cathedral, old ornamentation was rarely thrown out. Mundane or special, it was sold or passed along for reuse. For instance, the Jesuit superior general Mutio Vitelleschi circulated one of the ceiling stars that had been used to decorate the Holy House, sending it to Jesuits in Mexico City in 1615 to be used in a church. With or without Lauretan relics, the Loreto devotion thrived in Coimbra from the late sixteenth century onward. In the early eighteenth century, the Augustinian friar Agostinho de Santa Maria overlooked Casal and actually credited an earlier sixteenth-century bishop of Coimbra, João Soares, with founding Coimbra's major church dedicated to Loreto. Santa Maria, *Santuário Mariano*, tomo 6, p. 504. On Lauretan ceiling stars: ARSI Rom. 51, tom. 2, appendix (Mangioni), chapter 9.

Bishop Casal's actions well reflect episcopal reform, new policies of the Council of Trent, and Catholic *mind.* But when the cast of actors is extended beyond the high-ranking churchman, one notices a larger, shared *mood* behind Casal's return of the stone and ensuing consolation prize. The bishop was not the only one to substitute a makeshift structure dedicated to Loreto in lieu of the Holy House itself. Others were carrying the Holy House away from Loreto, also not in pieces, also not in the hypothetical, but in alternative hard format: in blueprints. Around 1625, fifty years after Bishop Casal's penitential procession, the Loreto sanctuary began selling floor plans of the Holy House as souvenirs for pilgrims. Printed in multiple languages, the series of loose-leaf broadsheets displayed wall-by-wall perspectives of the Holy House, with insets of text explaining construction materials and decorative features.[25] These paper souvenirs were affordable and convenient to carry or to reproduce as part of larger works such as the pilgrim Nicolà Albani's *Veridica Historia* (figure 5.1).[26] When considered together, bishop and blueprint demonstrate a deep-seated seventeenth-century impulse, not to *take*, but to *make* your own relic.

Pilgrims could purchase patterns of the Holy House in loose-leaf form, but they were also sewn into previously-bound books as appendices and stuffed into pamphlets. They spread in tandem with the burgeoning printed literature on Loreto, first and foremost through pilgrim manuals in which they were supplemented with extensive textual descriptions.[27] The text was frequently lifted verbatim from earlier shrine histories like that of the Jesuit Oratio Torsellino, who devoted several chapters of his much-read and widely circulated *Lauretanae Historiae* (Rome, 1598) to painting verbal sketches of the appearance and measurements of the Holy

25. As explained in the previous chapter on pilgrims, these broadsheets most likely were first produced as part of the celebrations at Loreto of Pope Urban VIII's jubilee year, in 1625. Ranucci and Tenenti, *Sei Riproduzioni della Santa Casa di Loreto in Italia*, p. 153.

26. The pilgrim Albani mentioned in chapter 4 above reprinted five pages of the series in his travel account *Veridica Historia* (Naples, 1743). For his book Albani may have duplicated the original souvenir broadsheets he picked up on his visit to Loreto, or it is also possible that he reproduced the engravings from the well-known and readily available work of the Jesuit Pietro Valerio Martorelli, *Teatro Istorico della Santa Casa* (Rome, 1732). One loose-leaf copy of the seventeenth-century floor plans can be found in the Bibliothèque Nationale Française in Paris: BNF Ms. FR 11758, folios 14–29 (A. Philippon, "Le Véritable plan," 1649).

27. In addition to Albani's 1743 pilgrimage manual noted previously, early modern Lauretan pilgrimage manuals that feature Holy House blueprints include: Bralion, *L'histoire de Nostre Dame de Laurette* (1665); Raffaelli, *Notizie della Santa Casa* (1714); Lucidi, *Notizie della Santa Casa* (1769); Gaudenti, *Storia della santa casa di Loreto* (1784).

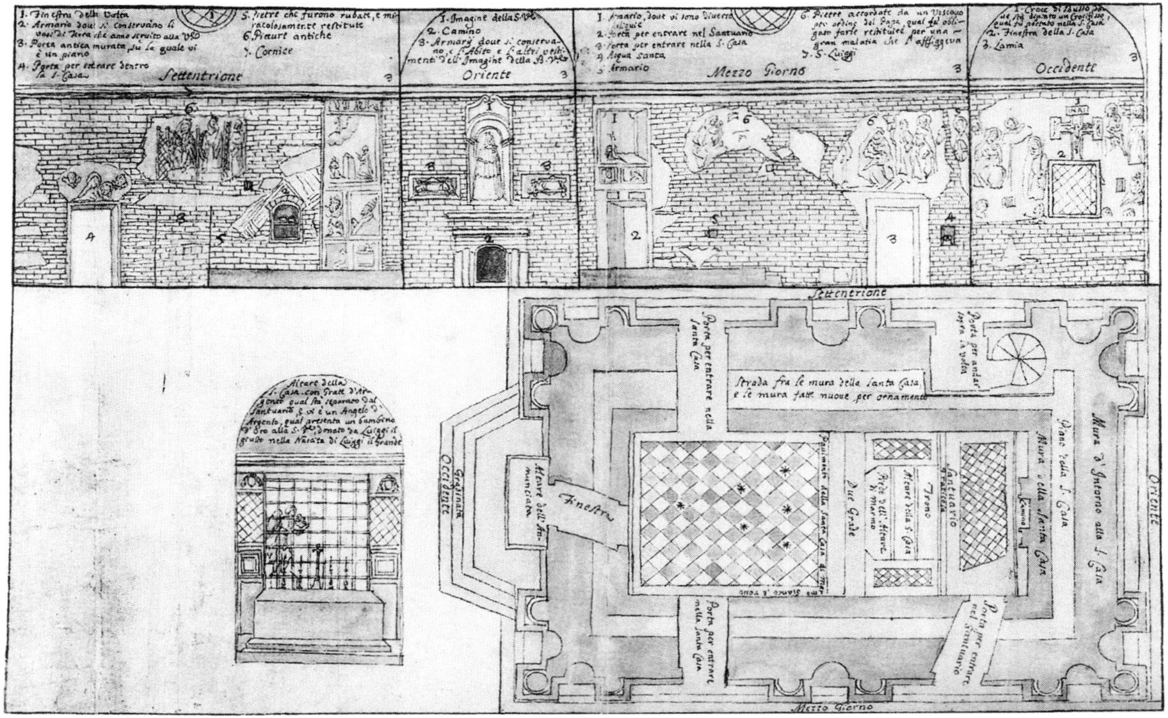

FIGURE 5.1. Blueprint of floor plan of Holy House of Loreto, published by Nicolà Albani (c. 1760) and reprinted in Albani, *Viaje de Nápoles* (Santiago de Compostela, 1993). Photo reproduced by permission of the Consorcio de Santiago.

House in various stages of its history.[28] These heavily explicated schemata allowed aspiring copyists to effectively build their own Holy House.[29] At the seminary of St. Sulpice in Illy, France, standard Holy House blueprints were stored alongside architectural plans that were used to fashion a chapel in the model of Loreto in the late seventeenth century.[30] The dimensions and decoration of St. Sulpice's constructed chapel of Loreto conformed to the information in the Holy House prints, showing that these rubrics were being used and not just filed away as keepsakes.

Blueprints were so effective at diffusing a standard model of Loreto's Holy House that it transforms one's sense of the relic, making it "tempting to see the chapel as having been *made* to be reproduced."[31] But here again, the existence of Bishop Casal's penitential procession serves as a reminder to not privilege strategic functions over lived experience. Casal did not set out to nearly die, change his mind, and then return his bit of Holy House in order to launch a deliberate campaign to teach Catholics to duplicate instead of dismantle. Similarly, there is no evidence that the floor plans of the original Holy House of Loreto were designed with actual replication in mind. Neither bishop nor blueprint vendors could have anticipated that the *Santa Casa* would go viral.

But it did. Armed with Holy House diagrams or detailed books, hundreds of Catholics set out to assemble Holy House replicas all over Europe in the 1600s in what is best described as a bout of Holy House mania.[32] Copies of Loreto's Holy House were first in vogue close to the Loreto sanctuary, in Italy. In the early 1600s, imitation chapels—lovingly

28. For instance, book 3, chapter 6: "A description of the carved-worke wherwith the most sacred House is adorned round about." Torsellino, *History of our B. Lady of Loreto*, pp. 237–40.

29. This pairing of text and architectural detail was also effective for other Christian monuments like the Holy Sepulcher. For instance, the woodcuts of Erhard Reuwich, an artist and German pilgrim to Jerusalem in 1483, provided more accurate eyewitness information about the Holy Sepulcher for people who wished to recreate it in Europe. Such early modern blueprints call to mind more recent architectural pattern books of the twentieth-century United States that allowed middle-class house owners to simply follow printed patterns to build their homes in architect-designed styles usually reserved for the wealthy. On Reuwich woodcuts: Morris, *Sepulchre of Christ and the Medieval West*, p. 326. On US pattern books: Guter and Foster, *Building by the Book*.

30. BNF Ms. FR 11758, fols. 1–11 ("Inscriptions," 1690).

31. Levy, *Propaganda and the Jesuit Baroque*, p. 204. Levy is speaking of Andrea Pozzo's 1695 design for a Chapel of St. Ignatius in Rome. An engraving of Pozzo's design was circulated independently by French printers and Jesuits for an international audience.

32. The phrase is borrowed from Justin Kroesen, who refers to a similar "Holy Sepulcher mania" of replication in the eleventh century. Kroesen, *Sepulchrum Domini through the Ages*, p. 19n41.

built to the same dimensions and of the same materials, and sometimes even brazenly claiming the same miraculous origins—were constructed in Varallo, Lombardy, Milan, Bergano, Cremona, and even Rome.[33] Such was the local proliferation of Lauretan Holy Houses that Pope Urban VIII (r. 1623–44) felt compelled to curtail their spread in order to bolster Loreto's increasingly contended and diffused authenticity.[34] But papal regulations did not restrain the regions at the fringes of the Protestant-dominated north.[35] On these contested frontiers, Holy House copies stood as clear markers of Catholicism, reinforcing Catholic sacrality in disputed zones.[36] By the early seventeenth century, on the borders of Bavaria alone,

33. Ranucci and Tenenti, *Sei Riproduzioni della Santa Casa di Loreto in Italia*. They focus on six lesser-known Italian reproductions at the Churches of San Paolo ad Aversa di Napoli, in Aversa (1630); San Clemente in Venice (1644); Santa Teresa del Bambin Gesù in Parma (1662); Santa Maria dell'Aiuto in Catania (early 1700s); San Pantalon, also in Venice (1744); and San Giovanni Battista, in Vescovana (c. 1750). In Rome, the confraternity of Piceni additionally graced their reconstructed *Santa Casa* with an identical copy of Loreto's black statue of the Virgin. That 1507 statue predated their Holy House chapel and was said to derive its miraculous powers from the original at Loreto. Like Holy House replicas, Marian confraternities such as Rome's group of Piceni did not originate with the Jesuits. They had roots in the Marian societies of the Middle Ages. But they did spread far afield at the hands of the Jesuits; one Jesuit-instigated confraternity to the Madonna of Loreto in Cuzco, Peru is discussed in chapter 7 below. On the Piceni confraternity in Rome: B. Ang. Ms. 1610/2 (*Statuti dell'archconfraternità della S. Casa di Loreto*, 1694). On Marian societies: Henderson, *Piety and Charity in Late Medieval Florence*, pp. 28–30.

34. Bulgarelli, "Holy House of Loreto," p. 89.

35. In England, Holy Houses surface surprisingly early. The Abbot of Glastonbury, Richard Bere (1494–1524), erected a replica chapel after visiting Loreto. He was followed by a Scotsman, Thomas Doughty, who constructed a copy in 1533 at the hermitage of Musselburgh. But I do not consider these examples here as they predate the 1600s explosion of copies that is the focus of this chapter. To the southwest, Iberia affords an interesting contrast. Devotion there seems to have centered more on images of the Virgin of Loreto rather than the Holy House copies so popular elsewhere. J. A. Sánchez Pérez inventoried ten chapels dedicated to Loreto that were built from 1500 to 1800 in Spain, none of which he associates with Holy House replicas: Almunia (Zaragoza); Aluenda (Zaragoza); Ballobar (Huesca); Higuera la Real (Bajadoz); Llardecáns (Lérida); Madrid; Muchamiel (Alicante); San Juan (Alicante); Sariñena (Huesca); and Zaragoza. Holy Houses and Loreto chapels in the Portuguese domains are discussed further in chapter 7. On England's replicas: Hamilton, "Ottomans, the Humanists and the Holy House of Loreto," p. 5. On Spanish replicas: Sánchez Pérez, *El Culto Mariano en España*, pp. 235–36.

36. In Bohemia and Moravia, Lauretan replicas were a "noble-cult phenomenon." Members of the aristocratic Lobkowitz family built the first Lauretan Holy House in the region in 1584 after a pilgrimage to Loreto; they were also behind the construction of Prague's famous and costly Holy House replica in 1626. Historian Howard Louthan observes that nearly 80 percent of *Santa Casa* replicas built in Czech lands were commissioned and funded by noble families rather than city councils or religious orders (personal communication, 3 March 2004). Members of the German ruling houses of Habsburg and Wittelsbach also undertook pilgrimages to Loreto and commissioned Holy House copies

there were more than fifty sites that advertised having reproductions of the *Santa Casa* of Loreto.[37] One of the most famous emerged in Prague, where Catholic devout replicated not only the humble brick Holy House, but also its entire Renaissance marble shell—carvings and all.[38]

Bryan Rennie, twenty-first-century professor of religion, describes how models of the sacred are often discredited when people get hung up on direct correspondence with reality or truth. Rennie notes the modern temptation to ask: "Does the blueprint of the house match the actual house?"[39] The myriad Holy House replicas raise this question of accuracy now as they did back in the seventeenth century. If they were not precisely like the revered Holy House of Loreto, could they be effective points of access for the divine? In *L'histoire de Nostre Dame de Laurette* (Paris: Georges Iosse, 1665), a guidebook for French pilgrims traveling to Italy, the Frenchman Nicolas de Bralion expressed this anxiety for exactitude.[40] The appendix of Bralion's book includes the telltale souvenir diagrams. In his preface, Bralion extends an invitation to "all who cannot make the trip" to Loreto

---

that underscored their connection to this prominent Catholic site. Bulgarelli, "Holy House of Loreto," p. 87.

37. Howard Louthan has counted forty-five chapels dedicated to Loreto that were built in Czech lands from 1589 to 1729 (personal communication, 3 March 2004). Sifting through Gumppenberg's *Atlas Marianus*, David Freedberg adds eighteen built in Bavaria just between the years of 1632 and 1675. Four of these northern sites where early modern replicas can still be visited are Loretta of Mikulov (1624), Loreto of Kosmonosy (early 1700s), and Loreta of Rumburk (1704) in the Czech Republic; and Lorettoberg (1557), near Freiburg, Germany. Freedberg, *Power of Images*, p. 113.

38. The replica was built from 1626 to 1631 under the patronage of Katerina Lobkowitz, and it stands inside the Capuchin monastery in the Prague Castle complex (Hradčany). Neubert and Royt, *Praga Caput Regni*, p. 9.

39. Rennie brings up this question in reference to the debate about Clifford Geertz's argument that religion is both a model *of*, and a model *for* life, simultaneously reflecting what is and also what might be. Scholars N. Frankenberry and H. H. Penner critique Geertz's concept by applying the correspondence theory of truth. In that context, Frankenberry and Penner propose the question of the matching house that Rennie interrogates. Rennie, "Myths, Models, and Metaphors," p. 341.

40. If the Vatican Library's copy of the original 1665 edition is any indication, Bralion's *L'histoire de Nostre Dame de Laurette* was read with interest and had a wide circulation. It is filled with handwritten annotations and the cover chronicles its passage through several owners and sales that took it as far afield as England in 1722 and 1777. Bralion's work is filed at the Vatican as: BAV R.G. Storia V 6432. Bralion had visited Rome as a young member of the newly founded French Congregation of the Oratory, a preaching-oriented group of priests who borrowed rules from the Oratorians established by St. Philip Neri (1515–95). Partly inspired by his fifteen-year Roman residency, when he returned to Paris, Bralion wrote five different guidebooks for Italy-bound French pilgrims. Brizay, "Pèlerins et pèlerinages," p. 203.

to use the diagrams to make a Holy House replica that could substitute for pilgrimage.[41] He does not propose this casually but exhorts his readers "to build chapels that *perfectly represent* this venerable Sanctuary."[42]

Bralion was excruciatingly specific about what he meant by "perfectly represent." First, he provided extra instructional detail for builders to faithfully render decoration such as inscriptions above the Holy House's doors.[43] Second, he described the material and building techniques for the interior wall of the house with such precision that one can today recognize the masonry pattern that he recommends as random ashlar.[44] Bralion finally encouraged correspondence to the original Holy House with respect to physical layout and cardinal orientation. Culling from Torsellino and other previous chroniclers of the Holy House, he listed precise

41. Bralion is bold with his pitch; other accounts of Loreto that included blueprints and details about how to reconstruct a Holy House stopped short of explicitly "inviting" readers to build such a chapel. For instance, Torsellino's shrine history simply lists one case of a man who built a replica: "For Friar Vincent a good and a godly man, & a deuout Priest of the Order of the Franciscans, returning from Loreto into France, in the Suburbs of Laual (a towne of the diocesse of Mayin) built a litle House like to the Chapell of Loreto, and called it the B. Virgin of Loreto, which at this day is exceedinglie reuerenced, both of the inhabitants and strangers." If Torsellino offers Friar Vincent's story by way of encouragement to the reader to build a Holy House, it is a gentle prod at best. The anecdote seems presented more for admiration than emulation. Massimo Bulgarelli also singles out the German Jesuit Wilhelm Gumppenberg's *Atlas Marianus* (Munich, 1672) as being a major source for the diffusion of Holy House copies overseas, since it inventoried scores of Holy House copies. But Gumppenberg, like Torsellino, did not directly exhort his readers to build such copies. Torsellino, *History of our B. Lady of Loreto*, p. 235; Bulgarelli, "Holy House of Loreto," p. 87.

42. "Enfin i'ay eu un troisième motif de representer en cet Ouvrage la sainte Chapelle de Laurette; qui a esté d'inviter en faveur de ceux qui n'en peuvent pas faire le voyage, à faire bastir des Chapelles qui *representassent parfaitement* ce venerable Sanctuaire, à l'imitation de celle qui se voit à Paris aux Filles de la Magdeleine, sur laquelle il s'en est fait une autre à Pontoise, qui y sert de Chapelle à l'Hospital des pauvres Enfermez, lequel y est estably depuis peu d'annèes." Bralion, *L'histoire de Nostre Dame de Laurette*, p. xxv. Emphasis added.

43. Ibid., p. 120.

44. "Les pierres dont est construite la sainte Chapelle, qu'il faudroit encore imiter, sont naturelles & vives de couleur de chastaigné, en rouge obscur, taillées grossierement en façon des briques; mais inégales de longueur et largeur, & en plusieurs endoits, avancent les unes plus que les autres, comme si elles estoient déplacés & sont d'environ trois doigts d'épaisseur." / "The rocks of which the holy Chapel is constructed, that it is also necessary to imitate, are natural and bright with chestnut color, in dark red, cut thickly in the manner of bricks; but unequal in length and width, and in several places, with some sticking out more than others, as if they were displaced and they are around three fingers of thickness." Ibid., pp. 121–22. Special thanks to Jeanne Kilde for noticing the random ashlar pattern described here.

measurements of height, width, depth, and relative position for each component of the structure. He gave dimensions for the external marble-carved walls, the walkway between old and new walls, the display niche for the statue of the Madonna of Loreto, the doors, the window, and even the internal trappings of armoires, a decorative cross, and a vase of holy water.[45]

Bralion's idea of spreading "perfect" Holy Houses throughout Europe did not come to pass in quite the explicit fashion he envisioned, even though he provided his readers with tools to copy well. The many replicas described below attest more to variety than perfection, and more to creativity than exactitude. A survey of these copies vindicates religious scholar Bryan Rennie instead, who argues that models are "not perfect copies" of the sacred but are best approached as if they were portraits by painters or sketches by anatomists, works that intend to capture some part of the real, but not to replace it.[46] Rennie's 2009 analysis recalls Bishop Casal in the 1580s. Unable to remove the perfect Holy House from Loreto, he did not endeavor to replace it so much as to evoke it in the small chapel that he erected back in Portugal. Prototypes circulated more to enable mood than accuracy in the seventeenth century. The mood, for both Bralion and bishop, was to express one's piety in hard copy. With a passion as fervent as relic collectors, replicators succeeded in moving Loreto's Holy House, and along with it, a Catholic devotion.

Actual Repetitions: Holy House Mania and the Jesuits

The French author Bralion's commitment to exactitude was unusual among his peers. Today preconceptions linger about the Renaissance as a watershed for modern architecture, heralding in periods of obsessive architectural accuracy. In practice, however, Catholics in the seventeenth century were engaged in a time-honored tradition of laxity when they copied. The Holy House of Walsingham and the Holy Sepulcher were two Renaissance precedents to the 1600s replicas of the Holy House of Loreto. In the cases of those two relics as well, variation between copies and the original was expected. Holy House builders inflected their structures to enhance tactile and emotional engagement. This preference to privilege touch led builders to make small changes in Holy House copies that were designed for placement in Europe's *Sacro Monte* or Sacred Mountain

45. Ibid., pp. 112–25.
46. Rennie, "Myths, Models, and Metaphors," p. 346.

pilgrimage destinations.[47] Most remarkably, the prevailing mood led Jesuits to alter their Holy House replicas. The architectural output of the Jesuits is as celebrated as their mission work and is repeatedly cited for its consistent accuracy and purposeful pedagogical intent. But the Jesuits were surrounded by old, superficially slapdash models of the holy, and contemporary duplicates of staggering variety of form and quality. While they strove to be mindful, their hard copies of Loreto's relic expressed mood and individual experience more than conformity or perfection. Moreover, the Jesuit copies surveyed below did not uniformly involve transplantation rituals that used these constructions to sacralize new spaces.[48] Instead, Loreto-inspired creations in Jesuit overseas missions followed European precedents and variants by exuding a portable sacrality that did not depend on place.

There was substantial precedent for aspiring Holy House replicators, Jesuit and pilgrim alike, to diverge from blueprints. Duplication of Catholic devotional images was an old art that had outlasted the Middle Ages without getting hung up on verisimilitude. Reproductions of famed icons and saints' statues ideally nodded to the original but allowed for variation as long as the parent type was recognizable.[49] The same was true for emulating sacred buildings.[50] Multiple sites could share this beneficial association-by-structure. For instance, England's Holy House of

47. Italy's fifteenth-century *sacromontes* long preceded theorist Mircea Eliade's symbolic category of "sacred mountain" as an *axis mundi* that connects the earth with heaven (*Sacred and Profane*). But Eliade's concept applies beautifully to these mountains that were intentionally designed to provide spiritual access, much like their sixteenth-century contemporary "altepetls" or water-hills across the Atlantic in Mexico. On altepetls as the Mexican pre-Christian and prototypical "sacred mountains": Carrasco, "Human Sacrifice/Debt Payments from the Aztec Point of View."

48. J. Z. Smith, *To Take Place*. In this path-breaking study, Smith persuasively demonstrates that it is people who make and move the sacred: when the faithful move, they sacralize their new locations through ritual. Sometimes Smith's observed dynamic is apparent among Jesuits and other seventeenth-century house builders, but just as often, Holy House copies suggest a dynamic of *detachment* from geographic space.

49. Freedberg comments that Catholic images were credible because they were "evident visual derivatives of well-known miraculous or miracle-working images," but also particular enough to be identified. Freedberg, *Power of Images*, p. 120.

50. David Friedman has noted that entire early medieval towns were conceived as recreations of better-known cities: "The likeness was not to be found in exact imitation; the qualities of the original that medieval planners considered significant could be captured in abstract physical schemes" (Friedman, *Florentine New Towns*, p. 200). Monasteries, too, were often laid out to echo the topography of Jerusalem. The architectural evocation of that Holy Land city bestowed an urban sacrality on these religious complexes. Morris, *Sepulchre of Christ and the Medieval West*, pp. 230, 240–41.

Walsingham and Italy's Holy House of Loreto surfaced roughly simultaneously.[51] Both residences of Mary, they coexisted through the centuries in part because Catholics commonly practiced and recognized loose iteration.

Minimal correspondence between exemplar and copy gave way gradually to the symmetry and realism associated with the Renaissance, but even then, "perfect representations" à la Bralion were not emulations as exact as modern audiences might expect. A good example of the historical trajectory of precision is the Holy Sepulcher, the tomb where Christ was buried. Like Loreto's *Santa Casa*, it underwent a vogue of replication in Europe, but five centuries previous to the *Santa Casa*'s heyday.[52] Whether pilgrims visited the actual site of the Holy Sepulcher, Jerusalem, or looked at a copy of the tomb at a European city across the Mediterranean, what they recognized as "the Holy Sepulcher" was not, actually, Christ's physical tomb. It was the distinctive *Anastasis Rotunda*, the enormous dome of the Jerusalem church that covered the sacred spot proclaimed to be that of the tomb.[53] Over time, the simulacra of the Holy Sepulcher changed. During the early medieval period, Holy Sepulcher imitations were not intended as carbon copies. They were true to one or two distinctive features of their model, in this case, the round contours of the church complex in Jerusalem.[54] Beyond this, their variety can also partly be explained by function: wooden Holy Sepulchers were moveable and useful for processions, whereas larger, more permanent Holy Sepulchers could act as private chapels.[55] But by the late fifteenth century, builders became concerned with

51. Waller, *Walsingham and the English Imagination*, pp. 16–17.

52. Kroesen suggests a reason for the frenzy of Holy Sepulcher replication in the eleventh century: the 1009 destruction of the original Holy Sepulcher complex by Muslims occupying the Holy Land. That event was followed by a boom of Holy Sepulcher replicas, perhaps instigated by returning crusaders. As discussed in chapter 2 above, the appearance of Loreto's Holy House in Italy in the thirteenth century, at a similar moment of post-Holy-Land ransacking, seems telling. Kroesen, *Sepulchrum Domini through the Ages*, p. 19n41.

53. For a thorough account of the excavations, buildings, destruction, and rebuilding of Jerusalem's Church of the Holy Sepulcher stretching back to Emperor Hadrian: Coüasnon, *Church of the Holy Sepulchre in Jerusalem*, pp. 13–14, 19–20.

54. For illustrations of medieval and early modern Holy Sepulcher replicas, see Morris, *Sepulchre of Christ and the Medieval West*, and Kroesen, *Sepulchrum Domini through the Ages*. They both classify the replicas as typical of medieval Christian art, as defined by Krautheimer, *Studies in Early Christian, Medieval and Renaissance Art*.

55. Kroesen, *Sepulchrum Domini through the Ages*, p. 62. Kroesen also tracks regional variation in Holy Sepulcher copies over time between England/Germany (more permanent structures), France/the Mediterranean (accompanied by Entombment sculptures), and central Europe (decorated with iconography focused on suffering): pp. 108–9.

correlating their replica with the original sepulcher in more than one respect. The copy that set the new standard for accuracy was commissioned by a German pilgrim, Georg Emerich, on his return from the Holy Land in 1465. He took an architect to Jerusalem with him and returned with sketches and dimensions that he used to erect a Holy Sepulcher replica in Görlitz. This replica continues to be singled out for being "as exact a copy as could be achieved."[56] It inspired more copies in a similar vein. People in nearby Sagan and Warsaw took measurements of the *Görlitz* sepulcher now, to erect their own models of the Holy Sepulcher.[57]

Yet the trend toward accuracy did not inexorably dead-end in Emerich's stricter imitation. The most celebrated Renaissance replica of the Holy Sepulcher suggests that while verisimilitude had gained importance, it did not preclude improvisation. Leon Battista Alberti designed a Holy Sepulcher in 1467 for the Chapel of San Pancrazio near the Rucellai Palace in Florence. Alberti's patron, Giovanni Rucellai, sent a group of woodcarvers and engineers to the Holy Land to research the exact design and measurements of the Holy Sepulcher. Alberti incorporated some of their eyewitness information, scaling his structure down, but preserving the proportions and sectional divisions of the Jerusalem church wall. He then put a classical finish on it and added wooden inlay.[58] Two centuries later, in 1659, the Bishop of Zagreb, Petar Petretic, took similar liberties when he commissioned a Holy Sepulcher to be made out of eight panels of embroidered cloth.[59] Alberti's and Petretic's Holy Sepulchers seems to prove art historian Evonne Levy's point that "while actual copies in the modern sense of the term became more possible and likely with the graphic reproductions now at architects' disposal, invention was key to imitation, mitigating outright copying at the moment it became truly possible."[60]

Replicas of Italy's Holy House of Loreto emerged in this period of mitigation. Bralion cried for accuracy, but in practice, most Lauretan Holy Houses were creations of local Albertis. The only two points of Bralion

56. Morris, *Sepulchre of Christ and the Medieval West*, p. 355.

57. Kroesen, *Sepulchrum Domini through the Ages*, pp. 118–19.

58. Franco Borsi comments that Alberti's replica actually resembles the chapels of S. Costanza and S. Stefano more than it does the Holy Sepulcher. He adds: "the Rucellai tomb is no pedestrian imitation of the Holy Sepulchre.... [He transformed] the medieval, oriental style of the original edifice in accordance with the classical canons that were more congenial to him." Borsi, *Leon Battista Alberti*, p. 83. Also: Morris, *Sepulchre of Christ and the Medieval West*, pp. 348–50.

59. The large panels were embellished with gold thread and silk and showcased sixteen biblical scenes. McWilliam, "Baroque in Croatia," p. 713.

60. Levy, *Propaganda and the Jesuit Baroque*, pp. 200–201.

that architects seem to have uniformly respected were layout and dimensions, information available on all the circulating blueprints of the *Santa Casa*. Effort was consistently made to approximate the size of the structure, and to fit it with three appropriately placed entrance doors and a window. But at Bralion's other suggestions for emulation—cardinal orientation, decoration, and materials—attention fluctuated. For instance, Holy Houses were constructed out of painted bricks, stucco, wood, marble, bronze, or any combination of the above.

Some recreated interior detail with care: in Aversa, the 1630 replica at the Church of San Paolo reproduced the cycle of faded murals of Mary's life that graced the inside of Loreto's Holy House.[61] However, not far across Italy, in the Church of San Clemente in Venice, a 1644 copy also boasted frescoes of Mary on the interior walls that did not resemble Loreto's series. A hundred years later, two Holy House copies were built almost in San Clemente's shadow—one at the Church of San Pantalon in Venice, another at the Church of San Giovanni Battista in nearby Vescovana. These relative newcomers looked to the neighboring San Clemente instead of to Loreto proper for their prototype. Their Marian frescoes were painted after the innovated murals in San Clemente's Holy House replica.[62]

Variants were upstaging the original and becoming prototypes in their own right. This was the case even in Aversa, with its accurate mural cycle. The instigator of Aversa's copy, Monsignor Carlo I Carafa dei Principi di Roccella, is said to have initiated his building project as a result of his visit to the court of Frederick of Hapsburg. Up north, he had seen replicas of the Holy House that prompted him to stop at the real deal on his way home, to research dimensions for building a copy of his own.[63]

The biggest point of variance between Holy House copies and Loreto's original was external appearance. Historian Massimo Bulgarelli groups the copies into three types: those that reproduced the entire marble exterior, with all the trappings; those that attempted to render the exterior but scaled it down, representing it with paint or reduced ornamentation; and those that ignored the marble exterior completely, basing themselves on the oldest form of the Holy House, the simple structure beneath the Renaissance encasement.[64] The first, most expensive and extreme category

61. Ranucci and Tenenti, *Sei Riproduzioni della Santa Casa di Loreto in Italia*, p. 23.
62. Ibid., p. 16.
63. Ibid., p. 23.
64. Bulgarelli, "Holy House of Loreto," pp. 87–88.

is also the most rare. It includes the Holy House of Prague (1626) and in Italy, the Holy Houses at the Churches of Santa Maria Corteorlandini in Luca, Italy (1667),[65] Santa Maria dell'Aiuto in Catania, and San Paolo ad Aversa di Napoli.[66] By contrast, the second category encompasses the most innovation. It includes Bohemia's Holy Houses of Pysely and Hlàsnà Lhota, and Italy's Holy Houses in Venice and Parma. Parma's 1682 copy in the Church of Santa Teresa del Bambino Gesù used chiaroscuro painting techniques and reliefwork to give the illusion of marble decoration.[67] But the final category was the one to travel the farthest, and is the topic of the remainder of this chapter.

Before turning to descriptions of some of these more remote improvisations, a word must be said on the feature that they most consistently duplicated of Loreto's Holy House: its interior. Jeanne Halgren Kilde has shown that some sacred buildings, such as the destroyed and rebuilt World Trade Center skyscrapers in New York City, can be conservative in their reconstructions and placement, "guarding against the change in meanings over time," ossifying or precisely preserving features of the original for commemorative purposes.[68] In the case of the Holy House of Loreto, the aspect that was repeatedly conserved and respected across copies, distance, and time was the crude inner wall of the original. This was the wall that had so captured the imagination of pilgrims including Montaigne, and had so obsessed Bralion that he expounded on how it was "cut roughly" of stones "unequal in length and width," with parts "stick[ing] out . . . as if they were displaced."[69] Mary had long been sought and found in the humblest of details.[70] Holy House builders consistently strove to commemorate the mood evoked by the Italian structure's plain interior.

65. Ibid.

66. The last even displayed a double of the cannonball taken to the Loreto shrine in 1511 by Pope Julius II. The cannonball marked the pope's survival of the siege of Mirandola. Ranucci and Tenenti, *Sei Riproduzioni della Santa Casa di Loreto in Italia*, p. 36.

67. Ibid., p. 16; on Bohemian examples, see Bulgarelli, "Holy House of Loreto," pp. 87–88.

68. "Sacralizing and memorializing efforts are often aimed at preserving specific meanings and guarding against the change in meanings over time, that is, guarding against 'forgetting,' as it is often characterized." Kilde, "Approaching Religious Space," p. 192. See too: Kilde, "Park 51/Ground Zero Controversy and Sacred Sites as Contested Space."

69. Bralion, *L'Histoire de Nostre Dame de Laurette*, pp. 121–22. Also see note 44 above.

70. For example, when the Siennese priest Gaspare di Bartolomeo journeyed to the Holy Land in 1431, he expressed this vividly in his reaction to the Fountain of the Virgin Mary. Bartolomeo ruminated: "[Mary] came to this fountain to wash the most holy swaddling clothes of her son, the sweet Jesu[,] and also the little one splashed in this water." The site prompted him to imagine Mary engaged in the most domestic of chores, washing her

It was a mood not left to the imagination by seventeenth-century hard copyists. They painstakingly recreated the humble wall for visitors to physically touch. The placement of some Holy House copies as centerpieces of hands-on, walk-through Catholic scenes shows how these objects were favored for the sensory experience they provided. For instance, Holy Houses were quickly incorporated into the participatory displays of two of Italy's Sacred Mountain sanctuaries, Varallo and Varese. Sacred Mountains were substitute pilgrimage sites that recreated the landscape of the Holy Land for Catholics who could not travel so far. They emerged around the same time as the Marian shrine of Loreto and gained popularity alongside it, with spin-off Sacred Mountains popping up across Europe from the fifteenth century onward.[71] The first Sacred Mountain in Europe was Varallo, created in 1486 by the Franciscan Bernadino Caimi, a former guardian of the Holy Sepulcher in Jerusalem.[72] Caimi had personally seen the sacred sites of the Holy Land. His desire to recreate the full experience of it for Catholics not fortunate enough to get there foreshadows Bralion's invitation to "all who cannot make the trip" to build their own Holy House.[73]

In 1572, a nonmarbled version of Loreto's *Santa Casa* was added to Varallo's scene of Mary's Annunciation. At the nearby Sacred Mountain of Varese, a Lauretan Holy House was also raised with a painted suggestion of the decorative portico. The copy was the starting point in Varese's chronologically ordered chain of Rosary stations, since it evoked the Annunciation that started Mary on her path as Mother of Christ, and alluded to the Nativity scene that followed.[74] Neither the Varallo nor the

---

baby's laundry. The sheer triviality of this task brought her to life for Bartolomeo. Siena, *Viaggio fatto al Santo Sepolcro 1431*, p. 154.

71. Sacred Mountain imitations sprang up like Holy Sepulchers all over the mountain range in the Lake District of northern Italy. They even specialized. Varallo rendered the Life of Christ; Oropa, the Life of the Virgin Mary; Orta San Giulio, the life of St. Francis; Varese, the fifteen mysteries of the rosary. Freedberg, *Power of Images*, p. 196.

72. Ibid., p. 193. Lightbown notes one earlier prototype of this idea assembled in Fabriano, Italy, in 1393 by two Augustinian friars and Holy Land pilgrims, Pietro and Giovanni Becchetti. Lightbown, *Carlo Crivelli*, p. 39.

73. Substitute pilgrimage existed for specific Holy Land sites including Mt. Sinai. In Abbotsbury, England, a chapel of St. Katherine acted as a "substitute Mount Sinai" in the late medieval period, drawing many pilgrims from the immediate area, many of them women for whom far-ranging travel was especially dangerous. Some of these pilgrims built smaller shrines to St. Katherine in the English countryside to commemorate their visits and to create a private space, even closer to home, where they could connect with St. Katherine. Lewis, "Pilgrimage and the Cult of St. Katherine of Alexandria in Late Medieval England," pp. 145, 159.

74. Bulgarelli, "Holy House of Loreto," pp. 85–87.

Varese Holy Houses were perfect representations in all respects. This is curious, since for Caimi, the creator of Varallo's Sacred Mountain, just as for Bralion, accuracy was paramount. Detail did not just matter for establishing authenticity. It mattered for *empathy*.

Caimi's goal in planning his Sacred Mountain exhibits was "to make the pilgrim present at the event,"[75] to recreate the Nativity, the Last Supper, and the Crucifixion as if they were "true events which took place in real locations."[76] At Varallo, Caimi used the topography of a mountaintop to evoke Jerusalem's landscape. Then, over the course of the sixteenth century, tableaux of life-like figures were added to his original three outdoor chapels. The more realistic the added statues, the more heightened was the emotional response they provoked. Hair, beards, painted eyes and blood, clothes, and props of carefully measured mangers, tables, crosses, and flickering torches—all this verisimilitude combined to collapse time and space and to "*produce again*, not reflect, illustrate, portray or image."[77]

Copies of the Holy House of Loreto therefore seem to have been welcome additions to Sacred Mountain panoramas, not for their precise correspondence to Holy Land realities, but for their shared power to evoke emotions associated with the sacred past. Viewers reported being moved to tears by the Sacred Mountains' walk-through scenes that helped them to experience biblical stories without having to extrapolate from a stained glass window or small engraving. It was a difference of sensory magnitude that brought Mary closer through the very ordinariness of particulars. People came back again and again to walk through the Holy Houses and peopled scenes.[78] One Milanese visitor to Varallo was so affected that he overlooked the builders' meticulousness of design and exclaimed, "The very simplicity of this enterprise, this structure with no art, and the noble site are superior to all antiquity."[79] This comment that counterintuitively

75. Morris, *Sepulchre of Christ and the Medieval West*, p. 361.

76. Freedberg, *Power of Images*, p. 118.

77. "[Such] striving for resemblance marks our attempts to make the absent present and the dead alive." Ibid., p. 201. Emphasis added. Freedberg comments that Franciscans like Caimi seemed obsessed with numbers, distance, and measurements and traces this to a favorite Franciscan text, *Meditations on the Life of Christ* (p. 118). But he is far more persuasive about the universal and psychological effects of verisimilitude at Varallo than he is about showing that Franciscans specifically had a penchant for accuracy.

78. One repeat visitor was the famous reformer of the Council of Trent, Archbishop Carlo Borromeo, who loved Varallo and dubbed it the "the New Jerusalem." Ibid., p. 193.

79. Girolamo Morone to Lancino Curzio, 1507, as quoted by Freedberg, *Power of Images*, pp. 125–26.

ignores artistry attests more than anything to the success of the *emotional* enterprise of copies of sacred structures.[80] The details that had the most profound impact were not marble embellishment or monumental architecture. They were on the smallest human scale, effective in making viewers feel they had stumbled upon a lived moment.

On a smaller scale than Europe's Sacred Mountains, calvaries, also known as Ways of the Cross or Stations of the Cross, also gained popularity in the 1500s. These were set up outside nearly every city and village so that locals could enhance their meditation by tracing Christ's final footsteps. Holy House copies were frequently part of those public stagings as well.[81] While designed to encourage meditation, these displays that so often featured Mary's residence were communal rather than private, and they drew people from all walks of life. Alessandro Nova has noted how rich and poor crossed paths there, sharing in the same scenes.[82] The placement of myriad copies of Loreto's Holy House at cavalries and Sacred Mountains demonstrates that these buildings were not the sole province of wealthy elites, or passive signposts of Catholicism. They were first and foremost intense avenues to emotional experience triggered by touch.

Perhaps for this reason, by the end of the seventeenth century, Europe's landscape was a kaleidoscope of colorfully varied *Santa Casa* depictions. Some of these solid, magically multiplicated refractions of Loreto's Holy House sprang up overseas as well, independently initiated by Jesuits who were motivated more by personal mood than by a corporate mind to convert. Their subgroup of copies merits closer consideration not because it contradicts the broader trends just described, but because it followed them so closely.

80. This emotional, participatory connection with Holy House copies is similar to what anthropologist E. Valentine Daniel associates with mood: a religious moment that is not dominated "by 'learning about'" or being lectured to, but rather by "being-in-the-world." Daniel, "Arrogation of Being," p. 181.

81. While Holy Houses were sometimes incorporated into Stations of the Cross, sometimes these local processional stops were linked to Loreto without the aid of Holy House replicas. For instance, between 1674 and 1680, a group of thirty wealthy Bohemian families created a Via Sancta, or Way of the Cross, that connected Prague to Stará Boreslav. Forty-four prayer stations were built along the northeasterly road between the cities. This number was chosen deliberately to correspond with the number of verses in the Litany of Loreto, which is discussed further in chapter 7. Ducreux, "L'ordre symbolique d'un pèlerinage tchèque," p. 94.

82. Nova, "'Popular' Art in Renaissance Italy." Maureen Flynn has described such joint religious experience in more caustic terms as "a spectator sport," pitched and staged for mass audiences. Flynn, "Baroque Piety and Spanish Confraternities," p. 244.

The best documented Jesuit Holy House replica on the American frontiers was erected by Pierre Chaumonot in Canada at the new Huron mission of Lorette in 1673. He had visited Italy's Holy House years before and may have been building in part from memory. But Chaumonot made such efforts to clone the original Italian Holy House of Loreto that one would think that he had read his countryman Bralion's appeal for exactitude. Chaumonot's colleague Bouvart enthused that the Canadian structure "resembled the true Loreto" in many regards.[83] Although blueprints of Loreto's Holy House were plentiful in Europe, as noted above, Chaumonot does not appear to have had one. He modeled his copy after the dimensions described by fellow Jesuit Oratio Torsellino in his book *Lauretanae Historiae* (1598).[84] Technically his copy came close to the dimensions of the original: Chaumonot's new Holy House of Lorette was forty feet long by twenty-five feet wide, as compared to the smaller thirty-one feet by thirteen feet of Italy's *Santa Casa*.[85] Chaumonot replicated the external appearance of Italy's original as well. He kept to the exact number of doors (three) and windows (two).[86] He also imported mud bricks for the walls, to simulate the commonness of the oft-touched ancient stones of Europe's relic.[87]

83. ASJCF no. 324 (1675 *Rélation du Père Martin Bouvart, S.J.*), fol. 13.

84. Chaumonot makes no mention of building from a floor plan in his biography where he describes, in some detail, the process of creating the replica. Historian André Sanfaçon deduces the use of Torsellino from the 1675 report of his Jesuit colleague, Bouvart. In that report, Bouvart follows up his description of Chaumonot's replica by noting details that they "observed" from Torsellino: "Turcellin estime que la pièce principale du logis est le côté du septrantrion, et assure que le seuil de la porte est de bois, ce que nous avons aussi observé dans la Lorette du Canada." / "Torsellino maintains that the main room of the house is on the north side, and identifies the threshold of the door as wood, which we also observed in the Lorette of Canada." ASJCF no. 324 (1675 *Rélation du Père Martin Bouvart, S.J.*), fol. 13. Also: Sanfaçon, "'A New Loreto in New France,'" 206.

85. ASJCF no. 324 (1675 *Rélation du Père Martin Bouvart, S.J.*), fol. 13. The difference can be blamed on Torsellino, who wrote: "The length of the sacred house, is about 40 foote; the breadth lesse than 20; and the height about 25." Torsellino, *History of our B. Lady of Loreto*, p. 14.

86. Loreto's Holy House began with only one access door that was later sealed; the three current doors were apparently added in the sixteenth century at the request of Pope Clement VII (1478–1534) to allow pilgrims safer access. The placement of the three extant doors does not correspond to the tripartite doors often used in Christian churches to denote the Holy Trinity. On the mythohistory associated with the three Holy House doors: Servants of the Pierced Hearts of Joseph and Mary, "Virgin Mary and the Holy House of Loreto." On tripartite doors: Kilde, *When the Church Became Theatre*, p. 67.

87. Bouvart explains how bricks were brought from the neighboring settlement of Beaupré, "between Château-Richer and Sainte Anne." ASJCF no. 324 (1675 *Rélation du Père Martin Bouvart, S.J.*), fol. 9.

One might expect *Jesuit* Holy Houses, in particular, to uphold the form and not just the spirit of Italy's original, and to resemble Chaumonot's. But in fact, Chaumonot was an exception. In the case of Lauretan Holy Houses, Jesuit design was far from uniform. This is surprising, since by the seventeenth century, Jesuit architecture showed outward signs of systemization. It has been noted that Jesuit churches of the 1600s displayed a "conceptual and artistic unity" unusual for the time.[88] Jesuit architects were chanting a familiar, rote chorus in their structures. Historians are quick to find reason for this in the centralized hierarchy of the Society of Jesus. Some of the first superior generals jumped in at each and every construction phase of the earliest Jesuit churches.[89] Following their lead, later Jesuit administrators in Rome vigorously adopted dual roles as monitors and distributors of Jesuit architectural agenda.

Rome-based leaders of the Society of Jesus are best known for their rigorous supervision of all matters touching on the Jesuits,[90] and architecture was no exception. As early as 1565, the Second General Congregation of the society agreed that plans for all Jesuit construction projects had to be submitted for approval by the superior general. Claudio Acquaviva (1543–1615) reinforced the policy when he became the fifth to assume that leadership post. In 1613, he sent a circular letter to Jesuit provincials adding to the policy. He asked that plans for new churches, colleges, professed houses, and all Jesuit-affiliated structures should be sent to Rome in duplicate, so that copies could be kept.[91] In practice, as Evonne Levy notes, this "centralized coordination" and record keeping bore most heavily on buildings that were actually paid for by the Jesuit administration in Rome.[92] In principle, however, Rome's aggregation of architectural blueprints created an image of the Society of Jesus that is aptly summed up by Jeffrey Chipps Smith, who exclaimed: "No other order went to such length to remain informed about and to exert at least nominal control over

88. J. C. Smith, *Sensuous Worship*, p. 200.

89. On their micromanaging the building of the Chapel of St. Ignatius in Rome: Levy, *Propaganda and the Jesuit Baroque*, pp. 91–108.

90. See, for instance, Jesuit historian John O'Malley's discussion of the purpose of frequent interviews between Jesuit superiors and novices in the early days of the society. He writes of how "supremely important [it was] for the superior to have complete knowledge of the inclinations and motions [of soul] of those who [we]re in his charge and to what defects or sins they ha[d] been or [we]re moved and inclined; that thus he m[ight] direct them better." O'Malley, *First Jesuits*, p. 355.

91. J. C. Smith, *Sensuous Worship*, pp. 106–7.

92. Levy, *Propaganda and the Jesuit Baroque*, p. 78.

all major building campaigns."[93] Jesuit provincials and superiors amassed hundreds upon hundreds of construction plans to send to Rome.[94]

Most of this enthusiastically submitted architectural information was cursorily examined, approved, and filed away. It was not practical for Rome to pronounce approval on all architectural projects, especially those farthest flung; the turnaround time was too long. It could take several years for correspondence to make a full conversational circuit across the Atlantic.[95] Regulation of establishments on the American frontiers was therefore left to intermediaries in the hierarchy, such as Jesuit provincials residing overseas.[96] But Rome's reaction to petitions from closer at hand offers a fascinating window on the psychology of Jesuit authority. In 1561, the rector of the Jesuit college of Loreto (Italy) petitioned to build another college in the nearby city of Macerata. The response from Rome was a gentle but firm version of "Think it out some more and get back to us."[97] The answer was neither yes or no. Levy suggests that this tactic of loose arbitration allowed space for individual architectural creativity. The tendency was for Jesuit superiors to open a dialogue with juniors with whom they disagreed, rather than to outright refuse them. In the ensuing

93. J. C. Smith, *Sensuous Worship*, pp. 106–7.

94. Ibid. For one sixty-year interval between 1580 and 1640, Smith turned up over a thousand drawings of Jesuit architectural projects in Paris, Rome, and Malta.

95. The 1683 annual report from the Jesuit expedition to California describing the founding of a California mission was shipped to Rome in early 1684. The copy of the letter in the Jesuit archives in Rome is annotated on the back with the date of Rome's reply: "Resp. 3 Nov. 1685." It seems that this date corresponds to when a Jesuit administrator in Rome wrote and sent a letter back to California. If one assumes the same length of time (two years) for the return transit of the reply across the Atlantic, the length of New Spain, and the Sea of Cortés separating California from Mexico, the California Jesuits would have heard back directly from Rome roughly four years after the 1683 events they reported. ARSI Mex. 17 (1683 *Relación* of the second Jesuit expedition to California), fol. 524v.

96. In the case of the 1683 California annual report, while it was en route from California to Rome, Jesuit superiors read it, copied it for their files, responded to it variously, and appended commentary. As filed in Rome, the report includes these intermediary responses and records of minor daily business, such as a later (1688) brief missive from Jesuit missionary Antonio de Roxas of the Sonora missions to the Jesuit provincial of New Spain, Bernabe de Soto, reporting his contribution of translators to aid the California efforts. The latter is filed in Rome for their information, though it was addressed to Bernabe de Soto in Mexico. ARSI Mex. 17 (1683 *Relación* of the second Jesuit expedition to California), fols. 512–24v.

97. Levy quotes the letter directly: "Beginning to build seems a matter requiring much thought, not so much beginning to build but the way of beginning, since this is a college to be built from its foundations, and therefore it will need to be planned with regard not only to the present, but also to the future." Levy, *Propaganda and the Jesuit Baroque*, p. 79.

exchange, administrative intervention could act as a "generative force" rather than a restrictive one.[98]

Superiors in Rome used the influx of information from the field to generate more than conversation. They selected architectural exemplars to recirculate. Eduardo Mercurian, superior general of the Society of Jesus from 1573 to 1580, enclosed standardized church dimensions in a letter to the provincial of Spain.[99] Perhaps encouraged by this impulse toward uniformity on the part of the hierarchy, a Jesuit architect, Giovanni de Rosis, published a helpful series of drawings around 1580 entitled *Plans for Jesuit churches*. Rosis's book included sketches of six variants on a longitudinal church.[100]

But even without Rosis's blueprints and Mercurian's stimulus, Jesuit architects were finding examples to follow. Jesuits looked first to their own ranks for models. Nearly one in every five Jesuit churches built in Italy before 1700 was designed to resemble the Jesuit architectural flagship, the Gesù Church in Rome.[101] Similarly, replicas of Loreto's Holy House became a leitmotif played out "in the [Jesuit] order's churches from Vilnius in Lithuania to Lima in Peru."[102] What one Jesuit recited or constructed was echoed and picked up by his colleagues.

Levy therefore credits the uniformity of Jesuit design in the early modern period to the "continuous solicitation of opinion,"[103] *from each other*, on architectural matters. Jesuit superiors were merely lynchpins in the process of collecting and redistributing ideas. As Claudio Acquaviva reassured indulgently during his generalate at the turn of the seventeenth century, "it is not necessary that the models of our churches all be done in the same way."[104] Jesuits in the field took advantage of this stretching room when it came to Loreto.

98. "We must rethink Jesuit discipline, principally the vow of obedience, as the site of a central tension in the Society: obedience . . . [was a] generative force." Ibid., p. 91.

99. Levy sees Mercurian's early generalate as an exceptional instance of Jesuit "flirt[ing] with standardiz[ed] design." In her broad survey of early modern Jesuit architecture, she rejects the notion that the Society of Jesus "imposed its own . . . design, because it simply did not have one." Ibid., pp. 195, 107.

100. Ibid., p. 196, fig. 86.

101. Ibid., p. 200. Levy counts 30 out of 160 Jesuit churches derivative of the Gesù.

102. Bulgarelli, "Holy House of Loreto," p. 87.

103. Levy, *Propaganda and the Jesuit Baroque*, p. 79.

104. The Jesuit superior general Acquaviva continued: "according to the convenience and circumstances that arise, things can be done in one manner or in another, whatever turns out best." There were some limits to this tolerance. For instance, the Jesuit Alessandro Valignano explicitly urged the Jesuits in Japan *not* to follow local construction methods. In his 1581 handbook for mission conduct, Valignano wrote: "in the construction of

In the 1690s, for instance, Jesuits put up a temporary chapel to serve their itinerant mission near Achao in Chiloé, off the coast of Chile. The superior of the mission, Michael Choller, replaced this with a permanent church that he named for Loreto. This wooden church took from 1723 to 1734 to finish. It had three aisles and interior columns and looked nothing like its Italian namesake. An Austrian furniture maker, Anton Miller, and a group of local carpenters helped to complete it. Art historian Gauvin Alexander Bailey notes that the structure resembled "a Tyrolean wayside chapel [more] than a Spanish colonial mission church."[105] He suggests that the Austrian provenance of the Jesuit builders explained the departure from local architectural patterns. These Jesuits looked to home for their church model, not to Lauretan blueprints.

The range of possibilities available to Jesuit duplicators of Loreto is most evident in the eclectic trail of Holy Houses left by one single Jesuit in particular: Juan Maria Salvatierra, a well-known Italian missionary serving in Mexico in the late 1600s. Salvatierra's varied buildings indicate a dimension to Holy House copies that goes beyond mind, mood, or the Jesuits. Viewed cumulatively, this Jesuit's full repertoire of Loreto replicas indicate that in the seventeenth century, the sacred had an astounding portability that trumped predispositions toward accuracy or positioning.

New Expression: The Frontier Replicas of Salvatierra and Company

The Jesuit Salvatierra's series of Holy House copies on the American frontier alter preconceptions about the expanding Catholic Church in the seventeenth century. They demonstrate that divergence from Old World or parent models was not, in fact, an aberration or a necessary stripping-down due to frontier context, as has sometimes been said.[106] Instead, just as has been shown with Holy House replicas in Europe, diversity among frontier copies was the hallmark of all transfers of this Catholic object.

---

churches it would be improper to imitate [the Japanese], since theirs are synagogues of Satan and ours are churches of God." Nonetheless, Jesuits in Japan built churches that had reception rooms for visitors and places to clean one's feet in order to welcome Japanese neophytes. Ibid., pp. 201 (Acquaviva); 186 (Valignano).

105. Bailey, "Cultural Convergence at the Ends of the Earth," pp. 212; 220.

106. Anthropologist George Foster's functional concept of a "stripping down process," whereby a conquering culture gets watered down or oversimplified in order to impose its customs, continues to hold sway. Foster, *Culture and Conquest*; on new critiques and revisions of Foster: Deagan, "Transculturation and Spanish American Ethnogenesis."

Salvatierra's alterations and implantations of Loreto's Holy House were as purposeful as they were varied. As the ensuing survey of his houses will demonstrate, this Jesuit engaged in both exact and inexact copying, sometimes cleaving to blueprints, sometimes building without architectural plan. Also, Salvatierra did not appear to give much care to selecting holy ground. Though Jesuit missionaries frequently distinguished themselves from other Catholic proselytizers by displaying adaptiveness to new places and peoples around the world, Salvatierra's Holy Houses in Mexico were not especially attuned to geography or to audience.[107] Finally and perhaps most importantly, Salvatierra was not exceptional or alone in his replicating style. Like Bishop Casal, he was in good company, surrounded by other Jesuit portagers and Catholic reproducers of devotion who were equally caught up in the mood for hard copy.

Juan Maria Salvatierra built three copies of the Holy House of Loreto during his time as a missionary in Mexico. He began by creating a marvel of exactitude like Chaumonot's, when he replicated the Holy House of Loreto at the Jesuit Colegio de San Gregorio in the environs of Mexico City in 1680. For this copy, Salvatierra worked off of a blueprint sent to him by his brother back in Italy.[108] A decade later, in the 1690s, he erected another scale copy in the college of Guadalajara, also with carefully calibrated measurements and attention to detail. But the most interesting architectural project Salvatierra left was his so-called replica of the Holy House at the mission of Loreto Conchó in Baja California in 1698. Unlike his previous replicas, the makeshift church that Salvatierra raised there bore little resemblance to Italy's *Santa Casa*.[109] It was a Holy House only in name. So was the more permanent structure that replaced it a year later, which Salvatierra also wrote of in his annual report as "la Santa Casa di Loreto."[110] That building was significantly larger than the *Santa Casa*, and its adobe walls were not doctored to imitate rough stone.[111]

107. Jesuit accommodation strategy, or adaptiveness to local traditions, has been primarily associated with China, although it was a tactic they applied in the Americas and in urban and rural European missions as well. On Jesuit accommodation in spheres beyond China: Hosne, "Tricky Concepts of 'Hispanicization' in Peru and 'Accommodation' in China."

108. Venegas, *Juan María de Salvatierra*, pp. 105–6.

109. As compared to other churches built in the California missions in this century, consensus is that Loreto's first church was of "typical mission construction," in no way different from other standard adobe churches erected speedily and simply on the frontier. Vernon, *Las Misiones Antiguas*, p. 14.

110. ARSI Mex. 17 (Salvaterra to Ugarte, 9 July 1699), fol. 607.

111. The first permanent church at Loreto Conchó was fifty-five by seventeen feet as compared to Italy's thirty-one by thirteen feet—close, but not nearly as close as Chau-

Salvatierra's most slipshod Holy House copy was not the result of carelessness or exhaustion. Like its predecessors, it had been preplanned. In 1697, when Salvatierra was given permission to go to California, a mission post that he had long desired, his friend and Jesuit colleague Juan Bautista Zappa wrote to him to urge him "not to forget to build there a saintly house to the Holy Lady of Loreto."[112] Friends of long standing, Zappa and Salvatierra had an informal agreement to build *many* Holy Houses of Loreto in Mexico.[113] Salvatierra responded to his friend's urging when he arrived at the remote outpost of Loreto Conchó in western California.[114] He wrote to the mainland requesting carpenters and supplies but decided not to wait for their arrival.[115] After a few months of using a tent on the beach as a rudimentary chapel, Salvatierra built a more permanent space for the California mission's church accoutrements. He wrote enthusiastically about this new shelter to another Jesuit friend, Juan de Ugarte: "Within the fort we built the Holy House of the blessed Virgin and the House of Loreto."[116]

Salvatierra's letter to Ugarte did not lament the lack of precision in the Loreto Conchó version of the Holy House, nor did it outline a plan for upgrade or compare it detrimentally against his own previous replicas. In fact, Salvatierra's matter-of-fact use of the tag "House of Loreto" to elevate his California mission site's first chapel was not unusual. It resembles the report of Pedro Marbán, first Jesuit superior at Loreto Moxos, the oldest

---

monot's replica, nor reflective of the dimensions made explicit on Loreto's blueprints. Jackson, *Missions and the Frontiers of Spanish America*, p. 195.

112. Ibid., p. 164.

113. Juan Bautista Zappa, also a Jesuit from Italy, was a longstanding friend of Salvatierra's from their early shared training back in Europe. Alongside Salvatierra, he distributed prints of the Madonna of Loreto and erected Holy House replicas in Mexico. The men appear to have mutually resolved to diffuse their homeland Madonna together, demonstrating historian J. Michelle Molina's observation that missionary practice derived primarily from personal relationships. Molina, *To Overcome Oneself*, pp. 104–30.

114. The casual placement of Lauretan architecture by Salvatierra contrasts with his deliberate choice of name for the Baja California site. Salvatierra named the Baja California mission "Loreto" because he associated the Virgin of Loreto with protecting the party from shipwreck; this naming decision is described further in chapter 7.

115. Salvatierra did petition the mainland, the Audiencia de Guadalajara in Mexico, in 1699 to request "an officially appointed mason, competent to build the Holy House of Loreto." This suggests that the final Holy House in Baja California was not exactly up to snuff with what he had envisioned. His request to the Audiencia was eventually turned down because of the extensive travel and cost it would require. Crosby, *Antigua California*, p. 267.

116. Salvatierra to Juan de Ugarte, 3 July 1698, as quoted by Crosby, *Antigua California*, pp. 34, 434n20.

and longest-lived Catholic community in the Amazon region by the mid-1700s. In its early days, in 1690, Marbán described Moxos Indians bursting out of the mission's first provisional chapel. He had to hold separate masses for men and women, and still the tiny church could not hold the overflow. Marbán spoke of the need for erecting a bigger church. Notably, in his letter regarding the matter, he did not use "iglesia," the common Spanish word for church, to describe Loreto's main building. He wrote instead of Loreto Moxos's "casa a la Santissima Virgen," or *house* dedicated to the Virgin Mary.[117] This alludes explicitly to the Madonna of Loreto's mythic *Santa Casa*, but as was the case with Salvatierra's rudimentary chapel at Loreto Conchó, the Loreto Moxos building bore no resemblance to the European prototype. Evidently, as was the case with so many Holy House copies in Europe, similarity was not the most important goal in reproducing the structure abroad.

Neither was placement. Here again, Salvatierra's physically different, but nominally connected, California Holy House is startling in its departure from expectation. The "casa di Loreto" in Baja California was neither an exact copy, nor was it carefully situated on previously holy ground. In fact, Salvatierra's positioning of Loreto's latest Holy House offshoot was hasty and reactive. He did not place it in a space that was previously sacred to the local Monquí. Previously, during his mission postings, Salvatierra had chosen to honor spots that were marked by an obvious divine or natural sign.[118] But in the case of Loreto Conchó, the selected construction site for the mission was the result of a bet with the expedition's ship captain, Juan Antonio Romero.[119] The two had drawn straws about where the party should land. Salvatierra had favored the site of a previous attempted mission, San Bruno; Romero had favored the Bay of San Dionisio. Although Salvatierra had prayed to the Madonna of Loreto to sway

117. ARSI Peru 21 (Marbán to P. Provincial F. Xavier, 4 June 1690), fols. 13–13v.

118. Salvatierra's Jesuit colleague Eusebio Kino was also attentive to signs. In late 1683, when a tree fell on an unfortunate squirrel and smashed the squirrel's body into the shape of a cross, Kino called the spot "Santissima Cruz" (the Most Holy Cross), and it was considered a miracle: "El paraxe y passo de la Ssa. Cruz tomo esta denominacion de lo que ayer milagrosamente sucedio al tiempo que derribaron un cordon seco pues al tiempo que cayo al suelo se aplasto una ardilla y formo con dicho tronco una cruz como si a proposito y con las manos se huvien echo y se puso y venero y quedo de aquella manera." / "The stop and road of the Most Holy Cross took that name from what miraculously happened yesterday when they were cutting down a dry tree which at the time that it fell to the ground, crushed a squirrel in such a form that its body was in the shape of a cross as if its hands had formed it purposefully and it was placed and venerated and stayed in that manner." ARSI Mex. 17 (1683 *Relación* of the second Jesuit expedition to California), fol. 521.

119. Crosby, *Antigua California*, pp. 25–26; 54–56.

the drawing in his favor, he lost to Romero. Perhaps Salvatierra construed the loss of the bet as the Madonna of Loreto's intervention to select for herself a new mooring. Nonetheless, it is clear that when the Jesuit constructed his replica, he did not do so on ground that he anticipated or already found to be sacred.

In contrast to Salvatierra, twentieth-century scholars of religion have privileged sacrality of place. They have repeatedly flagged *where* one places a sacred object as being a critical factor for bestowing the object with "numinous essence."[120] Mary's most celebrated entrenchments in the New World are generally understood to have succeeded in part because they reinforced preexisting perceptions of the landscape itself as holy. In Mexico, for instance, the Virgin of Guadalupe surfaced in a way that indelibly linked her to sacred terrain. She appeared to the Indian Juan Diego on the hill of Tepeyac, the former site of a temple to the Mexica mother goddess, Tonantzín.[121] The connection between place and spirituality preceded and outlasted Christianity's arrival.[122] This is a characteristic of religion that has been noted in Europe as much as it has in frontier zones in the Americas.[123] But in Loreto Conchó in 1697, Salvatierra seems to have cared as little for placement as he did for exactitude.

This is not to say that Salvatierra did not make an effort to sacralize, or to use the local surroundings to ground and sanctify the building. The Jesuit did draw from the alien landscape to construct this first mission

120. Salles-Reese, *From Viracocha to the Virgin of Copacabana*, pp. 5, 17. Interpretations like these draw on Mircea Eliade's concept of hierophany, when the divine manifests itself in space (*Sacred and the Profane*). For instance, Verónica Salles-Reese argues that Lake Titicaca in Peru has inherent sacred power that has transferred across occupying cultures and transitioning settlements. In contrast, Jonathan Z. Smith has criticized the centrality of "poles (or world trees, or mountains)" or fixed, holy landscape in religious analyses; he reinterprets an Australian ancestral myth to show how it hinges on moving itineraries, transformation, and memorializing instead. He builds on Victor Turner's theory that it is human ritual that infuses a space with the divine. For good overviews of current conversations about religious space: Kilde, "Approaching Religious Space"; J. Z. Smith, *To Take Place*, p. 10.

121. The association between the new Mary and the ancient Tonantzín existed from the earliest moments of the Guadalupan devotion. Leon-Portilla, *Tonantzin Guadalupe*.

122. On pre-Christian religious views of landscape and on continuities in Peru: Mills, "Naturalization of Andean Christianities." On Mexico, consider the enduring Nahua concept of "altepetl" (settlement or water-hill): López Austin, *Tamoanchan, Tlalocan*, pp. 218, 276. On the persistence of pre-Christian notions of sacred settings, see the discussion of Nahua cities as religious symbols in Carrasco, "City as Symbol in Aztec Thought."

123. On the topographical overlays of Christian and pre-Christian in medieval Spain: Christian, *Local Religion in Sixteenth-Century Spain*, and Christian, *Apparitions in Late Medieval and Renaissance Spain*.

church in a way that integrated it with its new setting. This was atypical for a man who had elsewhere erected replicas of imported or imitated European brick to denote Italy's Holy House of Loreto.[124] In contrast, Loreto Conchó's first permanent chapel was made entirely from *palo blancos* (*Lysiloma candida*), thirty-foot-high trees that grew in groves on the peninsula. Salvatierra described the outcome:

> On the eve of the Feast of the Nativity, Padre Piccolo consecrated the new cross and the church, both made of the wood of a white tree . . . which resembles that which on the mainland is called dragon's blood. This luxuriant and showy tree grows in great abundance in this valley. We have been able to build all structures within the fortification with these trees.[125]

The California setting and materials transformed the little mission. If it did not establish this "Loreto" as sacred, it did at least set it apart as something distinct, at once local and new.

Yet this adaptiveness, or responsiveness, to local sacred signifiers was minimal. Interestingly, once again, Salvatierra was not alone in his choice to not extensively adapt this Holy House for its new placement. Other Jesuits also treated Holy House copies differently from regular chapels that they worked hard to translate. For instance, in Canada, Salvatierra's Jesuit contemporary, Pierre Chaumonot, also had to find a place for a mission dedicated to Loreto in 1673. Like Salvatierra, Chaumonot was aware of Jesuit precedents in his particular frontier zone that he did not quite follow, because of a combination of personal choice and difficulties of application.

Chaumonot had begun his Canadian missionary career serving at Sainte-Marie-among-the-Huron. Sainte-Marie was the flagship mission for the Jesuits in Canada, established in 1639 on the shores of Georgian Bay, 750 miles to the northwest of Québec City. Founded at the zenith of Jesuit proselytizing to the Huron, it was intended to be permanent, though it lasted only ten years. Sainte-Marie was characterized by adaptiveness evident in its contrasting chapels. An early chapel was built for private use by Jesuits and French workers. In proper French style, this chapel had wooden floors and was unheated. But a second, later chapel was designed specifically for preaching to the newly Christianized Huron.

124. As noted previously, Salvatierra had built precise models of the Holy House in New Spain at the Jesuit College of San Gregorio in New Spain (1680), and in the Jesuit College of Guadalajara (1690s).

125. Salvatierra [1698] as quoted by Crosby, *Antigua California*, pp. 34, 434n20.

It was modified to make the converts feel comfortable. Modeled after a Huron longhouse, it had a dirt floor where the Huron could sit on the ground, and a large fireplace.[126] This welcoming chapel and the Jesuit mission were located in the Huron heartland, close to one of their major villages, Quieunonascaran.

But Chaumonot's 1673 Lorette mission and Holy House copy for the Huron differed from Sainte-Marie, distant as they were from Huron home territory. Lorette was situated on the outskirts of Québec City. Chaumonot intended for it to serve the 150 remaining survivors from the Sainte-Marie mission, which had been burned down in 1649 in the Huron-Iroquois conflagration.[127] The Holy House that Chaumonot erected there was a precise copy of the original at the Italian shrine. It showed no modifications for Huron preference. Its placement, like Salvatierra's at Loreto Conchó, was determined more by mission needs than by sensitivity to previous sacred landscape. Because the replica was to serve as the chapel for the mission village, it was positioned at the center of a square of Huron cabins. The cabins were built in traditional style but were neatly laid out in rows, after some shifting about to establish comfortable, orderly distance between them. In the standard pattern of Jesuit reductions or mission communities, the Jesuit planners insisted on geometric layout of housing as a way to establish the little chapel as a focal point for the community.[128]

It was serendipity that bestowed the Holy House of Lorette with an atmosphere of sacrality, not calculated Jesuit intention, planning, or situating. As with the Holy House of Loreto Conchó, *after* its construction, the natural surroundings were retroactively found to make the place special. The Jesuit Martin Bouvart noted during the construction of the Holy House of Lorette in Canada:

> After cutting down some large trees that block it, there will be a view of Québec. On that same side there is a beautiful river, with a stream of excellent water that forms a semi-circle around the village. Moreover, the elevation and evenness of the terrain, the purety of the air, the

126. Before the new Huron Christians attended this chapel, Jesuits would preach to them in their longhouses outside the walls of St. Marie: a gradation, to entice them into the chapel. It was a testament to Jesuit attachment to this intermediary chapel that the Jesuits buried the martyred Jesuit Jean de Brébeuf inside this chapel rather than in the French one. May 2005 visit to the reconstructed site and archaeological museum of Sainte-Marie among the Hurons, Huronia Historical Parks, Midland, Ontario, Canada.

127. Gérin, *La Seigneurie de Sillery et les Hurons de Lorette*, pp. 96–97.

128. The grid plan for Lorette resembles the configuration of Jesuit reductions in colonial Paraguay. "Plan of La Concepción Mission, Paraguay, in Late Colonial Times."

convenience of the fountains and other streams that are near, make this place one of the most agreeable in the entire country.[129]

Bouvart optimistically noted Lorette's situation, within view of Québec yet encircled by nature, betwixt and between. The meticulously crafted Lorette chapel and town took on a different light, placed in this liminal natural context. Bouvart quoted the reaction of Louis Taondechoren, one of the Huron catechists of the community, to the layout of the settlement:

> Remembering what he had heard about Loreto in Italy, [Taondechoren] added that all the cabins that he saw arranged around the chapel represented to him the grand temple that enclosed the Holy House of Loreto; and therefore [the Huron] should all consider the town as if it were a giant Cathedral, of which each cabin was a part.[130]

Although Chaumonot's Holy House used imported materials in its construction for precise representation of Loreto's parent relic, the natural surroundings gave it a power akin to Salvatierra's chapel far to the southwest, in Baja California. Both structures and sites named for Loreto were charged with significance not because of their authentic duplication of Italy's relic, nor because of their Jesuit instigators' attentiveness to previous sacred space or adaptation to local needs. Instead, what activated

129. "Ainsi dès le commencement de l'année 1673, les Hurons ayant apris les terres qu'on leur présentait, ou plutôt les ayant choisies eux-mêmes, on détermina où l'on placerait la chapelle et le village; on avait d'abord fait choix d'un grand platon qui est au delà du ruisseau où nos sauvages se fournissent d'eau, et on y avait fait abattre 30 arpents de bois, arborer une grande croix au milieu et bâti une maison de planches pour les ouvriers et pour mettre les matériaux à couvert, mais au printemps, apres la fonte des neiges, comme on s'aperçut que ce platon est d'un trop difficile accès à cause de la profondeur des fossés qui l'entourment, on choisit tout proche du côté de l'orient une autre plate forme beaucoup plus commode et beaucoup plus belle, d'où l'on aura la vue de Québec après qu'on aura abattu quelques grands arbres qui l'empêchent. Il y a de ce même côté une rivière assez belle, où se jette un ruisseau d'une eau excellente après avoir fait une espèce de demi-lune autour du village. D'ailleurs, l'élévation et l'egalité du terrain, la pureté de l'air, la commodité des fontaines et des autres ruisseaux qui sont proches, en rendent le séjour un des plus agréables de tout le pays." ASJCF no. 324 (1675 *Rélation du Père Martin Bouvart, S.J.*), fols. 7–8. Also: "Localization de la chapelle" (Corporation de la Chapelle Notre-Dame-de-Lorette et Ministère des Affaires culturelles du Québec), on-site display at the Église de l'Ancienne-Lorette, Loretteville, Québec, visited in June 2006.

130. "Entre les autres choses qu'il dit, ayant rapporté ce qu'il avait entendu de la Lorette d'Italie, il ajouta que toutes les cabanes qu'il voyait disposées autour de la chapelle, lui représentaient le grand temple qui renferme la sacrée maison de Lorette; qu'ainsi ils devaient tous considerer leur bourg comme une grande Eglise dont chaque cabane faisait autant de différentes parties." ASJCF no. 324 (1675 *Rélation du Père Martin Bouvart, S.J.*), fols. 8–9.

and empowered these very different and distant Holy House copies was their insertion into a new space. Their relatively unaltered *surfacing* somewhere new—their clumsy, but not thoughtless, intrusion in foreign landscapes—seems, oddly, to be what infused them with holy presence. They did not have to conform to blueprint, to precedent, or to setting. They simply had to evoke Loreto *in a new place*.[131]

The Jesuits were only one subset of Catholic builders and copyists in the seventeenth century, and likewise, the Holy House of Loreto itself needs to be framed in broader company. The features that surrounded its portability were remarkable but not unique. They can be observed in play in the construction of ordinary church buildings, in the Amazon missions of the Jesuits, for instance. There, in 1713, only thirty years after they broke ground for the "casa a la santissima Virgen" in Loreto Moxos, the Jesuits and Moxos Indians had completed wooden church-houses in fifteen of their sixteen mission towns.[132] They engaged in this work at the same time as they struggled to transplant failed and flooded settlements. In the Amazon basin, floods, raids, disease, agricultural mismanagement, or tribal conflicts led to residents abandoning settlements and attempting to join, or start, other ones.[133] The one constant in this capricious environment in the early 1700s appears to have been building churches. Every single time they relocated, the Moxos converts dutifully raised a new house dedicated to Mary, with little attention to blueprint or to previous sacrality of the landscape, but with much focus on the spirit of multiplication and resetting.

This broader impulse to participate in proliferation, to be part of new take-offs and landings, is part of what allowed the Holy House of Loreto and Catholicism at large to move. Copyists paid tribute to the relic's mobility through their alterations and fresh moorings. The *Santa Casa*'s transplantations and reappearances elsewhere, its very refractions, were part of its power. In each of its myriad offshoots, as in its original format, the Holy House of Loreto thrived on being touched, carried, and spread. The variety and extent of Loreto's Holy Houses in Europe and overseas suggest that there was more room for diversity and movement within

131. On the Huron mission's final anchorage at Jeune-Lorette, located near the sacred waterfall of Kabir Kouba: Vélez, "Les voyages outre-mer d'un nom," pp. 138–43.

132. ARSI Peru 21 (1713 *Relación de los Missiones de los Moxos*), fols. 175–79. The Moxos churches call to mind Tweed's analysis of religious space as "dwelling" or "home-making." Tweed, *Crossing and Dwelling*, pp. 103–11.

133. Vélez, "A South American Case Study: The Missions of Loreto Moxos," pp. 155–57 in "Catholic Missions to the Americas."

seventeenth-century Catholicism than is usually acknowledged. Furthermore, even within the orderly ranks of the Jesuits, the creation and construction of these houses was a little bit out of control. When reviewing the many hands involved in building these reliquaries, and the many modified forms they produced, one is left with an overwhelming sense of the tail wagging the Catholic dog. It was evidently not the *mind* of high church administrators or trained missionaries that fueled the spread of the Catholic religion. It was rather the *mood* that the elite shared with thousands of laypeople and new converts that spurred Loreto's continued flights: a mood for hard copy.

CHAPTER SIX

Anonymous Renovators of Icons

IN THE EARLY eighteenth century, a carved image stood in for the Virgin of Loreto at a church nearly six thousand miles across the Atlantic Ocean from her Italian shrine. The "large wooden statue of Our Lady" graced an altar at the first Jesuit mission among the Moxos Indians in the Spanish Viceroyalty of Peru (figure 6.1).[1] There was precious little to associate this three-dimensional Marian representation in the Moxos region with the dark, crowned statue back at the Loreto sanctuary (figure 6.2).[2] Closer to home, a more well-known, older piece of artwork also lacked clear attributes to associate it with the statue at Loreto. Around 1605 the Italian artist Michelangelo Merisi da Caravaggio (1573–1610) painted an image of the Virgin of Loreto for display in a chapel dedicated to her, the Cavalletti

1. "En el Altar mayor esta colocada una Ymagen grande de Bulto de Nra. Señora como Patrona y Tutelar de aquella Reduccion." / "On the main altar there is a large wooden statue of Our Lady as Patroness and Protector of this Reduction." ARSI Peru 21 (1696 "Relación de la Mision apostólica de los Moxos"), fols. 40v–41. There is no photograph of the Moxos mission statue of the Madonna of Loreto, but it is likely that it resembled the generic wooden statue in figure 6.1.

2. Much was done to connect the three-dimensional figure to Mary in general, however. The Jesuits placed a paired statue of the baby Jesus in a niche alongside so viewers might ponder Mary in her role as mother. At a side altar, they hung a painted canvas mural of Mary, Joseph, and Jesus to establish Mary as a part of the Holy Family. Every Saturday in front of her statue, the Jesuits sang a mass "to the most Holy Virgin," and the Moxos Indians recited a prayer about Mary's Immaculate Conception. ARSI Peru 21 (1696 "Relación de la Mision apostólica de los Moxos"), fols. 40v–41.

FIGURE 6.1. Typical Madonna statue used for Jesuit field mission (late 1600s). Photo: Dr. Severno Guardano, reproduced from Venegas, *Juan María de Salvatierra* (Cleveland, OH: 1929).

Chapel of Rome's Church of Sant'Agostino (figure 6.3).[3] Labeled simply "Madonna of the Pilgrims," this likeness of the Virgin of Loreto is white-skinned and dark-haired, an Italianate beauty. She stands at the thresh-

3. The lack of attributes has led to confusion in the naming of the painting. Today it is most often referred to as "Madonna dei Pellegrini" or "Madonna of the Pilgrims," though some still identify it as "Madonna di Loreto detta Madonna dei Pellegrini" or "The Madonna of Loreto called the Madonna of the Pilgrims." The painting was commissioned as an altarpiece for the chapel donated by the Bolognese Ermete Cavalletti (d. 1602), a leading

FIGURE 6.2. Wooden statue of Madonna of Loreto, currently inside the basilica of the Santa Casa of Loreto. Photo reproduced by permission of Alinari/Art Resource, NY.

old of a house, looking down at pilgrims who kneel at her feet while she carefully balances a well-fed, blond, and naked baby Jesus. Caravaggio's representation depicts Mary as "warmly human . . . a housewife,

---

member of one of Rome's pilgrimage-focused sodalities, the Confraternity of Santa Trinità dei Pellegrini. Ammannato, "Michelangelo Merisi Da Caravaggio"; Langdon, *Caravaggio: A Life*, p. 285.

FIGURE 6.3. *Madonna dei Pelligrini* (c. 1603–5). Painting by Caravaggio. Photo reproduced by permission of Scala/Art Resource, NY.

welcoming the pilgrims in a dark Roman *vicolo*."[4] But like the distant statue on the American frontier, Caravaggio's Madonna was white, not matching the dark shade of Loreto's miracle-working statue; it did not include features to explicitly identify it with Loreto; and it was composed locally instead of being exported directly from Loreto.

Scholars tend to separate imagery of the Americas from that of Europe, obscuring such parallels. Here, the iconography of Loreto is broadly defined to include all imagery associated with the Madonna of Loreto, across oceanic divides. The Italian shrine looms large in this assemblage because it originated the devotion and harbored some of its oldest art. But it did not direct the vast and quickly growing collection. Quite to the contrary, the shrine modified its art to follow external trends.

Most of these trends were not specific to Loreto. They involved generic images of Mary circulating around Europe and the wider world. Changes to Loreto's shrine image frequently involved making adjustments to the Virgin of Loreto so that she would fit a certain known Marian type. Like Caravaggio, the artists involved in this process sometimes made small but significant changes, almost by way of signature. If one is attuned to these subtle personalizations, the remarkable mutability of Catholic devotional art suddenly comes to light. There was a lively and ongoing articulation of difference underneath the superficial homogeneity of Catholic representations of Mary in the early modern period. Within this corpus, the Virgin of Loreto's image was never static. It coalesced slowly around myriad and diverse contributions of Catholic artists, few of them named and fewer still imagining themselves as revolutionaries.

Beneath the veneer of sameness and convention, images of Loreto were being thoughtfully edited by diverse artists. Art historian Maya Stanfield-Mazzi finds this sort of "*collective* envisioning of the Christian divine" happening in the South American Andes in the seventeenth century.[5] She highlights how colonial Catholic artwork in that zone of encounter showed a "bicultural resonance" between Spanish and Andean nascent Christians, an overlap of aesthetics that prevents clear classification of Andean artwork as either exclusively Spanish or "uniquely [pre-Christian] Andean invention."[6] Loreto's iconography provides examples that extend

4. Langdon, *Caravaggio: A Life*, p. 287. It is actually the dirty-soled feet of the pilgrims, painted large and in the foreground, that have attracted the most scholarly interest in this work. The feet call attention to the long journey of the disheveled man and the old woman who beseech Mary, who is also barefoot.

5. Stanfield-Mazzi, *Object and Apparition*, p. 97. Emphasis added.

6. Ibid., pp. 113, 140.

Stanfield-Mazzi's field of collaborative artistic revisionism from overseas Catholic frontiers back to Europe. In these culturally disparate regions, Catholics were nonetheless making similar choices about how to render or tweak the Madonna of Loreto. Local circumstances obviously affected and informed alterations, as did the availability of particular printed forms. But the biggest precipitant of change for the Virgin of Loreto's image was a shared awareness of a bigger outside stream of Marian representation. Even the Loreto sanctuary itself gestured toward these external currents. The Madonna of Loreto was most often adapted in the seventeenth century not because of a consciousness of the *right here*, of forces close by, but rather because of a sense of the *out there*, the broader forces at play in the wider world. To stay relevant to the *world*, to signify beyond her local anchorages, she had to be changed.

This chapter begins by examining how two peripheral artworks of the Virgin of Loreto, the eighteenth-century wooden statue from the Moxos missions and the seventeenth-century Roman painting by Caravaggio, each tapped into outside streams of Marian art. In the next section the same impetus for transformation is observed for the original icon of the Madonna of Loreto at the Italian shrine. Updates to this icon were spurred by an awareness of the world outside Loreto. The chapter concludes with a return to the frontier, to Canada, to consider some significantly named but lesser known Huron women converts who contributed to Mary's global public image. Overall, these case studies of modifications to the Virgin of Loreto reflect what mattered to people on both sides of the Atlantic about Mary at this time: she was alien, yet she was accessible; she moved, and she could also be moved.

Anchoring Ideal: A Moxos Mission Statue and Caravaggio Painting

The abovementioned Moxos statue (figure 6.1) and Caravaggio painting (figure 6.3) did not aim to perfectly imitate the miraculous black Madonna statue that was the focus of so many European pilgrimages to Loreto (figure 6.2). Furthermore, neither artwork appears to have elicited anxiety about provenance. It went unremarked that the prosaic wooden statue at the Jesuit mission of Loreto Moxos was not imported from Italy's Loreto.[7] The site's remoteness must have made such imports prohibitively

7. The Moxos Jesuits would have reported such special origins. Whenever artwork was a costly import, this was duly noted. In 1637, for instance, at the Jesuit College of Trujillo in

expensive. The Moxos missions lay nearly two thousand miles west of the viceregal capital of Lima. It took Jesuits over a year, one way, to make the arduous overland trek there.[8] Nor did the statue come from closer at hand, from a prestigious local urban center such as Cuzco.[9] It may have been carved by Inka or Moxos artists, or made in a local Jesuit-Moxos workshop, but there is no indication of the exciting religious hybridity that usually accompanied such collaboration: the statue did not fuse the unique attributes of Loreto's Madonna with pre-Christian indigenous aesthetics.[10]

Peru, António Vázquez excitedly wrote of the installation of "a statue of the Virgin of Loreto that was brought from Lima and cost four hundred pesos." There were no such entries for the early Marian image at Loreto Moxos. ARSI Peru 15 (1637 Letra Anua), fol. 107v.

8. Travel was so grueling that one Jesuit layman, José del Castillo, died in 1688 trying to find an easier connecting route between the Moxos missions and Cochabamba, the closest Spanish settlement to the north. To the east, the settlement of Santa Cruz was only relatively closer, three hundred miles distant. Loreto Moxos was situated six hundred leagues or eighteen hundred miles to the east of Lima, and one hundred leagues or three hundred miles to the west of Santa Cruz. In 1717–18, the journey from Lima took an average of fourteen months to make. On Castillo's death: Gutiérrez and Gutiérrez, "Territorio, Urbanismo y Arquitectura en Moxos y Chiquitos," p. 345. On the distance to Santa Cruz: ARSI Peru 21 (1713 *Relación de los Missiones de los Moxos*), fol. 175; Block, *Mission Culture on the Upper Amazon*, pp. 110–11.

9. It was not until the mid-1700s that the Jesuits established a satisfactory metropolitan source for religious art: Cuzco. While the Andean city was farther away than Santa Cruz, the former capital of the Inka empire was fast emerging as a center for colonial art. By the 1760s, Jesuits in the Moxos were sending to Cuzco for artwork for their churches: a 1767 inventory of San Ignacio de Moxos reported an order to Cuzco for a painting of the Resurrection. Gutiérrez and Gutiérrez, "Territorio, Urbanismo y Arquitectura en Moxos y Chiquitos," p. 306.

10. The statue of Mary was placed in Loreto Moxos decades before the establishment of a trade route to Cuzco. It therefore seems likely that it was actually made within the Moxos missions. The 1696 *Relación* reported some locally carved adornment in the Loreto reduction church produced by a workshop of "young men" led by Jesuit lay brother and woodworker Manuel Carrillo. Carrillo was inspired to start a workshop by the earlier efforts of the hapless José del Castillo, the fellow lay brother who had trained groups of Moxos Indians in carpentry before he met his death looking for a shortcut to Cochabamba (see note 8 above). In the early 1700s, Manuel Carillo turned the Moxos craftsmen toward constructing churches and religious art for the new missions of Trinidad, San Javier and San Ignacio. This art was not limited to wood. At the mission of Santa Rosa, a side chapel dedicated to Loreto was decorated with a mural series depicting the life of Santa Rosa. By the mid-eighteenth century, religious crafts fashioned in the Moxos, including rosaries made from bone, were an essential part of the profitable commerce between the Jesuit missions and Peruvian urban centers. On the hybrid religious iconography of the seventeenth-century Cuzco School of indigenous artists: *Virgin, Saints and Angels*; Spitta, *Between Two Waters*, pp. 78–84. On hybridity in Peruvian colonial Catholic artwork in general: Damian, *Virgin of the Andes*; Bailey, *Art on the Jesuit Missions in Asia and Latin America*. On local craftsmanship in the Moxos: ARSI Peru 21 (1696 "Relación de la Mision apostólica de los

But surprisingly and counterintuitively, conventional images like the one at Loreto Moxos were flashpoints for Catholic iconographical change. They were popular and accessible, two features that eased the reception of the Madonna of Loreto outside of her sanctuary, in Europe just as much as on the American frontiers. By virtue of its famous artist, *Madonna dei Pellegrini* cannot be deemed strictly conventional. But Caravaggio's Roman altarpiece was as popular and accessible in tone as the Moxos statue, to the point of divergence from the art displayed at the original Loreto shrine. Between 1604 and 1605, during his commission for the Cavalletti chapel, Caravaggio had made a pilgrimage to the Marian sanctuary. Yet curiously, his painting does not evoke the miraculous black statue of Mary, clad in a Dalmatica robe and set deep inside Loreto's Holy House. Instead, he painted a white Madonna dressed in red and blue, poised on the threshold of her home. This rendition also departs from the traditional two-dimensional iconography associated with the Virgin of Loreto that Caravaggio would have seen at the shrine. Paintings of the Madonna of Loreto in the fifteenth and sixteenth centuries showed her underneath a canopy surrounded by angels; angels are absent from Caravaggio's piece. In the seventeenth century, the Virgin of Loreto was also featured crowned as the Queen of Heaven, sitting atop a simple house held up by angels, holding the baby Jesus.[11] That was the official image adopted by bishops for the Loreto shrine seal (figure 3.1): Mary aloft, set divinely apart. But Caravaggio chose to render her crownless and terrestrial. This prominent Italian artist and Catholics at the Jesuit mission of Loreto Moxos alike preferred a Madonna of Loreto who was grounded, close enough to touch, and primed to move.

Changes to frontier statues of Mary are not usually explained as a matter of artistic preference, as is done for the European output of Caravaggio. Instead they are chalked up solely to convenience, market forces, or practical instructional goals. For instance, in the mid-1600s, the Jesuit Juan Bautista Zappa procured rote prints and medallions of the Virgin of Loreto en masse to distribute to Catholics in Mexico City.[12] Jesuits

---

Moxos"), fols. 40v–41; Gutiérrez and Gutiérrez, "Territorio, Urbanismo y Arquitectura en Moxos y Chiquitos," pp. 306, 310, 332, 352–53.

11. Belán, *Madonna*, pp. 170; 152. Perhaps because of the iconographical differences between Caravaggio's *Madonna* for the Church of Sant'Agostino and the statue of Loreto, Belán suggests that Caravaggio's painting shows Mary's mother, St. Anne, instead of the Lauretan Mary. But the St. Anne identification seems a stretch: Caravaggio's female figure holds a male baby, connoting Mary and Jesus rather than Anne and Mary.

12. Molina, "Visions of God, Visions of Empire," p. 186n15.

abroad clearly made the most of this cheap and readily available supply that referred liberally to a Mary larger than Loreto. But this tide of mass-produced, easily procured Catholic propaganda was as much the background in Europe as in the Americas.[13] Similarly, it has been argued that less detailed, more generic imagery of Mary made it easier to teach potential converts on the frontiers about Mary's role in the Catholic faith. Yet distilling religious complexity was the missionary's challenge and daily bread.[14] Even the simplest of Catholic symbols, such as the crucifix, could be difficult to unpack for newcomers to the faith, and could result in misunderstanding.[15] Therefore simplicity alone does not provide the most compelling explanation for why the anonymous artists at the Jesuit mission of Loreto Moxos would have chosen fewer identifying attributes to depict the Madonna of Loreto.

It is more likely that the Moxos artists, like Caravaggio, were not merely responding to *local* conditions and patrons, but were also influenced by broader, *distant* currents of representation of Mary. Some of these currents were tied to pilgrim experience, not to shrine iconography. Pilgrims to Loreto were encouraged to imagine Mary in her most human light, as a mother residing in the small house that one could visit at Loreto. Caravaggio took this a step further, rendering the Madonna of Loreto in a shadowed alleyway, barefoot and quietly casual, greeting *destitute* pilgrims.[16] For centuries, Mary had been presented as champion of the poor and downtrodden, and Caravaggio was not alone in attributing advocacy for

13. On affordable, standardized paper prayer cards in early modern Italy, the Netherlands, and Germany: Freedberg, *Power of Images*, pp. 115–16, 126.

14. In 1720, the Jesuit missionary Jaime Bravo attempted to introduce the Guaicuro Indians of California to Mary for the first time by erecting an enormous wooden cross and displaying a detailed oil painting of the Aragonese Madonna of Pilar on a pedestal. Although Bravo reported that the Guaicuro asked about the figure of St. James in a fighting posture in the foreground of the painting, he reported that "the whole picture was explained to them" and deemed the encounter a success. Bravo as quoted by Dunne, *Black Robes in Lower California*, p. 185.

15. In 1683 in the early days of the California mission, Jesuits had placed a statue of the crucified Christ in an early mission church. "When the Indians saw it they were terrified of it," the Jesuits reported. "They almost did not dare to talk with us or with each other except little and with great silences, asking who he was and who had killed him, and if this had been done by some cruel enemy of ours, and their caution [toward us] was great, judging that we treated people in this way." ARSI Mex. 17 (1683 *Relación* of the second Jesuit expedition to California), fol. 517.

16. Art historian Helen Langdon comments about Caravaggio's painting that "it was entirely new for the humble poor to appear centre stage, and the people [of Rome] 'made a great fuss over it.'" Langdon, *Caravaggio: A Life*, p. 289.

the poor to Mary in her Lauretan form.[17] In the early seventeenth century, a Camaldolese monk, Luigi Lazzari, proclaimed that Mary of Loreto threw open her doors to all, especially the dirty-soled. He observed that "everyone, everyone, rich, and poor, nobles, and plebes, wise, & ignorant, Princes, and Vassals, the righteous and the sinners, all come to be received inside the Holy House [of Loreto], even the Robbers, the Assassins in the street, the Hebrews, [and] the Turks should they commend themselves to the Patroness of Loreto."[18] Caravaggio expressed this open-armed outreach on canvas, with pilgrims sketched in. Catholics at the Moxos mission expressed it in wood, with themselves as kneeling pilgrims.

It is important to note that there were many streams of Marian imagery to choose from in the seventeenth and eighteenth centuries, and Mary as intercessor for the poor was only one of them. Caravaggio and the Moxos artists chose to overlook a prominent competing representation of Mary as disciplined. This alternative is well illustrated in a work by a contemporary of Caravaggio's, Rembrandt, who painted in the largely Calvinist society of the Netherlands. In his 1645 *The Holy Family with Angels*, Rembrandt shows Mary sitting quietly inside a modest house with a wood-beam ceiling (figure 6.4). She holds an open book on her lap. The baby Jesus sleeps inside a wicker cradle in the corner, minded by an angel who hovers above him. Joseph is the only active figure. He fills in the background, chopping wood industriously in the rear of the house.[19] Rembrandt's scene is strikingly different from Caravaggio's *Madonna dei*

17. Luigi Gambero describes two dimensions of Mary's association with poverty in the Middle Ages: she was taken as an exemplar for how to live in poverty during the Cluniac reforms of monastic life in the tenth century, and more commonly, she was put forward as the ultimate intercessor for the "most wretched," as in the twelfth-century writings of Philip of Harveng. Gambero, *Mary in the Middle Ages*, pp. 88–94, 177–84.

18. "Tutti, tutti, ricchi, e poveri, nobili, e plebei, savii, & ignoranti, Prencipi, e Vassalli, giusti e peccatori tutti vengono ricevuti dentro la Santa Casa, insino i Ladri, gl'Assassini di strada, gl'Hebrei, i Turchi se si raccomandano alla Padrona di Loreto." Lazzari, *Dodici Sermoni sopra la S. Casa di Loreto*, p. 131.

19. Belán, *Madonna*, fig. 130, p. 156. To be fair, not all seventeenth-century paintings of Holy Family domesticity were this predictable. See the wonderful *The Holy Family of Our Lady of Studzianna*, reproduced in Boyer, *Cult of the Virgin*, pp. 27–28. In that painting, Mary, Joseph, and Jesus are depicted as a wealthy family sitting down to dinner. All of them are dark-skinned, with Joseph darkest of all. Joseph tends to the child Jesus, who looks to be five or six. He holds a cup for the child, while Mary sits off to the side by herself, holding a pear. The painting was a gift from the Hapsburg emperor Ferdinand II to his daughter the queen of Poland. It was declared "miraculous" in 1671, and the clothing on each of its three figures is decorated with pearls. Today the painting still draws pilgrims to the Oratory of San Felipe Neri in Studzianna, Poland.

FIGURE 6.4. *Holy Family with Angels* (c. 1645). Painting by Rembrandt. Photo reproduced by permission of Scala/Art Resource, NY.

Pellegrini.[20] Rembrandt's Mary is seated indoors; Caravaggio's is standing at the door. Caravaggio's Madonna does not exude the domesticity or subservience associated so strongly with Mary elsewhere.

20. Depictions of the Holy Family such as Rembrandt's did not lead inexorably to women being constrained in stereotypical wifely or maternal roles. On how Holy Family devotions may have led to the empowerment of women: Villaseñor Black, "St. Anne Imagery and Maternal Archetypes in Spain and Mexico"; Geary, *Women at the Beginning*, pp. 61, 77.

Today's scholars have favored Rembrandt when characterizing the early modern period. Historian Gabriella Zarri has noted that depictions of Mary shifted between 1450 and 1650, with the Catholic Church increasingly putting Mary forward as a behavioral role model for women. Zarri highlights how Catholic women were steered away from prophecy, a religious sphere where they had previously been central. They were pushed instead toward "discipline."[21] Zarri's use of "discipline" is not as draconian as Michel Foucault's sense of the word in *Discipline and Punish* (1975). She refers to self-imposed monastic rigor, not external authority. But her term best connotes the increased restraint that many scholars have observed in Mary as she was rendered in the early modern era.[22] Maureen Flynn sees the Council of Trent as accelerating this process of subduing the Virgin Mary by regulating in favor of images of her that would "avoid presenting Mary in a role that would detract from the glory and authority of her son."[23] By the seventeenth century, Mary appeared across Europe as a "domestic deity," part of a reformulated patriarchal trinity of Joseph, Mary, and Jesus.[24]

But in the seventeenth and eighteenth centuries, the Italian Caravaggio and unnamed sculptors in the Moxos missions discarded this viable undercurrent when they represented the Madonna of Loreto. This

21. Zarri, "From Prophecy to Discipline, 1450–1650." Zarri attributes this "disciplining of religious behavior" to the reorganization policies of the Council of Trent and sees it peaking in the harsh asceticism of seventeenth-century nuns. Karen-Edis Barzman extends the Catholic Church's female-disciplining trend all the way into the nineteenth century in her article "Sacred Imagery and the Religious Lives of Women, 1650–1850."

22. Donna Spivey Ellington comments on Mary's remoteness in sixteenth-century sermons. In the sermons that Ellington surveyed in *From Sacred Body to Angelic Soul*, Mary is presented as "more distanced from the action, more spiritualized, more passive, and much more silent" than previously. Beth Kreitzer notes a similar passivity and restriction of Mary in Lutheran sermons, writing that by the end of the sixteenth century, "Gone was the powerful, merciful, mother Queen of Heaven, and in her place remained only the humble, chaste, obedient girl." On Mary in Catholic sermons: Ellington, *From Sacred Body to Angelic Soul*, p. 263. On Mary in Lutheran sermons: Kreitzer, *Reforming Mary*, p. 141. See, too, William Christian's assessment that Mary became more "stately, queenlike and dignified" over time: Christian, *Apparitions in Late Medieval and Renaissance Spain*, p. 215.

23. Flynn, "Baroque Piety and Spanish Confraternities," p. 242. Flynn notes that the Council of Trent restricted images of Mary as the Mother of Mercy shielding humanity along with those of Mary breastfeeding the infant Christ because both kinds of images depicted Mary as nurturing and sovereign rather than suffering and secondary.

24. Grieco, "Models of Female Sanctity," p. 163. Grieco argues that this replaced a "matriarchal trinity" of St. Anne, St. Elizabeth, and the Virgin. Karin Tilmans agrees, putting the decline of the cult of St. Anne, Mary's mother and teacher, in the early sixteenth

is remarkable considering that the latent potential was certainly there to make Loreto's Virgin into a poster girl for disciplined domesticity: after all, Loreto claimed the *Santa Casa*, a trapping that equipped Mary well to play the role of Holy House Mother. The shrine itself leaned in this direction. By the 1600s, it acquired new devotional trappings that emphasized the Lauretan Madonna's domesticity. The "sante scudelle," or holy dishware, for example, were discovered in the walls of the Holy House in the 1550s and promoted as secondary relics.[25] Because these plates were believed to have been touched and used by Mary and Jesus, they were seen as relics in their own right. Yet Caravaggio did not paint them; sculptors in the Moxos missions did not incorporate them in their work. Instead, artists like them continued to make choices that pulled the full corpus of Loreto iconography away from the passivity attributed so firmly to Mary in other quarters.

The more generic, whitened Madonna of Loreto presented by Caravaggio, artists at the Jesuit missions, and some of their contemporaries stressed undisciplined movement instead. Caravaggio painted Mary, the holy paragon of motherhood, as a human woman on the edge of social decorum. She stands barely balanced and unshod, on the doorstep, as if she were about to step away from the relative safety of the stoop. She is unchaperoned and with no interface between herself and her leaning petitioners. Her unsettling boldness does not sit comfortably with early modern protocols of exemplary behavior for women. Likewise, the wooden statue at Loreto Moxos was designed for portability and was altered and shaped by movement.[26]

As with the origin myth of the arrival of Loreto's Holy House, multiple countervailing attitudes were layered in the iconography of Loreto's Madonna over time. The remainder of this chapter considers how Catholics

---

century, at precisely this moment of what Grieco calls the "'viricentric' reorganization of religion and society." Tilmans, "*Sancta Mater versus Sanctus Doctus?*," pp. 331–51; Grieco, "Models of Female Sanctity," p. 162.

25. ARSI Rom. 122, tom. I (Borghese, *Relation*, 1604), fols. 180–81v. Some of the sacred plates were sequestered beyond the chaotic market of pilgrims. Two of them went to the newly founded Jesuit college in Loreto for safekeeping. The Jesuits had not had these treasures for very long when, in 1573, a hapless novice stumbled and managed to break one: ARSI Rom. 51, tom. II, appendix (Mangioni), chapter 9.

26. On the portability of colonial statuary: *Collecting across Cultures*; and Roberts, *Transporting Visions*.

deliberately altered her representations in order to keep her relevant and popular with new audiences between the fifteenth and eighteenth centuries. Change was an essential part of her image. The next section below considers the Marian icon inside Loreto's *Santa Casa* is a case in point. It did not remain static over the centuries. This parent image of the Virgin underwent an even more dramatic metamorphosis than her Holy House reliquary, shifting from a Byzantine-style painting into a three-dimensional statue. Over time, she was lifted off her iconic canvas, raised to her feet, and darkened. These modifications ran counter to what has been presented above as the larger trend to discipline Mary. They were reinforced by Jesuit introductions of new, whitened images of Loreto in the Americas. The final section turns to Huron women christened with the name "Mary" and explores how their lived actions paralleled and reinforced the iconography of Mary as undisciplined. Caravaggio's painting captured the Madonna of Loreto in the early 1600s as hovering at the doorway, primed for action. These Huron converts in the 1700s stepped Mary completely off the doorsill. Because of such human renovators of art who largely went unnamed, devotees of Loreto had access to imagery of Mary as separate from her house, alien but accessible, and above all, mobile.

Actual Conventions: The Loreto Shrine's Updated Madonna

There are two major changes evident in Lauretan iconography between the fifteenth and eighteenth centuries: one to medium, and one to color. These adjustments were reflected in the most celebrated public face of the Madonna of Loreto, the miracle-working image at her shrine (figure 6.2). In Italy, first, the Madonna of Loreto became identified with a statue in standing posture instead of an icon. Second, her depictions shifted in terms of color. From the fourteenth century onward, she was illustrated as alternately black or white. The shrine image was updated in this period to coincide with other well-liked Marian representations. Loreto's iconographical flexibility therefore also reveals what early modern artists considered most appealing about Mary: her realistic human features (associated with her new medium), and her otherworldly, regally divine nature (associated with her varying colors). These changes were anonymously implemented and received as normal, not revolutionary. In Europe as in the Americas in this time period, Catholic art did not have to buck convention in order to be special. What seems to twenty-first-century viewers to be radical or novel was most often rooted in long-standing tradition: for instance, blackness often denoted antiquity. Conversely, what seems traditional or conservative to us could indicate significant change: whiteness could denote divine otherness. Amid these complexities of meaning produced by casual alterations or new settings, in all her forms, the Madonna of Loreto was consistently welcomed as accessible, foreign, and uncontained, moving beyond and separate from her Holy House.

The Madonna of Loreto was first rendered as a painting of Mary on a wooden panel. This original image at Italy's Loreto shrine was doubly prestigious. It was Byzantine in style, and it was attributed to St. Luke the Evangelist. Like other Byzantine representations of Mary, she was two-dimensional, half length (depicted from the waist up), and dark toned. She enjoyed the best artistic provenance possible for a Marian icon: St. Luke was one of the apostles who was believed to have actually seen Mary. Moreover, he had purportedly painted only a few images of her.[27] Lucan Madonnas such as the one in Loreto therefore carried associations of antiquity and respectability.

At some point in the late 1400s, however, this icon at Loreto's shrine was significantly altered. The change occurred at the end of the fifteenth century, coinciding with the construction of a new basilica at the Adriatic shrine.[28] Loreto's two-dimensional icon was replaced by a three-dimensional statue. She retained her association with St. Luke but lost her Byzantine veneer. Girolamo Angelitta, a city official of Recanati, calmly reported this in his compiled history of the sanctuary. Angelitta wrote first of the icon. Loreto had an "Image of the Blessed Virgin . . . a picture of her made by the hand of St. Luke the Evangelist." Twenty pages later,

27. In the Orthodox Greek branch of the Catholic Church, images attributed to St. Luke were highly revered, and there were burgeoning numbers of these "originals" over time. Michele Bacci estimates the number of icons Luke supposedly painted eventually added up to the mystical number of seventy or seventy-two, equivalent to the number of apostles after Christ's ascension. Lucia Chiavola Birnbaum reports a more modest thirty-four images attributed to St. Luke, most of them concentrated in Russia and Italy (eight of them in Rome). Bacci, "With the Paintbrush of the Evangelist Luke"; Birnbaum, *Black Madonnas*, p. 105.

28. There is some disagreement over the date of this substitution. Ronald Lightbown dates it to between 1489 and 1518. However, Floriano Grimaldi dates it much earlier, in the fourteenth century. Lightbown's dates seem most plausible given the lack of mention of a statue in fifteenth-century Lauretan documents. Also, the flurry of construction at the shrine in the late fifteenth century might have provided suitable occasion for a change: a new image would have graced an entirely new basilica. Lightbown, *Carlo Crivelli*, p. 41; Grimaldi, *Devozione e Committenza nelle Marche*, pp. 29–33.

he seamlessly shifted his description, and the Lucan attribution, to the statue: "Luke the Evangelist . . . with his hands was Sculptor of the wood statue, that is inside [the *Santa Casa*]."[29] Angelitta was matter-of-fact. He did not draw excessive attention to the change. There had been an icon; now there was a statue; St. Luke had a hand in both.

Angelitta's conflation of image, statue, and St. Luke was neither careless nor terribly original. In Loreto—as in Florence, Siena, Montserrat, Rocamadour, Oropa, Tindari, and hundreds of other Marian sites—what appears to have mattered was that the presence of the Madonna, and her miracles, could still be felt through the substitute devotional object. Icons were often changed in order to insure that devotions to the Madonna they represented would persist beyond the finite lifespan of paint and fabric.[30] What Angelitta did—to maintain artistic provenance across objects, to transfer miraculous power from the old to the new—was a symbolic and routine gesture. He treated the switch in medium from icon to sculpture just as practically as the replacement of one icon by another icon.[31]

His acceptance of change as ordinary distracts, however, from a significant stylistic choice made at Loreto. After more than a century, the sanctuary chose to update its icon with the qualitatively different technology of sculpture. This sort of shift in type was less common than simply rotating icons, partly because of the technical conundrum it presented. St. Luke, purported creator of Loreto's Madonna, was not a sculptor; he was a painter of icons.[32] It took extra creativity to link St. Luke the painter to the new medium of sculpture, although at least four Marian sanctuaries also coped with this difficulty: the well-known shrines of Montserrat in Catalonia and Rocamadour in France, and Oropa and Tindari, closer afield in Italy, all swapped out Lucan icons for statues prior to the sixteenth century.[33]

29. "Imagine della Beatissima Vergine . . . un ritratto di lei fatto per mano di S. Luca Evangelista suo molto famigliare." / "Luca Evangelista, c'haveva meco molta domestichezza, con le sue mani fu Scultore de la statua di legno, che ci è dentro [della Santa Casa]." Angelitta, *L'historia*, pp. 21, 42–43.

30. In Florence, for instance, the original late thirteenth-century image of the Madonna of Orsanmichele was partly burned in a fire in 1304 and had to be replaced four years later by a second painting. Friedman, *Florentine New Towns*, pp. 191–94; Henderson, *Piety and Charity in Late Medieval Florence*, pp. 54, 206–7.

31. Similarly, sculpture was known to replace sculpture, as it did in Switzerland in 1465 when a fire destroyed the statue of the Virgin of Einsiedeln. Katz, "Regarding Mary," p. 90.

32. Bacci, "With the Paintbrush of the Evangelist Luke"; Cassagnes-Brouquet, *Vierges Noires*, pp. 68–69.

33. These sites varied in their postrenovation explanations of Luke's artistic role. In Montserrat's founding story, the carving of the statue was deflected to St. Nicodemus

Why did the Loreto sanctuary take on this change in medium? At the time the new statue was introduced, no fires, rot, or disasters were reported at the shrine. This suggests that the substitution was a matter of choice or taste rather than necessity. Taste mattered in renovation of Catholic imagery. For example, back in the late thirteenth century, high regard for things Byzantine had prompted Siena to change its famed Marian icon.[34] Three hundred years after this vogue for the Byzantine, Loreto responded to different popular currents, notably to European audiences' growing predilection for realism. Three-dimensionality was enjoying a heyday in European religious art that peaked in the 1600s. Pilgrims were drawn to Loreto and to the popular Sacred Mountains sites discussed in chapter 5 in order to see and touch rounded-out representations such as Loreto's own Holy House. These models were considered to be more effective than painting in helping the viewer to imagine the lives of holy individuals. Across the continent in Spain, life-sized, multicolored sculpture was also being privileged as a medium for evoking the humanity of Mary, Christ, and the saints.[35] Loreto's shift to three dimensions could be seen as part of this external trend.

---

with St. Luke credited only for painting it. At Rocamadour, the versatile Luke was simply promoted from painter to sculptor, responsible for both carving and painting. Oropa and Tindari also amplified Luke's artistic talents by ascribing their antiquated, dark Madonna sculptures to the painter saint. On Montserrat: Katz, "Regarding Mary," p. 90. On Rocamadour: Cassagnes-Brouquet, *Vierges Noires*, pp. 68–69. On Oropa: Birnbaum, *Black Madonnas*, p. 134. On Tindari: Begg, *Cult of the Black Virgin*, p. 246; it should be noted that although Begg counts Tindari as one of the black Virgin statues attributed to St. Luke, the Tindari sanctuary itself does not put forward that attribution.

34. Preference for the Byzantine style not only resulted in the alteration of major shrine icons but also led to adjustment of small objects of religious art. Benedetta Montevecchi describes a thirteenth-century French reliquary donated to the Loreto treasury: it was shaped like an enthroned Mary holding the baby Jesus. The style is like French statues, but the gilding and ornate carving led her to conclude that it was reworked in the Adriatic region to make it look more Byzantine. Likewise, Sienna's venerated painted panel, "Madonna degli occhi grossi" (Madonna of the big eyes), was replaced in the 1270s by a half-length painting of the Madonna done by Guido da Siena in Byzantine style, modeled after St. Luke's most famous icon of Mary, the *Hodegetria*. On the Loreto reliquary: Montevecchi, "Arte francese e Arte Adriatica." On the history of the Byzantine *Hodegetria*: Angelidi and Papamastorakis, "Veneration of the Virgin Hodegetria," p. 377. On the popularity of Byzantine iconography in Italy in particular: Cutler, "Pathos of Distance."

35. Maureen Flynn sees this peaking in the seventeenth century and specifically cites the larger Spanish cities of Valladolid, Sevilla, Granada, and Córdoba as harboring these life-sized polychromatic sculptures. Freedberg also gives a vivid example of freestanding terracotta statues north of Bologna in the 1460s that showed "the Bewailing of the Body of Christ" with a visceral realism that moved viewers to tears. Flynn, "Baroque Piety and Spanish Confraternities," p. 244; Freedberg, *Power of Images*, p. 237.

When they changed Loreto's icon for a statue, the anonymous renovators certainly showed attunement to aesthetic preferences beyond the sanctuary, in the Catholic world at large. But they also seem to have looked inward to consider the growing fame of Loreto's other relic, the Holy House. As noted previously, the Holy House's appeal came partly from its poor and humble interior. Loreto's shrine administrators introduced a small statue that seemed more appropriate to that kind of space than a Byzantine icon. Contrast the small sculpture they introduced with a famed Byzantine icon nearby in Rome, the "Regina Coeli" or "Queen of Heaven" at the Church of Santa Maria Maggiore.[36] At Rome's Santa Maria Maggiore, Mary was represented in the typical fashion for Byzantine icons: she was a queen. The painting attributed to St. Luke there is older and larger than Loreto's statue. It shows Mary only half length, but nevertheless the image towers five feet high and three feet wide. Mary wears a gold-trimmed dark blue mantle over a purple tunic, royal colors enhanced by the faded gold background. She is stately, opulent, and imperious in scale.[37]

The Madonna of Loreto sprang from just such a queenly image. But her new statue distanced her from this older Byzantine stream, setting imperial markers of majesty aside while retaining Lucan provenance. Loreto's new statue stood a modest three feet high. It was not full sized, but it was a full-figure Mary. She was slight, less than a foot wide and only a few inches deep. She stood crowned and held forward a similarly crowned baby Jesus, who held in his left hand a globe of the world topped by a crucifix.[38] Unlike the Byzantine icon of Santa Maria Maggiore, Loreto's updated statue deliberately confronted its viewers with a contrast between celestial role and earthly reality. It matched with its reliquary, the humble Holy House.

The new three-dimensional sculpture offered pilgrim visitors a tangible but stubbornly mundane measure for the Queen of Heaven. Along with her *Santa Casa* shelter, she was low, short, narrow, and humble enough to stand rather than sit in a throne.[39] She was also distinctly dark. The new

36. In the thirteenth century this icon was called "Regina Coeli." Today it is more commonly known as the "Salus Populi Romani" ("The Health of the People of Rome") because the Romans carried the image in procession seeking Mary's protection from plague in the late sixth century. Noreen, "Icon of Santa Maria Maggiore, Rome."

37. Pace, "Between East and West"; Noreen, "Icon of Santa Maria Maggiore, Rome."

38. For a rare photograph of this statue that was burned in a fire in 1921: Santarelli, *Tradizione*, p. 171. Today's statue was modeled after it and follows its scale and dimensions.

39. Perhaps the standing posture was adopted for the Madonna of Loreto to make her unique among Europe's black Madonnas, who tended to be represented seated and

sculpture of Loreto's Madonna was significantly darker than the original. The exact lightness of the first Marian icon at Loreto is disputed, but the late fifteenth-century sculpture was painted a definitive shade of brown.[40] The trend to darken this Italian Virgin culminated in the statue currently on display at the sanctuary. Today's statue is black (figure 6.2). It was designed in 1921 by Enrique Quattrini and Leopoldo Celani to replace the older sculpture, burnt irretrievably in a fire. Quattrini and Celani brought an ebony tinge to the Madonna of Loreto when they chose to carve their statue out of dark Lebanese cedar wood. The two artists followed a "vogue of darkening" of Marian images in Europe that was first articulated in Loreto in the 1490s.[41] At that time, the statue that was substituted for Loreto's early Byzantine-style painting was deliberately tinted brown.

Before exploring this adjustment to shade, it must be noted that the change in *medium* of Loreto's Madonna took firmer and more consistent hold within the global corpus of Marian imagery than its ephemeral colors. For instance, when the Jesuit Juan Maria Salvatierra introduced the Virgin of Loreto in Baja California in 1697, he used a typical wooden sculpture of Mary that he carried from Mexico City. She was white and stood

---

enthroned as queens in a pose called *Sedes Sapientiae*, or Seat of Wisdom. Standing Marys in the sixteenth century also generally represented the doctrine of the Immaculate Conception. Regardless of valence, the standing pose of Loreto's Madonna went serial more than other aspects of her iconography. It drew comment from the well-traveled Italian monk Luigi Lazzari, who proclaimed: "Gentlemen, I have walked the World, and in the many Churches of the Madonna of Loreto, which I have visited I have never seen a single one of her Images depicting her seated." Lazzari, *Dodici Sermoni sopra la S. Casa di Loreto*, p. 180. On imagery of seated Marys: Cassagnes-Brouquet, *Vierges Noires*, pp. 153, 117; Begg, *Cult of the Black Virgin*, pp. 13 and 80. On how standing Marys denoted the Immaculate Conception: Stratton, *Immaculate Conception in Spanish Art*; D'Ancona, *Iconography of the Immaculate Conception in the Middle Ages and Early Renaissance*.

40. Boyer claims that Loreto's Virgin began as "white and neoclassical in style." Lightbown and Santarelli refer to the same fifteenth-century source to conclude at odds about the same question. They both refer to the 1467–68 pilgrimage account of the priest Giacomo Ricci, who thus described the image he saw at Loreto: "Bello il volto e un poco nero con colore rosso." / "The face is beautiful and a little black with red coloring." Lightbown argues that Ricci's words could describe a contrast between hair and skin, and concludes that Ricci saw a Virgin with long blonde tresses. Santarelli reads Ricci literally and concludes that he saw a dark-skinned Virgin. Regardless of the shading of the original image, scholars concur that the statue that replaced it was darker. Boyer, *Cult of the Virgin*, p. 82; Lightbown, *Carlo Crivelli*, p. 41; Santarelli, *Tradizione*, p. 168.

41. Sophie Cassagnes-Brouquet coins the phrase "vogue du brunissement" in reference to statues of Mary in twelfth- and thirteenth-century France. Monique Scheer extends the trend outside of France and into the early modern period. Cassagnes-Brouquet, *Vierges Noires*, p. 153; Scheer, "From Majesty to Mystery."

around three feet tall (figure 6.1).[42] He did not use a painting or a dark-faced Madonna more reminiscent of Italy's original shrine image.

This was not a careless decision. Salvatierra had previously been very interested in precise duplication of Loreto's relics. In 1680, he had asked his brother in Italy to send him floor plans for Loreto's Holy House so that he could build an accurate replica of it at the Jesuit College of San Gregorio near Mexico City. At the same time that he asked his brother for exactitude regarding the Holy House, he requested from him a statue "like the one in the original Holy House of Loreto, of the Lady of Loreto, holding the child Jesus in her arms."[43] He did not specify color in his request, only posture and medium. Nor did his brother fulfill his request with a tinted sculpture. The medium of the Marian image was important to emulate; evidently, the blackness was not. The darkness of Loreto's shrine Madonna does not seem to have mattered as much as form in the Jesuit diffusion of the Loreto complex.

The difference in color between statues of Mary used in Europe and overseas has tended to be explained as the result of frontier circumstances and acculturating projects. A case in point, white sculptures of Jesus have been taken as symbols of white colonial power among nonwhite, conquered populations.[44] But when the iconography of the Madonna of Loreto is considered as a whole, with her color changes in Europe set alongside her American alterations, local situations and agendas cannot fully explain her transformations. Just as the Madonna of Loreto's shift in medium was partly a response to preferences out in the wider world, changes to her color were also informed by awareness of external trends

42. While presented in this chapter to evoke all standardized frontier mission statuary of Mary, figure 6.1 is a photograph of the actual late seventeenth-century statue that Salvatierra is believed to have brought with him to Baja California. Venegas, *Juan María de Salvatierra*, p. 149; Dunne, *Black Robes in Lower California*, p. 45.

43. Venegas, *Juan María de Salvatierra*, pp. 105–6. Salvatierra also transported other "paintings . . . and statues in relief" ("imagini a penello e statue di rilievo") to furnish Loreto Conchó's new church in California. This artwork was donated by patrons in Mexico City through the Jesuit Colegio de San Gregorio. It is not described in detail in Jesuit records and correspondences, so it was unlikely that it was imported or sent for especially to denote Loreto's Madonna; it probably represented Mary in general. ARSI Mex. 17 (Letter from Ugarte, 1699), fols. 608v–9.

44. For example, the "Cristos de Caña," statues of the crucified Christ made by native artists in Mexico in the colonial period, were originally viewed as signs of full-fledged adoption of Christianity until one fell and broke open during study in the twentieth century. Nahuatl texts and sketches of European paintings were found inside. Now these statues are taken, instead, as emblematic of religious transculturation. Carrasco, "Borderlands and 'Biblical Hurricane,' " pp. 365–66.

and conditions. Below, local factors contributing to color change are considered as only partial explanations for why the Virgin of Loreto was represented as a black Madonna in Europe, and a white Madonna in the Americas. Then an external dynamic common to both Europe and the Americas is explored: the need to designate this particular Madonna as alien. On the frontiers and in the metropole alike, Loreto's variant tones for Mary stressed otherness. In combination with the three-dimensional realism of her new medium, the Madonna of Loreto's foreign colors consistently delineated her uniqueness: she was human, yet she was a divinity.

In Europe, eyewitnesses reported that darkness generally signified antiquity. The Jesuit António Cordeiro wrote as much about Loreto in 1719:

> Inside [the Holy House] is the Image of Our Lady, and in her arms her Child Jesus, both with faces already a dark color because of time and antiquity; and the height of the Image of Our Lady is four palms, and it is a sculpture, not a painting, and one presumes it is made of wood, because one cannot see what it is made of.[45]

Cordeiro remarked on the color of the image before mentioning its other significant attribute, its sculpted form. He wrote more extensively about the Madonna's sculpted form than he did about her tint, but the tint clearly mattered to him as an indicator of age.

By the late 1400s in Italy, when the Loreto shrine traded its olive-tinted Byzantine icon for a significantly darker statue of the Madonna, "black Madonnas"—statues of Mary that were distinguished by their darkness—were the core of some of the best-known and oldest Marian sites in Europe.[46] In Spain, the shrine of Guadalupe in Extremadura displayed a black carving of Mary also attributed to St. Luke; the Montserrat shrine in Catalonia showcased *La Moreneta*, a black wooden statue of Mary enthroned. These popular Spanish pilgrimage destinations claimed origins

45. "E nella està a Imagem da Senhora, e em seus braços o seu Menino Jesus, cujos rostos de ambas as Imagens saõ jà de cor morena pela antiguidade do tempo; e a altura da Imagem da Senhora he de cuatro pamos, e he de vulto, e naõ de pintura, e se presume ser de maydera, pois se naõ ve de que he." Cordeiro, *Loreto Lusitano*, p. 172.

46. The "black Madonna" grouping includes miraculous icons as well as statues. I focus on the statues here because of their relevance to Loreto. However, three "black Madonna" icons are worth noting here for their origins in the same late medieval and early modern interval. They have all been described as Byzantine in style, a description also applied to the original image at Loreto. These include: the Virgin of Czestochowa, Poland (first documented in 1382 when the icon was slashed); the Virgin of Oettingen, Bavaria (dating from the early fourteenth century); and the Virgin of Kazan in Russia, venerated after 1579. Special thanks to Lucyna Bojanowska for drawing my attention to the Virgin of Czestochowa.

in the early centuries of Christianity, with their statues in place as early as the seventh and ninth centuries.[47] To the north, two more shrines publicized black Madonnas with origins more than a century old. Austria's Mariazell sanctuary had a twelfth-century Romanesque black statue of Mary; Brabant, Belgium showcased a walnut-wood statue of Our Lady of Hal, dated to the thirteenth century.[48]

But it was France that boasted the most dark, ancient Madonnas. If Loreto shrine administrators were looking to their northwestern neighbor for models of Marian iconography, they would have found black wooden statues cutting a swath across southern France from its Mediterranean to its Atlantic coast. The central region of France around the Massif Central mountain range has the largest concentration of black Madonna statuary in Europe. Most of the darkened Virgins date to the twelfth century, when darkening was a common artistic modification for wooden sculptures of Mary.[49] The oldest French exemplars are near Auvergne, France, but they spread outward to Bourgogne, Provence, Languedoc, and over the Pyrenees to Catalonia.[50] Chartres reputedly harbored one of the oldest black

47. The Guadalupe shrine associates its statue with four different dates. First it was carved by St. Luke (first century); then it was transferred from the Rome of Pope Gregory the Great (540–604) to the Seville of St. Leander (534–600); then it was buried in the eighth century to hide it from Muslims invading the Iberian peninsula; finally, it was rediscovered in 1326 by a cowherd who stumbled across it. Montserrat likewise gives an early and a later date to its statue, *La Moreneta*. The sanctuary reports that the statue was discovered in the ninth century, but it is officially recognized as dating from the later twelfth century. The discrepancy in dates might indicate a shift of medium similar to Loreto's. The black statues may have been introduced in the fourteenth and twelfth centuries, inheriting ascriptions of provenance from previous images, or newly acquiring them to bolster their authenticity.

48. These more recent sanctuaries were catapulted to European-wide fame because of their respective Madonnas' miraculous intervention in local battlefields. The first reports of Mariazell's statue coincide with the 1157 founding of the shrine by a Benedictine monk. The site rose to prominence more than a century later, after 1377, when King Ludwig I of Hungary defeated Bulgarian troops because Ludwig's troops prayed to the Madonna of Mariazell. Similarly, the statue of Our Lady of Hal significantly antedates her military fame. The statue was given by St. Elizabeth of Hungary to her daughter Sophia, Duchess of Brabant, in the 1200s. During a siege three centuries later, in 1580, Our Lady of Hal miraculously deflected thirty-two cannonballs away from her shrine.

49. Black Madonna statues were clearly not as marginal as they have been made out to be. For arguments on the exceptionality of black Madonnas: Birnbaum, *Black Madonnas*; Begg, *Cult of the Black Virgin*. Begg even felt the need to tabulate all the black Madonnas in Europe to demonstrate that these were a significant grouping. In central France after the twelfth century, however, they were evidently the norm.

50. These black Madonnas are all also sculpted sitting in thrones. Forsyth, *Throne of Wisdom*; Begg, *Cult of the Black Virgin*, pp. 13 and 80; Boyer, *Cult of the Virgin*, p. 38; Cassagnes-Brouquet, *Vierges Noires*, p. 117.

enthroned Madonnas in existence, installed there by the eleventh century.[51] Rocamadour's seated black Madonna sculpture has been dated as early as the ninth century and as late as the twelfth.[52] Loreto's statue may have been darkened to affiliate it with this respected, recognized, nearby pool of ancient black Madonnas.

In Europe, darkness also gestured to alterity, or foreign provenance. Though the black Madonnas technically radiated out of central France, the founding histories that sprang up around them pointed to another locus of origin across the Mediterranean Sea. Like the Virgin of Loreto, these French statues were believed to have come from the Holy Land. Most of France's twelfth-century black Madonnas were attributed to returning crusaders. The Virgin of Saint-Cristophe in Auvergne was reportedly brought directly from the Holy Land by the French knight Raoul de Scorailles in 1098.[53] The delivery of Notre-Dame-des-Neiges to Aurillac was also credited to a local crusader, back from Palestine. The French king St. Louis IX (1214–70) was reported to have himself carried the statue of Notre-Dame-de-Puy-en-Velay home from the Holy Land after his disastrous showings in the Seventh and Eighth Crusades.[54] Even *La Negrette*, the more recent Black Virgin of Espalion, was considered a travel trophy of the crusading lords of Calmont d'Olt.[55] In this noteworthy group of French sculptures, blackness denoted more than generalized antiquity: it indicated the *Christian* past rooted in the Holy Land. Perhaps not coincidentally, the ebony Virgins of French sculpture shared their dark connotation with the olive-tinted Madonnas of Byzantine iconographical fame. The exotic shades of each were construed as authentically evoking the eastern Holy Land of biblical times.

51. There are reports of this statue on display at Chartres as early as 1013. It was destroyed during the French Revolution. Today in Chartres Cathedral, the black statue of Notre-Dame-de-Pilier that replaced the lost statue is dated to the sixteenth century. Cassagnes-Brouquet, *Vierges Noires*, pp. 79, 130.

52. As with the Spanish sites and with Loreto, which all report a series of origin dates for their sculptures, it is likely that the later dates refer to a change in medium. The shrine of Rocamadour rose to prominence in the late twelfth century with the discovery of the body of St. Amadour. It seems likely that Rocamadour introduced a new sculpture of the Madonna in the twelfth century, to coincide with the Amadour innovation.

53. Cassagnes-Brouquet, *Vierges Noires*, p. 62.

54. Le Puy was the oldest and the most prominent of Auvergne's Marian pilgrimage sites. Today the Le Puy Madonna statue's origins are given as 1093, but Le Puy historians of the fifteenth and sixteenth centuries placed the origins of their enthroned Madonna so far back in biblical history that it predated Mary's own birth! Ibid., pp. 64, 68–69, 77.

55. Ibid., p. 109. But Cassagnes-Brouquet argues that this statue was most likely made locally, sculpted for a crèche scene in the Calmont castle chapel in the fifteenth century.

Black statues of Mary continued to be used to denote *Christian* antiquity in the early modern period. In places like Italy, however, the landscape was cluttered with sculpture of ancient, darkly painted Roman deities. In this context, one might imagine that a black Madonna would verge dangerously on suggesting the pre-Christian. One seventeenth-century devotee of Loreto—the Catholic monk Luigi Lazzari, introduced earlier in this chapter—worried that the Italian Madonna and her Holy House would be compared to the pre-Christian Roman goddess Diana. Loreto lay just across the sea from the oft-visited ruins of the ancient Roman Temple of Diana at Ephesus. Diana of Ephesus had been traditionally depicted in statues in black, standing glory, a style similar to the Madonna of Loreto's new sixteenth-century look.[56] Lazzari's anxiety that darkness might signify alternatives to Christianity was also voiced by one Jesuit on the American frontier who chose to distribute a whitened statue of the Madonna of Loreto instead of replicating the Italian shrine's distinctively dark Mary.

The French Jesuit Martin Bouvart, like the Italian priest Lazzari, was outnumbered by a large majority of Catholics on both sides of the Atlantic who were not reading color as a distinguishing feature between Christian and non-Christian. But the Jesuit's clear articulation of anxiety bears

56. The best known representation of Diana of Ephesus is a second-century Roman alabaster and bronze statue of the goddess, crowned and with a black face, hands and feet. Unlike Christian Madonnas, however, this Diana sculpture also features multiple breasts and a dress decorated with bulls, goats, deer, and a bee. Ephesus, on the western coast of modern-day Turkey, had the largest collection of Roman ruins on its side of the Mediterranean. It drew many visitors, including early antiquarians such as Cyriac of Ancona (1391–1452). The Temple of Diana had been one of the seven wonders of the ancient world. When Ephesus later emerged as a center for Christianity, the structure was targeted as a problematic symbol of persisting Greco-Roman religion. The Archbishop of Constantinople, John Chrysostom, commanded that the temple be razed in 406. Interestingly, current-day Ephesus is also known for another Holy House associated with the Virgin Mary that has become a popular pilgrimage site for both Christians and Muslims in the area. The Holy House of Ephesus is a small stone building similar in size to Loreto's *Santa Casa* and made of materials that have been dated back to the sixth or seventh century. It is located about seven kilometers from Selçuk, Turkey, overlooking the ancient Ephesian ruins. Loreto's house is associated with an earlier period in Mary's life when she welcomed the Annunciation; the House of Ephesus is purportedly Mary's final residence, where she lived before her death. However, the Ephesian Holy House devotion emerged long after the period discussed in this book. Although veneration of the structure has been extended back as early as the twelfth century, it was officially recognized beginning in the late 1800s. At that time a French priest, the Abbé Julien Gouyet, was inspired to identify it as Mary's house because of the writings of a visionary German nun, Catherine Emmerich (1774–1824). On the sculpture of Diana: Begg, *Cult of the Virgin*, p. 54. On the Roman ruins: *Ephesos Metropolis of Asia*; Strelan, *Paul, Artemis and the Jews in Ephesus*, pp. 44, 82. On the Holy House of Ephesus: A. Gallagher, "Mary's House in Ephesus."

mention here because it has dominated twentieth-century, race-conscious historiography of the Americas.[57] In the 1670s, Bouvart commented on the black Madonna of Loreto's pronounced whiteness in Canada. He described the customary light-colored statue of Mary that had been sent from France to furnish the replica Holy House that served as the chapel at Lorette-among-the-Huron. Bouvart emphasized the necessity of a color divide. He explained that the statue at Lorette was not black like Italy's original Virgin. If it had been, it might have encouraged the Huron to "resume the custom which we have made them abandon of blackening and staining their faces."[58] Bouvart did not want the newly converted Huron to associate the Virgin Mary with pre-Christian practice.

Bouvart's aside gets to the heart of the difference between readings of changing colors among Catholics in Europe and the Americas in the seventeenth century: whereas in Europe, black was selected to mean "old," in the Americas, white was selected to indicate "new." But symbolically, the inverse colors both emphasized remoteness. In the Catholic churches of Europe, *blackness* alluded to the temporally distant; Loreto's shrine statue was darkened to allude to an ancient, established Christian past. At Jesuit missions in the Americas, Mary's *whiteness* reminded viewers of spatial separation; lightened Madonnas conjured the far-removed European and American metropolitan centers that supplied newly arrived, novelty images. In each case, Catholics opted to paint the Madonna of Loreto in shades that indicated that she was *not from here*. On a religious level, the Virgin of Loreto's shifting hues acted to preserve the gap between the human and the divine. When the Lauretan Mary's color was altered, consciously or subconsciously, its contrast served to accentuate that she was other, former, foreign to the land. In Europe and the New World alike, this particular incarnation of Mary was special because she was an arrival from distant realms—human and celestial.

57. Monique Scheer notes that European explanations of black Madonnas changed in the late nineteenth century coinciding with the development of race theory when prior to this color was not equated with race. Scheer, "From Majesty to Mystery." For an in-depth study of how color changes did *not* clearly delineate race in the case of the Virgin of Guadalupe in Mexico and in Spain: Peterson, *Visualizing Guadalupe*. For how race has become tied into more general twentieth-century interpretations of black Madonnas, particularly in Mexico, the American Southwest, Brazil, and Cuba: Oleszkiewicz-Peralba, *Black Madonnas in Latin America and Europe*, especially chapters 2, 3, and 4. On the contrast between these earlier, alternate perceptions of the color of Mary and current-day interpretations at US Christian shrines of the black Madonna: Abrams, *God and Blackness*, p. 35; J. E. Clark, *Indigenous Black Theology*, pp. 157–61.

58. Bouvart, "De la Chapelle de Notre-Dame de Lorette en Canada," p. 13.

To say that color mattered on Loreto statues as a marker of the *alien*, above all, contradicts a common assumption about color as a signifier in zones of colonial power. Color continues to be interpreted primarily as a discriminator between European, indigenous, and African cultures, or as a straightforward demarcator of race. At the other extreme, the color of Catholic images has been taken to be a mere byproduct of market-driven forces such as availability or supply. The seventeenth-century coloring of Loreto's Madonna offsets both interpretations with its variety.

Color was not a fixed or predetermined category for the Virgin Mary. She was not rendered as consistently white in the New World and dark in the Old. In fact, as the case of Loreto shows, her shades fluctuated in both zones, challenging the premise that color was used to unambiguously and literally represent white conquerors versus dark conquered. For instance, Floriano Grimaldi, one of the foremost recent historians of Loreto, indicates that the vast majority of early modern paintings and prints of the Madonna of Loreto produced in Europe depict her tinted white.[59] The blackness of Loreto's miraculous statue did not carry over to the wider pool of Lauretan imagery circulating outside her home sanctuary, even in Europe. The profusion of *white* portraits of her seems connected to the sixteenth-century explosion of standardized paper images of Mary in Europe.[60] These affordable representations were highly homogenized, notwithstanding the particularities of local shrine images. Black-and-white woodcuts of Mary were recycled and repeated in print.[61] This booming seventeenth-century Catholic market of icons and statues did not cater separately to European, Indian, and creole audiences, or rather, it did not reserve a standard white Mary for acculturating the Indians while encouraging Europeans to adopt black statues.

Catholics on both sides of the Atlantic could choose from many alternative forms of Mary, and they did. For example, Diego de Ocaña, a

59. Grimaldi, *Devozione e Committenza nelle Marche*, pp. 29–33.

60. Freedberg, *Power of Images*, pp. 115–16, 126. Philip Soergel also surveys the output of German printing presses to conclude that the rise in printed materials such as apologetic pilgrimage books served to advertise shrines in Bavaria, confirming how print culture worked to fuel Marian devotion. Soergel, *Wondrous in His Saints*, pp. 5–13.

61. Recycled woodcuts did not indicate stagnation. Consider the clever recasting of image in one sixteenth-century French emblem book in which the woodcut for emblem 8, "The Unjust Prince," reappears wittily to illustrate emblem 20, "The Drunkard." In Mexico City centuries later, William Taylor also notes two simple woodcuts of Our Lady of Remedios and Our Lady of Guadalupe that were oft-repeated through the seventeenth and eighteenth centuries to different effect. Guerolt, *Le Premier Livre des emblèmes* (1550); Taylor, "Our Lady of Guadalupe and Friends," p. 19, fig. 2; p. 21, fig. 3.

Hieronymite alms collector and artist, wrote about altering the color of a Spanish face of Mary, the Virgin of Guadalupe. He was passing through the silver-mining center of Potosí in the Spanish Viceroyalty of Peru between 1601 and 1603. Among other responsibilities, Ocaña had been charged by the Hieronymite administrators of Extremadura's shrine with distributing images of the Guadalupan Madonna in South America. At the Hieronymite sanctuary in Spain, she was represented by a black statue. In his circuit of South America, Ocaña shifted her medium to paint and canvas. In Potosí, he painted her slightly brown to better evoke her statue in Spain. He remarked on the reception of his representation: "Since I painted her a little dark (un poquito morena), and the Indians are like that, they said that That Lady (aquella señora) was more beautiful than the other images, and [that] they loved her a lot because she was of their color."[62]

Ocaña made an opposite decision from the Jesuit Martin de Bouvart on the American frontiers. Ocaña chose to retain the dark color of Spain's Virgin of Guadalupe, while Bouvart chose to lighten the dark color of Italy's Madonna of Loreto. Yet their explicit commentary reveals a shared understanding between the two men of the role of color in religious iconography. Color was a fluid and secondary category. It could and had to be calibrated for particular audiences and moments. As mentioned above, the color of the Lauretan Madonna varied in European iconography. Likewise, overseas, Catholics could look to the exemplar of the black statue venerated at the Loreto sanctuary, or they could take some of Mary's readily available stock white imagery and modify it for effect.

In short, color was not what made this Madonna wonderful. It never attached distinctly enough to the Virgin of Loreto in the seventeenth century to be what identified her. Paradoxically, color also counteracted the effect of the new three-dimensional sculpted medium adopted by Loreto's shrine. Statues of Mary made this Catholic figurehead seem real and approachable. Her blackness and whiteness, on the other hand, instilled distance. Most alterations to the Virgin of Loreto's color in the early modern period intentionally maximized alienation. Viewers were not meant to look at her face and recognize themselves in its shades. At Italy's Loreto shrine, European pilgrims looked on a *black* Madonna; on the American frontier, Indian neophytes usually observed a *white* version.

62. Ocaña as quoted and translated by Kenneth Mills, "Diego de Ocaña's Hagiography of New and Renewed Devotion in Colonial Peru," p. 61. Technically, since Ocaña rendered the Virgin of Guadalupe in a shade of brown and not black like her statue, he was lightening her image.

The evanescent shades of the Madonna of Loreto, along with her altered media, demonstrate how Catholic iconography was perennially in flux. Images of the Virgin of Loreto followed a typical pattern. Alterations were obscured by the shrine's emphasis on continuity and by artists seamlessly fitting themselves into standardized streams of Marian imagery. However, adaptation was an unspoken but understood necessity if the Italian Madonna was to remain relevant. Behind the veneer of sameness and repetition, the changes to her iconography reflect shifting Catholic attitudes toward Mary. Between the fifteenth and eighteenth centuries, the Madonna of Loreto was humanized and three-dimensionalized. She was distanced through darkening and lightening of tone. This revitalization of medium and color was dictated as much by external tastes as it was by local strategy. As was the case for other aspects of Lauretan devotion ranging from pilgrimage to Holy Houses, personal preferences transformed its Madonna. Shrine administrators, independent artists, and Jesuits were all united in their desire for the Loreto devotion to reach the widest possible contemporary audience by means of her image. They modified her to keep her popular. Taken together, their works attest to their communal belief that Mary's global allure rested on these rearticulated and contradictory qualities: she was human, yet she was divine; she was old, yet she was new; she was close, yet she was distant; she was familiar, yet she was foreign. Truly the full sweep of iconographical change associated with the Madonna of Loreto did justice to Mary's complexity. So, too, did the full sweep of human contributors who pitched in to help renovate her image. Frequently overlooked as actors in that panorama of contributors are the women who coincidentally shared the Virgin's name.

New Expression: Marys and Maries Out in the World

In the 1670s, the Jesuit mission of Lorette in Canada was a hotbed of Maries. Jesuits and Huron parents had chosen to christen girls "Marie" so often that it seemed that their sheer numbers might summon Mary herself to the Canadian forest. In Europe as well, the name "Mary" remained one of the most popular names parents chose for their Catholic daughters. While women called Mary also possessed surnames, the first name they shared was so prevalent and universalizing that it affords them a certain degree of anonymity. It is difficult to track the impact of individual Marys in a sea of women and imagery bearing the same name. But like many other seventeenth-century women, those named Mary occasionally left traces similar to those just noted above in the discussion of Loreto's shrine image. Their life experiences emphasized their humanity, exoticized their differences, and involved mobility outside the domestic space of the home. For a small handful of them, the resemblance they bore to their namesake was so strong that it led others to perceive them as living representations of the Virgin Mary. There are real women hidden behind the idealized artistic portrayals of the Mother of God considered above. As we have seen with other components of the Loreto devotion, such realities are what bring Catholic exemplars—in this case, images of the Madonna of Loreto—their distinctive power and peculiarity.

The multiple Maries of Canada and Marys of Europe are therefore included last in this analysis as peripheral and inadvertent, but highly significant, contributors to the iconography of the Madonna of Loreto. In part because of the serendipity of a shared name, these women added to a full, diverse corpus of expressions of what Mary looked like and how she manifested herself on this earth. As such, they affected the Virgin of Loreto's vast stream of iconography as much as statue makers, icon producers, and artists like Caravaggio.

These women's biggest contribution to Loreto's public image was to underscore the strain of Catholic art that represented Mary in her real, human form as uncloistered. Here, that fringe branch of Marian iconography is first put in context alongside other competing contemporary depictions of the Virgin as domesticated. Second, a handful of Marys in Europe and Maries in Canada are surveyed to demonstrate how these women's choices and actions reflected and encouraged one type of visual rendition of the Mother of God over another. Third and last, a Jesuit firsthand account is used to consider the impact of a single real Marie, a Huron Catholic convert Marie Tsaouenté, on the changing image of her namesake. This closing case study suggests that women only tangentially associated with Italy's Madonna could, and did, affect how their contemporaries envisioned this sacred figure.

As noted earlier in this chapter, the Virgin Mary was pulled in two directions in the Counter-Reformation period, and Catholic women and the Madonna of Loreto along with her. On the one hand, Mary was turned into an exemplar for restraint and domesticity, as she appears in Rembrandt's 1665 painting, *Holy Family with Angels*, described previously (figure 6.4). In that work, Mary is safely sequestered with her family. A century before Rembrandt, in 1563, the Council of Trent had laid the groundwork for Rembrandt's indoor Virgin by decreeing that all female religious orders be enclosed, physically separated from the outside world.[63] Partly because of this reform policy, if Catholic women wanted to take to the streets to participate in social outreach or missionary work in the early modern period, they had to rely on the support and chaperoning of men or male religious orders.[64]

But as noted above, in spite of the Madonna of Loreto's pairing with a Holy House in which she could quite easily have been enclosed, the Italian Virgin's iconography drifted toward a divergent stream. Alongside the Catholic Church's literal and artistic bent to cloister, in the 1600s, the Virgin Mary was also being described daily in sermons as a radically mobile female.[65] Jesuits in particular emphasized this dimension of Mary in their sermons in the mission field.[66] Like the painter Caravaggio, they were not inventing this face of Mary wholesale. The Catholic Bible gave plentiful detail about how Mary's life was marked by upheaval and transit unusual for a woman. Her peregrinations began at her birthplace of either Nazareth or Jerusalem. The Gospels of Matthew, Mark, Luke, and John pick up Mary's journey with the conception of Jesus at Nazareth.[67] She rode a donkey onward to Bethlehem while pregnant, following her husband Joseph so that they could be counted in the Roman census. Shortly after delivering Jesus, Mary fled to Egypt to hide from King Herod. She, Joseph, and Jesus made the arduous trek back to Nazareth from Egypt over several years. When Jesus was crucified in Jerusalem, Mary found her way there, too, to stand at the foot of his cross. In the early eighteenth century, an English writer, Thomas Allen, devoted thirteen entire pages to describing these "Travels of the Blessed Virgin Mary," but even with that much space, he only got her as far as Hermapolis in Egypt.[68] Sermons, biblical accounts, and books like Allen's were corroborated by the stories

63. This policy was the product of Session XXV, Cap. V of the Council of Trent. Hsia, *World of Catholic Renewal*, p. 33.

64. Hsia, *World of Catholic Renewal*, p. 33; Donnelly, "6. The Quest for Active Women's Orders"; Caffiero, "From the Late Baroque Mystical Explosion to the Social Apostolate"; Lierheimer, "Female Eloquence and Maternal Ministry."

65. Vélez, "Urban Driftwood."

66. There was often a positive response to this emphasis from women in particular: In 1696, Jesuit Diego de Eguiluz reported that more Moxos women than men were attending the Jesuits' Saturday masses specifically dedicated to the "Santissima Virgin." See: ARSI Peru 21 (1696 "Relación de la Mision apostólica de los Moxos"), fols. 40v–41.

67. Mary makes a final biblical appearance in the book of Acts. She is associated as well with the "woman of the apocalypse" in Revelations. Further details of her early life can be found in the apocryphal "Infancy Gospel" or "Protoevangelium" of James.

68. There, "304 miles from Jerusalem . . . the two wearied Travelers [Mary and Joseph] at length arrived" and apparently dropped from exhaustion along with Thomas Allen, who

and experiences of pilgrims. The Holy Land was strewn with sites where Mary had paused or resided. Even Mary's houses were not stationary; her Holy House hopped its way from Nazareth to Loreto, Italy. A pilgrim bent on visiting Mary could traverse for himself the vast distances crossed by the Holy Mother and her associated relics. Mary had certainly not lived a life of conventual enclosure.

But in the very diverse arena of Marian representation, it was not a given that the artists and renovators of the Madonna of Loreto would highlight this aspect of Mary over the other. For every mobile woman serendipitously named Mary, there was probably another of that name who chose to stay in the home, in a cloister, or within a sheltered local community.[69] There were countercurrents stressing Mary as a stay-at-home mother and wife. Still, a vast and noticeable majority chose to render the Virgin of Loreto, in particular, on the threshold of her Holy House, about to step into the outside world, à la Caravaggio instead of after Rembrandt. Why?

The missing piece of the puzzle lies, perhaps, in some of the company kept by the creators of Loreto's imagery. In Europe as well as in distant mission fields, self-appointed iconographers were surrounded by living, breathing Marys who *moved*, just like their biblical namesake.[70] Whether these women consciously chose to travel or were forced to do so because of trying personal circumstances, their wanderings contributed to global interest in Mary as someone who moved. Marys roaming far from the hearth were so visible that they may have influenced the direction of the stream of iconography related to the Virgin Mary, deflecting it toward mobility. In Europe, for instance, the well-known adventuress Marie de l'Incarnation

---

left Mary to stagger off in pursuit of the Wise Men. Allen, *Travels of our Lord and Saviour Jesus Christ*, p. 13.

69. For instance, in the late 1600s, two Huron parents approached the Jesuits to request that their daughter, Marie-Anne Garihonnentha, be taken in by the Ursulines at their convent in Québec. The parents were directly inspired to cloister their daughter because of how the Jesuits had spoken of Mary in a sermon (*Relations Inédites de la Nouvelle-France*, pp. 300–305). On how the French female order, the Ursulines, managed to combine both active lives out in the world with cloistered lives: Keller-Lapp, "Devenir des Jésuitesses."

70. Of course there were many women *not* named Mary who were also finding inspiration in her mobile example at the time. Notably, Marguerite Bourgeoys (1620–1700) founded a Canadian branch of France's Congrégation de Notre Dame (Our Lady), and sailed to Montréal in the mid-seventeenth century in order to establish schools for Catholic girls. She felt justified in her actions "because the Virgin Mary was [also] a traveler, a teacher, one 'who had shared all the fruits of the primitive church with the apostles.'" Deslandres, "In the Shadow of the Cloister," p. 137. Also: Simpson, *Marguerite Bourgeoys and Montreal*.

(1599–1672) found in Mary the validation she needed to follow men in undertaking projects of defiantly uncloistered Catholic evangelization. She embarked on a transoceanic voyage from France that was worthy of her namesake in order to establish a school to teach indigenous girls Catholicism in Québec, Canada.[71] Around the same time, Mary Ward (1585–1645), an English former nun, left her contemplative order of Poor Clares to found the Institute of the Blessed Virgin Mary, later known as the Sisters of Loreto. Their ministry involved emulating the Jesuits in their work out in the world.[72] Likewise, in the Spanish Viceroyalty of Río de la Plata (now Argentina) in the late eighteenth century, one woman, María Antonia de Paz y Figueroa, took informal vows to live like a Jesuit, worked alongside them doing community outreach, and then took over their duties when they were expelled from her town of Santiago de Estero.[73]

It must be noted that Jesuits did not necessarily sanction these radical Maries, Marys, and Marías. The Jesuits were the only Catholic order of the early modern period to never develop a branch of sisters. This was a decision made by the founder of the society, Ignatius Loyola, after what he saw to be a failed test run of some women whom he had allowed to take vows.[74] This is not to say that Jesuits ignored the many Catholic women who joined them in the field and in their labors.[75] But it is to say that they

71. Hsia, *World of Catholic Renewal*, p. 151; Lierheimer, "Female Eloquence and Maternal Ministry." On the impact of Atlantic crossings on Ursuline notions of enclosure: Keller-Lapp, "Maritime Habits." On Marie de l'Incarnation: N. Z. Davis, "New Worlds: Marie de l'Incarnation."

72. L. Gallagher, "Mary Ward's 'Jesuitresses.'" The Ursuline sisters also defended this spirit of *female* apostolic activism so apparent in Mary's travels and accompanied the first cohorts of Jesuits sent to Canada. Founded by a Franciscan tertiary, St. Angela Merici (c. 1474–1540), in Italy in 1532, this teaching order of women preceded the formal establishment of the Society of Jesus. See Hsia, *World of Catholic Renewal*, p. 37; Donnelly, "6. The Quest for Active Women's Orders," pp. 301–2; Deslandres, "In the Shadow of the Cloister," p. 137.

73. Fraschina, "Jesuit *Beata*."

74. Foremost among them was Isabel Roser, wealthy Barcelona widow and benefactress of Ignatius. She took vows with the Jesuits in 1545, but only two years later, Ignatius went to the pope to secure permission to release her from them. Elizabeth Rhodes notes that Ignatius's decision has been blamed on Roser's "domineering" and "feisty" personality. She went on to join a Franciscan convent in Barcelona. Rhodes, "Join the Jesuits, See the World," pp. 45–46n4.

75. For instance, the Ursulines constantly noted Jesuit efforts to pull them into the world, though not always with appreciation. In a 1639 letter to the Ursulines at Rouen chronicling her Atlantic crossing, Cécile Richer de Ste.-Croix wrote of her exasperation at her Jesuit shipmates (including Pierre-Joseph-Marie Chaumonot) for repeatedly interrupting the Ursulines' prayers by bursting into their cabin to announce worldly minutiae such as the ship's near-avoidance of icebergs. Keller-Lapp, "Maritime Habits," p. 6.

usually distinguished sharply between their flesh-and-blood female contemporaries and Mary, the roaming apostle—the symbolic Mother of God who participated alongside them in their evangelizing efforts, figuratively and often literally traveling with them in statue or painted form. For the most part, Jesuits advised human women to *not* hit the road like the divine Mary had, but instead to be moderate, disciplined, and domestic in the way they expressed devotion.[76] At first glance, it would seem that Jesuits were trained to impart Rembrandt instead of Caravaggio, to encourage the image of a cloistered Mary rather than a Madonna on the brink.

This is why it is so remarkable that in certain remote mission fields, such as in eastern Canada, Mary intrudes in Jesuit writings in decidedly active, transitory form. The movement that Jesuits charted repeatedly for Canada's living "Maries" was conversion, a shift toward Christianity. Although Jesuits baptized many Huron girls as "Marie" during their infancy, they were pleased to remark on how many of these babies had grown admirably into the name.[77] By the mid-1600s, "Marie" had come to designate the best of the "good Christian women" in the Huron mission community.[78] There was Marie-Thérèse Oüareonha, who gave the blanket off her back to an Iroquois girl, starting the girl down the road to conversion with this simple act of generosity.[79] There was also Marie Magdaleine Gachinnontée. Her brother, who had not yet converted to Christianity and lived among the nearby Ottawa, sent her a gift. By way of thanks, Marie Magdaleine sent him a letter saying that the best gift he could give her would be to convert to Christianity.[80] Marie Ouendraka, the widow of Ignace Tsaouenhohoui, turned down the Jesuits' offer of food to her during a

76. On Jesuits advocating female restraint: Molina, *To Overcome Oneself*, pp. 50–66 ("Women's Devotional Labor"); Jacobson Schutte, "Little Women, Great Heroines."

77. On Jesuit "sacred biographies" of women in seventeenth-century Canada: Greer, "Colonial Saints."

78. The Jesuits used "good Christian woman" to refer to a wide range of Christian behavior, from the upstanding to the simply satisfactory. For instance, when Pierre-Joseph-Marie Chaumonot appeared in court to attest to the character of a young Huron woman, Genevieve, who was charged with drunkenness, he called her a "good Christian woman" ["c'estoit une bonne Chrestienne"] and recommended better treatment for her than prison while her case was decided. ASJCF Fonds Joseph Chaumonot BO-258, Cahier 3, doc. 17 (Jugement du Conseil Souverain), pp. 337–38.

79. *Relations Inédites de la Nouvelle-France*, p. 297. This act was all the more touching given that the Iroquois were long-standing enemies of the Huron.

80. Though Mary Magdalene was a disciple of Jesus as distinct from the Virgin Mary, Christ's mother, the Jesuits included a "Marie Magdaleine" in their lists of virtuous Maries. LAC Collection Félix Martin (1611–1776), MG18-H27, "De la Mission des Hurons de N. D. de Lorette en 1676," fol. 60; Jansen, *Making of the Magdalen*, pp. 29–30.

famine of 1675, admirably suffering so other villagers could eat. She even redirected the Jesuit fathers' charity effort, suggesting other places where the food would better serve.[81] These Huron women shone for their proactive Christian deeds.

It can be argued that Jesuits were predisposed to see shades of the Virgin Mary everywhere, which is why they projected her on to these good Christian Maries. Jesuits were steeped in the Holy Mother's life and lore. For one, in the seventeenth century, Jesuits and Catholics more broadly were conditioned to recognize Mary in maternal suffering. Though Mary had many forms, the one that rang from most Catholic pulpits in the 1600s was an iteration of the *Mater Dolorosa*, or the Sorrowing Mother.[82] The *Mater Dolorosa* devotion originated in the Middle Ages alongside plague and famine.[83] In the thirteenth century, it was articulated in its most enduring form in the hymn "Stabat Mater Dolorosa." The verses of that hymn present Mary standing helpless at the foot of the cross, watching her only son suffer and die. Even more than Christ's final agonies, this snapshot of Mary was believed to have special power to wrench hearts and redirect lives.[84]

Schooled in this language of pain, the Jesuits in Canada were primed to read Mary in the suffering of Huron mothers, even those who did not share the Madonna's name. They set these women's brave forbearance in Marian light, highlighting their acceptance of difficult situations. "This mother had never seemed so admirable as she did in the resignation with which she witnessed the death of her dear [son] Ignace," a Jesuit reported in 1675.

> When she saw he was in danger, she went to offer the Holy Virgin a porcelain necklace, to tell her that she was presenting her son to her. Then, speaking to her [spiritual] Director, she told him, "My tears escape in spite of myself, because I do accept with all my Heart the privation of my children in punishment for my sins."[85]

81. *Relations Inédites de la Nouvelle-France*, p. 83.

82. Warner, "Mater Dolorosa."

83. This was another aspect of Mary that appears to have resonated especially with women, who sponsored and collected *Mater Dolorosa* imagery. Katz, "Regarding Mary," p. 82.

84. For one particularly vivid illustration of how Jesuits incorporated the concept of suffering Mary into their preaching: Renzoli, *Sermoni sopra la Passione*, pp. 132, 241–42.

85. "Cette mere n'a jamais paru plus admirable qu'en la resignation qu'elle a témoignée en la mort de son cher Ignace. Lorsqu'elle le vit en danger, elle alla offrir à la Sainte Vierge un beau collier de porcelaine, pour lui dire qu'elle lui présentait son fils. Ensuite, parlant à son Directeur, elle lui dit: 'C'est malgré moi qu'il m'échappe quelques larmes, car j'accepte

Huron mothers like this one were imitating Mary at her most trying and unpleasant moment. They surrendered their children and reined in their grief. They even approached Mary as a figure who might help them come to terms with their loss. The Jesuits did not orchestrate or imagine these emotional moments. They witnessed them, and in the genuine misery of their neophytes, they saw the sermons of the Passion brought to life.[86]

It is not entirely surprising that Jesuits were moved when their converts' experience and resilience echoed the familiar trials of Mary. But it is unexpected that they also glimpsed Mary among the Huron outside of this deeply instilled context of suffering. The behavior of *real* Maries stretched the Jesuits, leading them to revisit the mobility of the female divine, and indirectly transforming their vision of Mary. In order to perceive the traces of this influence, Jesuit records must be considered as more than a navel-gazing inroad into the internal mindset of the Jesuits. Like other Catholic writing, Jesuit letters point beyond themselves. Actual Maries could be preserved in Jesuit prose in the same way as Nikolà Frankopan, Ignace Tsaouenhohoui, and even their own Juan Maria Salvatierra: these names designated real authors, pilgrims, and house builders whose unsolicited actions were in critical dialogue with Catholic ideals. None of those individuals can be reduced to imaginary characters or objects of imposition, performing just for the spiritual enlightenment or purposes of missionary scribes.[87] In the context of this chapter about independent artists, readers are asked to see the ensuing Huron Marie described in a Jesuit letter as more than an image constructed by a Jesuit. Instead, they are invited to approach her as a fellow painter, like the other anonymous artists aggregated above. Marie Tsaouenté was a *representer* of the Virgin Mary, at the same time as she was seen, by others, to evoke that divine figure. Notably, Marie Tsaouenté was choosing to render herself, to inflect her Mary, in the *same* way as her contemporary across the Atlantic, the Italian Caravaggio: not as a figure of suffering or domesticity.

---

de tout mon Coeur la privation de mes enfants en punition de mes péchés.'" *Relations Inédites de la Nouvelle-France*, p. 215.

86. It is worth noting that Jesuits in Canada did not always see suffering women as symbolic of Mary. Jérôme Lalemant wrote of an Algonquin woman who was held captive by the Iroquois but escaped. Lalemant called her an "Amazon." He lamented that she was not Christian: "She had no thought of suffering . . . for her God, for she had never heard of Him." Lalemant, "Some Iroquois Surprised after Defeating the Algonquins," pp. 109, 111.

87. On taking Jesuit dialogue as serious historical evidence rather than simply rhetoric: Ginzburg, "Alien Voices."

Marie Tsaouenté stood out to the Jesuits above all the other good Christian Maries of the Lorette mission. They called her "La Précieuse" (The Precious One). She had studied the catechism and the Catholic faith so industriously that the Jesuits trusted her to teach and train other Indians at Lorette. "On top of this," wrote one Jesuit, "because so many Christians reside in her cabin . . . she assembles them around her every evening to repeat holy stories that the Jesuits told her and speeches they gave. Then she makes them say their prayers aloud and sing a spiritual song before they can retire to bed."[88] Within the domestic living space of her cabin, Marie Tsaouenté did the work of a Jesuit missionary.[89]

She also arbitrated in an awkward French and Huron encounter in 1675. A French orphan boy had drowned in a river near Lorette. The French wanted to bury him, but Christian burial was very different from traditional Huron death rites.[90] Concerned that the Hurons would be offended, the Jesuit François Vaillant approached Marie Tsaouenté and asked what she thought. Tsaouenté answered with tremendous confidence:

> No, my Father, [I am not offended] . . . to the contrary, I judge that you French, you have a better understanding of the honor that needs to be paid when we bury the dead with so much ceremony. Because when I saw yesterday the French throwing earth on the eyes, nose, mouth and other parts of the body of this child, I said to myself: "This is exactly what the Fathers have shown us, that there is nothing in man except the soul that is precious; and for the rest, there is nothing but earth and dust, and consequently the body separates from the soul, and does not need to be separated from the earth, since it is nothing but earth."[91]

88. "De plus, comme dans la cabane où elle demeure il y a un grand nombre de chrétiens . . . elle les assemble tous les soirs autour d'elle pour leur répéter les histories saintes qu'ont racontées les Pères et les discours qu'ils ont pronouncés. Ensuite elle leur fait faire les priers tout haut et chanter quelque cantique spirituel avant qu'ils se retirent pour prendre leur repos." *Relations Inédites de la Nouvelle-France*, p. 316.

89. François Vaillant's willingness to praise these activities for Marie Tsaouenté within a domestic space recalls the work of an "anonymous Jesuit" of late sixteenth- or early seventeenth-century Peru. That Jesuit also saw indigenous women as keys to transmitting Andean Catholicism within the family. This was also true in Japan, where Jesuits trained a cadre of women catechists to assist them in the 1600s with preaching, disputation with Buddhist priests, teaching, translation, baptism, confession, and more. On Peru: Mills, "Naturalization of Andean Christianities," pp. 530–31. On Japan: Ward, "Jesuits, Too," p. 643.

90. On Huron rituals of death: Brébeuf, "Of the Solemn Feast of the Dead [1636]," pp. 61–69.

91. "Non, mon Père, répondit-elle; au contraire, je jugeai que vous autres Français, vous aviez bien plus de connaissance de l'estime qu'il faut faire de chaque chose que nous

Vaillant observed that Tsaouenté then turned to the Indians standing around and continued expounding on her understanding of Christian death. He added wryly, "Then she made a beautiful speech about immortality and the nobility of our soul, to which there was nothing to add."[92]

There are at least two possible readings of Vaillant's description. The first one is to exclusively credit the author of the text, the Jesuit Vaillant. Marie Tsaouenté is thus reduced to a ventriloquist's puppet, spouting what the Jesuit wanted her to say. Before dismissing this reading, it must be noted that it is one that has been repeatedly applied to the mythohistory of Loreto. To offer an extreme instance of it, in 1531, author Girolamo Angelitta introduced the Virgin Mary in his first printed history of the Loreto shrine by quoting her words. He described her appearance to a hermit near Loreto. Refracted through Angelitta, Mary purportedly thundered at the hermit:

> Go tell this to the people of Recanati, whose country I chose from among all the nations to locate my seat . . . that [this] place is Holy, and terrible, because it is a Temple of God, in which the word was made flesh, and in which for a time there conversed Christ God the man, Author and writer of the law, and the Trinity, and the Angels, and I, of power exalted by a Chorus of Angels as humble Mother, & Virgin.[93]

Sixty years later, perhaps unsure how to handle Mary's reported apparition, the Jesuit historian Oratio Torsellino revised Angelitta's account. He drained out the voice of Mary, reporting this same encounter secondhand and as if it were a dream:

---

qui enterrons nos morts avec tant de cérémonie. Car quand je vis hier les Français jeter de la terre sur les yeux, le nez, la bouche, et les autres parties du corps de cet enfant; je dis en moi-même: 'Voilà justement ce que nos Pères nous ont tant de fois enseigné, qu'il n'y avait dans l'homme que l'âme qui fût précieuse; que pour la reste, ce n'était que terre et poussière, et par consequent le corps étant séparé de l'âme, il ne doit plus être séparé de la terre, n'étant lui-même que terre.'" *Relations Inédites de la Nouvelle-France*, pp. 78–79.

92. "Ensuite elle fit un beau discours sur l'immortalité et la noblesse de notre âme, auquel il n'y avait rien à ajouter." Ibid.

93. "Narra questo al popolo di Racanati, il cui paese fra tutte le nationi ho eletto, per locar vi la sede mia . . . che 'l luogo è Santo, e terribile, perche è Tempio di Dio, in cui il verbo si fece carne, & in cui per tanto spatio conversarono in terra Christio Iddio huomo, Autore e compitore della legge, e la Trinità, e gli Angioli, e io dal potente essaltata sopra i Chori de gli Angioli, humilissima Madre, & Vergine." Angelitta, *L'historia*, pp. 43–44.

> For the second yeare after the comming of the sacred House into Italy, our B. Lady appearing unto [a hermit] in his sleepe, and bidding him be of good comfort, told him that in Italy she had chosen a seat for the little House wherein her selfe did live on earth.[94]

Here, the voice of Marie Tsaouenté could be similarly excised and presented with a tacit question mark. It could be said that a Huron, Marie, appeared to a Jesuit, Vaillant, and brought him comfort by repeating his lesson that the Catholic God knows best. It could be left there.

But such a reading gives too little attention to the distant echo and possibility of a real (or divine) Marie having spoken. This analysis of Loreto's mythohistory has repeatedly offered a second kind of reading, potentially riskier because it cannot be fully substantiated, but also fruitful in the extra information it reveals. By this alternative reading, Marie Tsaouenté is not exclusively an invention of the Jesuit mind. She is an actual Huron woman called Marie who knows how to speak in Christian terms. She breaks into the historical record; the record does not enclose her into silence.

What does a real Marie Tsaouenté contribute to our understanding of the changing seventeenth-century imagery of Mary? First, she speaks, loudly, of an alternative to the Catholic seventeenth-century streams of good Christian women as grieving in silence, enclosed in the home, or in familiar form and color. Standing at the door of her cabin, consulted by a Jesuit, Marie Tsaouenté—alien to Europeans, yet also familiar—brings history and iconography together. This Huron Marie so deeply resembles Caravaggio's Virgin of Loreto, perched on the stoop of her mysterious Holy House (figure 6.3), that she brings the Italian artist's idealized painting to life. In her words to the petitioning Jesuit Vaillant, Marie "La Précieuse" ruminates on the movement of the soul, the "precious" spiritual core freed of the physical weight of its body. Is Mary—is Marie, in the end, the real mover of Catholic devotion? She leaves the Holy House behind and steps forward. Angels, pilgrims, and Jesuits were united in finding ways to portage Loreto's house, but in the end, one is left with this arresting universal symbol captured in paint, image, and prose: a female voice, the human woman who has endured more than seems possible, the black or white figure hovering in the liminal zone, defying boundaries, crossing the oceans.

Mary came to life in the Jesuit missions in the Americas in the seventeenth century for the same qualities that had put her Holy House at

94. Torsellino, *History of our B. Lady of Loreto*, pp. 63–64.

Loreto on the map two centuries earlier: she could move, literally and figuratively; she could be as human as she was divine, and as familiar as she was foreign; and she could weather many changes to remain popular and accessible. Underacknowledged renovators including painters, statue makers, Jesuit missionaries, and above all, Catholic women called attention to this versatility, whether they did so deliberately through artistic projects, or subconsciously in how they wore or honored a name. Cumulatively, these impromptu iconographers favored a mobile and independent Virgin. In this way, they contributed to the creation of a visual stamp for the Madonna of Loreto that was very different from the official seal of the Loreto sanctuary that opened this book in chapter 3 (figure 3.1). On the official seal from the late 1500s, the Virgin Mary sits placidly and quietly on her flying Holy House, ready to be transported by others. In most of her representations in the 1600s, however, in the European heartland near her shrine and on the American frontiers alike, the Madonna of Loreto was detached from her house, ready to fly again of her own volition. The new Marie of Lorette stood, and remains, as crucial counterpoint to competing renditions of Mary as disciplined and domestic.

CHAPTER SEVEN

Counters, Namers, and Processers

AGOSTINHO DE SANTA MARIA (1642–1728), a Descalced Augustinian friar from Portugal, spent the last three decades of his life taking inventory of sites dedicated to Mary.[1] Santa Maria focused his late seventeenth-century work on places named for Mary in Portuguese dominions. He cast his net wide when collecting Marys, reporting on hundreds of regional advocations. Santa Maria was not alone in trying to make sense of the diffuse Catholic labeling overseas by tallying. Jesuits such as Wilhelm Gumppenberg, Francisco de Florencia, and António Cordeiro also produced encyclopedic compilations of Marian sanctuaries across the world. Their projects suggest that mission names counted in the early modern period *because they were actually counted.* Cataloguers presented oft-repeated designations like "Nuestra Señora del Pilar" and the "Madonna of Loreto" as proof that Catholic belief had spread beyond European regions and out into the world.[2]

Counters like Santa Maria did not invent this claim that Marian names indicated devotion. The assumption was based on the actions of two other groups of Catholics: the namers themselves and the processers. Catholics who assigned the names of Mary abroad were aware that their actions would be read as belief, and some even anticipated being counted. Processers require a lengthier introduction, as they are a category with double meaning. Today, the verb "process" is associated with crunching

1. Santa Maria, *Santuário Mariano.*

2. Evonne Levy draws a contrast between perceptions of Catholic belief in Europe versus overseas. She describes paintings copied by artists at Japanese seminaries as radiating Catholic belief but then comments that "in Europe, feats of imitation were not usually taken as signs of belief." I argue otherwise here: *especially* in Europe, imitation conveyed Catholicism. Levy, *Propaganda and the Jesuit Baroque*, p. 203.

large amounts of numerical figures and is tied to computers or to the bureaucratic paperwork of organizations like the Internal Revenue Service, which processes United States tax returns. But the verb "process" can also indicate people who participate in a procession, in this case, a Catholic ritual of carrying a statue of Mary or a saint outside the church space. The first sense of the word involves collecting information and the second sense disseminating it, but in both usages, people "process" or find serious significance in preexisting data. Names matter to processers. Moving in procession is kindred to counting and naming because like those sister actions, it involves finding deep meaning in a discrete unit (in this case, a Catholic name). In the case of Loreto, namers imparted this Marian tag overseas knowing that it would be recognized by fellow Catholics; processers took it out of churches, demonstrating and enacting living devotion; and counters took namers and processers at their word, making inventories of when and where they used "Loreto."

The three groups are considered together here because they cross-validated each other. Their complicity sidesteps hierarchies of power. The counters highlighted in this chapter did not monitor namers for correction, in the infamous sense of the Panopticon in Michel Foucault's *Discipline and Punish* (1975). Nor did the processers in this chapter take the names given to them and consciously or subconsciously resist them, in the now-canonical manner of the peasants in James Scott's *Weapons of the Weak* (1985). This is not to say that such power dynamics did not exist in the seventeenth-century Atlantic world, but rather to showcase a large and diverse group of Catholics who performed outside those parameters, voluntarily writing themselves and others into global registries. These Catholics repeatedly selected, invested in, and recorded the designation "Loreto." While they did so in part to be heard by an audience of fellow humans and devout, they also counted, named, and processed in order to be heard by the divine, by the Madonna of Loreto and God themselves.

This chapter begins with counters including the Augustinian Santa Maria and the Jesuits Wilhelm Gumppenberg, Francisco de Florencia, António Cordeiro, and Miguel Venegas. This assortment of atlas makers, inventory compilers, and biographers shows the diversity and quantity of individuals engaged in the counting project of the seventeenth century. It was these counters who fixed and publicized the notion that the spread of Loreto was collective and intentional. Attention then turns to some of the namers featured by the above writers, including the Jesuits Juan Maria Salvatierra and Antonio de Orellana. Finally, it examines Jesuit records that point to the Inka of Cuzco and the Monquí of California, whose processions in honor of Loreto brought the name currency and freshness. While links and common impulses between these groups of counters, namers, and processers are duly noted, the variations between them are just as telling. There were many ways to make Loreto count in the seventeenth century, and that variety allowed for dramatically wide participation.

Anchoring Ideal: Counting Loreto in Seventeenth-Century Marian Atlases

The Madonna of Loreto appeared in the Augustinian Santa Maria's ten-volume global inventory of Mary fifteen times.[3] Though that may seem a drop in the bucket among thousands of sites described, Santa Maria thought it significant. He wondered at the extent of the spread of this particular Italian devotion. He even posited a divine reason for it:

> I believe that just as the Angels moved the Madonna of Loreto from Dalmatia [to Italy] . . . because the Dalmatians did not know how to esteem such a great treasure; so, too, did they take the Sacred Image [of Loreto] to another part, where she would receive the following and veneration she deserves.[4]

Santa Maria saw angels behind the spread of "Loreto." His reference to them evoked the mysterious voyage of the original Marian shrine complex of Loreto, but he extended the story. He noted that three centuries after the miraculous transport of the Holy House of Loreto from Nazareth to Dalmatia to Italy, its Madonna continued to travel, quite purposefully, to other places. The proof lay in the repeated surfacing of her name around the world. To Santa Maria, every site named for her suggested successful movement. Each Loreto signaled new, even potentially better Catholic devotees.

Notably, Jesuits were not the angels or the stars in Santa Maria's picture of Loreto's triumphant expansion. By his count, they were barely there at all. Santa Maria mentioned only one Jesuit propagator of the

3. Santa Maria, *Santuário Mariano*, tomos 1–10. Ten of Santa Maria's sites were in Portugal, three in Brazil, one in Asia, and one in the Philippines.

4. "Creyo, que assim como os Anjos a levàrao da Dalmacia a Senhora do Loreto, que elles haviào trazido de Nazareth; porque não souberão os Dalmatas estimar hum tão grande thesouro: assim tambem levariào esta Sagrada Imagem a outra parte, aonde se lhe desse todo o culto, & veneração que ella merece." Santa Maria speaks here of the origins of a Loreto chapel in Portugal's bishopric of Algarve. Ibid., tom. 6, pp. 432–33.

devotion, in the distant Philippines: Francisco Colin (1592–1660), who erected a chapel to Loreto while serving as rector at the Jesuit College of St. Joseph in Manila.[5] Santa Maria attributed most of the other Loretos he inventoried to Catholic devout who dedicated family chapels to her.[6] Beyond such chapels, he credited other religious orders with establishing convents and monasteries in her name. For two "Loretos," he singled out the Franciscans. He described a Holy House replica constructed by the Capuchins in 1575 at their Convent of San Antonio in Tancos, Portugal.[7] He also told of a sculpture of the Madonna of Loreto that was purportedly brought to the area of Chincheo, China (the Bay of Amoy)[8] by a Franciscan friar, Odorico.[9] Santa Maria's collection challenges the notion that transporting Loreto overseas was a peculiarly *Jesuit* initiative.[10]

Nevertheless, while Jesuits were certainly not the only ones naming, counting, or processing Loreto, many Jesuit counters made much of their society's affinity to this Madonna. Some even went so far as to suggest that the Jesuits were, indeed, her seventeenth-century angelic transport. Jesuit counters inflected their tallies differently from Santa Maria, as evidenced in the writing of four Jesuit contemporaries, Gumppenberg, Florencia, Cordeiro, and Venegas.

5. Ibid., tom. 8, p. 380. Francisco Colin worked in the Philippines for thirty-five years during part of which he served as Jesuit provincial of that region (1639–44). He is also known for his published work about Jesuit evangelization in that province, *Labor evangélica* (Madrid, 1663). Lach and Van Kley, *Asia in the Making of Europe*, p. 353; Cushner, "Early Jesuit Missionary Methods in the Philippines," p. 366.

6. Santa Maria, *Santuário Mariano*, tomos 1–10. Ten of the fifteen were private family chapels.

7. This is the only Holy House replica that Santa Maria mentions. The Capuchins, like the Jesuits, cultivated the Lauretan devotion strongly from their earliest emergence as an order in the 1520s. Ibid., tom. 3, pp. 500–507; Regni, *Loreto e i cappuccini*.

8. On the location of Chincheo: *South China in the Sixteenth Century*, pp. 313–26.

9. Santa Maria, *Santuário Mariano*, tom. 8, pp. 22–24. Santa Maria refers to the legendary and beatified Italian Franciscan, Odorico da Pordenone (1286–1331), who traveled through Tibet and China in the 1320s and wrote of his adventures. Odorico lived a century or more before the Loreto devotion's consolidation and popularity in Italy. It appears that Jesuits in China were trying to explain and validate the presence of an old, previously venerated statue that was taken to be Mary by searching for early Christian roots for it. In their story of provenance, Odorico is given the role frequently bestowed on St. Thomas the Apostle, who was believed by Jesuits such as Manuel da Nóbrega (1517–70) to have brought Christianity to the Americas centuries before European contact. On the travels of Odorico: [Odoric of Pordenone], *Travels of Friar Odoric*. On St. Thomas the Apostle and belief in his presence in the Americas: Vigneras, "Saint Thomas, Apostle of America."

10. On the many non-Jesuits who transported Loreto overseas: Vélez, "Les voyages outre-mer d'un nom."

Wilhelm Gumppenberg (1609–75) was the most well-known of these chroniclers of Mary. Later collectors of Marian devotions like Santa Maria based their own surveys on Gumppenberg's relatively slim four-volume *Atlas Marianus sive de Imaginibus Deiparae per Orbem Christianum miraculosis* (Ingolstadt, 1657–59). Santa Maria cited Gumppenberg, although he had arrived at a more subdued conclusion about Loreto in the world. Gumppenberg asserted that the Madonna of Loreto was the most common image of Mary in the world.[11] The German Jesuit spoke from personal experience. He had made a pilgrimage to the shrine of Loreto in 1632. He also lived in the German north during a time of heightened popularity of this Italian Madonna.[12] He collected twelve hundred different images of Mary for publication. Though his book had greater scope than any previous inventories of Marian sanctuaries, the bulk of Gumppenberg's images were taken from the Loreto-infused German region he knew best.[13]

It was not his emphasis on Loreto that made fellow counters like Santa Maria turn to Gumppenberg, however. The Jesuit's work counted Catholicism in a new way, novel even among the ranks of the Society of Jesus, where information gathering was a finely honed aspect of training. As historian Trevor Johnson notes, "numbers counted [to the Jesuits], and the Jesuits duly counted numbers."[14] But Jesuits focused on counting certain phenomena to the exclusion of others. They counted the crowds they drew in rural missions and the number of people they baptized in American missions. They also counted their own, keeping track of the growing ranks of Jesuit novices as a mark of their success and even noting how many Jesuits showed special devotion to Mary.[15]

11. Gumppenberg even used a woodcut of the Madonna of Loreto seated atop the *Santa Casa* as a frontispiece for his work. By Gumppenberg's measure, the Virgin of Loreto was only slightly ahead of the Roman image of Mary at Santa Maria Maggiore in terms of worldwide diffusion. Noreen, "Icon of Santa Maria Maggiore, Rome," p. 664n11.

12. Freedberg comments that during Gumppenberg's lifetime, there were eighteen chapels to Loreto built in Bavaria alone. This surge in popularity is considered in chapter 5 with regard to Holy House replicas. Freedberg, *Power of Images*, p. 113.

13. Liechtenberger, *Encyclopédie des sciences religieuses*, p. 311.

14. Johnson, "Blood, Tears and Xavier-Water," p. 190.

15. In 1650, Hippolyte Marracci published the stories of three hundred Mary-favoring Jesuits in his *Bibliotheca Mariana*. This has since been followed up by the Jesuit Carlos Sommervogel's multivolume *Bibliotheca Mariana de la Compagnie de Jésus* (Paris, 1890), an exhaustive bibliography of all Jesuit publications related to Mary. For more recent scholarly notice of Jesuit devotion to Mary: Levy, *Propaganda and the Jesuit Baroque*, p. 17; Liechtenberger, *Encyclopédie des sciences religieuses*, p. 311.

But this was not Gumppenberg's project any more than it was Santa Maria's. Gumppenberg did not count Jesuits, converts, or crowds. He counted Mary as she appeared in image and miracle, in name and in place. The four were inextricably woven together in his *Atlas*.[16] Gumppenberg's primary innovation in collating images, miracles, and names was to fix these to precise places on the world map. He chose a cutting-edge title for his compilation: *Atlas Marianus*, an atlas of Mary. "Atlas" was only just making the shift in general meaning from the globe-burdened figure of Greek mythology to a collection of maps. Gerardus Mercator had published his *Atlas, Sive Cosmographicae Meditationes De Fabrica Mundi* (Duisburg, 1585–95) a mere half century earlier. The more recent two-volume *Atlas Novus* (Netherlands, 1635–58) was more likely the inspiration for Gumppenberg's title, coinciding, as it did, with Gumppenberg's extended period of research into Marian sanctuaries. The *Atlas Novus* was designed by the Dutch cartographers Willem and Joan Blaeu, father and son. They had created and bound maps with the ambition of charting and naming the whole globe.[17] Gumppenberg included no maps, but his aim was the same. He meant to show the entire world as colored by Mary's presence.

With regions thus shaded in, patterns were apparent: particular Madonnas surfaced and resurfaced. Loreto, Italy, was no longer a discrete Marian sanctuary. It was aligned with Loreto in Manila, in Chincheo, in Portugal, and elsewhere. Though the Madonna of Loreto was one of many Marys featured in Gumppenberg's inventory, her recurrence in places like the Moxos missions in the Amazon River basin transmitted a sense of her as a global presence. Gumppenberg's atlas brought her fame by displaying her many offshoots all in one book, and all of a piece. Later writers of Marian inventories followed suit, reacting to Loreto's newly mapped aura of fame.

16. His diverse images of Mary have captured the most recent scholarly interest: Noreen, "Icon of Santa Maria Maggiore, Rome"; Freedberg, *Power of Images*; Scheer, "From Majesty to Mystery." In the seventeenth century, however, Santa Maria focused not on Gumppenberg's images but on his accounts of miracles. For an entertaining, abbreviated selection from Gumppenberg's assortment of Marian miracles: Michael P. Carroll, *Madonnas That Maim*, p. 73.

17. The Blaeu cartographers followed up the *Atlas Novus* with its better known sequel, the magnificently illustrated eleven-volume *Atlas Maior* (Netherlands, 1662–67). The *Atlas Novus* also found wide usage, though, especially in regions that had previously not been mapped with precision. Stone, "Origins and Sources of the Blaeu Atlas"; [Blaeu], *Atlas Maior of 1665*.

Francisco de Florencia (1619–95), a Mexican creole, may have been inspired by Gumppenberg's collection to create an iconographical map of his own home region of New Spain (Mexico). After spending a decade in Europe procuring Jesuits to serve in New Spain, Florencia returned home and spent ten years researching locally venerated Madonnas to compile his *Zodiaco Mariano* (1755). Between 1685 and 1695, Florencia produced histories of Nuestra Señora de los Remedios, the Virgins of Guadalupe, Loreto, Zapopan, and San Juan de los Lagos, and also the Crucified Christ of Chalma and the Archangel San Miguel.[18] Florencia celebrated the Catholicism of his region in the same way as Gumppenberg had emphasized his local circuits in Germany. Interestingly, Loreto appeared in both of their accounts. But in Florencia's *Zodiaco*, she appears as a European import alongside Marian advocations that had emerged in Mexico. The Jesuit deliberately mixed old and new designators in order to establish his territory as part of a larger Christendom. In this context, his Catholic predecessors who brought familiar Marian names to New Spain had left him handy tickets of entry to the global Catholic community.

Florencia was not alone in using imported, recycled Virgins to put his homeland on the Catholic world map. His contemporary across the Atlantic in Portugal the Jesuit António Cordeiro (1641–1722) also made a hobby of Marian cartography. Cordeiro had even studied Santa Maria's ten volumes on Mary in the Portuguese empire.[19] But while Santa Maria, Gumppenberg, and Florencia each strove to be comprehensive in their surveys of Mary's presence, Cordeiro focused in on two specific Madonnas. He wrote a multivolume work provocatively entitled *Loreto Lusitano, Virgem Senhora da Lapa* (Lisboa, 1719; "The Portuguese Loreto: Our Lady the Virgin of Lapa").[20] In *Loreto Lusitano*, Cordeiro attempted to promote

18. Dyck, "Patriotic Tradition of Francisco de Florencia's *Zodiaco Mariano*." Jason Dyck argues that Spanish America was "patriotically invented by Creole religious scholars through sacred maps of miraculous images." I have argued instead that patriotism (nationalism) is only the tip of the iceberg. Florencia *was* after promoting the particularities of New Spain with creole pride, but he did this in a distinctly expansive, *Catholic* way. He used integration and repetition rather than separation. Florencia's *Zodiaco Mariano* is as much about seeing connections between New Spain and the Catholic world as it is about setting New Spain apart.

19. Cordeiro cited Santa Maria in his work. Cordeiro, *Loreto Lusitano*, p. 172.

20. Ibid. This work is lesser known than Cordeiro's other published history, which focused on the Azores: Cordeiro, *História Insulana* (1717). On Cordeiro's publications: Wessels, *Early Jesuit Travellers in Central Asia*, p. 8.

the local Portuguese devotion to the Virgin of Lapa by comparing her to the Virgin of Loreto.[21] He used the fame of the latter to exalt the former.[22]

Cordeiro drew two main parallels between the devotions of the Madonnas of Lapa and Loreto.[23] First, he asserted that they were both world renowned; second, he explained how they were both the special project of the Jesuits. In discussing these commonalities, he spent remarkably little time on the Portuguese Virgin of Lapa. Instead he wrote pages and pages about the Italian Loreto, as if by stressing her fame, Lapa—and the Jesuits—would benefit by simple association.[24] In the Old World, just as in the New, the name Loreto counted to Jesuits as a way to connect with mainstream Catholicism.

But Cordeiro took his counting and linking a step further than his fellow Jesuits Gumppenberg and Florencia. He argued that the Virgin of Loreto was so well known *because of the Jesuits*. Cordeiro did this not by counting Loretos as his predecessor Santa Maria had done, but by actually counting Jesuits. He enumerated the exemplary Jesuits whom he felt had displayed an affinity for Loreto: St. Francis Xavier; St. Francis Borgia;

21. Cordeiro, *Loreto Lusitano*, pp. 173–76. The sanctuary of the Virgin of Lapa is in the mountains of the Portuguese interior in today's district of Viseu. Though it had drawn pilgrims since at least the fifteenth century for its miracle-inducing image of Mary, it was a full century before the shrine took new life at the industrious hands of the Jesuits who moved into Lapa in the seventeenth century. They built and expanded the shrine chapel and founded a Jesuit college there in 1685.

22. Cordeiro was not the only one to cross-promote Marian shrines. In 1517, an anonymous broadside was printed and distributed at the Marian sanctuary of Ettal in upper Bavaria that had a woodcut illustration of the Virgin of Ettal surrounded by the names of *four* prominent Marian pilgrimage sites as well as her own: Loreto (Italy), Einsiedeln (Switzerland), and Aachen and Altötting (Germany). Philip Soergel concludes that this was an "advertisement attempt[ing] to lend luster to the less well known Ettal." Soergel, *Wondrous in His Saints*, p. 38.

23. Cordeiro drew other comparisons as well though he did not belabor them. He noted the similarity between the two Virgins' origin stories, commenting on how both devotions indicated Christian military victory over Muslims and growing European nationalism. In Lapa's case, this was expressed through her mythohistory's glorification of the Portuguese kings. Cordeiro, *Loreto Lusitano*, pp. 173–74 and iii–v.

24. Cordeiro's analogy does not appear to have brought the Virgin of Lapa much broader acclaim. However, she did gain some unexpected publicity from non-Jesuit circles across the Atlantic in the early eighteenth century. At that time, Portuguese settlers in Brazil established a large mining district, Minas Gerais. One district of Minas Gerais was named after the Virgin of Lapa. So the Portuguese Madonna found global recognition by the late 1700s owing to booming trade in green tourmaline gemstones mined at the municipality of Virgem da Lapa, Brazil. Ramos, "Slavery in Brazil."

Pedro Fabro, one of the first nine Jesuits; and St. Ignatius Loyola.[25] Cordeiro then counted the number of Jesuit seminaries and students in Europe: twenty-three of them, with two thousand students. To Cordeiro, these sums were proof that Mary had given Jesuits a mandate to teach, and to teach about Loreto. This use of current numbers to backdate or bolster a divine mission may seem strange to twenty-first-century reasoning. But to Cordeiro, the numbers amounted to logical evidence.[26] The Jesuits counted as teachers because they could literally be counted in the schools.

They could also be counted in the original Loreto sanctuary in Italy. As noted in chapter 3, the Jesuits had established a college of confessors there in the late sixteenth century. According to Cordeiro, when listening to penitent pilgrims at Loreto, the Jesuit confessors

> assumed the posts that the very Angels had set up . . . [because] God ordered that the second Apostles of the Society of Jesus should follow, in those positions, the Saints of the Heavens, so that in Heaven they would come to fill the empty chairs of the fallen Angels.[27]

Cordeiro saw the Jesuits associated with the Loreto devotion as filling the shoes of the apostles and, even more dramatically, as taking on the role of angels. By his account, by liberally but purposefully planting the name Loreto abroad, Jesuits rode the coattails of the flying Virgin they promoted so passionately.

Santa Maria had written of angels carrying Loreto across the globe. Cordeiro wrote of Jesuits as angels because of their work with Loreto. The conflation of angels and Jesuits around Loreto could be dismissed as mere poetic self-aggrandizement were it not for myriad other tallies from the time. Atlases, catalogs, and inventories do indeed show sizeable

25. Cordeiro, *Loreto Lusitano*, pp. 191–92 (Xavier); 202 (Borgia); 189 (Fabro); 188 (Loyola).

26. "Com razão logo dizemos que quiz a Virgem Senhora que a Companhia ensinasse em seminarios, collegios e escolas a seculares publicas, que lhes ensinasse a todos as letras Divinas, & humanas para o espiritual fruto, que dahi (como jà vimos) se seguio." / "It is therefore with reason that we say that the Virgin Mary wanted the Society to teach in seminaries, colleges and schools to secular publics, to teach them all the Divine word and the humanities for spiritual fruit, which ensued from their instruction (as we have already seen)." Ibid., p. 226.

27. "Assim quis [a Santa Madre Igreja Romana] que houvesse Collegio da Companhia em Loreto, como ha, & que dos Padres do mesmo Collegio fossemos Penitenciarios, como sâo, substituindo as cadeyras que alli tinhao instuido, & começado a ler, os mesmos Anjos; ordenando Deos que os segundos Apostolos da sua Companhia de Jesus succedessem em ler cadeyros, aos Santos do Ceo, & de modo que no ceo venhâo a alcançar as cadeyras, que os máos Anjos perderão." Ibid., p. 179.

numbers of Jesuits energetically transporting and imparting Loreto, Lapa, and other Catholic devotions around the world. So does a more personal genre: Jesuit biography. Some Jesuit biographers such as Miguel Venegas (1680–1764) also counted Loreto in the lives of their subjects. The more intimate gaze of a biographer allows a closer interrogation of what was happening on the ground when the name of Loreto was being applied and invoked. This is a useful counterpoint to the distant, aggregative perspectives of the tabulators considered above. The works of Santa Maria, Gumppenberg, Florencia, and Cordeiro retroactively cast the group of diffusers of Loreto in mythical light, as deliberate players in a joint project to publicize an Italian Madonna. If biographers could isolate a single namer's experience, perhaps the case study of one would show the process of Loreto's spread as more organic, and less contrived.

The Jesuit biographer Miguel Venegas disappoints in this regard. He was drawn to count Loreto when he researched his subject and colleague the missionary Juan Maria Salvatierra; he celebrated this one man's use of Loreto as much as Gumppenberg celebrated his scores of Lauretan images. Venegas was born in Puebla, Mexico, and spent his life there, occupying his last decades with compiling histories of the Jesuits of that region, especially western Mexico and Baja California.[28] He had himself wished to serve in the California missions, but illness prevented him. Venegas ended up posted at a quiet backwater, the Jesuit *hacienda* of Chicomocelo. His writing served as an outlet for him to experience fieldwork vicariously by reconstructing the lives of Jesuit colleagues such as Juan Maria Salvatierra and Juan Bautista Zappa.[29] When he had gathered all the materials available on Zappa and Salvatierra, Venegas saw a common design in their careers: the Madonna of Loreto.[30]

Venegas capitalized on the recurring theme that he saw, making it the lynchpin of his biography of Salvatierra in particular. He dedicated his posthumous account of Salvatierra's life to the Virgin of Loreto, addressing

28. Of these, the best known is his six-hundred-page manuscript "Empresas Apostólicas," which was edited and much abbreviated by fellow Jesuit Andrés Marcos Burriel to be published as *Noticia de la California* (1757).

29. Venegas also wrote the posthumous biography of Juan Bautista Zappa (*Vida y Virtudes*, 1754). His biographies of Salvatierra and Zappa and much of his other work are collected in the five-volume *Obras Californianas del Padre Miguel Venegas, S.J.*

30. Venegas researched meticulously for his biographies of both men, circulating questionnaires to missionaries who had known them and drawing extensively on their archived correspondence. Mathes, "Ethnohistoric Evidence," p. 47.

his prologue directly to her.[31] It was not just his book, but Salvatierra's entire life that Venegas presented as a tribute to this Italian Madonna, whom he likely saw as the force behind all of Salvatierra's deeds. He infused purpose and pattern into Salvatierra's experience of her. For instance, Venegas told of how Salvatierra fell ill while returning from Mexico City to Loreto Conchó, Baja California, in 1717. He had to stop at one of his former posts, the college of Guadalajara. Carried inside on a litter, Salvatierra asked to be taken immediately to the copy of Loreto's Holy House that he had erected at that site.[32] Here, Venegas and Salvatierra seem to agree about this Madonna's special powers.

But for other moments of Salvatierra's life, Venegas diverged from his subject's perspective, playing up human deliberation. This is evident in Venegas's detailed description of how Salvatierra's remains were exhumed eight years after his death by the Jesuit provincial of Mexico, Gaspar Rodero. Rodero did so in order to personally transfer Salvatierra's remains to the inside of Guadalajara's Holy House of Loreto chapel.[33] Venegas's repeated emphasis on moments like this make Salvatierra's piecemeal plantings of Loreto retrospectively seem to be a full-fledged Jesuit initiative.

Like Cordeiro with his numbers, Venegas did not invent this idea of the propagation of Loreto being a special project to the Jesuits in particular. He took it from his source material. The Jesuit missionary Salvatierra had himself noted that his Holy Houses of Loreto were only a few among many that were being built by others in his order. Salvatierra had written of contemporaneous copies of the Holy House that he knew of "in Tepotzotlán, Querétaro, Guadalajara, San Luis Potosí, and even in the most distant Missions."[34]

But from the steps-removed distance of a counter, Venegas took Salvatierra's observation further. Like the compilers of Marian atlases who painstakingly inventoried place names, Venegas felt that the cumulative effect of Lauretan structures built by Jesuits had great significance. Combining the output of Salvatierra and his friend Zappa, Venegas noted that their buildings were "a very excellent way of inspiring devotion for the

31. "To the most Holy Mary, Mother of God, Lady of armies and Conqueress of New Kingdoms in her Sacred Image of Loreto." Venegas, *Juan María de Salvatierra*, pp. 51–52.

32. Ibid., pp. 219–20.

33. Ibid., pp. 231–32. A later rector of the college of Guadalajara, Felipe Badillo, moved Salvatierra's remains one last time, from the chancel of the Holy House chapel to the niche in one of its walls, directly below the statue of the Madonna of Loreto.

34. Salvatierra's c. 1680 letter to his brother as paraphrased by Venegas, *Juan María de Salvatierra*, p. 105.

Most Holy Virgin."[35] As if to illustrate this, he told of another Italian Jesuit who had carried off to the Philippines some of his collected papers pertaining to Salvatierra.[36] This unnamed Jesuit had been looking for a missionary to emulate in his new work in the Philippines, and he saw his fellow countryman Salvatierra as a good model. Venegas loaned him the papers so the young missionary could learn from Salvatierra's example.

This exchange of papers suggests that Salvatierra's actions—including the building of Lauretan Holy Houses—were under scrutiny by many in the Society of Jesus. Salvatierra's life was being mined by Jesuit colleagues for ideas on how best to proselytize.[37] Because of this demand for success stories from the field, within months of his death, Salvatierra's internal experiences of the Italian Virgin had been transformed into a published manifesto of her importance to Jesuit mission everywhere. But in this process of amplification, biographers, counters, and readers lost some of the sense of coincidence and spontaneity so evident in Salvatierra's own accounts of his actions. The actual experiences reported by namers themselves are crucial correctives to the anchoring claims of Loreto's counters. What did it mean to namers to repeat and implant "Loreto" overseas? Why did they choose to disseminate "Loreto" in particular?

Actual Patterns: Naming as Litany in the Jesuit Missions to the Americas

Catholic inventories assiduously tracked Loreto's namers as they set forth from an Italian hilltop to Atlantic seaports, from the cities and rural outposts of New Spain to the northern forests of the Huron, and from the remote Moxos missions in Peru back, at last, to metropolitan printing presses. The circular trajectory at first confounds notions of European or Catholic centralized authority and then reinforces it—if mostly in name. Yet the orderly printed compilations of counters whitewash the more chaotic reported experiences of the namers themselves. Naming in the seventeenth century, the heyday of imperial overseas expansion, tends to be associated with territorial conquest, imposition, and in the famous

35. Venegas, *Juan María de Salvatierra*, p. 105.

36. Ibid., pp. 56–57.

37. Venegas encouraged this by sharing his research into Salvatierra's life and also by direct exhortation. He stated outright that the purpose of his biography and, by extension, of Salvatierra's own life, was to "act as a stimulant, particularly among the Jesuits, to [the] devotion and worship" of the Madonna of Loreto. Ibid., p. 53.

terminology of Patricia Seed, "possession."[38] But there were many reasons for choosing the name Loreto in the 1600s that did not include asserting cultural or religious supremacy. Picene merchants from the coast near Italy's Loreto sanctuary named their ships and settlements after Loreto to commemorate their origins and to give thanks to the Madonna of their home coast. French and Huron Catholics took on the name Loreto as an additional appellation; they were not assigned the name but chose to claim it and fought to use it to mark their new connections to particular Catholic communities.[39] In this section, Jesuits posted to Mexico and the Amazon River basin, the frontiers of Spanish America, are considered as another group of namers who had distinctive reasons for applying Loreto abroad that cannot be reduced to establishing European authority. These Jesuits rarely cited promotion of Loreto, their own Society of Jesus, the Catholic Church, or European empires as their primary or exclusive motive for choosing the name Loreto. Instead, they told of the consolation and effectiveness of repeating a familiar name. Jesuit namers indicated that above all else, the repetition of Loreto made them feel that they were part of a global chorus that was heard not just by humans, but by God.

This section opens with the Juan Maria Salvatierra's casual and varied applications of Loreto's name in the Mexican field, which contrast with this Jesuit's more calculated project of replicating Loreto's Holy House described in chapter 5, and with his biographer Venegas's interpretations. Namers including Salvatierra often alluded to litany, a personal spiritual experience hinged on repetition, as the impetus for their choice of the name Loreto. Later counters like Venegas, however, emphasized the masterful Jesuit strategy of the namers instead, finding retroactive justification for namers' choices. By contrast, the Jesuit namers' own reported reasons are taken seriously here: unlike their later chroniclers, they wrote that invoking Loreto was first and foremost an act of meaningful repetition directed to Mary and God, and only secondarily a means to magnify or instruct. Both dynamics—repetition and instruction—informed Jesuit naming choices overseas, but the namers spoke mostly of the former.

Salvatierra is considered alongside his Jesuit colleagues to the south, in the Moxos missions of the Spanish Viceroyalty of Peru. Those Jesuits' stated reasons for naming a mission site Loreto differ from Salvatierra's, but in both cases, Jesuits were not ham-fistedly imposing the name, blindly following church policy, or simply selecting the name to use for

38. Seed, *Ceremonies of Possession*; Greenblatt, *Marvelous Possessions*, pp. 56, 60.

39. Vélez, "Les voyages outre-mer d'un nom."

doctrinal instruction. In Peru and Mexico alike, Jesuit namers wrote instead of the circular act of repeating Loreto in order to be recognized. This desire for recognition was felt twofold. Part of the urgency was individual, stemming from the need to be heard by God, a process that was linked to the litany. Part of it can also be attributed to a desire to be heard by human contemporaries, as if the namers were themselves aware of the counters waiting to tally them. The Society of Jesus was a relatively late arrival to Spanish America, a group tardiness that prompted their members to seek publicity in a mission field where they—like many of their converts—felt new to the quickly changing scene.[40] Pronouncing Loreto abroad was a way to be heard by both divine and human spheres.

The Jesuit Salvatierra can first be seen mobilizing the name Loreto in Mexico to catch divine attention, to seek help, not to dominate or convert. His biographer, Venegas, vividly recreated a moment in which this Jesuit was moved to purposefully recall Loreto for reassurance. In Venegas's vignette, Salvatierra was rector of the Jesuit college of Tepotzotlán near Mexico City when one of the Jesuit novices, Joseph Toledo Chipi, fell gravely ill. Salvatierra carried him to the chapel of Loreto inside the college. Venegas recounted:

> the Venerable Father [Salvatierra] . . . firmly enjoin[ed Chipi] to commend himself devoutly to the Most Holy Virgin. He laid the sick man on the platform before the altar then kneeling down began to recite the litanies of Our Lady, the sick one replying to each verse, "Pray for me." An admirable thing truly! Just as the litanies were finished the sick man was completely restored to health to the surprise of all in the house, who a short time before despaired of the man's life.[41]

It is a touching scene: a man on the brink of death, barely able to speak, using the reassuringly familiar prompts of an oft-repeated prayer, the Litany of Loreto, to beg Mary to save his life. Salvatierra brought the novice as close as he could to Mary in her incarnation of the Madonna of Loreto.

40. The first Jesuits were dispatched to Brazil in 1549, less than a decade after the founding of the Society of Jesus. In addition to their youth as a missionary operation, Jesuits arrived to the New World several decades after Franciscan missionaries, who were in the vanguard of Spanish occupation of the Americas, with their famous "Twelve Apostles" arriving in Mexico City in 1524. The repercussions of Jesuits being among the newest Catholic missionaries to the Americas affected Jesuit internal policies as well as their approaches to conversion in different regions. For just one example, there is the case of how Jesuits chose to publicly discipline one of their own, a mestizo Jesuit Blas Valera, in Peru in the late 1590s, only a few decades after Jesuit arrival: Hyland, *Gods of the Andes*, chapter 2.

41. Venegas, *Juan María de Salvatierra*, pp. 313–14.

He urged Chipi to recite a litany named for her, inside the chapel dedicated to her, right at the altar. According to Salvatierra as filtered through Venegas, it was the effectiveness of Chipi's prayer—his earnest and desperate chanting of the Litany of Loreto—that incited Mary, the Virgin of Loreto, to restore his health.[42]

It was this litany, named for Italy's Madonna, that Jesuits repeated abroad far more often than the myriad copies of her icon and house. Most Jesuits shared with Salvatierra and Chipi the firsthand experience of finding reassurance and hope, if not healing, in the power of its repetition. The Litany of Loreto was compiled and published in Dillingen in 1558 by the Jesuit provincial of upper Germany, Peter Canisius (1521–97). Canisius's litany was only one of many Marian litanies developed in the 1500s. Litanies had their origins in the collective chanting of Latin prayer, a practice that dated back to late antiquity. They were lists of attributes of a saint, Mary, or Christ designed to be recited and thus committed to memory.[43] But the Litany of Loreto received a boost in popularity from German Jesuits, who were eager to endorse this latest articulation of prayer as conceived by one of their most respected members. They rehearsed it in mass and en masse, performed it on rural missions, printed and distributed it on affordable broadsheets, illustrated it with woodcuts, and set it to music.[44] Its popularity spilled out of Germany, where it had become the most well-known of Marian litanies in the course of only three decades. Pope Sixtus V acknowledged its prominence by formally sanctioning the Litany of Loreto in 1587, and offering a generous plenary indulgence of two hundred days' respite from purgatory to each Catholic who recited it fully.[45]

Although the Jesuit Canisius named his litany after Loreto, there was nothing in his prayer to denote the particularities of Mary as she was presented at the namesake Adriatic hilltop shrine. Three quarters of the Litany of Loreto is formulaic. It opens and closes with brief appeals to God, the Holy Spirit, Christ, and Mary.[46] In between there are forty-two

42. Salvatierra's intervention parallels an odd incident involving the author of the Litany of Loreto himself. In Altötting, Germany in 1570, the Jesuit Peter Canisius performed an exorcism on two women by directing them to recite the Litany of Loreto and placing them on a church altar. Soergel, *Wondrous in His Saints*, pp. 122–25.

43. Seventeenth-century litanies found precedent in the rosary, which has thirteenth-century origins: Winston-Allen, *Stories of the Rose*.

44. They also depicted it pictorially in churches. J. C. Smith, *Sensuous Worship*, pp. 147, 156; Bailey, *Between Renaissance and Baroque*, p. 178.

45. Tavard, *Thousand Faces of the Virgin Mary*, p. 95; J. C. Smith, *Sensuous Worship*, p. 228n76.

46. J. C. Smith, *Sensuous Worship*, pp. 145–46; p. 227n51.

descriptive phrases about Mary. Volumes have been written about the significance of this rich array of Marian titles, but most noteworthy here is that none of the litany's titles single out the Italian devotional complex (house with icon) of the Madonna of Loreto.[47] They refer to Mary in general. Her universal qualities are accentuated by the overall effect of repetition, through which the varied symbols and adjectives are drummed out by the return to four recurring phrases. Consider what the reciter of the Litany of Loreto would pronounce over and over again, with only a brief interruption to the series: "Mother," nine times; "Virgin," six times; "Queen," eight times; "pray for us," forty-two times. *Mary—Mother, Virgin, Queen—**pray for us***. This was the essential message imparted by the "repetition, sheer repetition"[48] in the Litany of Loreto.

It has been argued that this sort of droning "oral recital of prayers . . . [was an] effective means of impelling the members of society toward cultural and political integration."[49] But impelling falls short of describing the power of the Litany of Loreto, as Salvatierra's use of it to intervene for his sick protégé Chipi demonstrates. Those who invoked Mary through this litany or through the word "Loreto" found the act meaningful precisely because of the reiterative nature of the call. It was effective because it chimed in with a familiar Catholic chorus that amplified its volume, increasing the chances that Mary might hear. Salvatierra chose to use the name "Loreto" for one of his mission sites in the same way in which he, and other Jesuits, recited the Litany of Loreto and built replicas of Loreto's Holy House. They copied, and they repeated, nine times, six times, forty-two times: *Mary. Mother. Virgin. Queen.*

47. Though theological and historicizing interpretations abound for the symbols in the Litany of Loreto, psychologist David Richo's take on the subconscious feminine focus of the Litany's Marian titles provides the most compelling explanation for its enduring popularity. The titles of Mary in the Litany of Loreto include: "Holy Mary," "Holy Mother of God," "Holy Virgin of Virgins"; "Mother of Christ," "Mother of Divine Grace," "Mother most pure," "Mother most chaste," "Mother inviolate," "Mother undefiled," "Mother most admirable," "Mother of our Creator," "Mother of our Savior"; "Virgin most prudent," "Virgin most venerable," "Virgin most renowned," "Virgin most powerful," "Virgin most merciful," "Virgin most faithful"; "Mirror of justice"; "Seat of wisdom"; "Cause of our joy"; "Spiritual vessel"; "Vessel of honor"; "Singular vessel of devotion," "Mystical rose," "Tower of David," "Tower of ivory," "House of gold," "Ark of the covenant," "Gate of heaven," "Morning star," "Health of the sick," "Refuge of sinners," "Comfort of the afflicted"; and finally, "Queen of angels," "Queen of patriarchs," "Queen of prophets," "Queen of apostles," "Queen of martyrs," "Queen of confessors," "Queen of virgins," "Queen of all saints." Richo, *Mary within Us*; J. C. Smith, *Sensuous Worship*, pp. 145–46.

48. Freedberg, *Power of Images*, p. 126. Freedberg hammers home the lingering aura left by repetition.

49. Cruz and Perry, "Introduction," p. x.

These conventions of repetition surface in a letter written by Salvatierra to explain his choice to designate a new mission site in Baja California as Loreto. Before turning to Salvatierra's description, however, it is worth noting how much his impulse toward litany contrasts with how his biographer, Venegas, presented his actions. Venegas made it seem that Salvatierra had been following a deliberate program to advance the specific devotion of Loreto. He pitched Salvatierra's broadcasting of Loreto in a fashion reminiscent of what one of today's art historians, Evonne Levy, calls "propaganda." Levy embraces the loaded term "propaganda" to describe highly visible Jesuit architecture. She specifies the work that this early modern architecture did for the Jesuits: it promoted its Jesuit creators, but at the same time, it effaced them, pointing beyond them to spur adherence to Catholicism.[50] It is in this regard that Levy's analysis of architecture as propaganda is most applicable to the Jesuit practice of repetitive naming. Jesuits including the biographer Venegas described mission names (and litanies) in the same manner as they did new churches. They recognized that the appellations were highly visible, and they pitched them to a wide audience in a way that was self-promoting but that always pointed beyond their society to the larger institution of the church and to God himself.

What the propaganda-attuned might miss in their after-the-fact analysis, however, is a palpable randomness, sometimes desperation, inherent in some moments of naming.[51] This was as evident in a remote mission post in California as it was at the altar of the Jesuit college of Tepotzotlán. At frantic moments, repetition could stand to comfort as much as to instruct. Salvatierra reported both impulses when he narrated his California naming in a letter written soon after the event. En route to a new mission site in Baja California, the expedition's ship, the *Santa Elvira*, encountered a stretch of bad weather offshore. Salvatierra feared for his life and for that of the crew. He reported that it was a moment when the Virgin of Loreto made herself felt:

> The Most Holy Virgin of Loreto has worked great miracles throughout this journey with the frigate . . . so much so that all [on the expedition], with one voice . . . called the trip a miracle, seeing themselves

50. Levy considers how Jesuit projects "advanced the interests of the Society" while at the same time "point[ing] incessantly, uncomfortably to its signified [Catholic lesson], at the expense of the signifier." Levy, *Propaganda and the Jesuit Baroque*, p. 77.

51. Mircea Eliade acknowledges this randomness with his concept of "hierophany," the manifestation of the sacred, with his subtext that hierophanies are mysterious, not part of the profane world, and unexpected. Eliade, *Sacred and the Profane*, p. 11.

> many times lost, and in a single moment, saved. One time it particularly seemed to all that survival was impossible. Around the feast day of the Nativity, a storm and strong current dragged the ship with all speed towards a white sand spit. . . . The [men] declared themselves lost, but on calling upon the Most Holy Virgin of Loreto, they found themselves saved from danger.[52]

Spared disaster in the shallows by the Madonna of Loreto's intervention, the ship eventually found a safe harbor.[53] It appears that Salvatierra was waiting for precisely such a moment of group recognition for the Madonna. He continued: "It seemed to all that the discovery of the Port was a special favor of the Virgin, which is why they gave the place the name of the Port of the Madonna of Loreto."[54]

Salvatierra's language here is typically self-effacing: he declares the naming a group affair, not his alone, not even occurring at his behest. *All* could see the Madonna's hand in events; all sensed her presence, and thus all agreed to recognize her. However, in order for all to see, someone—in this case, Salvatierra—had to actively name and publicize her. During the establishment of the California mission, Salvatierra's letters brim with attributions of her intervention, particularly in ocean-related crises. Through recitations of the Litany of Loreto and direct petitions in public

52. "La Santissima Vergine di Loreto ha operato gran maraviglie in desto viaggio con la Galeota e col bastello sino all'arrivo del desto Hiaqui, in modo, chi tutti ad una voce, come quelli chi vi si sono trovati, chiamano quel viaggio de miracoli, vedendosi molti volte perduti, et in un subito, liberati. Una volta singolarmente parve' a tutti impossibile adarne salvi. Vicino alla festa della natività, la tempesta e la corrente molto gagliarda portarano con tutt'impeto la Galeota sopra un Renaio bianco, il quale poco a poco s'andava chiudendo con l'onde grosse del mare, et esta in alcresi andava viando sopra il d. Renaio. Si scimarano tutti perduti, ma nell'invocare la Santissima Vergine di Loreto si trovarano liberi dal' pericolo." ARSI Mex. 17 (Salvaterra to Ugarte, 1697), fols. 583–84. The Feast of Nativity to which Salvatierra refers is most likely 8 September, the Feast of the Nativity of the Virgin Mary.

53. There was more lag time between near-shipwreck and the finding of a safe port than Salvatierra's letter makes it seem. The California expedition left the Mexican coast on 10 October 1697 with two ships: the *Santa Elvira* and *El Rosario*. The ships were looking for a previous mission site, San Bruno. Winds separated the ships during the crossing, though. The *Santa Elvira* emerged from the wave-tossing alone and first attempted to shelter in Concepción Bay, and again at the waterless and abandoned San Bruno, before stopping twenty miles south of San Bruno in the more promising bay of San Dionisio on 19 October. The name "Loreto" was given to this third landing site in San Dionisio Bay. Vernon, *Las Misiones Antiguas*, pp. 11–13.

54. "Parendo a tutti, che l'inventione di quel Porto fosse in specialissimo favore della Vergine, e percio gli diedero il nome del Porto della Madonna di Loreto." ARSI Mex. 17 (Salvaterra to Ugarte, 1697), fols. 583–84.

prayer, he had been fastidiously promoting the Madonna of Loreto as the harbinger of the nascent colony's safety from the sea.[55]

Promote as he may, Salvatierra had little control over the location on which the name Loreto was imposed. Nature wreaked havoc on the expedition to Baja California with the end result that Salvatierra's chosen name was affixed to a place hastily and without premeditation. First, the expedition's ships were separated by a storm at sea; next they confronted a dearth of fresh water. By the time they dropped anchor at their preliminary target site, the abandoned mission of San Bruno, tempers were flaring. Salvatierra wished to remain at San Bruno until they found water, but Captain Juan Antonio Romero, in charge of the expedition's surviving ship, the *Santa Elvira*, disagreed. He thought they should head farther down the coast instead. Romero remembered from a previous expedition a better-watered spot in the Bay of San Dionisio. The two leaders resolved the dispute by drawing lots, with Salvatierra praying to the Madonna of Loreto to arbitrate.

She did not arbitrate in the Jesuit's favor. Romero's lot was drawn, and Salvatierra was forced to concede.[56] The group ended up twenty miles south of the area that had been previously surveyed and chosen by the Jesuit Eusebio Kino, in a small harbor the Cochimí and Monquí inhabitants called "Conchó." Here, at a place already named, Salvatierra repeated Loreto. Notwithstanding that this was not the precise location where Mary had intervened to save them from shipwreck, or the site where a devout Jesuit had prayed for her to bestow her blessing, Salvatierra renamed Conchó as "Loreto" the day after their party arrived. On 19 October 1697, he consecrated their anchorage to the Italian Madonna's protection. Perhaps because of this hastiness, the newly given name never replaced the old one. The Jesuit Salvatierra had pronounced a site "Loreto" when it already had a well-established Indian name, "Conchó."[57] For the first decades of that Loreto mission, there was a double appellation at play, with Jesuits themselves referring to the spot variously as "Loreto," "Conchó," or "Loreto

55. Two years after their tumultuous arrival at the Port of Loreto, Salvatierra still enthusiastically discerned the hand of Loreto's Madonna behind every safe docking of the desperately needed supply ships from the Mexican mainland. See Salvatierra's letter of 22 October 1699 to Don José Miranda, Royal Treasurer of Guadalajara, quoted in: Dunne, *Black Robes in Lower California*, p. 66. On Salvatierra's habit of carrying a statue of Mary with him in his travels: Vélez, "Urban Driftwood," pp. 63–64. On the affinity of Italian mariners with the Virgin of Loreto: Vélez, "Les voyages outre-mer d'un nom," pp. 123–26.

56. Crosby, *Antigua California*, pp. 25–26; on Juan Antonio Romero, pp. 22, 54–56.

57. Vernon, *Las Misiones Antiguas*, p. 13.

Conchó."[58] This reality is far from Patricia Seed's carefully orchestrated and purportedly successful imperial ceremonies of possession. The awkwardness of Salvatierra's overlay seems to trump propagandistic imposition and intent.

Salvatierra's clumsiness was neither accidental nor exceptional. It was the norm for many Jesuit field situations. To the south, where Jesuits also named a mission in the Amazon basin after Loreto, the new Catholic tag was likewise affixed to an older indigenous referent. In 1681, the Jesuits named their first permanent mission among the Moxos Indians "Nuestra Señora de Loreto" or "Loreto Moxos."[59] Notably, unlike Salvatierra, who harked from Milan, none of the Moxos Jesuits were Italian, so none associated the Madonna of Loreto with their native regions. Loreto Moxos was founded by six Jesuits who were primarily of Spanish origin.[60] Pedro Marbán (1647–1713), soon to become superior of the Loreto mission, was recruited from Lérida, in Catalonia.[61] The cattle-herding Cipriano Barace (1641–1702) was also born and raised in Spain, in Navarre.[62] They were accompanied by Peruvian creole Antonio de Orellana (1653–1712), who hailed from the town of Pisco, south of Lima.[63] Rounding out the group, of unknown provenance but with common Spanish names, were Joseph de Vega and Jesuit lay brothers Antonio Fernández and Manuel Carrillo.[64]

58. Relative to other mission sites in California such as the confusingly dubbed St. Francis-Xavier-Viggé-Biaundo, the name "Loreto" took well. The former was first founded on a plateau that was called "Viggé" by the Indians and then moved next to a water source that the Indians called "Biaundó." Though the Jesuits christened the place as the Mission of St. Francis Xavier, that name never replaced the older Indian designations for the landscape. Ibid., p. 14.

59. ARSI Peru 21 (Orellana, Annual Report, 1688), fols. 3–4v.

60. The six are named by Jesuit Antonio de Orellana in his 1688 annual report. Ibid.

61. Marbán was later known for his writing of a Moxos language vocabulary (*Arte de la Lengua Moxa, con su vocabulario, y catechismo*, Lima, 1701). Sommervogel, *Bibliothèque de la Compagnie de Jésus*, tom. 5, p. 517.

62. Cipriano Barace is best known of this group because of his martyrdom. He was killed by Baures Indians in 1702. He also founded the mission of Trinidad and pioneered cattle herding in the region. Barace was honored for this with a 1986 commemorative postage stamp in Bolivia. Sommervogel, *Bibliothèque de la Compagnie de Jésus*, tom. 8, p. 1760; "Father Cipriano Barace, S.J."

63. Antonio de Orellana worked at the Moxos missions for thirty-one years before retiring to Arequipa, Peru, to serve as rector of the Jesuit Collegium Maximum there. He was the architect of many of the buildings in the early missions. Sommervogel, *Bibliothèque de la Compagnie de Jésus*, tom. 5, p. 1931; Block, *Mission Culture on the Upper Amazon*, p. 60.

64. Manuel Carrillo is the only one of these lay brothers to be singled out repeatedly in the founding of the missions. He was a carpenter who ended up training Moxos Indians in construction techniques. Gutiérrez and Gutiérrez, "Territorio, Urbanismo y Arquitectura en Moxos y Chiquitos," p. 353.

This group of Jesuits had been working for almost a decade to proselytize among the Moxos Indians and to organize them into a newly settled Catholic community devoted to the Virgin Mary. They chose to locate this first mission on the site of an old Moxos village that they had been using as a mission camp. There, they pulled together three different Moxos communities whose members had approached the Jesuits in part because of their proffered protection against slave traders from Santa Cruz.[65] The Jesuit choice of location was crucial. It was a gesture of continuity for their Moxos converts. But having offered this reassurance, the Jesuits then established difference by overlaying an imported Catholic name.

Already this situation was different from Salvatierra's haphazard acceptance of location for Loreto Conchó. Just as Jesuit counters were not all in lockstep with their methods of counting Mary, Jesuit namers repeated Loreto in different ways. The Peruvian Jesuit Antonio de Orellana left a lengthy explanation detailing why his cohort of Jesuits chose to name their first mission town after the Madonna of Loreto:

> After nearly seven years of labor, effort and diligence to prepare [the Moxos Indians] for this state, at last the desired and planned time came, and with our new colleagues having arrived in the year 1682, we began the Baptisms on the day of Our Lady of the Annunciation. This was the happiest of portents because this reduction was dedicated to the Most Holy Virgin from the start and now for having achieved this first triumph on the day of the first mystery of our Redemption that was celebrated in the Most Holy House of Loreto, the town was given this advocation. More than 500 souls were baptized on this day, and later the others who were left in the Town who were more than 600.[66]

Orellana's professed reason for the name choice was not salvation from shipwreck that he attributed to his regional Madonna, nor was it an explicit Jesuit program to promote Loreto. It was repetition, providentially

65. Block, *Mission Culture on the Upper Amazon*, p. 37. Loreto was founded in 1682, only a year after a slave-raiding expedition from Santa Cruz captured many Moxos Indians from the upper Mamoré region.

66. "Llego pues el tiempo desiado i pretendido despues de cassi siete años de travajos, fatigas e diligencias p.a ponerlos en cite citado, y aviendo llegado los nuevos compañeros el año de 1682 se dio principio a los Baptismos el dia de N.S. de la Anunciazion. Felisissimo pronosticco por estar desde sus principios esta reduccion dedicada a la Ss. Virgen y agora por averse conseguido este primer triunfo en dia del primer misterio de Nra. Redempcion que se celebro en la Ss. Casa de Loreto se le dio al Pueblo esta advocazion. Baptisaron-se este dia mas de 500 almas, y despues en otros los que restavan del Pueblo que eran mas de 600." ARSI Peru 21 (Orellana, Annual Report, 1688), fols. 3–4v.

inspired by the liturgy, and perhaps by Mary herself, as she loomed behind calendrical coincidence. The ritual calendar of the Catholic Church conveniently offered up the day of the Annunciation (25 March), the occasion when the Virgin Mary was visited by the angel Gabriel. On that day, Gabriel told Mary that she would bear the child of God. Such a momentous day was an auspicious occasion for baptisms, and the inhabitants of the new settlement had at last been schooled enough in Christianity to be ready for that sacrament. So the Jesuits chose to baptize the town along with the majority of its inhabitants on this day associated with the Madonna and her Holy House, now in Loreto.

The Moxos Jesuits' careful positioning resembles the counter Gumppenberg's *Atlas Marianus*. Instead of fixing Loreto in space, however, they fixed it in time. They also situated it among other missions. Orellana, Salvatierra, and other Jesuit namers comported themselves as if their repetitions took place on a wider stage, with their choices taking significance because they were not solitary. Loreto was one star in a constellation of twenty-five mission names chosen by the Jesuits in the Moxos. The full constellation was thoughtfully assembled for effect. Unlike Salvatierra's personal ascription of Loreto, in the Moxos, Loreto did fill some propagandistic purposes by reflecting universal Catholic themes rather than regional ones, by guiding Catholic behavior, and by calling attention to the Society of Jesus as an order proud of its currency and newfound local knowledge. To better understand the effect of the reaffixed name Loreto in the Moxos, it should be viewed in context of its surrounding missions.

What other names were Jesuits choosing for their missions? In the twelve years after founding Loreto Moxos, the Jesuits in the Amazon basin established five more missions that became anchors for proselytizing in the region: Santissima Trinidad de los Mayunianas (1687), San Ignacio de los Punuanas (1689), San Francisco Xavier (1691), San Joseph de los Maharenos (1693), and San Francisco de Borja de Churimanes (1693).[67] By 1713, the indigenous designations had been dropped in Jesuit correspondence and the missions were referred to in shorthand by their easily recognizable Catholic referents.[68] To these missions were added ten more:

67. ARSI Peru 21 (1696 "Relación de la Mision apostólica de los Moxos"), fols. 39v–54. The Jesuits' first six reductions were the longest lasting and also the only missions that were cohesive in terms of language, as they all served Moxos-speaking populations.

68. On rare occasions, the indigenous referent actually trumped the Christian overlay. One of the Jesuit missions in Paraguay remained "Itapúa" from the moment of its founding (BAV, VAT LAT 8215 [Cardiel, *Breve Noticia*], pp. 58v–63). The Jesuit missions in Baja California also present an interesting case. Sixteen out of eighteen of their missions had

in the immediate area, San Pedro Apostól, Santa Rosa, and Exaltación de la Cruz; to the east, Concepción, San Joaquín, and Juan Bautista; and to the west, another San Joseph, San Luis, San Pablo, and Santissimos Reyes.[69] Nine more missions were named over the eighteenth century. These last offshoots included Santos Desposorios, San Martín, Santa Ana, San Miguel Arcángel, Santa María Magdalena, San Nicolás, and San Simón y Judas.[70] The mission of Loreto Moxos is best understood in this company, although at first glance, when it is aligned with these other local designations, it seems a bizarre aberration.

The most evident theme in the full group of names chosen by Jesuits for the Moxos missions is Catholic transcendence of region, or universality. Other than Loreto, none of the appellations pinpoint specific locations in Europe or the Holy Land. The majority of Moxos mission names are biblical, referring to the shining stars in Christianity's main text. Four of the missions evoke the Holy Family; seven of them refer to the apostles and early followers of Christ; five more refer to generic Christian concepts such as the Trinity.[71] This ratio is similar to that of other Jesuit mission zones where universal biblical monikers were preferred. To the south in Paraguay,

---

indigenous names that were used at founding (the only exceptions being the relatively late Santa Rosa, 1734 and Todos Santos, 1752). Listed here in order of founding, the Baja California missions with Cochimí designations included: Loreto Conchó (1697); San Francisco Javier de Biaundó (1699); San Juan Bautista de Ligüí, also known as Malibat (1705); Santa Rosalía de Mulegé (1705); San José de Comondú (1708); La Purísima Concepción de Cadegomó (1719); Nuestra Señora de Guadalupe de Huasinapí (1720); Nuestra Señora del Pilar de la Paz Airapí (1720); Nuestra Señora de los Dolores Apaté (1720); Santiago el Apostól Aiñiní (1724); San Ignacio de Kadakaamán (1725); San José del Cabo Añuití (1730); San Luis Gonzaga Chiriyaqui (1737); Santa Gertrudis de Cadacamán (1751); San Francisco de Borja Adac (1762); and Santa María Cabujakaamung (1766). Crosby, *Antigua California*, pp. 398–402.

69. ARSI Peru 21 (1713 *Relación de los Missiones de los Moxos*), fols. 175–79.

70. Gutiérrez and Gutiérrez note that only seventeen of the twenty-five missions were still being used at the moment of the Jesuit expulsion in the 1770s: Loreto, Trinidad, San Ignacio, San Francisco Javier, San Francisco de Borja, Desposorios, San Pedro Apóstol, Santos Reyes, Concepción, Exaltación, San Joaquín, San Martín, Santa Ana, San Miguel Arcángel, Santa María Magdalena, San Nicolás, and San Simón y Judas. Gutiérrez and Gutiérrez, "Territorio, Urbanismo y Arquitectura en Moxos y Chiquitos," p. 334.

71. Holy Family names include: Joseph (twice used); Ana (Anne), Mary's mother; and Joaquin, Mary's father. Apostles and early followers' names include: Pedro (Peter), Pablo (Paul), the pair of Simon and Judas, Juan Bautista (John the Baptist), Miguel Arcángel (Michael), Maria Magdalena, and the Santissimos Reyes (the Three Kings). Generic Christian concept names include: Trinidad (the Trinity of Father, Son, and Holy Ghost): Exaltación de la Cruz (Exaltation of the Cross); Concepción (the Immaculate Conception); and Santos Desposorios (the Holy Spouses).

for instance, fourteen of twenty-three Jesuit missions were graced with names of biblical characters.[72] To the west, in Baja California, one of every five Jesuit missions referred to the Holy Family or the apostles.[73] As in the Moxos, Jesuits in those zones showed a preference for the most generic versions of these biblical names. For example, missions named for the Virgin Mary were not usually named for regional Madonnas like the Virgin of Guadalupe.[74] Instead, Jesuits opted for the all-purpose "María Mayor" or "Nuestra Señora de la Fe" (Our Lady of the Faith).[75] One could see this as calculation: Jesuit missionaries were consistently choosing names that stressed the broad applicability and biblical roots of the Catholic Church as opposed to its European provinciality. But it is also reminiscent of the Litany of Loreto, with its reassuring repetition of familiar titles.

At first glance, the peculiar designation of Loreto seems to jar in this rote company. Yet it sits more comfortably alongside a smaller subset of names that one might also notice in the above list of Moxos missions: hip, current, *Jesuit* names. Jesuits were peppering the litany of universal Christian titles in the Moxos region with a few select names of their own. Enter

72. BAV, VAT LAT 8215 (Cardiel, *Breve Noticia*), pp. 58v–63. In an inventory of Paraguay missions that had to relocate several times after founding, Cardiel lists twenty-three different naming examples in Paraguay. I group these by theme for easier comparison with Moxos names. Paraguay missions called generically after Mary and her family included: S. Maria la Mayor; Nuestra Señora de la Fe; Jesús; San Joseph; and Santa Ana. Those named for apostles and biblical figures were: Santiago (St. James); Santo Thomé (St. Thomas); Santissimos Apostoles; San Miguel (Michael the Archangel). Another three missions denoted Christian concepts: Santissima Trinidad; Candelaria (named for 2 February, the Catholic feast day of Candlemas); Cruz (Cross), which eventually got subsumed into the town of Yapeyú; Concepción; and Santo Angel. These names account for more than half of the Paraguay roster. Some of the remaining missions on Cardiel's list are discussed further below (note 79).

73. Baja California had a Santa María and *two* San José missions (de Comondú and del Cabo Añuití), along with a San Juan Bautista (John the Baptist) and a Santiago el Apostól (St. James the Apostle). There was also the catch-all mission of Todos Santos (All Saints). Crosby, *Antigua California*, pp. 398–402.

74. Perhaps because it was close to the Mexican mainland, Baja California had a mission named for Nuestra Señora de Guadalupe (1720), but it also had the more generally named Santa María, La Purísima Concepción (the Immaculate Conception), and Señora de los Dolores (Our Lady of Sorrows). Ibid.

75. This was also the case farther to the west in Peru, where Jesuits favored another broad-spectrum face of Mary, "Our Lady of the Rosary." Records from the 1630s from the Jesuit college in Urubamba, Peru, repeatedly mention Jesuits bestowing the name "Our Lady of the Rosary" on confraternities and churches (ARSI Peru 15 [Vázquez to Vitelleschi, 1637], fol. 89v and ARSI Peru 15 [Durán, 1639], fol. 143v). "Our Lady of Sorrows" was also popular in South America, even reaching the Jesuit Chiloé missions. Bailey, "Cultural Convergence at the Ends of the Earth," p. 228.

the Moxos region as you might the towering nave of the Jesuits' flagship Church of the Gesù in Rome, and the Moxos mission names present a similar gallery of very recently deceased and canonized Jesuits for contemplation.[76] There is San Ignacio, denoting Loyola; San Francisco Xavier; San Francisco Borja; and San Luis, named for Aloysius (Luis) Gonzaga (1568–91), an Italian Jesuit known for working with plague victims.[77] Jesuits in Paraguay and Baja California followed suit.[78] Those missionaries also named sites for Ignatius, Gonzaga, and even the Jesuit martyrs of Japan.[79]

Like the Jesuit saints, the Virgin of Loreto was part of early Jesuit history, a history that was still less than a century old in the mid-1600s, when the missions were named. Jesuits born in Europe were familiar with the Loreto advocation through pilgrimage to her shrine, a practice they were encouraged to undertake during their novitiate; Jesuits born overseas would have known of her because of the omnipresent Litany of Loreto. Indeed, by the time the Moxos missions were established, the Jesuits

76. Jesuit organization and efforts directly resulted in Xavier and five other Jesuit candidates being granted the status of sainthood between 1540 and 1770. Considering that the early modern saints numbered only twenty-seven, Jesuits scored a whopping one new saint for every five. Capuchins (a branch of the Franciscans) and Theatines (also relatively new, like the Jesuits) were the only religious orders to come close to this proportion of new saints. Hsia, *World of Catholic Renewal*, p. 127.

77. The frescoed dome of the Gèsu Cathedral is divided into four quadrants featuring God; Francis Xavier (1506–52), pioneer of Jesuit missions to Asia; Francis Borgia (1510–72), one of the early superior generals of the Society of Jesus; and Ignatius Loyola (1491–1556), founder of the order. It took over a century for construction and decoration of the church to be completed. At the time, it was the largest ecclesiastical undertaking in Rome.

78. As far away as Cuzco, Peru, Jesuit churches proudly displayed the luminaries of the Jesuit family. In Cuzco, the Jesuit church even displayed the unsainted, with its entrance painting commemorating the marriage of Don Martín García de Loyola, governor of Chile and relative of the Jesuit founder Ignatius, to Beatriz Clara Coya, the last legitimate heir to the Inka royal family. In spite of the harmonious, celebratory cast of this painting, this was a forced marriage with Beatriz put forth as a "war trophy." Timberlake, "Painted Colonial Image," p. 591n1.

79. Four Baja California missions were named after Jesuit saints: San Francisco Javier de Biaundó, San Ignacio, San Luis Gonzaga, and San Francisco de Borja (Crosby, *Antigua California*, pp. 398–402). Paraguay missions named for Jesuits in the seventeenth century included: San Ignacio Guazú and San Ignacio Mini; San Luis Gonzaga; and the Santissimos Martires del Japón (BAV, VAT LAT 8215 [Cardiel, *Breve Noticia*], pp. 58v–63). The last alludes to Christians crucified between 1587 and 1632 because of a persecution edict in Japan. Though most of the victims of this were Japanese laymen, the missionaries among them garnered much attention in Europe, and Jesuits dominated their number. The reported death toll varies but it ranges between thirty-six and fifty-five Jesuits, twenty-five to thirty-six Franciscans, twenty-one to thirty-eight Dominicans, and five to twenty Augustinians, all of whom died during this outbreak of anti-Catholic violence. Delplace, "Japanese Martyrs."

there might even have known of a specific case when one of their own had applied the Italian Madonna's name to a mission. Paraguay boasted the earliest and most notorious Jesuit mission dedicated to Loreto. Loreto of Guairá had been established there in the early 1600s by two Italian Jesuits, Giuseppe Cataldini (1571–1653) and Simone Mascetti (1577–1658).[80] The mission garnered publicity and sparked controversy in 1631 when the mission superior, Peruvian Jesuit Antonio Ruiz De Montoya (1585–1652), relocated twelve thousand Guaraní Indians down the Paranapanemá River to escape raids by slavers from São Paulo, Brazil.[81] Reports of Paraguay's Loreto of Guairá in full flight would have reached Rome and recirculated once more to Jesuits abroad through newsletters and friends.[82]

One could take the perspective of the Jesuit counter Venegas and the modern historian Evonne Levy, both noted previously, and stop to marvel at the successful propaganda of Jesuits choosing a name that magnified their fledgling society. But in the Amazon basin, the name Loreto Moxos also functioned in two other ways: it was a happy reminder of the diversity and the pedagogical possibilities available to seventeenth-century Catholic namers. For instance, in their desire to honor the calendar, the Moxos Jesuits could have chosen to christen the town with a more technical ceremonial tag for Mary, "Our Lady of the Annunciation." But the Jesuit selection of "Loreto" shows that in and of itself, the Catholic liturgy did not invite generic naming. It was a list that served both as calendar and color wheel. As the official compilation of all important Catholic occasions and celebrations, the liturgy included the full spectrum of recognized regional saints. Calendrical coincidence therefore resulted in the comparatively original nomenclature of the colonial Paraguayan Jesuit mission of Nuestra Señora de Candelaria, named for the 2 February festival of Candlemas (Candelaria in Spanish).[83] The liturgy may also have been the inspiration

80. Cataldini harked from the city of Ancona and Mascetti from the town of Castilenti. Both Italian cities lay close to Loreto, making it likely that Cataldini and Mascetti experienced the Madonna of Loreto firsthand through a visit to her original shrine center. Ruiz De Montoya, *Spiritual Conquest* (1639), pp. 38–39, 211n39 and n40.

81. Ibid., pp. 15, 104–13.

82. For instance, Paraguay and Loreto surfaced in a 1641 exchange between the Jesuits Pierre-Joseph-Marie Chaumonot in Canada and Filippo Nappi in Rome. Chaumonot thanked Nappi for informing him that one of his colleagues, Angelo de Magistris, was being sent to serve in Paraguay. He noted happily that Magistris was a fellow devotee of the Madonna of Loreto. Angelo de Magistris celebrated his first mass as a priest in an Italian replica of Loreto's Holy House, just like Chaumonot himself. See ARSI Gall. 109, tom. I (Chaumonot to Nappi, 13 August 1641), fols. 112–13.

83. BAV, VAT LAT 8215 (Cardiel, *Breve Noticia*), pp. 58v–63. Nuestra Señora de Candelaria was associated with 2 February, Candlemas, but she also had strong regional

behind two missions named for the relatively obscure San Nicolás in the Moxos region and Paraguay respectively.[84] Like the many synonymous titles for Mary in the Litany of Loreto, these more colorful references still proudly designated Catholicism. They were not meant to stand alone, but to cumulatively indicate Catholic presence by dint of repetition.

A name like Loreto might also instruct. Jesuits favored names that could serve as guides to Catholic behavior. For example, in the Moxos, Jesuits called another of their missions "Exaltación de la Cruz," a name that reminded the devoted that they should be celebrating the cross, Christianity's most prominent symbol.[85] Such idealistic, conceptual names were favored not only by missionaries, but by other Catholic urban planners building towns and cities in the colonial Americas.[86] Vasco de Quiroga (1470–1565), first Bishop of Michoácan in Mexico, named two of his utopian planned communities "Santa Fe," or Holy Faith.[87] This kind of name broadcast the hope of what town residents might become: good Catholic citizens. In the case of Loreto, both a Jesuit biographer, Venegas, and a Jesuit namer, Salvatierra, flagged the teaching possibilities for the name Loreto because of its link to the Holy House. In Canada, the Jesuit Chaumonot made manifest the associated teaching tool by building a replica Holy House of Loreto in tandem with naming his mission site Lorette.

---

associations. Some of the Paraguayan Jesuits were Spanish and may have favored her name out of loyalty to home as well as calendar. She was the patroness of the Canary Islands, site of her shrine. Hernán Cortés reportedly introduced her to the Americas because he wore a medal of her around his neck ("Nuestra Señora de la Candelaria"). Interestingly, Our Lady of Candelaria's sixteenth-century popularity was largely due to the efforts of Alonso de Espinosa, a Dominican friar from Guatemala who traveled back to the Canary Islands to write of miracles associated with her image. He wrote a widely read account of this Marian devotion entitled *The Guanches of Tenerife* (Seville, 1594).

84. BAV, VAT LAT 8215 (Cardiel, *Breve Noticia*), pp. 58v–63; Gutiérrez and Gutiérrez, "Territorio, Urbanismo y Arquitectura en Moxos y Chiquitos," p. 334. Perhaps the calendar also explains the more obscure nomenclature of the two Baja California missions, Santa Rosalía in 1705 and Santa Gertrudis in 1751 (Crosby, *Antigua California*, pp. 398–402). San Nicolás likely refers to St. Nicholas, fourth-century Bishop of Myra, whose feast day is 6 December. His feast day falls at what seems to be another auspicious and convenient moment for baptizing new converts, since the early December date heralds in the upcoming rituals and celebrations of the Christmas season.

85. "Cruz" was also a name used by Jesuits in Paraguay; see n72 above.

86. Christophe Pourtois situates Jesuit mission planning as part of a larger, seventeenth-century movement of urban utopia building particular to South America. Pourtois, "From the City of the Caesars to the Demystified City," p. 11.

87. The "hospital-pueblos" of Quiroga were loosely inspired by Sir Thomas More's *Utopia* (1516). Zarandona, "Biography of Vasco de Quiroga"; Verástique, *Michoacán and Eden*.

Yet curiously, the Jesuits in the Moxos do not seem to have taken advantage of the didactic possibilities behind the name Loreto. Jesuit namers in the Moxos missions in 1682 might have envisioned using Loreto's associated relic as an instructional tool to bring the Catholic calendar to life, for Orellana even mentioned the Holy House of Loreto specifically as the scene of the liturgical event of the Annunciation. But the Jesuits at the Moxos mission of Loreto never built a Holy House replica. Seventeenth-century Jesuits are often characterized as having "dogged intentionality" to instruct, fueled by the reforms of the Council of Trent.[88] This was not apparent in the Moxos, though, where Jesuit teaching around Loreto never went further than applying the name.

In sum, the Jesuit namers considered above picked Loreto for many reasons: to commemorate salvation from a shipwreck, to call attention to an auspicious date of founding, to highlight recent Jesuit history, to showcase Catholic variety, or to allow for teaching possibilities. But apparent in all these situations, Jesuits were intoning Loreto as part of a comforting litany that they knew was being recited simultaneously by many others. Invoking Loreto in this way, as a means to connect to the wider Catholic world, differs from the strategy that counters most often ascribed after the fact to namers. Miguel Venegas, António Cordeiro, and other tabulators including today's historians have sometimes interpreted the name Loreto as a calculated imposition that brought positive publicity to Jesuits, to the Italian Madonna, and to the Catholic Church as a whole, and that contributed to European possession of new territory. But as demonstrated above, namers in the field were frequently acting less out of preplanned strategy to expand than from a devotional impulse in the moment. Caught wanting help or divine good favor, individuals drew on Loreto as a well-known line in a global chorus. Repeating Loreto was deemed as a particularly effective way to join the Catholic song and thereby catch divine attention.[89] Chanting it seems to have mattered most to the newly arrived or conscripted, people who looked to affiliate themselves with older religious streams. In

88. J. C. Smith, *Sensuous Worship*, p. 3. The Jesuits have been singled out for their adherence to the pedagogical reforms of the watershed Council of Trent in the mid-sixteenth century. Edicts from that meeting emphasized the importance of pedagogy and downplayed the specificities of regional devotions, creating ample precedent for stressing the universal. For Trent's pedagogical and devotional reforms: O'Malley, *Trent: What Happened at the Council*. On Jesuit identification with the Council of Trent: Pomplun, *Jesuit on the Roof of the World*, pp. 7–8.

89. Robert Orsi makes a compelling argument that St. Jude needs his followers as much as they need him; this understanding is the glue of the relationship between Catholic devotees of St. Jude and the divine saint himself. Orsi, *Thank You, St. Jude*.

this atmosphere, Jesuits were not so different from their converts: both parties drew on the name Loreto for its well-established track record.

New Expression: Processing "Loreto" in Cuzco, Peru, and Baja California

Names counted, and were being marked, in more than printed inventories and missionary circuits, and by more than Jesuits. In the city of Cuzco, Peru, in 1647, the Jesuit António Vázquez reported an instance of the name "Loreto" being advertised in conjunction with a local celebration of a Marian holy day, the Feast of the Assumption (15 August). Vázquez spent a busy day attempting to moderate requests from eager Catholic Inka to ratchet up the pomp of the planned festivities. Finally he threw up his hands and declared the occasion to be "a party [belonging to] the Indians."[90] The Inka who approached Vázquez belonged to a *cofradía*, or confraternity, only recently instigated by the Jesuit college of Cuzco in the 1630s, and dedicated to the Madonna of Loreto.[91] Though it was the Jesuits who had selected the name Loreto for the new association of Catholic Inka laymen, it was these Inka who set about to put their organization on the map with an energy reminiscent of the Augustinian cataloguer Santa Maria and the Jesuit missionary Salvatierra. These Inka broadcast the name of the Virgin of Loreto through public procession in the city streets. Their processing action aligns them with counters like Santa Maria and namers like Salvatierra, all of them parties seeking to make the Madonna of Loreto matter by mobilizing her name in new spaces.

What was distinctive about how indigenous converts used the name Loreto overseas, as opposed to Jesuits? The performance of Cuzco's cofradía of Loreto during the 1647 Feast of Assumption offers some clues that suggest more similarities than differences in how Loreto was being appropriated. For one, young cofradías—much like the relatively new Society of Jesus—felt a keen pressure to exhibit themselves well in a processional

90. "Era fiesta de yndios." ARSI Peru 15 (1637 Letra Anua), fols. 104–5v.

91. "Cofradía" is used interchangeably in this chapter to designate confraternities and congregaciónes. All were Catholic associations of laypeople organized around prayer and community service. Though confraternities in Cuzco had been organized well before this, in the Jesuit annual reports that I saw, Jesuit confraternities dedicated to *Loreto* in Peru appear to have emerged in a wave in the 1630s. I surmise that the confraternity that Vázquez describes had not existed in Cuzco for more than a decade. In addition to the one in Cuzco, Jesuits founded a confraternity to Loreto out of their college in Huamanga and another in their College of Huanbelica. The Huamanga cofradía is discussed further below in notes 97–99. On Huanbelica: ARSI Peru 15 (1649 Letra Anua), fol. 225 v.

forum that was crowded with a great variety of Catholic symbols. In her analysis of a series of paintings illustrating the Corpus Christi processions in Cuzco in the 1670s, Carolyn Dean notes the competitiveness of Inka cofradías over visual display.[92] In the paintings Dean surveys, alongside the city's parishes, three of Cuzco's confraternities are depicted carrying floats, richly ornamented with symbols that called attention to their respective devotions.[93] The local prestige of these groups is also indicated by the number of participants they mustered.

Just as the Jesuits repeated the name Loreto to fix their missions onto the map of Catholicism, members of these Inka confraternities chose to repeat the name Loreto with the understanding that it would be an action witnessed and interpreted. Because they worked with a name that was given to them, however, these indigenous converts are not referred to as namers here, but rather as *processers*. They did not bestow a new name on a particular place but instead activated a given name, making it public enough to be noticed and counted. The processers highlighted here publicized Loreto by literally forming Catholic processions in her honor. This section begins by recounting how one Jesuit, Nicolás Durán, understood the Inka processers in Cuzco's confraternity of Loreto. It finishes with a look at a parallel procession at another mission named for Loreto, Loreto Conchó. That procession included Monquí converts and the Jesuit namer discussed above, Juan Maria Salvatierra. It was a procession noted and counted by Salvatierra's Jesuit biographer, Miguel Venegas. Seventeenth-century counters, namers, and processers of Loreto thus finish together on the same page.

In 1647 in Cuzco, the Jesuit António Vázquez was impressed by the final product of the eager Inka cofradía of Loreto. But his colleague Nicolás Durán was deeply unsettled by it. The Inka members of the confraternity had spent weeks planning an elaborate procession that gained them citywide recognition.[94] Their procession involved several companies of Inka

92. Corpus Christi is a late May–early June celebration of the Body of Christ, or the Holy Eucharist. It was especially popular in early modern Iberia. As such, it was one of the first Catholic holy days to be introduced in Cuzco after the Spanish conquest, and by the late sixteenth century it was recognized as Cuzco's most important religious festival. Dean, *Inka Bodies and the Body of Christ*, p. 31.

93. The confraternities in the Corpus Christi or Santa Ana series of paintings were dedicated to "the four saints" (two unidentified and two Jesuit—St. Ignatius and either St. Francis Xavier or St. Francis Borgia); St. John the Baptist and St. Peter; and Santa Rosa and "La Linda" (a Cuzco advocation of Mary). Ibid., pp. 64–80.

94. Perhaps in part because of this small cofradía's highly visible processions, the Madonna of Loreto became a familiar part of Cuzco's devotional scene. By the late eighteenth

dressed as Moors and Christians, entire troops of children costumed as angels, and six statues of Jesuit saints. In the midst of this boisterous convoy, a flower-and jewel-bedecked Madonna of Loreto borne on a float miraculously staggered through the streets unscathed.[95] Durán wrote, "The emotion of the Cuzco Indians for the Most Pure Queen of the Angels to whom they have dedicated two cofradías is so great that it is necessary to put a brake on [their] excessive devotion." He continued anxiously:

> They decorate their chapel to Our Lady so that it is only slightly less [grand] than our church. . . . People do not dare compete with the Indians . . . [whose] processions are so magnificent, that all agree that they beat out those of Corpus and the other festivities in the city[,] although their cofradía and chapel are dedicated [merely] to the Virgin of Loreto.[96]

Before addressing Durán's concern, it should be noted that the Inka processers he noticed were not unique to Cuzco, the old Inka ceremonial capital that has been exceptionalized as much as the Jesuit order. Indigenous processers were remarked on at other sites on the American frontiers. For instance, the Jesuit provincial Francisco Lupercio de Zurbano charted the trajectory of recognition for a new cofradía dedicated to the

---

century she was even being pulled into the regular rituals of cofradías not named for her. In 1783, Cuzco residents in the parish of Santiago founded a cofradía nominally dedicated to their titular neighborhood saint, St. James, but they included the Madonna of Loreto as a corollary. They set aside several days each month for the group to honor her alongside St. James. Bradley and Cahill, *Habsburg Peru*, pp. 138–39.

95. "Fue milagro sin duda desta Sta Ymagen, y el no aver sucedido entre tantos fuegos desgracia ninguna y el no averse perdido de tanta riquesa como avia en los sanctos en los altars arcos triunfales y angeles adornados todos con perlas y joyas un tan solo alfiler." / "It was a miracle beyond doubt of this Holy Image, that no disgrace happened amidst so many fires, and that not a single pin on her was lost amidst so much richness that was present in the sanctuaries, on the altars and triumphal arches and with angels decorated with pearls." ARSI Peru 15 (1637 Letra Anua), fols. 104–5v.

96. "Digo solo q es tan grande el afecto de los indios de Cuzco con la purissima Reyna de los Angeles a quien tienen dedicadas dos cofradias q es necesario poner freno a su mucha devocion . . . adornan su capilla de N.S. q es poco menor q nra. Yglesia y esta aun lado de ella todos los dias de sus festividades con tanta curiosidad q afirman las personas de quanta de hazer publico, q no se atreven a competir con los Yndios Los quales no perdonan a travajo en orden a servir a su Patrona, y Reyna con altars colgaduras retablos, laminas, targas, danças, juegos, y fuegos, olores, y perfumes, cera y luces, y arcos triumphales, q hazen de diversidad de flores buscadas, y traidas de muchas leguas de la ciudad. Las proceciones son tan lucidas, q todos afirman vencer a las de Corpus y demas festividades de la ciudad aunq su cofradia, y capilla estan dedicadas a la Virgen de Loreto." ARSI Peru 15 (1639–40 Letra Anua), fols. 166v–67.

Virgin of Loreto to the south of Cuzco. This group of Indians burst onto the Catholic scene in the colonial city of Huamanga (today known as Ayacucho). In 1638, they organized a well-received procession for Mary's feast day of the Annunciation.[97] A few years later, they petitioned to build a chapel in her honor.[98] Eventually, the group funded a stone chapel to house a beautiful image of the Madonna of Loreto, gracing the premises with "excellent paintings and . . . the best music in the bishopric."[99] In Huamanga, as in Cuzco, urban Indian confraternities began with Jesuits guiding them to the name "Loreto" and encouraging them to carry this particular incarnation of Mary in procession. Then, once publicly recognized through processions as devoted to Catholicism, the confraternity members proceeded to erect chapels and sponsor artwork, building off of a foundation of respect from the broader Catholic community.

It was Durán's discomfort, not the Cuzco Inka processing of Loreto, that was unusual. He voiced a worry that the Inka had mastered the same kind of display as the Jesuits themselves, that they were speaking the same Catholic language of repetition. But both the counters and namers of his own time and twenty-first-century scholars have contradicted his assessment. Durán's anxiety first stands in contrast to the interpretation of the compilers of Marian inventories and Jesuit mission namers who instead saw Loreto's presence in Inka quarters as something to celebrate.[100]

97. "Se vio [en la fiesta de Huamanga] la piedad devocion y alientos en el divino servicio de los de la Cong.on de Nra. Señora de Loreto a cuyo exemplo se movieron los q no son della para mostrar su afecto y piedad con la Reyna de los Angeles y se advirtio quan poderosas son estas demonstraciones para atraer los coraçones a Dios." / "One could see [in this festival of Huamanga] the piety, devotion and warmth in divine service of those of the congregation of Our Lady of Loreto by whose example others who were not members were moved to show their affection and piety to the Queen of Angels and through which it was noted how powerful these demonstrations are for drawing hearts towards God." ARSI Peru 15 (1637 Letra Anua), fol. 115.

98. ARSI Peru 15 (1646 Letra Anua), fol. 205v.

99. "Nros. ministerios estan en este Coll.o [de Huamanga] bien acreditados, porq se acude a ellos con charidad y zelo, en las Congregaciones de Seglares y estudiantes y en la Cofradia de los Yndios se hacen las fiestas de nra. Señora con aparato lucim.to y devocion con frequencia de sacramentos; los Indios han labrado una capilla sumptuosa de piedra y Boveda donde han puesto un Retablo de cedro y una Imagen muy Hermosa de nra. S.a del Loreto. Estan todas los lienços adornados de excelentes pinturas y tienen la major musica q se halla en aqueste obispado." ARSI Peru 15 (1649 Letra Anua), fol. 223v.

100. There could have been a theological, or pedagogical, worry behind Durán's criticism here; perhaps the Jesuit thought that Cuzco residents were better off reflecting on Christ instead of Mary. However, though this was one of the concerns that figured in the Council of Trent, it was the Jesuits themselves who chose the advocation "Loreto" as a contemplative designation for the Inka confraternity instead of opting for a more general appellation for Mary or for Christ.

Durán's perspective also differs from prevalent interpretations by modern scholars of colonial religious processions who approach rituals like this Cuzco procession as declarations of cultural occupation.

Today's historians have fixated on the actors in Cuzco rituals to either construe Europeans as dominating Indian space, or Indians as taking over European space. Both of these poles should be tested against Durán to clarify the uniqueness of his position. These two modern poles are not revisited to dismiss them, because both stances do illuminate power dynamics that contributed to these rituals. But in their extreme forms, these historians' camps can blind readers to the shared language and name that so obsessed Durán.

The European domination thesis has been most famously articulated by Patricia Seed, who wrote of how Europeans used processions to dominate new peoples in what she refers to as ceremonies of possession. Seed describes a series of processions by a French expedition to the Tupí-inhabited region of the Amazon River basin in 1612. French officials, Capuchin friars, sailors, soldiers, and local Tupí paraded together on several occasions, carrying a cross and singing the litany. Like the processions in Cuzco, these gatherings were theatrically staged with ecclesiastical props, costumes, and script. They were collective, with indigenous participation cementing alliance with the newcomers. Seed posits that the repeated "physical actions" of the French-Tupí processions "enacted colonial authority" over the region.[101]

Seed's description somewhat resembles the events surrounding the introduction of the Madonna of Loreto to Baja California in the late 1600s, when the Italian Madonna was celebrated at the mission of Loreto Conchó in multiple processions that escalated in scale. On Christmas day in 1697, banners, arches, and decorations were set up throughout the town. Her statue was carried into a new chapel while the soldiers fired an honorary salvo on their guns.[102] The next year, before being walked through the settlement followed by the Monquí residents, soldiers, and Jesuits, the Lauretan Virgin was dressed with a necklace of pearls, a silver crown, and silk from Milan.[103] On the day of her Nativity (8 September) in 1700, she was again held aloft and carried around the town with her followers in

101. Seed, *Ceremonies of Possession*, p. 68.
102. Dunne, *Black Robes in Lower California*, p. 54.
103. Ibid., p. 59.

tow.[104] These moments in Baja California suggest that the "authority" on display in these rituals cannot be summed up as uniquely French (as Seed contends) or political. But it does suggest that authority could have a specific Catholic face.

In one Baja California mission, that face was the Virgin of Loreto. She animated the scene like a sixteenth-century monarch making a royal entry.[105] Her statue was greeted with artillery salvos and triumphal arches as if she were Phillip II of Spain (1527–98) on one of his grand tours of Europe.[106] She paced the town slowly and repeatedly in the manner of Elizabeth I (1533–1603), who patiently made an entrance to London in 1559, stopping frequently at appointed stations throughout the city.[107] Catholic processions liberally borrowed political flourish to create a sense of holy authority. Yet of course, the mute Madonna statue on parade could not exchange witty banter with local officials as did the queen of England.[108] This technicality changed the tenor of Catholic processions. It intensified audience collaboration. Whether in Europe or on the American frontiers, the onus was on Catholic participants to breathe life into their ruler.[109] They did this by physically escorting her through the streets.

Here, in the subtext of enlivening pantomime, historian Carolyn Dean observes an opening for asserting indigenous control of ritual space, an opening that contradicts Seed's reading of European dominance. Dean notes the similarities between the celebration of Corpus Christi in Cuzco and the pre-Christian Inka solstice festival of Inti Raymi. Beyond the

104. The Jesuit Salvatierra felt that on this occasion the Madonna at last ended her circuit in a chapel that did her justice. He wrote that the ceremony finished when she was returned to "a new adobe house, all white-washed and adorned with paintings, statues, an altarpiece, and a canopy. It resemble[d] a veritable paradise." Salvatierra as quoted by Crosby, *Antigua California*, p. 270.

105. I call attention to sixteenth-century pageantry here for its relative recency to the events of this chapter. Imperial Rome set an obvious earlier precedent for both royal and Catholic pageantry. For example, after military victories, Roman emperors made triumphant entries into the city. Beard, *Roman Triumph*; E. B. Smith, *Architectural Symbolism of Imperial Rome and the Middle Ages*.

106. Harris, *Aztecs, Moors and Christians*, p. 198.

107. Anglo, *Spectacle, Pageantry and Early Tudor Policy*, pp. 344–60.

108. Manley, "Scripts for the Pageant."

109. Theater allowed more flexibility for bringing Mary to life. Onstage, Mary could actually be given a voice. For instance, in 1538 at the Franciscan mission of Tlaxcala in New Spain, a male actor dramatized Mary in a play written for the festival of Our Lady of Assumption. After delivering Mary's lines in Nahuatl, he was hoisted away into the clouds by a stage pulley. Harris, *Aztecs, Moors and Christians*, pp. 132–33.

Catholic gestures, she sees in Cuzco's early modern processions "a performed remembrance of the Inkaic past."[110] David Cahill has a similar interpretation of a Cuzco procession to the Madonna of Loreto in 1692. He describes how the 1692 procession was led by Don Juan Sicos Inga, the alcalde mayor of the Inka nobles. Sicos Inga may have carried a banner of the Virgin of Loreto, but he also wore Inka ceremonial livery.[111] Cahill concludes that the Lauretan procession was just another of many civic and ecclesiastical "occasions on which the Inca nobles [could] sall[y] forth in full finery."[112] Judging from Dean's and Cahill's accounts of the Cuzco scene, Durán might have felt threatened by the zealousness of the Inka converts' Catholic display because of its pre-Christian undertones.

However, centuries prior to Dean and Cahill, in the late 1640s in Cuzco this was not Durán's complaint at all. He spoke of the Lauretan procession instead as if it were a competitive upset in a shared arena. He did not speak of the Inka as playing old games beneath a Christian veneer. Instead, he saw them playing the imported game of Catholicism better than the veterans. These Christian rookies were supposed to be learning and rehearsing the Catholic language of procession, but instead, they were owning it. They were using it to successfully summon Mary, to attract her intervention.

Durán acknowledged that the Inka devotion to the Madonna of Loreto in the mid-1600s was especially potent. He even concluded that their connection to her was strong because they were Indians, a feature that he perhaps thought had caught Mary's eye for its novelty and local rootedness. Durán wrote:

> It has been noticed and remarked as a special benefit, that when the Image of the glorious Queen of the Angels is taken in procession through the streets[,] *in return for the warm esteem of these natives her children[,] she has spared the [whole] city from affliction with typhoid fever*. Because a few years ago[,] Cuzco was wracked by this illness[,]

110. Dean is careful to note that this subtext existed "concomitantly [with a message of] triumph of Christianity" (Dean, *Inka Bodies and the Body of Christ*, p. 81). Max Harris arrives at a similar point via a different route. He pays tribute to what Philippe Buc has declared to be the "dangers of ritual" by uncovering a slew of context that allows competing readings of colonial religious processions. Harris looks at rituals to find "public transcripts," "conscious hidden transcripts," and "unconscious hidden transcripts." He concludes that whether they knew it or not, "indigenous Catholic performers . . . resist[ed] . . . and grie[ved]" their conquest when they participated in these rituals. Harris, *Aztecs, Moors and Christians*, p. 26; Buc, *Dangers of Ritual*.

111. Cahill, "Virgin and the Inca," pp. 612–13.

112. Ibid., p. 637.

> but today it is much more rare[,] and one barely ever sees any person of note die of it.[113]

Thus, in spite of his reservations about the dramatic opulence of the Inka-organized processions, Durán read them as authentic and highly effective expressions of Catholic belief.

Durán's reading unmasks him as a Catholic counter amid processers. By his reckoning, competitive actions did not designate difference, but *sameness*; such behavior was neither submissive nor undercutting, but *shared*. The Inka were processing in order to be counted, and Durán duly read and registered their repetition of Loreto as intended.[114] Furthermore, the Inka were not processing simply to catch the eye of human counters or to magnify their own human cohort, but to solicit the help of the divine Madonna of Loreto herself.

Another Jesuit counter, Miguel Venegas, reported on a Loreto procession with a similar focus on communal language and holy target. He collected information on one of Salvatierra's homecomings. In 1706, Salvatierra and six Monquí converts from the mission of Loreto Conchó returned from a long trip to Mexico City to raise funds for their mission. During the last leg of their travels, all the Monquí fell ill. One of them died in Salvatierra's arms. Their ship nearly capsized in strong winds when they crossed back over the Gulf of California.[115] Carried away by their emotional first actions on shore, Salvatierra's biographer Venegas cast their landing in terms of a pilgrimage made in thanks for the miracle of survival:[116]

113. "Ase advertido y notado como especial beneficio, q despues q la Ymagen de la gloriosa Reyna de los Angeles pasea estas calles en estas procesiones *en pago del afecto destos naturales sus hijos ha librado esta ciudad del rigor de las tabardillas*. Porq siendo el Cuzco los años atras infestadissimo deste mal ya oy es mucho menos y apenas se ve muerte de persona de importancia." ARSI Peru 15 (1639–40 Letra Anua), fols. 166v–67, emphasis added. On the seventeenth-century "[fiebres] tabardillas" (or "tabardillo") identified now as murine or exanthematic typhus: Varela Hernández and Jaramillo, "Dermatology from the Discovery of America to the Colony," p. 116.

114. Such religious processions—with dual goals of being counted by fellow devotees and paying tribute to the divine—continue today. Consider, for instance, the procession back to Taiwan made by Taiwanese immigrants to San Francisco, to honor their goddess Ma-Tsu, chronicled in: Lee, *Happy Birthday Mazu, Empress of Heaven, Goddess of the Sea.*

115. Crosby, *Antigua California*, p. 83.

116. Diana Webb also notes the resemblance between pilgrimages and the heartfelt penitential processions of northern Italy after a plague in 1399. She tells of "bands of white-clad penitents" beseeching Mary by taking her in procession "from church to church, from shrine to shrine, from town to countryside and back." Though Webb notes that these group circuits were technically image-wielding processions, she implies that the term falls short of conveying the earnestness and urgency behind the demonstration. She also refers

> On the third of February they left that harbor and amid great rejoicing arrived at the longed-for land of California, where all fulfilled the vows they had made to go barefooted from the beach to visit the sanctuary of the Most Holy Virgin of Loreto, there to offer her various tokens of their devotion.[117]

Venegas elevated the tiny frontier chapel at Loreto Conchó to the status of "sanctuary of the Most Holy Virgin of Loreto," as if it held the magnetism of Italy's ancient pilgrimage center. Perhaps, to this group, it did. If so, the pull was instilled by a combination of name and procession. As noted above in the list of Marian processions used to introduce Loreto at this site in Baja California, the Monquí had been schooled to shoulder the Virgin of Loreto on roundabout travels, to take her out into the streets with them, and then to return her home. They were well acquainted with this ceremonial procedure to showcase their queen and thus display their possession of Catholicism. But their barefoot visit to the familiar Virgin of Loreto immediately upon disembarking suggests more than social conditioning. These men's metaphorical procession to Mexico City had been long and unsettling; their survival must have felt a miracle. Reassuring themselves of Mary's presence and thanking her for her protection was a crucial part of their homecoming. The statue of the Virgin of Loreto inside their small home church was the starting point and ending point of their recent circular journey. It was not a journey of forced conformity, but of chosen companions and shared prayers.

Venegas's representation of Monquí and Jesuit together, in step at a remote Loreto offshoot, calls to mind what is most striking about his counting and Durán's reportage of the actions of the Inka cofradía of Loreto. Unlike modern scholars who tend to emphasize cultural difference, seventeenth-century Jesuits and other Catholic counters were mostly attuned to sameness. Likewise, the Inka processers in 1647 and the Monquí and Jesuit processers of 1706 may have found their actions charged with significance precisely because they were similar to majority Catholic actions. Be they European or indigenous, faithful devotees used and counted on the name "Loreto" with equal hope for results. This is, finally, what Catholic confraternities in procession had in common with the namers who preceded them, and the counters who later scrutinized and charted

---

to them as "quasi-pilgrimages," "highly stylized journey[s]" undertaken for personal reasons. Webb, *Patrons and Defenders*, p. 18.

117. Venegas, *Juan María de Salvatierra*, p. 209.

their traces on the world map: a conviction that a name could, and often did, accurately denote religious devotion *and* successfully reach divine ears. Loreto was believed to signal genuine belief because sometimes the name really did mark bona fide miracles.

In 1990, American pop singer Bette Midler made the lyrics of a Julie Gold song famous: "God is watching us from a distance." Three centuries before, Catholics showed analogous awareness of an audience more important than human posterity. The Virgin of Loreto, and by extension, Christ and God, were hearing a constant litany of names, and seeing repeated iterations of houses and icons in the 1600s. Their divine attention was bigger than Loreto or any of its material manifestations, and more significant than any single glamorized subgroup of Loreto's invokers, Jesuit or indigenous. Counting, naming, or processing Loreto put Catholics and hopeful newcomers in a large, active network that spanned the globe and reached beyond it to the heavens. In a network that large, synchronicity—in repeated names, not only in gesture or objects—was the glue that held the whole together. The creation of religious community cannot be understood if one looks only at difference, disharmony, and violence. But it can be illuminated if one counts what many people chose to purposefully, voluntarily, and visibly make the same.

PART IV

New Departures

CHAPTER EIGHT

Reconstructing Catholic Expansion

THIS HISTORY BEGAN with a house falling from the sky on a winter evening in the thirteenth century. Like a stone dropped in a puddle, the reverberations of its landing extended far, breaking boundaries of time and region. The event has been deemed a miracle. But its miraculous qualities present a challenge to skeptical historians, the humanities scholars especially trained to tell true stories verified by hard evidence. Can miracles be productively approached as *history*? The case of Loreto demonstrates: Yes. If one knows how to read them, layered myths like the Holy House's 1295 arrival are not only repositories of accurate details about the past, but they also beautifully capture how story is the backbone of history. Embellished ideals and real encounters build interdependently, one on the other, for the preservation of the whole. This final chapter opens by recapitulating the three entry points for analysis that have been tested in this book: beginning with anchoring ideals, looking for actual patterns, and finding late expressions. These strategies have been applied here to historically examine miraculous data to determine what happened in the remote past. Now they will be brought to bear to reconstruct Loreto's origins. Taken seriously as historical proof, the prototype miracle of Loreto illuminates how Catholicism moved and continues to move.

Anchoring Ideals: The Persistence of Old Agendas

Each chapter of this study has opened with a moralizing narrative that amplifies a piece of Loreto's past. Instead of focusing on the distortions or inaccuracies of this subgenre of miracle narratives, these introductory sections have considered the power of these founding instructional tales to preserve truths and to inspire in lasting ways. For instance, in the 1580s, a Catholic ideal took physical form in a shrine seal that turned the paired Madonna of Loreto and her flying Holy House into a public brand for the peaceful expansion of Catholicism (chapter 3). Later seventeenth-century authors took this brand as a starting point for their published reports about Loreto. The Jesuit Louis Richeôme's 1604 book *Pèlerin de Lorete* laid out idealized directives for how Catholic pilgrims should mentally prepare for and make sense of pilgrimage (chapter 4). Richeôme's orderly meditations stood as goals for pilgrims engaged in more chaotic and troubled approaches to Loreto. Adding to the crowded field of stamps and printed books, Bishop Casal staged a penitential procession that likewise purported to teach a memorable lesson to Catholics. He returned a stone that he had taken from the Holy House of Loreto to model for pilgrims that they should not take pieces from the original relic, but should find alternate means to commemorate its presence, such as building scale replicas (chapter 5). Wood and painted canvas were prototypes for the Madonna of Loreto, who underwent many anonymously instilled transformations to stay relevant to changing audiences (chapter 6). Even tallies of the name Loreto in seventeenth-century atlases could stand as models. These compilations of Loreto missions around the world encouraged others to draw on a variety of Catholic names to designate their religious affiliation (chapter 7). A seal, a manual, a procession, a statue or painting, and an atlas: All stood as thoughtfully crafted maps for how the Loreto devotion should spread.

If these alluring prototypes were studied in detached isolation, they would mislead. Most were created in Europe. All attempted to freeze or permanently anchor only a few facets of a complicated devotion. All report triumph, broadcasting successful transit, continued potency or survival. Taken alone, these artifacts of Loreto would seem to point to the traditional interpretation of how Catholicism moved: it was a European export, carried outward in carefully regulated ways and imposed stiffly. But this book has repeatedly demonstrated otherwise. Grounding narratives must be viewed first, as their prominence demands, but they should be considered as embedded in the broader contexts that inspired them. In reality, they never appeared alone. The chapter introductions demonstrate that each of these exalting showpieces of Loreto's mythohistory was itself grafted atop earlier incarnations of Loreto's past, and already leaning outward to future branchings. Every epic anchorage emerged in direct conversation with actual moments that were less glamorous and less provincial than seems first indicated.

Actual Convergences: Movements, Additions, and Real Situations

The book's chapters therefore move on from ideals to urge readers to look for the contrast between such glittering narratives and the gritty historical record. The dissonances between ideal and real recur across time and space. They converge around three patterns that were observed at the start of this study as jarring elements within Loreto's very own origin myth (chapter 2). First, there were journeys, or *movements* of the objects at the center of the Loreto devotion. Second, there were pairings, or *additions* of new objects and meanings to the corpus. Third, there were lived experiences, or *real situations* among individuals that served to bring devotional trappings to life. Movements, additions, and real situations were incorporated into Loreto's history from its genesis.

For example, the real situations of two Jesuits, Raphael Riera and Oratio Torsellino, prompted them to inflect their histories of Loreto based on what they personally observed at the Marian pilgrimage site in the late 1500s (chapter 3). The accounts of these "Actual Eyewitnesses" added layers of new, recent details to the founding myth of Loreto, connecting that distant landing to current events. Similarly, the "Actual Encounters" of two pilgrims, Nicolà Albani and the Jesuit Pierre Chaumonot, shaped how these men perceived Loreto and carried it forward (chapter 4). Their serendipitous detours to the shrine of Loreto saved their lives, so both found ways to add to the mushrooming corpus of Loreto: Albani published his account and blueprints of the Holy House, and Chaumonot constructed a copy of the Holy House in the Canadian mission field. Because these individuals were themselves in motion, their journeys unseated Loreto from its Adriatic cradle. Notably, Albani and Chaumonot stand in counterpoint to anchoring ideals. These men were not following printed pilgrimage guidelines like Richeôme's when they first stumbled into Loreto, yet their spiritual encounters there led them to feel authorized to publish or write about pilgrimage, and to extend its circuits beyond Italy.

Albani's and Chaumonot's actions were also part of a larger stream of "Actual Repetitions" that directly informed the oft-broadcast morality tale of Bishop Casal, which was used to order listeners not to reverently rip the sacred Holy House of Loreto to pieces, but rather to leave it intact where it stood. Catholics found a creative alternative in physically replicating the structure of the Holy House. They left multiple copies of it strewn across Europe and even in the frontiers of the Americas, in the wake of Jesuit missionaries whose architectural ambitions were more often personal than pedagogical (chapter 5). Again, these Holy House builders were not in lockstep with Casal's ideal.

Parallel refractions and disobediences occurred for the image of Mary at the heart of Loreto's Holy House. Over the centuries, the dark icon at the Loreto shrine was updated into an even darker statue; when carried overseas, statues of Loreto's Madonna were whitened (chapter 6). Though they were largely anonymous and happening below the radar, these surface modifications were not undertaken in defiance. They were seen as useful additions to the original paired relics back in Italy, and they were seen as consistent with Loreto's idealized mythohistory, which stressed that her relics were foreign arrivals, alien, and also perennially on the move.

Loreto's incessant journeying was further magnified by the "Actual Patterns" of naming new and often remote outposts after Loreto, whether or not these sites sported a house replica or icon variant (chapter 7). For some Jesuits posted overseas, repeating the name "Loreto" in their mission zones marked them as part of a large and ever-growing Catholic chorus. They were not exactly following strict templates when they chose to impart "Loreto," yet they freely contributed to its overseas distribution.

Cumulatively, these spontaneous reiterations of name, icon, and house show the importance of movements, additions, and real situations to the diffusion of Catholicism. But their presence and great variety in the seventeenth century also present a tension, when read alongside the opening ideals. There is an uncomfortable acceleration to Loreto's new drifting that seems on the edge of control, even for the self-appointed authors, pilgrims, architects, artists, and counters who were taking part in the driving. Closer looks at this acceleration have been necessary to better understand its nature.

Reading Backward: From New Expressions to Old Founding Texts

Each chapter has concluded by taking a more in-depth look at the connections between one historical episode from a later moment, and the older mythohistory. These linkages between times suggest that more recent and well-chronicled episodes can illuminate past mysteries. The episodes were chosen not simply to highlight connections, however, but also to interrogate some of the more radical stretches and adaptations of the devotion of Loreto. In contrast to the first assortment of anchoring ideals, the "New Expressions" that end each chapter have featured frontier zones where empires and cultures collide: Dalmatia, Québec, Baja California, the Amazon Basin, and the city of Cuzco, Peru. If these expressions were reviewed in isolation, just as with the ideals mostly originating in Europe, the grouping would mislead. One might construe these episodes to be replacing Europe's foundational templates with entirely new models from the frontier. But the new incarnations are presented here as deeply entangled with the early mythohistory, self-consciously attached to it by the actual histories that bridge this analysis. Without the first Holy House dropping from the sky, and the real intermediaries who portaged it elsewhere, these later expressions would not take the powerful forms that they are shown, here, to assume.

Nikolà Frankopan is a case in point. He surfaces in the Jesuit Oratio Torsellino's published history of Loreto as one of the Catholic leaders who helped the Dalmatians cope with the Holy House's unexpected departure to Italy (chapter 3). Torsellino's Frankopan was based on several Slavic Catholics of this name from Trsat, who reached across the Adriatic Sea to honor and sponsor the Loreto shrine. Although none of the Frankopans created bishop's seals or compiled histories of Loreto, these men's actions reinforced and wrote in a Slavic dimension to Loreto's past; they were part of a growing stream of authors extending Loreto's narrative. Similarly, the Huron Catholic Ignace Tsaouenhohoui was not an official pilgrim following the rubric laid out in Richeôme's manual, nor did he designate himself a pilgrim after intense encounters, like Albani and Chaumonot (chapter 4). But the Jesuit wanderer Chaumonot saw himself reflected in the pilgrim-like trajectory of this Huron as he stumbled into Christian sites in Canada with desperation, and departed from them spiritually recharged. His real encounters were not projected or imposed fictions. Ignace's gestures of pilgrimage, like the Frankopans' motions of authorship, breathed life into the Loreto devotion and added a Huron leg to it.

Another extension was added by the Jesuit Juan Maria Salvatierra when he built a rudimentary replica of the Holy House of Loreto in Baja California, at the nascent mission to the Monquí Indians of Conchó (chapter 5). The structure was different in form and geographically distant from the Holy House in Italy that Bishop Casal had attempted to preserve in his penitential procession. Yet its spiritual pull on Salvatierra and the Monquí converts was as potent as that of the original. Similarly, in the Moxos missions of the Amazon, later manifestations of the Holy House stretched the sphere of influence of earlier ones.

Loreto's iconography was also dramatically transformed by overseas activities. Jesuit missionaries wrote about pious female converts called Marie at the Canadian mission of Jeune-Lorette (chapter 6). These flesh-and-blood women can be viewed as living contributors to the ever-changing stream of images of Mary. In fact, they reflect many of the adaptations to the image of the Madonna of Loreto that were encapsulated in Caravaggio's classic seventeenth-century painting: she was humanized, raised to her feet, and brought outside her household.

In the same manner, the real Inka Catholics of Cuzco and Monqui converts of Baja California animated the name Loreto that was being tallied by atlas makers and repeated by Jesuits across their missionizing fields (chapter 7). These new Catholics took Loreto to the streets in procession. In doing so, they gave the name meaning not just for themselves, but for their Catholic contemporaries back in Europe who painstakingly tracked the devotion's spread.

The exemplars in these last chapters show that it is not just categories of human actors such as "author" and "pilgrim" that need to be made more expansive to reflect realities in the historical record. The categories of "holy house," "icon," and even "atlas" take on new significance when one factors in the human activity that kept them vibrant. Changes, continuities, and overseas leaps start to make sense when viewed in this much wider frame spanning first landings, latest permutations, and above all, multitudes of people.

What Really Happened in Loreto, Italy, around 1300?

Loreto's elusive origin myth was the trigger for this whole endeavor. Can the above strategies of historical decipherment help to answer the still-unsolved questions about Loreto's early days? It is worth recalling the enigma of Loreto's first mysterious anchorage before applying the ideals, actualities, and new expressions to the task of its interpretation. Multiple written sources from two centuries after the event agreed that two objects were discovered on the Adriatic coast of Italy in the winter of 1295: a small structure made of foreign materials, and an image of Mary. The Virgin Mary herself appeared to a hermit to mark the space as "holy, and terrible," to explain that the structure was her own house flown by angels over the sea, and to comment that the house had stopped on the opposite coast, in Dalmatia, before arriving at Loreto (chapter 1). Although the Holy House and icon were encased and fixed in prose and marble, they jumped oceans again in later centuries. Jesuit missionaries named frontier sites in the Americas after Loreto and transported copies of its Holy House, icon, and name. This mythohistory elicits many questions, but the two that loom largest remain: What really happened in Loreto, Italy, around 1300? What can this early anchorage tell us about how Catholicism moves, yesterday and today?

What follows is largely conjecture, but it is based on the three patterns evident from the later historical record of actual events and new expressions of the 1600s and early 1700s. First, there was movement: not the movement of solitary relics, but of groups of Catholics. Second, there were additions: Catholic attributions of provenance were frequently assigned after the fact, and not aimlessly. Finally, there were real experiences: latecomers embraced newly arrived Catholic expressions and asserted ownership over them because they had strong personal encounters or associations with them.

Movement is the first clue recognizable in the origin narratives and historical records surrounding Loreto. What, or who, was moving along the Italian coast around 1300? It does not seem that it was the Holy House or its associated icon. Neither object shows the hallmarks of being "holy detritus," abandoned and shunted from place to place until someone reclaimed it.[1] Nor does it appear that these relics were expressly sent for from an exotic foreign market. The most likely candidate for such importation would be the Byzantine icon at the center of Loreto's earliest church. But by 1300, Italy already had a long tradition of obscuring the local origins of religious artwork, especially art in the Byzantine style.[2] By effacing the boundaries between the Italian and Byzantine in this period, Italians could claim to share a classical and Christian legacy with the empire to the east.[3] Loreto's icon emerged at a time when Byzantine

1. Barry, "Religious Statues Left Behind Find Their Own Patron Saint"; Vélez, "Urban Driftwood."

2. Art historian Anthony Cutler has noted "the Italian refusal to distinguish local productions from those of the east Christian world," especially in the 1300s. Cutler, "Pathos of Distance," p. 24.

3. While Western or Roman Catholicism and Byzantine Eastern Orthodox Christianity did share a long history, by the fourteenth century, attitudes toward depicting Mary differed between these branches of the church. But the eighth-century Byzantine iconoclast movement continues to cause exaggeration of the difference between icon usage in the West versus the East. On the variety of ways icons were approached in the Byzantine empire: Maguire, *Icons of Their Bodies*. On the historiography of iconoclasm: Brubaker, *Inventing Byzantine Iconoclasm*.

images were so popular that they were being produced internally for local markets. Furthermore, Loreto's first icon does not seem to have come from Dalmatia. Descriptions of it bear little resemblance to Slavic Madonnas of the thirteenth century.[4] Also, Catholics from Illyria in the 1200s tended to favor images of regional favorites such as St. George and St. Veneranda, so it is unlikely that they brought over a painting of Mary.[5] Therefore, it seems plausible that these objects originated precisely where the mythohistory stepped off to explain them: near Recanati. This assumption illuminates a different side of Christianity that has reappeared often in this study, a Christianity of fortuitous convergence, not of transfer.

There is a well-documented drifting group of Catholics who converged on the Italian coast in the early fourteenth century: Slavic migrants. Just as the relics existed in Italy before they acquired fame, the Slavs were an early and normal presence on the Italian coast. Notably, by the mid-thirteenth century, there was a large enclave of Dalmatian merchants resident in Recanati, the city just west of Loreto. Recanati had established a small port to trade with Dalmatia.[6] The city hosted one of the largest Adriatic trade fairs in the Marche region every fall, drawing seafaring merchants from Venice, Milan, and Genoa as well as Dalmatia.[7] Dalmatians came to the Marches through the ports of Ancona and Recanati, but many of them also settled around these cities to engage in other trades.[8] By the 1400s, Dalmatian farmers, builders, cobblers, weavers, innkeepers, and tailors were all reported in the vicinity of Loreto.[9] Dalmatians also frequently ventured

4. For instance, two miniature images of Mary from Serbia in the 1200s differ from the regal Byzantine posture; they are Madonnas *de tendresse*, tender maternal images. Grabar, *Deux Images de la Vierge dans un Manuscrit serbe.*

5. Lightbown, *Carlo Crivelli*, p. 27.

6. Grimaldi, *Pellegrini*, pp. 258, 270. Recanati, like Ancona, established reciprocity with cities on the Dalmatian coast from an early date: in 1206 and in 1229, for instance, Recanati renewed pacts with the port of Ragusa on the opposite Adriatic shore. Grimaldi remarks especially on the trans-Adriatic trade in livestock: sheep, cattle, and horses were the goods most frequently shuttled between Dalmatia and the Marche.

7. Lightbown, *Carlo Crivelli*, p. 23.

8. Emigration also went the other way. In the 1400s, Reinhold Mueller points to a veritable brain drain from the Italian city of Venice to the Dalmatian city of Ragusa. Ragusa aggressively recruited its doctors and school teachers from Venice as well as relying on the imported labor of Venetian sailors and indentured servants. Mueller, "Aspects of Venetian Sovereignty in Medieval and Renaissance Dalmatia."

9. Lightbown, *Carlo Crivelli*, p. 27; Grimaldi, *Pellegrini*, pp. 260–61. These manual laborers make an interesting contrast with the Dalmatian population in Venice in the 1400s. Dalmatians in Venice dominated more elite trades of skilled artisanry including shipbuilding and painting. The well-known *Scuola Dalmata* of fresco painters was based at Venice's San Giorgio degli Schiavoni parish. Wolff, *Venice and the Slavs*, pp. 60–61.

to the Italian Marches to join the Franciscan order, which had retreats for hermits scattered through the mountains west of Loreto.[10] One of these pockets of Dalmatian immigrants seems well-positioned to have inspired or fueled the nascent devotion's as-yet-unconsolidated history.

In early 1460, twelve years before Tolomei's first published account of Loreto's origins, a large group of expelled *schiavoni* made a new home for themselves in Castelnuovo, a village extension of the town of Loreto.[11] The Castelnuovo Slavs had been driven out of Recanati because of the plague. The plague was a persistent blight in the Marche in the fifteenth century.[12] Outbursts of the plague decimated the population and led to certain groups of immigrants like the Lombards being invited in to resettle empty lands.[13] In contrast, the Slavic immigrants on Italy's eastern coasts tended to be expelled from towns whenever plague threatened. Urban centers commonly self-quarantined themselves in times of epidemic, but Dalmatians and Albanians seem to have been particularly pinpointed as carriers of the plague, which was believed to have arrived in western Europe through the Balkans.[14] In 1456, Recanati decreed twice that all schiavoni must leave the city because they were carriers of the plague. The next epidemic of plague followed hard on the heels of the first; in 1460, the schiavoni were again ordered to leave.[15] Many of the expelled

10. Grimaldi, *Pellegrini*, pp. 260–61. Grimaldi procures this data on Dalmatians from wills and testaments.

11. Ibid., pp. 258–59. Grimaldi notes that while Slavic immigrants are first recorded as living in Loreto earlier than this, in 1435, this is a relatively late date for Slavic settlement in the area. In Recanati, city registers refer to a Slavic ghetto ("fundus sclavunici") much earlier, by the end of the thirteenth century.

12. Lightbown, *Carlo Crivelli*, p. 34. The plague struck Recanati in 1426, 1427, 1429, 1433, 1435, 1436 and then again in 1456, 1460, 1462, 1468, 1475, 1476, 1478, 1479, 1481, 1483, 1484, 1485, 1486, 1494 and 1495. Grimaldi observes that the devotion to the Madonna of Loreto grew tremendously during the plague years of the fifteenth century because she, along with the saints Sebastian and Roch and the Madonna of Misericordia, was seen to offer protection from the plague. *La Madonna di Loreto nelle Marche*, pp. 20–23.

13. Lightbown, *Carlo Crivelli*, p. 27. Lombards were invited into the plague-reduced city of Jesi in the Marches in 1471.

14. Dalmatians were blamed for the plague up through the eighteenth century. Lightbown quotes the Florentine humanist Matteo Palmieri, who wrote of the plague of 1448–51 that "it was a great pestilence, which took its rise in Asia and then spread through Illyria and Dalmatia into Italy" (ibid., p. 34). Wolff notes that three hundred years later, in 1783, the shipboard doctor Francesco Falier chronicled the plague outbreak in Dalmatia as if Dalmatia were "a bulwark against Oriental infections that menaced even the civilization of Italy. If the line of quarantine could not be reliably held in the mountains of Dalmatia, it had to be maintained along the coast of the Adriatic." Wolff, *Venice and the Slavs*, p. 279.

15. Grimaldi, *Pellegrini*, p. 259. The first decree of 1456 was in January; it was repeated eleven months later, in December.

could not return to the Balkan coast. They simply resettled in the outskirts of Recanati, supporting themselves as agricultural laborers.

Such was the group that arrived in Loreto to begin anew. Little is known of them, except that at the time they came to Loreto, the town was drastically diminished in population because of the plague. New arrivals, even foreigners, would therefore have had the opportunity to play a role in the community. Soon after these Slavic refugees from Recanati relocated to Castelnuovo, two wills were filed by Loreto residents specifying that donations and pilgrims be sent to *both* the Madonna of Loreto *and* the Dalmatian Madonna of Trsat.[16] The mention of both Marian shrines suggests that some of the recent Dalmatian arrivals may have come from the environs of Trsat. People residing in Loreto—not pilgrims, but regular inhabitants—were starting to connect the two Adriatic devotions in practice.

One last puzzle piece snapped into place in Loreto's Castelnuovo neighborhood in the late fifteenth century. More Slavs arrived, war refugees from the continuing exodus of Slavs to Italy after the 1453 fall of Constantinople to the Ottomans. Well into the 1470s, coinciding with each new Ottoman advance, waves of Dalmatian and Albanian refugees poured into Italy's ports on the Adriatic.[17] Most of these refugees were Catholic. Many of them even brought magnificent relics along that they had salvaged from their embattled churches: the head of the Apostle Andrew; the cross of Zaccarias; the foot of St. Anne.[18]

Loreto's governor, Pietro Tolomei, sat down to compile the first definitive history of Loreto at this moment of influx of Dalmatian Catholics (chapter 3). Here one can discern the other historical patterns of additions and of lived experience that have recurred in this study. Tolomei wrote one hundred years before the Jesuit Oratio Torsellino published his descriptions of weeping Slavs at the shrine. Unlike the Jesuits of the

16. Ibid., pp. 266–69. These wills are the earliest written documents connecting the two Marian shrines. One dates to 7 August 1462 and the other to 28 February 1475. It is unclear whether the authors of the wills were part of the new Slavic neighborhood or Italians.

17. On Dalmatian refugees: ibid., p. 259. On ten separate surges of Albanian immigration into Italy between 1380 and 1478, corresponding with Ottoman advances: Lightbown, *Carlo Crivelli*, p. 27. On the Venetian government's measures to support the Albanian and Dalmatian refugees of the 1470s: Pullan, *Rich and Poor in Renaissance Venice*, p. 212.

18. Hamilton, "Ottomans, the Humanists and the Holy House of Loreto," pp. 11–12. These relics were brought by wealthy Catholic exiles from throughout the crumbling Byzantine Empire, not just from the Balkans. Thomas Palaeologus, brother of the last Byzantine emperor, Constantine XI, brought the head of the Apostle Andrew to Rome; Giovanni Asan, prince of Morea, brought the cross of Zaccarias to Genoa; and Leonardo Tocco brought the foot of St. Anne to Naples to put in his private chapel.

1550s, Tolomei was not faced with groups of sobbing pilgrims. But he did oversee the streets of Castelnuovo that were crowded with Slavic refugees of plague and war. He may even have attended mass with these Catholic devout who had fled from Dalmatia and been driven from Recanati before they at last found sanctuary at Loreto. Did their journey of stuttering and interrupted starts provide the backbone for his reconstruction of the Madonna of Loreto's travels? Perhaps he asked them about their countryman, the legendary Nikolà Frankopan of Trsat. Maybe they told him about building and rebuilding provisional chapels as they paused in forests and forded waters trying to find a safe refuge. Or perhaps they simply captured his imagination as they strode into Castelnuovo uninvited in the manner of the Huron war refugee Ignace Tsaouenhohoui, who led his relatives back to the protection of the walled city of Québec that had shut them out. No matter the details, Governor Tolomei's brief early narrative suggests that he saw the Madonna of Loreto in these refugees. He did not simply invent them to embellish his narrative. He folded this very visible living group into his history of Loreto's origins because their real situations were making the Holy House vibrant and present. Slavs remained in the mythohistory that they helped to build; some of them wept to remain there. They appear in the record as much of a fixture as the *Santa Casa* and the Madonna. Here at last, hidden well inside burgeoning narrative encasements, one glimpses the genesis of Italy's Lauretan devotion.

Look, again, at the recurring patterns evident in this reconstruction of Loreto. There was the *movement* of Dalmatian refugees in the fourteenth and fifteenth centuries. They recharged the local atmosphere with their fervor to find a spiritual home away from home. They became associated with an icon of Mary that was probably painted in the 1200s near Recanati, and with the small church that housed her there too. By the mid-1400s, there was an *addition*: locals composed a backstory to these Italian relics, linking them to the Dalmatian Catholics at the same time as they envisioned these objects' more distant connections to the Holy Land. Finally, there was a *real situation*: Slavic immigrants and local Italian speakers coexisted in and apportioned the Catholic space around Loreto. As they did so, they jointly remembered a devotional past that involved them both. The memory also glorified what united Italians and Slavs across cultural, linguistic, and oceanic divides. Both Catholic groups believed in a Holy Mother who stayed with them, even if that necessitated flight.

Here were the formative ingredients of the Loreto devotion and its mythohistory: deeply devout foreigners moving in to reside with old-timers; two existing sacred objects in the Marche, provenance pending;

and an uncoordinated, late but roughly simultaneous appropriation of the objects by both Italians and Dalmatians in the immediate vicinity. These hypothetical origins for Loreto correspond to the elements that frequently combined to explain the process of the devotion's movement in the seventeenth and eighteenth centuries: uprooted and earnestly spiritual aliens, Jesuit and Indian, moving on the American frontiers; sacred objects and structures needing added explanations; and an imperfectly synchronized but mutual grab for the devotional helm by all parties involved, in order to give meaning to their current lived experience.

In its most idealized form, with a flying house falling from the sky, the Madonna of Loreto's mythohistory sounds like a parable. It turns out to be a strikingly accurate one for rendering a lesson about how Catholics moved. Numerous Catholic devotees of Loreto literally charted miraculous escape routes out of desperate situations of fear, violence, forced coexistence, and death, somehow reintegrating themselves into new, faith-filled communities. Trailing the footsteps of such refugees was an odd and uncomfortable road for Catholic expansion to take, and an even stranger one to glorify. But the historical record shows that whenever and wherever these experiences of flight and landing repeated, the Loreto devotion could find new roots. In microcosm, Loreto shows that the history of Christianity is above all a history of *physical movement*.[19]

Were all these linkages across time and space necessary to reconstruct these movements around Loreto in 1300? The methodology here has not been presented simply as a means to explain a discrete local event, but as a way to understand how and why that event continued to travel and resonate over time. Loreto is not a small hometown story relevant only to the Italian hilltop where it began. Its movement and repetitions in later years show a capacity for portability, resilience, and adaptation that makes the Catholic religion and so many other religions vital for twenty-first-century folk to study.

It is not the claim of this work that the Loreto devotion uniquely encapsulates every way in which Catholicism spread. But Loreto's journeys stand as crucial counterpoint to stubborn notions that the Catholic religion expanded predominantly through imperial combat in this age of encounters. There are many recent and relevant studies of Christianity

19. Peter Brown highlights this dynamic in early Christianity, countering the stereotype of "timeless cult site[s]." He paints a picture of changing, mobile Christianity: "We are often on the roads of Gaul and Italy. New things are always happening. New forms of *gloria* are 'revealed,' 'shine forth.'" Brown, *Relics and Social Status in the Age of Gregory of Tours*, pp. 12–13.

and violence, shedding light on components of Catholicism—political and spiritual—that need to be understood.[20] There are also studies that flag how the ravages of epidemics catalyzed conversion.[21] Yet the traumas of military might and disease alone cannot convincingly explain how, and why, Catholicism took hold and persisted in so many disparate regions, Europe included. The spread of Loreto calls attention to alternative dynamics that existed in places where Catholicism took root. War and death could be key factors in such zones, as noted in many of the case studies above, yet they played out there concurrently alongside other collaborative processes.

The mythohistory of Loreto as reconstructed here offers at least three more take-away messages about how Catholic devotions moved nonaggressively in the sixteenth, seventeenth, and eighteenth centuries, the period of Catholicism's widest global expansion. Two have grounded this study, but the third requires further comment.

First, Catholicism was *additive*. Divergences from Old World or parent models were not aberrations or stripping down, but a crucial and deliberate part of these Catholic objects' renewed potency. There was more room for diversity and alterations within early modern Catholicism than is usually acknowledged.

Second, Catholicism at this time hinged on *personal experience*, earthly as much as otherworldly. There were real tactile, physical, and individual components to the Holy House and its icon. These Catholic objects, in their original formats and in their myriad offshoots, were meant to be touched, carried, and spread. That was part of their power.

Finally, stemming from the two above historical patterns of addition and personal experience, it can be observed that the creation and authorship of this segment of Catholic devotion was a little bit out of control. When reviewing the many hands involved in building Loreto's reliquaries, one gets a sense of growing mass participation, and one sympathizes with the desperation of some parts of the Catholic Church bureaucracy, in this period of church reformation, to retroactively reign in, monitor, and authenticate some of this wildfire spread of spirituality and Catholic self-identification. It was never simply a battle between high-ranking orthodox authority versus less elite, popular masses, however. As has been

20. To name just a few: Armstrong, *Fields of Blood*; Buc, *Holy War, Martyrdom and Terror*; France, *Crusades and the Expansion of Catholic Christendom*; Boxer, *Church Militant and Iberian Expansion*.

21. Cook, *Born to Die*, pp. 2, 211; Reff, "Jesuit Mission Frontier in Comparative Perspective," p. 27.

demonstrated here, the expansion of Catholicism cannot be adequately explained as either top-down or bottom-up. There were multiple, simultaneous modes of regeneration stemming from, and entangling, all corners of society. European or indigenous, male Jesuit or female neophyte, old Catholic or new convert, each fresh contributor had to bridge with other spheres for validation.

An Old Miracle of Mass Participation and the New Age of Wikipedia

Oddly, with this last observation about mass participation, it is especially easy to recognize ourselves in the early twenty-first century. We are engaged in similar processes of tolerating and regulating replication today; we also worry about hidden and unqualified contributors, lest their creative embellishments cause us to lose touch with the real. At the same time, we invite amateur participation on a wider scale than ever before for the task of recording and transmitting human knowledge. To name just one contemporary analogy, there is our own modern shrine to information, the Internet, and one of its more recent manifestations, Wikipedia. Wikipedia is a universe of copied and recopied memes, a vast collection of pooled little "Holy Houses" of knowledge. We turn to it for vetted, supposedly cross-checked information, to copy archived memories, yet we also turn to it to edit, add, link and cross-link, and alter. *We* do this—you, and me—not just trained or credentialed authorities sitting far away in some elite metropolitan center.

A comparison between the construction of Loreto's mythohistory and today's Wikipedia entries is illuminating, both for the similarities and differences that rise to the fore. Like the corpus of Loreto chronicled here, Wikipedia is massive, with over four million articles in the English edition alone. Both Loreto's founding narrative and Wikipedia are free to read, post, or access. Both have "no authors in any conventional sense. Tens of thousands of people—who have not gotten even the glory of affixing their names to it—have written collaboratively" to produce them.[22] Surprisingly, given the extent of this open invitation to participate, malicious vandalism is less common in the formation of both displays than one might expect.[23] Both also include what in Wikipedia terminology is

22. Rosenzweig, "Can History Be Open Source?," p. 117.

23. Ibid., pp. 132–33. Rosenzweig presents impressive statistics from Wikipedia itself on the "short life" of vandalism on Wikipedia.

a GFDL, a General Free Documentation License, which states: "You may copy and distribute the Document in any medium, either commercially or non-commercially, provided . . . you give credit to Wikipedia and allow others to reuse and refashion your revised version."[24] Though not stamped in legalese on its house and icon, Loreto's "documents" also came with partial license to copy and refashion.

For Wikipedia, however, there is a strict policy for aspiring contributors that has two emphases that seem at cross-purposes with sixteenth- and seventeenth-century Catholic Church aims: conventionality and neutrality. As an encyclopedia and not a living religion, Wikipedia urges its authors to summarize accepted wisdom, but not to innovate or "break new ground."[25] In contrast, the "New Expressions" sections in this book have highlighted how new ground, in Loreto's case, was a crucial factor in allowing the devotion to thrive and spread. Another disparity is that Wikipedia requires a "Neutral Point of View" for its articles, a balanced representation of multiple perspectives rather than a single one. Wikipedia's NPOV policy, its cornerstone of avoiding bias, has come under much scrutiny and has been found to be more of an ideal than a reality.[26] But that ideal of neutrality is publicly trumpeted, enforced, and regulated in magnificent contradistinction to the ideal publicized by the Catholic Church's equivalent to editorial staff (some of the first authors, Jesuits, and Tridentine bishops mentioned previously in this book). Early modern Catholic editors nominally sought to present one unified voice for the church, not multiple voices; ironically, the mythohistory of Loreto that they helped to shape still reveals multiple voices. Similarly, while Wikipedia's editors seek the opposite—to represent "differing views"—recent studies have shown that their encyclopedia format ends up favoring very few voices, verging on conformity.[27]

24. Ibid., p. 123.

25. Ibid., p. 121.

26. To note just one recent study: Greenstein and Zhu, "Is Wikipedia Biased?" Greenstein and Zhu statistically analyzed twenty-eight thousand Wikipedia entries about US politics and concluded that Wikipedia is, indeed, biased, and that the overall slant of Wikipedia has changed over time.

27. Rosenzweig, "Can History Be Open Source?," p. 122; also pp. 136–37: "*Wikipedia* can act as a megaphone, amplifying the (sometimes incorrect) conventional wisdom. . . . As a result, as the blogger John Morse observed, 'when you search Google for some obscure term that *Wikipedia* knows about, you might get two dozen results that all say the same thing—seemingly authoritative until you realize they all spread from a snapshot of Wiki—one that is now severed from the context of editability and might seem more creditable than it really is.'"

Interestingly, in spite of opposite end goals, the mythohistory of Loreto and Wikipedia end up squeezing many voices into one more authoritative, eminently quotable end product. This congruence may be due to their shared process of communal construction. That process has been hyperanalyzed for troubleshooting purposes in the case of Wikipedia. The catalog of anxieties expressed about Wikipedia's joint formulations resembles the concerns broached over the centuries about Loreto. Both Wikipedia and Loreto's mythohistory lean toward the popular rather than the academic; both produce articles (or in Loreto's case, houses, icons, and missions) of varying length and quality; their biggest contributors tend to be white male English-speaking geeks (tech-savvy or Jesuit, respectively); they "sometimes get things wrong in one place and right in another"; and their circuits of distribution often run into political blocks to access that restrict instead of democratize.[28]

These challenges have often been chalked up to how the Internet, or World Wide Web, has changed procedure. But the changes described by online editor John Grabowski about one of Wikipedia's forerunners, the *Encyclopedia of Cleveland History*, have all been tracked here in the pre-Internet evolution of Loreto. Grabowski discusses having to grapple with fast growth, updating incoming entries constantly, needing to maintain a public profile and presence, and having to address matters of design and style. The outcome of Grabowski's process of production for a twenty-first-century online encyclopedia is the same as that of Loreto: the resulting compilation has "essentially become a living entity, one that need[s] continual oversight and hence a staff."[29]

Growth, in this case, seems to beget growth. Prior to 1700, the need for oversight and staff led to crowd sourcing just as it has in the past few decades. What remains as mysterious now as it was in earlier centuries is people's willingness to participate. Roy Rosenzweig, professor of history and new media, mused about this dynamic for Wikipedia: "somehow thousands of dispersed volunteers who do not know each other have organized a massive enterprise."[30] Why? The many case studies of Loreto's volunteers gathered here suggest that participation in a collaborative network of this sort was self-reinforcing. Participation not only fueled Catholicism, but it also invigorated participants. Bystanders could view a miracle like Loreto with curiosity, but it was *participants* who could tweak

28. Ibid., pp. 126, 127, 128, 138 (on restrictions to Wikipedia in China).
29. Grabowski, "Past as Prologue," p. 40.
30. Rosenzweig, "Can History Be Open Source?," p. 125.

the mythohistory, transmit it, and use it to access the divine. To make it work, one had to step inside the system. This is, curiously, also one of the dynamics of Wikipedia that has been remarked on positively of late: "the benefit of Wikipedia may be greater for its active participants than for its readers."[31]

We live with a dangerous hubris, today, that we are part of an entirely new global age, living in a world more interconnected and smaller than ever before. This can cause us to forget that seven hundred years ago, objects—some of them sacred commodities—were circulating across continents and oceans, crossing political and cultural borders with familiar alacrity. The process of "translation," the movement of revered objects in protective cases, has a long history.[32] It is an overwhelmingly communal history that shows these objects being created by, harbored by, and passed between multiple and varied groups. As we try to navigate through the confusion and sift through the rampant copying of our own times, it would serve us well to remember the centuries of precedents. We should revisit old, time-tested strategies for spreading and managing ideas on the run, for connecting disparate peoples by way of physical media, for distributing and retaining beliefs and cultural memories, and for doing this in compelling and lasting ways. Perhaps the collective portaging of an Italian devotion to the world centuries ago can help us to better understand why people self-enlist in the universalizing project, and why we synchronize or vary our contributions to it. Our circle of acknowledged producers of religion and history must be expanded to accurately reflect the complex, as yet growing accumulation of human encounters.

31. Classicist James O'Donnell as quoted by ibid., p. 139. This is also the observation of high school teacher Elizabeth Ann Pollard, who assigned her students the task of revising controversial Wikipedia articles on witchcraft. She found that her students' participation in the online community and peer review process of Wikipedia taught them to "manage complexity" and "take responsibility" in ways they would not have done for traditional individual research projects. The process empowered them not just to be historians but to change historical transcripts. Pollard, "Raising the Stakes," p. 21.

32. With regard to Catholic relics, *translatio* was a category coined in the Middle Ages to contrast relics that had physically moved to an entirely new site with those that had arrived through *inventio*. *Inventio* marked a relic's surfacing (or resurfacing) at a chosen site, as did the Holy House of Walsingham, Mary's house that surfaced in England by means of an unusually detailed vision to a noblewoman. *Translatio* described journeys such as that of the Holy House of Loreto, Mary's house that derived its importance and fame from its epic transit. The distinction between the two houses was not technically one of authenticity, because both were seen as sacred and closely connected to Mary. They differed, rather, in how they had arrived: the Holy House of Walsingham appeared (*inventio*), while the *Santa Casa* traveled (*translatio*). For the medieval roots of these terms: Webb, *Patrons and Defenders*, pp. 14–15.

BIBLIOGRAPHY

Unpublished Primary Sources

ARCHIVUM ROMANUM SOCIETATIS IESU, ROME, ITALY (ARSI)

Gall. 109 (*Historia Missionis Canaden. 1611–1659*), tom. 1.
 fols. 112–13 (Letter from P.-J.-M. Chaumonot to Filippo Nappi, August 1641).
Ital. 159, tom. 2 (*Epist. Ital. 1585*).
 fols. 36–37v (Letter from Alessandro Leni to Alberto Ariosto, 13 June 1585).
 fols. 43–44 (Letter from Hippolito Voglia to P. Acquaviva, 14 June 1585).
 fols. 47–48v (Letter from Francesco Mercato to P. Acquaviva, 16 June 1585).
 fols. 55–57 (Letter from Alessandro Leni to P. Acquaviva, 13 June 1585).
 fols. 64–65v (Letter from F. Mercato to Nicolas Bobadilla in Rome, 19 June 1585).
Ital. 160 (*Epist. Italiae 1585–92*).
 fol. 276 (Letter from Oratio Torsellino to Claudio Acquaviva, 7 May 1592).
 fol. 297 (Letter from Oratio Torsellino to Claudio Acquaviva, 28 May 1592).
Ital. 161 (*Epist. Italiae 1592–6*).
 fol. 12 (Letter from Oratio Torsellino to Claudio Acquaviva, 18 June 1592).
 fol. 14 (Letter from Oratio Torsellino to Rector of Loreto, c. 1592).
 fols. 21–22v (Letter from Oratio Torsellino to Claudio Acquaviva, 21 June 1592).
 fols. 145–46 (1592 *Memoriale interna alle cose del Collegio Illirico*).
 fols. 208–12 (Letter from Jacobus Borghi to Oratio Torsellino, 30 December 1594).
Mex. 17 (*Mexicana Documenta e Historia, 1600–1700*).
 fols. 512–24v (1683 *Relación* of the second Jesuit expedition to California).
 fols. 580–95 (Giovanni Salvaterra to P. Procurator J. Ugarte, 27 November 1697).
 fols. 596–608 (G. Salvaterra to Juan Ugarte, 9 July 1699).
 fols. 608v–9 (Letter from Juan de Ugarte, 1699).
Peru 15 (*Peruana Litterae Annuae, Tom. IV, 1630–51*).
 fol. 89v (Letter from António Vázquez to P. Vitelleschi in Rome, 1637).
 fols. 99–126 (1637 Letra Anua de Provincia del Peru [António Vázquez], 25 May 1638).
 fol. 143v (Letter from Nicolás Mastrilo Durán, 1639).
 fols. 157–74 (1639–40 Letra Anua de Provincia del Peru [Nicolás Mastrilo Durán], 26 May 1641).
 fols. 193–211 (1646 Letra Anua de la Provincia del Peru).
 fols. 213–27 (1649 Letra Anua de la Provincia del Peru).
Peru 21 (*Peruana Historia III, 1633–1700*).
 fols. 3–4v (Antonio Orellana, annual report, 1688).
 fols. 13–13v (Pedro Marbán to P. Provincial F. Xavier, 4 June 1690).
 fols. 32–65 (1696 *Relación de la Mision apostólica de los Moxos en esta Provincia del Peru de la Compañía de Jesus . . .*, Diego de Eguiluz).
 fols. 175–79 (1713 *Relación de los Missiones de los Moxos de la Compañia de Jesús en la Provincia del Perú . . .*, Alonso Messia).
Rom. 51, tom. 2 (*Romana. Relat. Visit. 1583–1589*).
 Appendix (P. Valentino Mangioni, *Informatione delle cose del Collegio della Compagnia di Giesù in Loreto*, 1624).

Rom. 122, tom. 1 (*Romana Fundat. Collegior. III L-M*).
fol. 6 (Anonymous summary of founding of Collegio Penitentieri).
fols. 180–81v (Giacomo Borghese, S.J., *Relation*, 1604).

ARCHIVUM SOCIETATIS IESU—PROVINCE DU CANADA FRANÇAIS, ST. JÉROME, QUÉBEC, CANADA (ASJCF)

Doc. no. 324, fols. 1–23 (1675 *Rélation du Père Martin Bouvart, S.J.*: "De la Chapelle de Notre Dame de Lorette en Canada. Établissement de la devotion de Lorette").
Fonds Joseph Chaumonot BO-258.
BO-258-01: "Destruction de la Huronie [1649–50]." pp. 505–23.
Cahier 3, doc. 17, pp. 337–38 ("Jugement du Conseil Souverain / Intervention du Père Chaumonot pour une Huronne en prison," 24 avril 1665).

BIBLIOTECA ANGELICA, ROME, ITALY (B. ANG)

Ms. 1610/2 [no. reg. 26953]. (*Statuti dell'archconfraternità della S. Casa di Loreto*. 1694).

BIBLIOTECA APOSTOLICA VATICANA, VATICAN CITY (BAV)

Vat. Lat. 8215. (Iosephus Cardiel, S.J., *Breve Noticia de las Missiones del Paraguay* [c. 1750]).

BIBLIOTHÈQUE NATIONALE DE FRANCE, PARIS, FRANCE (BNF)

Lorraine 270 (*Affaires Ecclésiastiques*, tome 2: Portions Congrues).
fols. 171–80 (Papal Indulgences, c. 1600).
Ms. FR 11758 (*Plan de l'église de la Vierge*, 1650–90).
fols. 1–11 ("Inscriptions qui estoient au mois de septembre 1690 à Nostre Dame de Lorette, bastie dans le grand clos de Messieurs du seminaire de St. Sulpice à Illy," 1690).
fols. 14–29 (A. Philippon, Ingénieur Ordre du Roy, "Le Véritable plan, et pourtrait de la Maison Miraculeuse de la Ste. Vierge, ainsy qu'elle se voit à présent à Lorette . . . ," 1649).

LIBRARY AND ARCHIVES CANADA, OTTAWA, ONTARIO, CANADA (LAC)

Collection Félix Martin (1611–1776), MG18-H27.
fols. 53–62 ("De la Mission des Hurons de N. D. de Lorette en 1676").

Published Primary Sources

Albani, Nicolà. *Veridica Historia o' sia Viaggio da Napoli a S. Giacomo di Galizia fatto dal Sig.r Nicolà Albani. Nativo della Città di Melfi Dove dà Notizia delle*

Città, Terre, Casali, Castelli e quanti luoghi che nel detto Viaggio vi sono, com'anche tutto le Meraviglie, e Curiosità che in essi si vedono, con far noto ancora le disgrazie a lui successe nel detto Viaggio, e che miracolosamente sia stato liberato. Tomo Primo e Secondo. Ed in fine v'è la Tavola di tutte le miglia che sono da Napoli a S. Giacomo di Galizia In Napoli, 1743.

Allen, Thomas. *The Travels of our Lord and Saviour Jesus Christ: From his Infancy to his Ascension into Heaven. To which are prefixed the Travels of the Blessed Virgin Mary; the Wise Men out of the East, and of St. John the Baptist, and thereunto subjoined, the Travels of St. Peter the Apostle, St. John the Evangelist, and St. Paul the Apostle: With an Account of their Labours, Dangers and Sufferings, which they underwent for the Profession of the Christian Faith. . . .* London: A. Bettesworth and C. Hitch, 1735.

Angelitta, Girolamo. *L'historia della Traslatione della Santa Casa della Madonna a Loreto.* Giulio Cesare, trans. Macerata: Sebastiano Martorelli, 1580.

[Blaeu, Joan]. *Atlas Maior of 1665.* Peter van der Krogt, ed. Köln: Taschen Books, 2005.

Bouvart, Martin. "De la Chapelle de Notre-Dame de Lorette en Canada [Lorette, Mars 1 et 2, 1675]." Vol. 60, miscellaneous document 140. *The Jesuit Relations and Allied Documents: Travels and Explorations of the Jesuit Missionaries in New France, 1610–1791.* Reuben Gold Thwaites, ed.; Tomasz Mentrak, transcriber. http://moses.creighton.edu/kripke/jesuitrelations/. Accessed 13 April 2018.

Bralion, Nicolas de. *L'histoire de Nostre Dame de Laurette.* Paris: Georges Iosse, 1665.

Brébeuf, Jean de. "Of the Solemn Feast of the Dead [1636]." *The Jesuit Relations: Natives and Missionaries in Seventeenth-Century North America.* Allan Greer, ed. Boston: Bedford/St. Martin's, 2000, pp. 61–69.

Chaumonot, Pierre-Joseph-Marie. *Pierre Joseph Marie Chaumonot, S.J.: Autobiography and Supplement* [1688]. William Lonc, S.J., trans. Midland, Ontario: Steve Catlin, 2002.

Cordeiro, António, S.J. *História Insulana das Ilhas a Portugal Sujeytas no Oceano Occidental* [Lisboa, 1717]. Terceira (Açores): Secretaria Regional de Educação e Cultura, 1981.

———. *Loreto Lusitano, Virgem Senhora da Lapa: Residencia milagrosa do Real Collegio de Coimbra da Companhia de Jesus em a Provincia da Beyra, Bispado de Lamego. . . .* Lisboa Occidental: Filipe [Felipe] de Sousa Vilela [Villela], impr., 1719.

Diderot, Denis, and Jean le Rond D'Alembert. "Pèlerinage." *Encyclopédie, ou Dictionnaire raisonné des sciences des arts et des métiers.* Neuchâtel, France: Chez Samuel Faulche, 1765. Tom. 12, pp. 282–83.

Espinosa, Alonso de. [*The Guanches of Tenerife* (Seville, 1594)] *The Holy Image of Our Lady of Candelaria and the Spanish Conquest and Settlement by the Friar Alonso de Espinosa of the Order of Preachers.* Sir Clements Markham, trans. and ed. London: Hakluyt Society, 1907.

Gaudenti, Antonio. *Storia della santa casa di Loreto esposta in dieci brevi ragionamenti fra un sacerdote custode di S. Casa ed un divoto pellegrino, coll'aggiunta delle rarità più osservabili nel tempio Lauretano. . . .* Loreto: F. Sartori, 1784.

Giuseppe Maria, Vescovo di Vaisson. *Predica in Lode della Santa Casa di Loreto . . . A dì 17. Giugno 1656 . . . nella nuova Chiesa della Madonna di Loreto già di San Gio: in . . . , Mercatello di Roma.* Ancona: Stamperia Camerale, 1670.

Guerolt, Guillaume. *Le Premier Livre des emblèmes.* Lyons: Balthazar Arnoullet, 1550.

Gumppenberg, Wilhelm, S.J. *Atlas Marianus.* Munich, 1672.

The Jesuit Relations and Allied Documents: Travels and Explorations of the Jesuit Missionaries in New France, 1610–1791. Reuben Gold Thwaites, ed. Cleveland, OH: Burrows Brothers, 1899.

Lalemant, Jérôme. "Of the Persecutions Excited against Us [1640]." *The Jesuit Relations: Natives and Missionaries in Seventeenth-Century North America.* Allan Greer, ed. New York: Bedford/St. Martin's, 2000, pp. 90–91.

———. "Some Iroquois Surprised after Defeating the Algonquins; A Woman Kills an Iroquois and Escapes [1647]." *The Jesuit Relations: Natives and Missionaries in Seventeenth-Century North America.* Allan Greer, ed. Boston: Bedford/St. Martin's, 2000, pp. 106–11.

Lazzari, Luigi. *Dodici Sermoni sopra la S. Casa di Loreto, con la vita del Patriarca San Benedetteo, e la Predica del Padre San Romoaldo.* Roma: Ignatio di Lazeri, 1669.

[Lengherand, Georges.] *Voyage de Georges Lengherand, Mayeur de Mons en Haynaut, à Venise, Rome, Jérusalem, Mont Sinaï, et le Kayre, 1485–1486, avec introduction, notes, glossaire, etc. par le Marquis de Godefroy Ménilglaise, Membre de la Société des Bibliophiles de Mons. . . .* Mons, France: Masquillier et Dequesne, 1811.

Loyola, Ignatius. "The Autobiography: Pilgrimage to Jerusalem [1523]." *Ignatius of Loyola: The Spiritual Exercises and Selected Works.* George E. Ganss, S.J., ed. New York: Paulist, 1991, pp. 65–112.

———. *The Spiritual Exercises of St. Ignatius: Based on Studies in the Language of the Autograph.* Louis J. Puhl, S.J., trans. Chicago: Loyola Press, June 1968.

Lucidi, Antonio. *Notizie della Santa Casa di Maria Vergine Venerata in Loreto, Raccolte da un Canonico di questa sacrosanta Basilica estratte dall'Angelita, Torsellino, Seragli, Renzoli ed altri rari scrittori. Aggiuntovi Tutti i presziosi doni, che conservasi nel suo Tesoro in le Poste per diverse parti del Mondo. . . .* Loreto: Federico Sartori, 1769.

Martorelli, Pietro Valerio. *Teatro Istorico della Santa Casa nazarena della B. Vergine Maria e sua ammirabile traslazione in Loreto.* Rome: Antonio de Rossi, 1732, 2 vols.

"Mission des Hurons a Notre-Dame de Foye et a Notre Dame de Lorette pendant les années 1673–1674." *Relations Inédites de la Nouvelle-France (1672–1679) pour faire suite aux anciennes relations (1615–1672) avec deux cartes geographiques.* Félix Martin, S.J., ed. Tome I. Paris: Charles Douniol, ed., 1861, pp. 295–318.

Misson, Maximilien. *Nouveau voyage d'Italie fait en 1688.* La Haye, 1691.

Montaigne, Michel de. *Journal de voyage* [1580–81]. François Rigolot, ed. Paris: Presses Universitaires de France, 1992.

[Odoric of Pordenone.] *The Travels of Friar Odoric: 14th Century Journal of the Blessed Odoric of Pordenone.* Sir Henry Yule, trans. Grand Rapids, MI: William B. Eerdmans, 2002.

"Plan of La Concepción Mission, Paraguay, in Late Colonial Times." *Colonial Latin America: A Documentary History.* Kenneth Mills, William B. Taylor, and Sandra Lauderdale Graham, eds. New York: SR Books, 2004, pp. 314–15 (Fig. 30).

Raffaelli, Pietro Paolo. *Notizie della Santa Casa della Gran Madre di Dio Maria Vergine adorata in Loreto. . . .* Padua: Stamperia del Seminario, 1714.

Ragueneau, Paul. "Of the Capture of the Villages of the Mission of St. Ignace, in the Month of March of the Year 1649." *The Jesuit Relations: Natives and Missionaries in Seventeenth-Century North America*. Allan Greer, ed. Boston: Bedford/St. Martin's, 2000, pp. 112–18.

Relations Inédites de la Nouvelle-France (1672–1679) pour faire suite aux anciennes relations (1615–1672) avec deux cartes geographiques. Félix Martin, ed. Tome I. Paris: Charles Douniol, 1861.

Renzoli, Cesare P., S.J. *La Santa Casa Illustrata e Difesa*. Macerata: Michele Angelo Silvestri, 1697.

———. *Sermoni sopra la Passione di Nostro Signore Gesù Cristo*. Ancona: Stamperia Camerale, 1687.

Riera, Raphael. *De' miracoli della B. V. M. di Loreto*. Macerata: Sebastiano Martellini, 1573.

Rousseau, Jean-Jacques. "Les Confessions." *Collection complète des oeuvres de J. J. Rousseau, citoyen de Genève*. P. A. du Peyrou, ed. Genève, 1782–89. Tom. 11 and 12.

Ruiz De Montoya, Antonio. *The Spiritual Conquest Accomplished by the Religious of the Society of Jesus in the Provinces of Paraguay, Paraná, Uruguay and Tape* [1639]. C. J. McNaspy, S.J., trans. St. Louis, MO: Institute of Jesuit Sources, 1993.

Santa Maria, Agostinho de, O.E.S.A. *Santuário Mariano e história das imagens milagrosas de Nossa Senhora, e das milagrosamente aparecidas, em graça dos pregadores e dos devotos da mesma Senhora*. Lisboa: António Pedrozo Galvão, 1707–23.

"Scritura di Autore Anonimo sopra la verita del miracoloso trasporto della S. Casa della B. Vergine Maria di Nazaret dalla Dalmatia a Loreto nella Marca (1695)." *Pélerinage du Grand Duc de Toscane Cosme III et de son fils Jean-Gaston suivi de la lettre d'un anonyme sur la Santa Casa*. Louis-Antoine de Porrentruy, Capuchin, compiler. Rome: Imprimerie A. Befani, 1907, pp. 17–51.

Siena, Mariano da. *Viaggio fatto al Santo Sepolcro 1431 [con] in appendice, Viaggio di Gaspare di Bartolomeo*. Paolo Pirillo, ed. *Corpus Peregrinationum Italicarum*, 1 (1.1). Pisa, Italy: Pacini Editore, 1991.

Tolomei, Pietro di Giorgio, detto Il Teramano. "Translatio miraculosa Ecclesiae Beatae Mariae Virginis de Loreto [c. 1472]." Giuseppe Santarelli, *Indicazioni documentali inedite sulla traslazione della S. Casa di Loreto*. Loreto: Congregazione Universale della Santa Casa, 1985, pp. 104–7.

Torsellino, [Oratio]. *The history of our B. Lady of Loreto translated out of Latyn, into English*. Saint-Omer: English College Press, 1608.

Tosi, Clemente. *I Tre Voli della Santa Casa di Loreto nel Piceno: Discorso Sagro*. Roma: Francesco Moneta, 1655.

Venegas, Miguel. *Juan María de Salvatierra of the Company of Jesus; Missionary in the Province of New Spain, and Apostolic Conqueror of the Californias*. Marguerite Eyer Wilbur, trans. and ed. Cleveland, OH: Arthur H. Clark, 1929. [Translation of Miguel Venegas. *El Apóstol Mariano representado en la vida del V. P. Juan Maria de Salvatierra* . . . . Mexico: Imprenta de Doña Maria de Ribera, 1754.]

———. *Noticia de la California y de su conquista temporal, y espiritual hasta el tiempo presente*. Madrid: Viuda de M. Fernández, 1757.

———. *Obras Californianas del Padre Miguel Venegas, S.J.* Edición y Estudios por Dr. W. Michael Mathes; Bibliografías e Indices por Profra. Vivian C. Fisher y Profr.

Moisés Coronado. 5 vols. La Paz: Universidad Autónoma de Baja California Sur, 1979.

———. *Vida y virtudes de V. P. Juan Bautista Zappa de la Compañía de Jesús*. Barcelona: Pablo Nadal, 1754.

Virginis Mariae Loretae Historia [Giacomo Ricci]. Giuseppe Santarelli, ed. Loreto, Italy: Congregazione Universale della Santa Casa, 1987.

Secondary Sources

Abrams, Andrea C. *God and Blackness: Race, Gender and Identity in Middle Class Afrocentric Church*. New York: New York University Press, 2014.

Albani, Nicolà. *Viaje de Nápoles a Santiago de Galicia*. Isabel González, trans. Biblioteca Facsimilar Compostelana. Santiago de Compostela, Spain: Consorcio de Santiago, 1993.

Alden, Dauril. *The Making of an Elite Enterprise: The Jesuits in the Portuguese Assistancy, 16th to 18th Centuries*. Minneapolis: Associates of the James Ford Bell Library, University of Minnesota, 1992.

Alfieri, Nereo. "Il sacello della Santa Casa." *Il Santuario di Loreto: Sette Secoli di storia arte devozione*. Rome: Autostrade, 1994, pp. 35–42.

Altman, Ida. *Contesting Conquest: Indigenous Perspectives on the Spanish Occupation of Nueva Galicia, 1524–1545*. University Park: Penn State University Press, 2017.

Ammannato, Cinzia. "Michelangelo Merisi Da Caravaggio (Milano 1571–Porto Ercole 1610) / 99. Madonna di Loreto detta Madonna dei Pellegrini." *Imago Mariae: Tesori d'arte della civiltà cristiana*. Pietro Amato, ed. Rome: De Luca Edizioni d'Arte, 1988, pp. 143–46.

Angelidi, Christine, and Titos Papamastorakis, "The Veneration of the Virgin Hodegetria and the Hodegon Monastery." *Mother of God: Representations of the Virgin in Byzantine Art*. Maria Vassilaki, ed. Milan: Skira editore, 2000, pp. 373–87.

Anglo, Sydney. *Spectacle, Pageantry and Early Tudor Policy*. Oxford: Clarendon, 1969.

Armstrong, Karen. *Fields of Blood: Religion and the History of Violence*. New York: Knopf, 2014.

Le Arti nelle Marche al Tempo di Sisto V. Paolo Dal Poggetto, ed. Milan, Italy: Silvana Editoriale, 1992.

Artioli, Laura. "Le long de la via Emilia: Les hôpitaux de pèlerins entre XVIe et XVIIIe siècle." *Rendre ses voeux: Les identités pèlerines dans l'Europe moderne (XVIe–XVIIIe siècle)*. Phillipe Boutry, Pierre-Antoine Fabre, and Dominique Julia, directeurs. Paris: Ecole des Hautes Etudes en Sciences Sociales, 2000, pp. 15–38.

Axtell, James. "The Art of Reduction." *The Invasion Within: The Contest of Cultures in Colonial North America*. New York: Oxford University Press, 1986, pp. 43–70.

Bacci, Michele. "With the Paintbrush of the Evangelist Luke." *Mother of God: Representations of the Virgin in Byzantine Art*. Maria Vassilaki, ed. Milan: Skira editore, 2000, pp. 79–89.

Bailey, Gauvin Alexander. *Art on the Jesuit Missions in Asia and Latin America, 1542–1773*. Toronto: University of Toronto Press, 1999.

———. *Between Renaissance and Baroque: Jesuit Art in Rome, 1565–1610*. Toronto: University of Toronto Press, 2003.

———. "Cultural Convergence at the Ends of the Earth: Unique Art and Architecture of the Jesuit Missions to the Chiloé Archipelago (1608–1767)." *The Jesuits II: Cultures, Sciences and the Arts, 1540–1773*. John O'Malley, Gauvin Alexander Bailey, Steven Harris, and T. Frank Kennedy, eds. Toronto: University of Toronto Press, 2006, pp. 211–39.

———. "The Iconography of Jesuit Saints in the Church of San Pedro in Lima." *Studies: An Irish Quarterly Review* 104: 416 (Winter 2015–16), pp. 468–80.

Baker, Kelly J. *Gospel According to the Klan: The KKK's Appeal to Protestant America, 1915–1930*. Lawrence: University Press of Kansas, 2017.

Bangert, William V., and Thomas M. McCoog, S.J. *Jerome Nadal, S.J., 1507–1580: Tracking the First Generation of Jesuits*. Chicago: Loyola University Press, 1992.

Baniulyte, Ausra. "Italian Intrigue in the Baltic: Myth, Faith and Politics in the Age of Baroque." *Journal of Early Modern History* 16 (2012), pp. 23–52.

Barry, Dan. "Religious Statues Left Behind Find Their Own Patron Saint." *New York Times*, 10 March 2012, p. 2.

Barthes, Roland. *Mythologies [1957]: The Complete Edition, in New Translation*. Richard Howard and Annette Lavers, trans. New York: Hill and Wang, 2013.

Barzman, Karen-Edis. "Sacred Imagery and the Religious Lives of Women, 1650–1850." *Women and Faith: Catholic Religious Life in Italy from Late Antiquity to the Present*. Cambridge, MA: Harvard University Press, 1999, pp. 231–48.

Beans, George H. "A Note from the Tall Tree Library: A Sixteenth-Century Airway Map." *Imago Mundi* 16 (1962), p. 160.

Beard, Mary. *The Roman Triumph*. Cambridge, MA: Harvard University Press, 2007.

Begg, Ean. *The Cult of the Black Virgin*. New York: Arkana/Penguin Books, 1996.

Belán, Kyra. *Madonna: From Medieval to Modern*. New York: Parkstone, 2001.

Birch, Debra J. *Pilgrimage to Rome in the Middle Ages: Continuity and Change*. Woodbridge, Suffolk, England: Boydell, 1998.

Birnbaum, Lucia Chiavola. *Black Madonnas: Feminism, Religion and Politics in Italy*. Boston: Northeastern University Press, 1993.

Blick, Jeffrey P. "The Iroquois Practice of Genocidal Warfare (1534–1787)." *Journal of Genocide Research* 3: 3 (2001), pp. 405–29.

Block, David. *Mission Culture on the Upper Amazon: Native Tradition, Jesuit Enterprise, and Secular Policy in Moxos, 1660–1880*. Lincoln: University of Nebraska Press, 1994.

Blum, Rony. *Ghost Brothers: Adoption of a French Tribe by Bereaved Native America: A Transdisciplinary Longitudinal Multilevel Integrated Analysis*. Montreal: McGill-Queen's University Press, 2005.

Borsi, Franco. *Leon Battista Alberti: The Complete Works*. New York: Electa/Rizzoli, 1989.

Bouvier, Virginia Marie. *Women and the Conquest of California, 1542–1840: Codes of Silence*. Tucson: University of Arizona Press, 2001.

Boxer, C. R. *The Church Militant and Iberian Expansion, 1440–1770*. Baltimore: Johns Hopkins University Press, 2001.

Boyer, Marie-France. *The Cult of the Virgin: Offerings, Ornaments and Festivals*. London: Thames and Hudson, 2000.

Bracewell, Catherine Wendy. *The Uskoks of Senj: Piracy, Banditry, and Holy War in the Sixteenth-Century Adriatic*. Ithaca, NY: Cornell University Press, 1992.

Bradley, Peter T., and David Cahill. *Habsburg Peru: Images, Imagination and Memory.* Liverpool, UK: Liverpool University Press, 2000.

Braudel, Fernand. *The Mediterranean and the Mediterranean World in the Age of Philip II.* Vol. 1. Sian Reynolds, trans. New York: Harper and Row, 1972–73.

Brizay, F. "Pèlerins et pèlerinages dans les guides et récits de voyage français en Italie au XVIIe siècle." *L'image du pèlerin au Moyen Age et sous l'Ancien Régime.* Pierre André Sigal, directeur. Gramat, France: Association des Amis de Rocamadour, 1994, pp. 203–12.

Brockey, Liam Matthew. "The Cruelest Honor: The Relics of Francis Xavier in Early Modern Asia." *Catholic Historical Review* 101: 1 (2015), pp. 41–64.

———. *Journey to the East: The Jesuit Mission to China, 1579–1724.* Boston: Harvard University Press/Belknap, 2008.

Brown, Peter. *The Cult of the Saints: Its Rise and Function in Latin Christianity.* Haskell Lectures on History of Religions. Chicago: University of Chicago Press, 1982.

———. *Relics and Social Status in the Age of Gregory of Tours.* Stenton Lecture 1976. Berkshire, England: University of Reading, 1977.

Brubaker, Leslie. *Inventing Byzantine Iconoclasm.* Studies in Early Medieval History. London: Bristol Classical, 2012.

Bruwaert, Edmond. *Vie de Jacques Callot, graveur lorrain, 1592–1635.* Paris: Imprimerie Nationale, 1912.

Buc, Philippe. *The Dangers of Ritual: Between Early Medieval Texts and Social Scientific Theory.* Princeton, NJ: Princeton University Press, 2001.

———. *Holy War, Martyrdom and Terror: Christianity, Violence and the West.* Philadelphia: University of Pennsylvania Press, 2015.

Bulgarelli, Massimo. "The Holy House of Loreto: The Sacred Building and Its Copies." *Lotus International* 65 (New York: Rizzoli International, 1990), pp. 78–89.

Burgess, Clive. "'Longing to Be Prayed For': Death and Commemoration in an English Parish in the Later Middle Ages." *The Place of the Dead: Death and Remembrance in Late Medieval and Early Modern Europe.* Bruce Gordon and Peter Marshall, eds. New York: Cambridge University Press, 2000, pp. 44–65.

Burkardt, Albrecht. "Voyage de dévotion et quête du miracle à travers les procès de canonisation de saints français de la première moitié du XVIIe siècle." *Rendre ses voeux: Les identités pèlerines dans l'Europe moderne (XVIe–XVIIIe siècle).* Phillipe Boutry, Pierre-Antoine Fabre, and Dominique Julia, directeurs. Paris: Ecole des Hautes Etudes en Sciences Sociales, 2000, pp. 501–30.

Burke, Peter. "The Jesuits and the Art of Translation in Early Modern Europe." *The Jesuits II: Cultures, Sciences and the Arts, 1540–1773.* John O'Malley, Gauvin Alexander Bailey, Steven Harris, and T. Frank Kennedy, eds. Toronto: University of Toronto Press, 2006, pp. 24–32.

Caffiero, Marina. "From the Late Baroque Mystical Explosion to the Social Apostolate, 1650–1850." *Women and Faith: Catholic Religious Life in Italy from Late Antiquity to the Present.* Cambridge, MA: Harvard University Press, 1999, pp. 176–204.

Cahill, David. "The Virgin and the Inca: An Incaic Procession in the City of Cuzco in 1692." *Ethnohistory* 49: 3 (Summer 2002), pp. 611–49.

Caldari Giovannelli, Claudia. "Il Cardinale Antonio Maria Gallo a Loreto e Osimo." *Le Arti nelle Marche al Tempo di Sisto V*. Paolo Dal Poggetto, ed. Milan, Italy: Silvana Editoriale, 1992, pp. 85–93.

Campbell, Joseph, and Bill Moyers. *The Power of Myth*. New York: Anchor Books, 1991.

Cantù, Francesca. "Il Generalato di Claudio Acquaviva e l'identità misionaria della Compagnia di Gesù: Note e prospettive sulle missioni americane." *A Companhia de Jesus na Península Ibérica nos séculos XVI e XVII: Espiritualidade e cultura*. Actas do Colóquia internacional, Maio 2004. Vol. 1. Porto: Centro inter-universitário de História da espiritualidade da Universidade do Porto, 2004, pp. 151–70.

Carpenter, Roger. "Making War More Lethal: Iroquois vs. Huron in the Great Lakes Region, 1609 to 1650." *Michigan Historical Review* 27: 2 (Fall 2001), pp. 33–51.

Carrasco, Davíd. "Borderlands and 'Biblical Hurricane': Images and Stories of Latin American Rhythms of Life." *Harvard Theological Review* 101: 3/4 (July–October 2008), pp. 353–76.

———. "City as Symbol in Aztec Thought." *City of Sacrifice: The Aztec Empire and the Role of Violence in Civilization*. Boston, MA: Beacon, 1999, pp. 15–48.

———. "Human Sacrifice/Debt Payments from the Aztec Point of View." *The History of the Conquest of New Spain*, by Bernal Díaz del Castillo, Davíd Carrasco, ed. Albuquerque: University of New Mexico Press, 2008, pp. 463–64.

Carroll, Michael P. *Madonnas That Maim: Popular Catholicism in Italy since the Fifteenth Century*. Baltimore: Johns Hopkins University Press, 1992.

Carroll, Michael Thomas. *Popular Modernity in America: Experience, Technology, Mythohistory*. Albany: State University of New York Press, 2000.

Cassagnes-Brouquet, Sophie. *Vierges Noires*. Rodez, France: Editions du Rouergue, 2000.

"Census Returns of the Jedi." *BBC News*, 13 February 2003. http://news.bbc.co.uk/2/hi/uk/2757067.stm. Accessed 19 May 2015.

Charles, Michael B. "Remembering and Restoring the Republic: *Star Wars* and Rome." *Classical World* 108: 2 (Winter 2015), pp. 281–98.

Chevalier, Elisabeth. "Le pèlerin de Lorette d'après les principaux guides de langue française utilisés au XVIIIe siècle." *L'image du pèlerin au Moyen Age et sous l'Ancien Régime*. Pierre André Sigal, directeur. Gramat, France: Association des Amis de Rocamadour, 1994, pp. 213–20.

Chevalier, Ulysse. *Notre-Dame de Lorette: Étude historique sur l'authenticité de la Santa Casa*. Paris: Picard, 1906.

Christian, William A. *Apparitions in Late Medieval and Renaissance Spain*. Princeton, NJ: Princeton University Press, 1989.

———. *Local Religion in Sixteenth-Century Spain*. Princeton, NJ: Princeton University Press, 1989.

Clark, Anne L. "Guardians of the Sacred: The Nuns of Soissons and the Slipper of the Virgin Mary." *Church History* 76: 4 (December 2007), pp. 724–49.

Clark, Jawanza Eric. *Indigenous Black Theology: Toward an African-Centered Theology of the African-American Religious Experience*. New York: Palgrave MacMillan, 2012.

Clark, Roland, Luke Clossey, Simon Ditchfield, David M. Gordon, Arlen Wiesenthal, and Taymiya R. Zaman. "The Unbelieved and Historians, Part III: Responses and

Elaborations." *History Compass* 2017, e12430. https://doi.org/10.1111/hic3.12430. Accessed 10 May 2018.

Claster, Jill N. *Sacred Violence: The European Crusades to the Middle East, 1095–1396*. Toronto: University of Toronto Press, 2009.

Clendinnen, Inga. *Ambivalent Conquests: Maya and Spaniard in the Yucatan, 1517–1570*. New York: Cambridge University Press, 2003.

Clossey, Luke. *Salvation and Globalization in the Early Jesuit Missions*. New York: Cambridge University Press, 2008.

Clossey, Luke, Kyle Jackson, Brandon Marriott, Andrew Redden and Karin Vélez. "The Unbelieved and Historians, Part I: A Challenge." *History Compass* 14 (2016), pp. 594–602.

———. "The Unbelieved and Historians, Part II: Proposals and Solutions." *History Compass* 15 (2017), e12370. https://doi.org/10.1111/hic3.12370. Accessed 10 May 2018.

Collecting across Cultures: Material Exchanges in the Early Atlantic World. Daniela Bleichmar and Peter Mancall, eds. Philadelphia, PA: University of Pennsylvania Press, 2011.

Collis, Patrick A. "The Preface of the *Acta Sanctorum*." *Catholic Historical Review* 6 (Washington, DC: Catholic University of America, 1921), pp. 294–307.

Cook, Noble David. *Born to Die: Disease and New World Conquest, 1492–1650*. New York: Cambridge University Press, 1998.

Coüasnon, Charles. *The Church of the Holy Sepulchre in Jerusalem*. J.-P. B. Ross and Claude Ross, trans. Scweich Lectures of the British Academy (1972). London: Oxford University Press, 1974.

Coupe, Laurence. *Kenneth Burke on Myth: An Introduction*. New York: Routledge, 2005.

Crémoux, Françoise. "Réalité et représentation: L'image du pèlerin dans l'Espagne du XVIe siècle à travers les recueils de miracles de Guadalupe." *L'image du pèlerin au Moyen Age et sous l'Ancien Régime*. Pierre André Sigal, directeur. Gramat, France: Association des Amis de Rocamadour, 1994, pp. 221–30.

Crosby, Harry W. *Antigua California: Mission and Colony on the Peninsular Frontier, 1697–1768*. Albuquerque: University of New Mexico Press, 1994.

Cruz, Anne G., and Mary Elizabeth Perry. "Introduction." *Culture and Control in Counter-Reformation Spain*. Anne J. Cruz and Mary Elizabeth Perry, eds. Hispanic Issues 7. Minneapolis: University of Minnesota Press, 1992, pp. ix–xxiii.

Cuffel, Alexandra. "'Henceforward All Generations Will Call Me Blessed': Medieval Christian Tales of Non-Christian Marian Veneration." *Mediterranean Studies* 12 (2003), pp. 37–60.

Curzi, Valter. "La committenza Gallo: Il Pomarancio a Loreto." *Le Arti nelle Marche al Tempo di Sisto V*. Paolo Dal Poggetto, ed. Milan, Italy: Silvana Editoriale, 1992, pp. 94–99.

Cushner, Nicholas P. "Early Jesuit Missionary Methods in the Philippines." *Americas* 15: 4 (April 1959), pp. 361–79.

Cutler, Anthony. "The Pathos of Distance: Byzantium in the Gaze of Renaissance Europe and Modern Scholarship." *Reframing the Renaissance: Visual Culture in Europe and Latin America, 1450–1650*. Claire Farago, ed. New Haven, CT: Yale University Press, 1995, pp. 23–45.

Damian, Carol. *The Virgin of the Andes: Art and Ritual in Colonial Cuzco*. Miami Beach, FL: Grassfield, 1995.

D'Ancona, Mirella Levi. *The Iconography of the Immaculate Conception in the Middle Ages and Early Renaissance*. Monographs on Archaeology and Fine Arts 7. College Art Association of America, 1957.

Daniel, E. Valentine. "The Arrogation of Being." *Macalester International* 8: 171–91.

Darnton, Robert. *The Great Cat Massacre and Other Episodes in French Cultural History*. New York: Vintage Books, 1985.

Davis, Natalie Zemon. "New Worlds: Marie de l'Incarnation." *Women on the Margins: Three Seventeenth-Century Lives*. Cambridge, MA: Harvard University Press, 1997, pp. 63–139.

Davis, Robert C. "Counting European Slaves on the Barbary Coast." *Past and Present* 172 (August 2001), pp. 87–124.

Deagan, Kathleen. "Transculturation and Spanish American Ethnogenesis: The Archaeological Legacy of the Quincentenary." *Studies in Culture Contact: Interaction, Culture Change and Archaeology*. James G. Cusick, ed. Center for Archaeological Investigations, Occasional Paper no. 5, pp. 23–43.

Dean, Carolyn. *A Culture of Stone: Inka Perspectives on Rock*. Durham, NC: Duke University Press, 2010.

———. *Inka Bodies and the Body of Christ: Corpus Christi in Colonial Cuzco, Peru*. Durham, NC: Duke University Press, 1999.

De Boer, Wietse. *The Conquest of the Soul: Confession, Discipline and Public Order in Counter-Reformation Milan*. Leiden: E. J. Brill, 2001.

Deflem, Mathieu. "Ritual, Anti-structure and Religion: A Discussion of Victor Turner's Processual Symbolic Analysis." *Journal for the Scientific Study of Religion* 30: 1 (March 1991), pp. 1–25.

Delplace, Louis. "Japanese Martyrs." John Booby, trans. *New Advent Catholic Encyclopedia*, 2007. http://www.newadvent.org/cathen/09744a.htm. Accessed 13 April 2018.

De Queiroz, Alan. *The Monkey's Voyage: How Improbable Journeys Shaped the History of Life*. New York: Basic Books, 2014.

Deslandres, Dominique. "In the Shadow of the Cloister: Representations of Female Holiness in New France." *Colonial Saints: Discovering the Holy in the Americas, 1500–1800*. Allan Greer and Jodi Bilinkoff, eds. New York: Routledge, 2003, pp. 129–52.

Devens, Carol. "Separate Confrontations: Gender as a Factor in Indian Adaptation to European Colonization in New France." *American Quarterly* 38: 3 (1986), pp. 461–80.

"Devoción a María." *Diccionario Histórico de la Compañia de Jesus: Biográfico-Tematico*. Charles E. O'Neill and Joaquín Maria Dominguez, S.J., directors. Madrid: Universidad Pontificia Comillas, 2001, pp. 1014–16.

De Vries, Hent. "Of Miracles and Special Effects." *International Journal for Philosophy of Religion* 50 (2001): 41–56.

Dierkens, Alain. "Du bon (et du mauvais) usage des reliquaires au Moyen Age." *Les reliques: Objets, cultes, symboles*. Edina Bozóky and Anne-Marie Helvétius, eds. Turnhout, Belgium: Brepols, 1999, pp. 239–52.

Diotavelli, Daniele. "Medaglie e sigilli." *Le Arti nelle Marche al Tempo di Sisto V*. Paolo Dal Poggetto, ed. Milan, Italy: Silvana Editoriale, 1992, pp. 71–72.

Ditchfield, Simon. *Liturgy, Sanctity and History in Tridentine Italy: Pietro Maria Campi and the Preservation of the Particular*. New York: Cambridge University Press, 1995.

———. "Martyrs on the Move: Relics as Vindicators of Local Diversity in the Tridentine Church." *Martyrs and Martyrologies*. Diana Wood, ed. Studies in Church History 30. Cambridge, MA: Blackwell, 1993, pp. 283–94.

———. "'Of dancing Cardinals and Mestizo Madonnas': Reconfiguring the History of Roman Catholicism in the Early Modern Period." *Journal of Early Modern History* 8: 3–4 (2004), pp. 386–408.

———. "Tridentine Worship and the Cult of Saints." *Cambridge History of Christianity*. Vol. 6, *Reform and Expansion, 1500–1660*. R. Po-Chia Hsia, ed. New York: Cambridge University Press, 2007, pp. 201–24.

Donnelly, John Patrick, S.J. "6. The Quest for Active Women's Orders." *Handbook of European History 1400–1600: Late Middle Ages, Renaissance and Reformation*. Vol. 2, *Visions, Programs, Outcomes*. Thomas A. Brady Jr., Heiko A. Oberman, and James D. Tracy, eds. Grand Rapids, MI: William B. Eerdsman, 1995, pp. 301–4.

Donohue, J. Augustine. "The Unlucky Jesuit Mission of Bac, 1732–1767." *Arizona and the West* 2: 2 (Summer 1960), pp. 127–39.

Doyle, Mark. *Fighting Like the Devil for the Sake of God: Protestants, Catholics and the Origins of Violence in Victorian Belfast*. Manchester, UK: Manchester University Press, 2009.

Ducreux, Marie-Elizabeth. "L'ordre symbolique d'un pèlerinage tchèque dans l'espace habsbourgeois au XVIIe siècle: Stará Boleslav." *Rendre ses voeux: Les identités pèlerines dans l'Europe moderne (XVIe–XVIIIe siècle)*. Phillipe Boutry, Pierre-Antoine Fabre, and Dominique Julia, directeurs. Paris: Ecole des Hautes Etudes en Sciences Sociales, 2000, pp. 87–122.

Duhamelle, Christophe. "Les pèlerins de passage à l'hospice zum Heiligen Kreuz de Nuremberg au XVIIIe siècle." *Rendre ses voeux: Les identités pèlerines dans l'Europe moderne (XVIe–XVIIIe siècle)*. Phillipe Boutry, Pierre-Antoine Fabre, and Dominique Julia, directeurs. Paris: Ecole des Hautes Etudes en Sciences Sociales, 2000, pp. 39–56.

Dunne, Peter Masten, S.J. *Black Robes in Lower California*. Berkeley: University of California Press, 1968.

Dursteler, Eric. "On Bazaars and Battlefields: Recent Scholarship on Mediterranean Cultural Contacts." *Journal of Early Modern History* (2011), pp. 413–34.

Dyck, Jason. "The Patriotic Tradition of Francisco de Florencia's *Zodiaco Mariano*." Paper presented for session 11, "Marian Images in Spain and the New World." Society for Spanish and Portuguese Historical Studies Conference, Fort Worth, TX, 5 April 2008.

Ehrman, Bart. *Forged: Writing in the Name of God: Why the Bible's Authors Are Not Who We Think They Are*. New York: Harper Collins, 2012.

Eire, Carlos. "The Good, the Bad, and the Airborne: Levitation and the History of the Impossible in Early Modern Europe." *Ideas and Cultural Margins in Early Modern*

Germany: Essays in Honor of H. C. Erik Midelfort. Margorie Elizabeth Plummer and Robin Barnes, eds. Farnham, VT: Ashgate, 2009, pp. 307–23.

Eliade, Mircea. *The Sacred and the Profane: The Nature of Religion*. Willard R. Trask, trans. New York: Harper and Row, 1961.

Ellington, Donna Spivey. *From Sacred Body to Angelic Soul: Understanding Mary in Late Medieval and Early Modern Europe*. Washington, DC: Catholic University of America Press, 2001.

Elliot, John. "Concerto Barroco." *New York Review of Books* 9 April 1987, pp. 26–29.

Endo, Shusaku. *The Samurai*. Van C. Gessel, trans. New York: New Directions, 1997.

Ephesos Metropolis of Asia: An Interdisciplinary Approach to Its Archaeology, Religion, and Culture. Helmut Koester, ed. Valley Forge, PA: Trinity Press International, 1995.

Fabre, Pierre-Antoine. "'Ils iront en pèlerinage . . .': L''expérience' du pèlerinage selon l''Examen général' des *Constitutions* de la Compagnie de Jésus et selon les pratiques contemporaines." *Rendre ses voeux: Les identités pèlerines dans l'Europe moderne (XVIe–XVIIIe siècle)*. Phillipe Boutry, Pierre-Antoine Fabre, and Dominique Julia, directeurs. Paris: Ecole des Hautes Etudes en Sciences Sociales, 2000, pp. 159–88.

Fancy, Hussein. *The Mercenary Mediterranean: Sovereignty, Religion, and Violence in the Medieval Crown of Aragon*. Chicago: University of Chicago Press, 2016.

"Father Cipriano Barace, S.J. (1641–1702), Founder of Trinidad, Bolivia." *Jesuit Stamps 1898–2016*. Peter Fennessy, S.J., compiler. https://www.manresa-sj.org/stamps/1_Barace.htm. Accessed 24 November 2017.

Fenton, William N. "Problems Arising from the Historic Northeastern Position of the Iroquois." *Smithsonian Miscellaneous Collections: Essays in Historical Anthropology of North America* 100 (Washington, DC: Smithsonian Institution, 1940), pp. 180–81.

Fernandes, Naresh. "Tomb Raider." *Transition* 84 (2000), pp. 4–19.

Fine, John A., Jr. *When Ethnicity Did Not Matter in the Balkans: A Study of Identity in Pre-nationalist Croatia, Dalmatia and Slavonia in the Medieval and Early-Modern Periods*. Ann Arbor: University of Michigan Press, 2006.

Fine, Jonathan. *Political Violence in Judaism, Christianity and Islam: From Holy War to Modern Terror*. Lanham, MD: Rowman and Littlefield, 2015.

Flynn, Maureen. "Baroque Piety and Spanish Confraternities." *Confraternities and Catholic Reform in Italy, France and Spain*. John Patrick Donnelly, S.J., and Michael W. Maher, S.J., eds. Kirksville, MO: Thomas Jefferson University Press, 1999, pp. 233–45.

Forsyth, Ilene H. *The Throne of Wisdom: Wood Sculptures of the Madonna in Romanesque France*. Princeton, NJ: Princeton University Press, 1972.

Foster, George M. *Culture and Conquest: America's Spanish Heritage*. New York: Wenner-Gren Foundation, 1960.

France, John. *The Crusades and the Expansion of Catholic Christendom, 1000–1714*. New York: Routledge, 2005.

Frankenberry, Nancy, and Hans Penner. *Language, Truth, and Religious Belief: Studies in Twentieth-Century Theory and Method in Religion*. Atlanta, GA: Scholars Press, 1999.

"The Frankopan Family, Princes of Krk." Punat, Croatia: Marina Punat, 2014. http://www.marina-punat.hr/en/arhiva/227-kr%C4%8Dki-knezovi-frankopani. Accessed 19 May 2015.

Fraschina, Alicia. "A Jesuit *Beata* at the Time of the Suppression in the Viceroyalty of Río de la Plata: María Antonia de Paz y Figueroa, 1730–1799." *The Jesuits II: Cultures, Sciences and the Arts, 1540–1773*. John O'Malley, S.J., Gauvin Alexander Bailey, Steven J. Harris, and T. Frank Kennedy, S.J., eds. Toronto: University of Toronto Press, 2006, pp. 758–71.

Frazier, Alison Knowles. *Possible Lives: Authors and Saints in Renaissance Italy*. New York: Columbia University Press, 2005.

Freedberg, David. *The Power of Images: Studies in the History and Theory of Response*. Chicago: University of Chicago Press, 1989.

Friedman, David. *Florentine New Towns: Urban Design in the Late Middle Ages*. Cambridge, MA: MIT Press, 1988.

Gallagher, Amelia. "Mary's House in Ephesus, Turkey: Interfaith Pilgrimage in the Age of Mass Tourism." *Vicentian Heritage Journal* 33: 2 (2016), article 2.

Gallagher, Lowell. "Mary Ward's 'Jesuitresses,' and the Construction of a Typological Community." *Maids and Mistresses, Cousins and Queens: Women's Alliances in Early Modern England*. Susan Frye and Karen Robertson, eds. New York: Oxford University Press, 1999, pp. 199–217.

Galpern, A. N. *The Religions of the People in Sixteenth-Century Champagne*. Cambridge, MA: Harvard University Press, 1976.

Gambero, Luigi. *Mary in the Middle Ages: The Blessed Virgin Mary in the Thought of Medieval Latin Theologians*. San Francisco, CA: Ignatius, 2005.

Ganss, George E., S.J. *Spiritual Exercises of Saint Ignatius Loyola: A Translation and Commentary*. St. Louis, MO: Institute of Jesuit Sources, 1992, pp. 1–14.

Geary, Patrick. *Furta Sacra: Thefts of Relics in the Central Middle Ages*. Princeton, NJ: Princeton University Press, 1990.

———. "Oblivion between Orality and Textuality in the Tenth Century." *Medieval Concepts of the Past: Ritual, Memory, Historiography*. Gerd Althoff, Johannes Fried, and Patrick Geary, eds. New York: Cambridge University Press, 2002, pp. 111–22.

———. *Women at the Beginning: Origin Myths from the Amazons to the Virgin Mary*. Princeton, NJ: Princeton University Press, 2006.

Geertz, Clifford. *The Interpretation of Cultures*. New York: Basic Books, 1973.

———. "Shifting Aims, Moving Targets: On the Anthropology of Religion." *Journal of the Royal Anthropological Institute* 11: 1 (2005), pp. 1–15.

Gérin, Leon. *La Seigneurie de Sillery et les Hurons de Lorette*. Des Memoires de la Société Royale du Canada, Deuxième Serie (1900–1901): tome 6, section 1. Ottawa, Canada, 1901.

Gharib, Georges. *Le Icone Mariane: Storia e culto*. Rome: Città Nuova Editrice, 1987.

Giannatiempo López, Maria. "Antonio Calcagni e la porta sud di Loreto." *Le Arti nelle Marche al Tempo di Sisto V*. Paolo Dal Poggetto, ed. Milan, Italy: Silvana Editoriale, 1992, pp. 236–45.

Ginzburg, Carlo. "Alien Voices: The Dialogic Element in Early Modern Jesuit Historiography." *History, Rhetoric, and Proof: The Menahem Stern Jerusalem Lectures*. Hanover, NH: University Press of New England, 1999, pp. 71–91.

———. *The Cheese and the Worms: The Cosmos of a Sixteenth-Century Miller*. John Tedeschi and Anne Tedeschi, trans. Baltimore: Johns Hopkins University Press, 1980.

Golub, Alex, and Jon Peterson. "How Mana Left the Pacific and Became a Video Game Mechanic." *New Mana: Transformations of a Classic Concept in Pacific Languages and Cultures*. Matt Tomlinson and Ty P. Kawika Tengan, eds. Acton: Australian National University Press, 2016, pp. 310–38.

Gomez-Géraud, Marie-Christine. "Entre chemin d'aventure et parcours d'initiation: Le pèlerin de Lorette de Louis Richeôme." *L'image du pèlerin au Moyen Age et sous l'Ancien Régime*. Pierre André Sigal, directeur. Gramat, France: Association des Amis de Rocamadour, 1994, pp. 231–40.

Gonneau, Pierre. "Les pérégrinations de Vasilij Grigorovic Barskij, 1723–1747." *Rendre ses voeux: Les identités pèlerines dans l'Europe moderne (XVIe–XVIIIe siècle)*. Philipe Boutry, Pierre-Antoine Fabre, and Dominique Julia, directeurs. Paris: Ecole des Hautes Etudes en Sciences Sociales, 2000, pp. 217–38.

Grabar, André. *Deux Images de la Vierge dans un Manuscrit serbe*. L'art Byzantin chez les slaves 4. Paris: Librairie Orientaliste Paul Geuthner, 1930.

Grabowski, John J. "The Past as Prologue: Authority and *The Encyclopedia of Cleveland History*." *Public Historian* 35: 2 (May 2013), pp. 36–45.

Greenblatt, Stephen. *Marvelous Possessions: The Wonder of the New World*. Chicago: University of Chicago Press, 2017.

Greenstein, Shane, and Feng Zhu. "Is Wikipedia Biased?" *American Economic Review* 102: 3 (May 2012), pp. 343–48.

Greer, Allan. "Colonial Saints: Gender, Race and Hagiography in New France." *William and Mary Quarterly* 7: 2 (April 2000), pp. 323–48.

Gregory, Brad S. *Salvation at Stake: Christian Martyrdom in Early Modern Europe*. Cambridge, MA: Harvard University Press, 1999.

Grieco, Sara F. Matthews. "Models of Female Sanctity in Renaissance and Counter-Reformation Italy." *Women and Faith: Catholic Religious Life in Italy from Late Antiquity to the Present*. Cambridge, MA: Harvard University Press, 1999, pp. 159–75.

Griffith, James. *Beliefs and Holy Places: A Spiritual Geography of the Pimeria Alta*. Tucson: University of Arizona Press, 2015.

Grimaldi, Floriano. *Devozione e Committenza nelle Marche: La Madonna di Loreto*. Loreto: Delegazione Pontificia per il Santuario della Santa Casa di Loreto, 1997.

———. *Pellegrini e pellegrinaggi a Loreto nei secoli XIV–XVIII*, supplemento n. 2 al "Bollettino Storico della Città di Foligno." Loreto, Italy: Tecnostampa, 2001.

———. "Il Vescovo Rutilio Benzoni a Loreto e Recanati." *Le Arti nelle Marche al Tempo di Sisto V*. Paolo Dal Poggetto, ed. Milan, Italy: Silvana Editoriale, 1992, pp. 127–28.

Gros-Louis, Charlotte, and Céline Gros-Louis. *La Chapelle Huronne de Lorette, 1730–1980*. Québec: Bibliothèques nationales du Québec et du Canada, 1980.

Grosso, Michael. "Evidence of St. Joseph of Copertino's Levitations." Supplemental web material for "Chapter 1: Empirical Challenges to Theory Construction," in *Beyond Physicalism: Toward Reconciliation of Science and Spirituality*, Edward F. Kelly, Adam Crabtree, and Paul Marshall (eds.). Lanham, MD: Rowman and Littlefield, 2015. https://www.esalen.org/sites/default/files/resource_attachments/Ch-1-Supp-Joseph.pdf. Accessed 14 October 2017.

———. *The Man Who Could Fly: St. Joseph of Copertino and the Mystery of Levitation.* Lanham, MD: Rowan and Littlefield, 2015.

Guter, Robert P., and Janet W. Foster. *Building by the Book: Pattern-Book Architecture in New Jersey*. New Brunswick, NJ: Rutgers University Press, 1992.

Gutiérrez da Costa, Ramón, and Rodrigo Gutiérrez Viñuales. "Territorio, Urbanismo y Arquitectura en Moxos y Chiquitos." *Las Misiones Jesuíticas de Chiquitos*. Pedro Querejazu, ed. La Paz, Bolivia: Fundacion BHN, 1995, pp. 303–402.

Hamilton, Bernard. "The Ottomans, the Humanists and the Holy House of Loreto." *Crusaders, Cathars and the Holy Places*. Brookfield, VT: Ashgate, 1999, pp. 1–19.

Hansen, Ron. "Saint Ignatius of Loyola, the Pilgrim." *A Tremor of Bliss: Contemporary Writers on the Saints*. Paul Elie, ed. New York: Riverhead Books, 1995, p. 112.

Harline, Craig. *Miracles at the Jesus Oak: Histories of the Supernatural in Reformation Europe*. New York: Doubleday, 2003.

Harris, Max. *Aztecs, Moors and Christians: Festivals of Reconquest in Mexico and Spain*. Austin: University of Texas Press, 2000.

Hayes, John F. *Wilderness Mission: The Story of Sainte-Marie among the Hurons*. Toronto: Ryerson, 1969.

Henderson, John. *Piety and Charity in Late Medieval Florence*. Oxford: Clarendon, 1994.

Henningsen, Gustav. "The Witches' Flying and the Spanish Inquisitors; or, How to Explain (Away) the Impossible." *Folklore* 120: 1 (April 2009), pp. 57–74.

Herbert, T. Walter. *Faith-Based War: From 9/11 to Catastrophic Success in Iraq*. New York: Routledge, 2014.

Hjarvard, Stig. "The Mediazation of Religion: A Theory of the Media as Agents of Religious Change." *Northern Lights: Film and Media Studies Yearbook* 6: 1 (June 2008), pp. 9–26.

Ho, Engseng. *The Graves of Tarim: Genealogy and Mobility across the Indian Ocean*. Berkeley: University of California Press, 2006.

Hosne, Ana Carolina. "The Tricky Concepts of 'Hispanicization' in Peru and 'Accommodation' in China." *The Jesuit Missions to China and Peru, 1570–1610: Expectations and Appraisals of Expansionism*. New York: Routledge, 2013, pp. 71–96.

Hsia, R. Po-Chia. *The World of Catholic Renewal, 1540–1770*. New York: Cambridge University Press, 2005.

Hyland, Sabine. *Gods of the Andes: An Early Jesuit Account of Inca Religion and Andean Christianity*. University Park: Pennsylvania State University Press, 2011.

Jackson, Robert H. *Missions and the Frontiers of Spanish America: A Comparative Study of the Impact of Environmental, Economic, Political, and Socio-cultural Variations on the Missions in the Rio de la Plata Region and on the Northern Frontier of New Spain*. Scottsdale, Arizona: Pentacle, 2005.

Jacobson Schutte, Anne. "Little Women, Great Heroines: Simulated and Genuine Female Holiness in Early Modern Italy." *Women and Faith: Catholic Religious Life in Italy from Late Antiquity to the Present*. Cambridge, MA: Harvard University Press, 1999, pp. 144–58.

Jansen, Katherine Ludwig. *The Making of the Magdalen: Preaching and Popular Devotion in the Later Middle Ages*. Princeton, NJ: Princeton University Press, 2001.

Johnson, Trevor. "Blood, Tears and Xavier-Water: Jesuit Missionaries and Popular Religion in the Eighteenth-Century Upper Palatinate." *Popular Religion in Germany and Central Europe, 1400–1800*. Bob Scribner and Trevor Johnson, eds. New York: St. Martin's, 1996, pp. 183–202.

———. "Holy Fabrications: The Catacomb Saints and the Counter-Reformation in Bavaria." *Journal of Ecclesiastical History* 47: 2 (April 1996), pp. 274–97.

Judging Faith, Punishing Sin: Inquisitions and Consistories in the Early Modern World. Charles H. Parker and Gretchen Starr-LeBeau, eds. New York: Cambridge University Press, 2017.

Julia, Dominique. "Aveux de pèlerins." *Rendre ses voeux: Les identités pèlerines dans l'Europe moderne (XVIe–XVIIIe siècle)*. Phillipe Boutry, Pierre-Antoine Fabre, and Dominique Julia, directeurs. Paris: Ecole des Hautes Etudes en Sciences Sociales, 2000, pp. 439–56.

———. "Compostelle, Lorette, Rome: L'image du pèlerin d'après les archives de la répression." *L'image du pèlerin au Moyen Age et sous l'Ancien Régime*. Pierre André Sigal, directeur. Gramat, France: Association des Amis de Rocamadour, 1994, pp. 241–52.

———. "Curiosité, dévotion et *politica peregrinesca*: Le pèlerinage de Nicola Albani, melfitain, à Saint-Jacques-de-Compostelle, 1743–1745." *Rendre ses voeux: Les identités pèlerines dans l'Europe moderne (XVIe–XVIIIe siècle)*. Phillipe Boutry, Pierre-Antoine Fabre, and Dominique Julia, directeurs. Paris: Ecole des Hautes Etudes en Sciences Sociales, 2000, pp. 239–314.

Juschka, Darlene M. "Whose Turn Is It to Cook: Communitas and Pilgrimage Questioned." *Mosaic: An Interdisciplinary Critical Journal* 36: 4 (December 2003), pp. 189–204.

Juster, Susan. *Sacred Violence in Early America*. Philadelphia: University of Pennsylvania Press, 2016.

Kadic, Ante. "St. Francis Xavier and Marko Marulic." *Slavic and East European Journal* 5: 1 (Spring 1961), pp. 12–18.

Katz, Melissa. "Regarding Mary: Women's Lives Reflected in the Virgin's Image." *Divine Mirrors: The Virgin Mary in the Visual Arts*. Melissa R. Katz, ed. New York: Oxford University Press, 2001, pp. 19–129.

Kaufman, Suzanne K. *Consuming Visions: Mass Culture and the Lourdes Shrine*. Ithaca, NY: Cornell University Press, 2005.

Keller-Lapp, Heidi. "Devenir des Jésuitesses: Les missionaires Ursulines du monde Atlantique." L'Autre Visage de la Mission: Les Femmes. Sarah A. Curtis, ed. *Histoire et Missions Chrétiennes* 16 (December 2010), pp. 19–52.

———. "Maritime Habits: Ursuline Atlantic Voyages to the New World, 1639–1727." International Seminar on the History of the Atlantic World, 1500–1825, Cambridge, MA, August 2006.

Kilde, Jeanne Halgren. "Approaching Religious Space: An Overview of Theories, Methods, and Challenges in Religious Studies." *Religion and Theology* 20 (2013), pp. 183–201.

———. "The Park 51/Ground Zero Controversy and Sacred Sites as Contested Space." *Religions* 2: 3 (2011): 297–311.

———. *When the Church Became Theatre: The Transformation of Evangelical Architecture and Worship in Nineteenth-Century America*. New York: Oxford University Press, 2002.

Klapisch-Zuber, Christiane. "Holy Dolls: Play and Piety in Florence in the Quattrocento." *Women, Family and Ritual in Renaissance Italy*. Lydia Cochrane, trans. Chicago: University of Chicago Press, 1987, pp. 310–30.

Knaap, Anna C. "Meditation, Ministry, and Visual Rhetoric in Peter Paul Rubens's Program for the Jesuit Church in Antwerp." *The Jesuits II: Cultures, Sciences and the Arts, 1540–1773*. John O'Malley, Gauvin Alexander Bailey, Steven Harris, and T. Frank Kennedy, eds. Toronto: University of Toronto Press, 2006, pp. 157–81.

Koldeweij, A. M. "Lifting the Veil on Pilgrim Badges." Ruth Koenig, trans. *Pilgrimage Explored*. J. Stopford, ed. Woodbridge, Suffolk: York Medieval, 1999, pp. 161–88.

Krautheimer, Richard. *Studies in Early Christian, Medieval and Renaissance Art*. New York: New York University Press, 1969.

Kreitzer, Beth. *Reforming Mary: Changing Images of the Virgin Mary in Lutheran Sermons of the Sixteenth Century*. New York: Oxford University Press, 2004.

Kripal, Jeffrey. *Authors of the Impossible: The Paranormal and the Sacred*. Chicago: University of Chicago Press, 2010.

Kroesen, Justin E. A. *The Sepulchrum Domini through the Ages: Its Form and Function*. Margaret Kofod, trans. Sterling, VA: Peeters, 2000.

La Basilica della Santa Casa di Loreto: Indagini archeologiche, geognostiche e statiche. Floriano Grimaldi, ed. Ancona: Soprintendenza per i beni ambientali e architettonici delle Marche, 1986.

Lach, Donald F., and Edwin J. Van Kley. *Asia in the Making of Europe*. Vol. 3, *A Century of Advance*, book 1, *Trade, Missions, Literature*. Chicago: University of Chicago Press, 1993.

Laflèche, Guy. *Les saints martyrs canadiens. 5. Le martyre de la nation huronne et sa défaite avec Dollard des Ormenaux*. Montréal: Editions du Singulier, 1995.

Laine, James W. "Mind and Mood in the Study of Religion." *Religion* 40 (2010), pp. 239–49.

Landi, Sandro. "Législations sur les pèlerinages et identités pèlerines dans la péninsule italienne, XVIe–XVIIIe siècle." *Rendre ses voeux: Les identités pèlerines dans l'Europe moderne (XVIe–XVIIIe siècle)*. Phillipe Boutry, Pierre-Antoine Fabre, and Dominique Julia, directeurs. Paris: Ecole des Hautes Etudes en Sciences Sociales, 2000, pp. 457–72.

Langdon, Helen. *Caravaggio: A Life*. New York: Farrar, Straus, and Giroux, 1998.

Latourelle, René. *Compagnon des Martyrs canadiens: Pierre-Joseph-Marie Chaumonot*. Québec: Éditions Bellarmin, 1998.

Lee, Jonathan H. X. *Happy Birthday Mazu, Empress of Heaven, Goddess of the Sea*. East Meets West Educational Film Production, 2008.

Leon-Portilla, Miguel. *Tonantzin Guadalupe: Pensamiento nahuatl y mensaje cristiano en el Nican Mopohua*. Mexico City: El Colegio Nacional y el Fondo de Cultura Económica, 2000.

Levy, Evonne. "'A Noble Medley and Concert of Materials and Artifice': Jesuit Church Interiors in Rome, 1567–1700." *Saint, Site and Sacred Strategy: Ignatius, Rome and Jesuit Urbanism*. Thomas M. Lucas, S.J., ed. Vatican City: Biblioteca Apostolica Vaticana, 1990, pp. 47–61.

———. *Propaganda and the Jesuit Baroque*. Berkeley: University of California Press, 2004.

Lewis, Katherine J. "Pilgrimage and the Cult of St. Katherine of Alexandria in Late Medieval England." *Pilgrimage Explored*. J. Stopford, ed. Woodbridge, Suffolk: York Medieval, 1999, pp. 145–60.

Lidov, Alexei. "Miracle-Working Icons of the Mother of God." *Mother of God: Representations of the Virgin in Byzantine Art*. Maria Vassilaki, ed. Milan: Skira Editore, 2000, pp. 47–57.

Liechtenberger, Frédéric. *Encyclopédie des sciences religieuses*. Tome 7. Paris: Librairie Sandoz et Fischbacher, 1888.

Lierheimer, Linda. "Female Eloquence and Maternal Ministry: The Apostolate of Ursuline Nuns in Seventeenth-Century France." Doctoral diss., Princeton University, 1994.

Lightbown, Ronald. *Carlo Crivelli*. New Haven, CT: Yale University Press, 2004.

Longman, Timothy. *Christianity and Genocide in Rwanda*. New York: Cambridge University Press, 2011.

López Austin, Alfredo. *Tamoanchan, Tlalocan: Places of Mist*. Bernard Ortiz de Montellano and Thelma Ortiz de Montellano, trans. Niwot: University Press of Colorado, 1997.

La Madonna di Loreto nelle Marche: Immagini devote e liturgiche. A cura di Floriano Grimaldi, M. Paola Mariano, e Katy Sordi. Ancona: Centro Beni Culturali della Regione Marche, 1998.

Maguire, Henry. *The Icons of Their Bodies: Saints and Their Images in Byzantium*. Princeton, NJ: Princeton University Press, 2000.

Maniura, Robert. *Pilgrimage to Images in the Fifteenth Century: The Origins of the Cult of Our Lady of Czestochowa*. Rochester, NY: Boydell, 2004.

Manley, Lawrence. "Scripts for the Pageant: The Ceremonies of London." *Literature and Culture in Early Modern London*. New York: Cambridge University Press, 1995, pp. 212–93.

Martin, Félix, S.J. "Précis historique sur la mission Huronne et sur les migrations de ce peuple jusquà nos jours." P.F.J. Bressani, S.J., *Relation Abrégée de quelques missions des Pères de la Compagnie de Jésus dans la Nouvelle France* [Macerata, 1653]. Félix Martin, S.J., trans. and ed. Montréal: Presses à Vapeur de John Lovell, 1852, pp. 316–18.

Martin, James, S.J. *Jesus: A Pilgrimage*. New York: HarperOne, 2014.

"Mary's Trsat." Opatija, Croatia: Kvarner County Tourism Office, 2015. http://www.kvarner.hr/hodocastiti-svetistima/en/trsat.html. Accessed 19 May 2015.

Mathes, W. Michael. "Ethnohistoric Evidence." *The Prehistory of Baja California: Advances in the Archaeology of the Forgotten Peninsula*. Don Laylander and Jerry D. Moore, eds. Gainesville: University Press of Florida, 2006, pp. 42–66.

McCoog, Thomas M., S.J. *The Society of Jesus in Ireland, Scotland, and England 1541–1588: Our Way of Proceeding*. New York: Brill Academic, 1996.

McWilliam, Neil. "Baroque in Croatia: Zagreb Museum of Arts and Crafts." *Burlington Magazine* 135: 1087 (October 1993), pp. 712–13.

Meacham, Jon. "The Birth of Jesus." *Newsweek*, 12 December 2004. http://www.newsweek.com/birth-jesus-123591. Accessed 13 April 2018.

———. "Who Killed Jesus?" *Newsweek*, 15 February 2004. http://www.newsweek.com/who-killed-jesus-131113. Accessed 13 April 2018.

Mills, Kenneth. "Diego de Ocaña's Hagiography of New and Renewed Devotion in Colonial Peru." *Colonial Saints: Discovering the Holy in the Americas.* Allan Greer and Jodi Bilinkoff, eds. New York: Routledge, 2003, pp. 51–75.

———. "The Naturalization of Andean Christianities." *The Cambridge History of Christianity.* Vol. 6, *Reform and Expansion, 1500–1660.* R. Po-Chia Hsia, ed. New York: Cambridge University Press, 2007, pp. 508–39.

Molina, J. Michelle. *To Overcome Oneself: The Jesuit Ethic and Spirit of Global Expansion, 1520–1767.* Berkeley: University of California Press, 2013.

———. "Visions of God, Visions of Empire: Jesuit Spirituality and Colonial Governmentality in New Spain, 1571–1767." Doctoral diss., University of Chicago, 2004.

Montevecchi, Benedetta. "Arte francese e Arte Adriatica, secc. XIII, fine-XV (?) / 31. Reliquiario a gruppo scultoreo con la Madonna col Bambino." *Imago Mariae: Tesori d'arte della civiltà cristiana.* Pietro Amato, ed. Rome: De Luca Edizioni d'Arte, 1988, pp. 87–88.

Morris, Colin. *The Sepulchre of Christ and the Medieval West: From the Beginning to 1600.* New York: Oxford University Press, 2005.

Mueller, Reinhold C. "Aspects of Venetian Sovereignty in Medieval and Renaissance Dalmatia." *Quattrocento Adriatico: Fifteenth-Century Art of the Adriatic Rim.* Charles Dempsey, ed. Villa Spelman Colloquia 5. Bologna, Italy: Nuova Alfa Editoriale, pp. 29–56.

Myers, W. David. *"Poor, Sinning Folk": Confession and Conscience in Counter-Reformation Germany.* Ithaca, NY: Cornell University Press, 1996.

Neubert, Karel, and Jan Royt. *Praga Caput Regni: The Sights of Prague and Its Neighborhood.* Prague: Odeon, 1991.

Newhaiser, Anna Kaisa, Miguel Farias, and Nicole Tausch. "The Functional Nature of Conspiracy Beliefs: Examining the Underpinnings of Belief in the *Da Vinci Code* Conspiracy." *Personality and Individual Differences* 51: 8 (December 2011), pp. 1007–11.

Nilson, Ben. "The Medieval Experience at the Shrine." *Pilgrimage Explored.* J. Stopford, ed. Woodbridge, Suffolk: York Medieval, 1999, pp. 95–122.

Noreen, Kirstin. "The Icon of Santa Maria Maggiore, Rome: An Image and Its Afterlife." *Renaissance Studies* 19: 5 (2005), pp. 660–72.

Nova, Alessandro. "'Popular' Art in Renaissance Italy: Early Response to the Holy Mountain at Varallo." *Reframing the Renaissance: Visual Culture in Europe and Latin America, 1450–1650.* Claire Farago, ed. New Haven, CT: Yale University Press, 1995, pp. 112–26.

"Nuestra Señora de la Candelaria." *Las Rutas de Angelica* blogspot. Angélica Zambrano, compiler. 2 February 2008. http://lasrutasdeangelica.blogspot.com/2008/02/nuestra-seora-de-la-candelaria.html. Accessed 22 November 2017.

Olds, Katrina. *Forging the Past: Invented Histories in Counter-Reformation Spain.* New Haven, CT: Yale University Press, 2015.

———. "How to Be a Counter-Reformation Bishop: Cardinal Baltasar de Moscoso y Sandoval in the Diocese of Jaén, 1618–1646." *Entre el cielo y la tierra: Las élites eclesiásticas en la Europa Moderna,* special monograph volume of *Mágina: Re-*

vista Universitaria, vol. 13. María Amparo López Arandia, ed. Jaén: Universidad Nacional de Educación a Distancia "Andrés de Valdelvira," 2009, pp. 197–213.

Oleszkiewicz-Peralba, Malgorzata. *Black Madonnas in Latin America and Europe: Tradition and Transformation*. Albuquerque: University of New Mexico Press, 2009.

Olin, John C. "The Idea of Pilgrimage in the Experience of Ignatius Loyola." *Church History* 48: 4 (December 1979), pp. 387–97.

Oliver, Jeanne. *Croatia*. New York: Lonely Planet, 2005.

———. "Croatia Traveler." Croatian National Tourist Board. http://www.croatiatraveller.com/Kvarner/Trsat.html. Accessed 19 May 2015.

Olvaeson, Tim. "Collective Effervescence and Communitas: Processual Models of Ritual Society in Emile Durkheim and Victor Turner." *Dialectical Anthropology* 26: 2 (2001), pp. 89–124.

O'Malley, John W., S.J. *The First Jesuits*. Cambridge, MA: Harvard University Press, 1993.

———. *Trent: What Happened at the Council*. Cambridge, MA: Harvard University Press, 2013.

Oreskovic, Luc. "La dévotion à la *Santa Casa*: Célébrer la translation entre Trsat et Loreto au XVIIe siècle." *Cahiers du Centre de Recherches Historiques (Revue électronique du CRH)* 41: 2008, pp. 73–88. http://ccrh.revues.org/3410?lang=en. Accessed 19 May 2015.

Orsi, Robert. "Abundant History: Marian Apparitions as Alternative Modernity." *Historically Speaking* 9: 7 (September/October 2008), pp. 12–16.

———. *Thank You, St. Jude: Women's Devotion to the Patron Saint of Hopeless Causes*. New Haven, CT: Yale University Press, 1996.

The Oxford Handbook of Religion and Violence. Mark Juergensmeyer, Margo Kitts, and Michael Jerryson, eds. New York: Oxford University Press, 2013.

Pace, Valentino. "Between East and West." *Mother of God: Representations of the Virgin in Byzantine Art*. Maria Vassilaki, ed. Milan: Skira, 2000, pp. 425–35.

Paiva, José Pedro. "Bishops and Politics: The Portuguese Episcopacy during the Dynastic Crisis of 1580." *e-Journal of Portuguese History* 4: 2, W (2006). https://www.brown.edu/Departments/Portuguese_Brazilian_Studies/ejph/html/issue8/pdf/jpaiva.pdf. Accessed 13 April 2018.

Pasulka, Diana Walsh. *Heaven Can Wait: Purgatory in Catholic Devotional and Popular Culture*. New York: Oxford University Press, 2015.

Pavicic, Jurica, Nikisa Alfirevic, and Vincent John Batarelo. "The Management and Marketing of Religious Sites, Pilgrimage and Religious Events: Challenges for Roman Catholic Pilgrimages in Croatia." *Religious Tourism and Pilgrimage Festivals Management: An International Perspective*. Razaq Raj and Nigel D. Morpeth, eds. Cambridge, MA: CAB International, 2007, pp. 48–63.

Pavone, Sabina. *The Wily Jesuits and the Monita Secreta: The Forged Secret Instructions of the Jesuits, Myth and Reality*. John P. Murphy, trans. St. Louis, MO: Institute of Jesuit Sources, 2005.

Payne, Craig. *Where Myth and History Meet: A Christian Response to Myth*. Lanham, MD: University Press of America, 2001.

Peterson, Jeanette Favrot. "Creating the Virgin of Guadalupe: The Cloth, the Artist, and Sources in Sixteenth-Century New Spain." *Americas* 61: 4 (April 2005), pp. 571–610.

———. *Visualizing Guadalupe: From Black Madonna to Queen of the Americas.* Joe R. and Teresa Lozano Long Series in Latin American and Latino Art and Culture. Austin: University of Texas Press, 2014.

Petrovich, Michael B. "Croatian Humanists and the Writing of History in the Fifteenth and Sixteenth Centuries." *Slavic Review* 37: 4 (December 1978), pp. 624–39.

The Pilgrim's Guide to Santiago de Compostela: A Critical Edition. Jeanne Krochalis, Paula Lieber Gerson, Annie Shaver-Crandell, and Alison Stones, eds. Studies in Medieval and Early Renaissance Art History 14. London: Harvey Miller, 1998.

Pinch, William R. "The Corpse and Cult of Francis Xavier, 1552–1623." *Engaging South Asian Religions: Boundaries, Appropriations and Resistances.* Matthew N. Schmalz and Peter Gottschalk, eds. State University of New York Press, 2012, pp. 113–32.

Plate, S. Brent. "Stones." *A History of Religion in 5 ½ Objects: Bringing the Spiritual to Its Senses*, Boston: Beacon, 2014, pp. 23–60.

Pollard, Elizabeth Ann. "Raising the Stakes: Writing about Witchcraft on Wikipedia." *History Teacher* 42: 1 (November 2008), pp. 9–24.

Pomplun, Trent. *Jesuit on the Roof of the World: Ippolito Desideri's Mission to Tibet.* New York: Oxford University Press, 2009.

"The Pope Visits Our Lady of Trsat, the 'Croatian Nazareth.'" Vatican City, 8 June 2003. http://www.croatia.org/crown/articles/7632/1/E-Croatian-Nazareth-EWTN-News-Story.html. Accessed 19 May 2015.

Pourtois, Christophe. "From the City of the Caesars to the Demystified City." *Cruelty and Utopia: Cities and Landscapes of Latin America.* Jean-François Lejeune, ed. Princeton, NJ: Princeton Architectural Press, 2005, pp. 11–12.

Provost, Georges. "L'image du pèlerin dans le clergé des XVIIe et XVIIIe siècle: L'exemple de Bretagne." *L'image du pèlerin au Moyen Age et sous l'Ancien Régime.* Pierre André Sigal, directeur. Gramat, France: Association des Amis de Rocamadour, 1994, pp. 273–86.

Pullan, Brian. *Rich and Poor in Renaissance Venice: The Social Institutions of a Catholic State, to 1620.* Cambridge, MA: Harvard University Press, 1971.

Ramos, Donald. "Slavery in Brazil: A Case Study of Diamantina, Minas Gerais." *Americas* 45: 1 (July 1988), pp. 47–59.

Ranucci, Maria, and Massimo Tenenti. *Sei Riproduzioni della Santa Casa di Loreto in Italia: Aversa—Parma—Catania—Venezia / San Clemente—Venezia / San Pantalon—Vescovana.* Loreto: Congregazione Universale della Santa Casa, 2003.

Reff, Daniel T. "The Jesuit Mission Frontier in Comparative Perspective: The Reductions of the Río de la Plata and the Missions of Northwestern Mexico, 1588–1700." *Contested Ground: Comparative Frontiers on the Northern and Southern Edges of the Spanish Empire.* Donna J. Guy and Thomas E. Sheridan, eds. Tucson: University of Arizona Press, 1998, pp. 16–27.

Regni, Pietro Vittorino. *Loreto e i cappuccini: Storia, Devozione e servizio della Santa Casa.* Loreto: Congregazione Universale della Santa Casa, 1995.

Remensnyder, Amy. "Topographies of Memory: Center and Periphery in High Medieval France." *Medieval Concepts of the Past: Ritual, Memory, Historiography.* Gerd

Althoff, Johannes Fried, and Patrick Geary, eds. New York: Cambridge University Press, 2002, pp. 193–214.

Rennie, Bryan. "Myths, Models, and Metaphors: Religion as Model and the Philosophy of Science." *Religion* 39 (2009): pp. 340–47.

Rhodes, Elizabeth. "Join the Jesuits, See the World: Early Modern Women in Spain and the Society of Jesus." *The Jesuits II: Cultures, Sciences and the Arts, 1540–1773*. John O'Malley, S.J., Gauvin Alexander Bailey, Steven J. Harris, and T. Frank Kennedy, S.J., eds. Toronto: University of Toronto Press, 2006, pp. 33–47.

Richo, David. *Mary within Us: A Jungian Contemplation of Her Titles and Powers*. Berkeley, CA: Human Development Books, 2007.

Richter, Daniel K. "Iroquois vs. Iroquois: Jesuit Missions and Christianity in Village Politics, 1642–1686." *Ethnohistory* 32: 1 (1985), pp. 1–16.

———. "War and Culture: The Iroquois Experience." *William and Mary Quarterly* 40: 4 (October 1983), pp. 528–59.

Rittgers, Ronald K. "'He Flew': A Concluding Reflection on the Place of Eternity and the Supernatural in the Scholarship of Carlos M. B. Eire." *A Linking of Heaven and Earth: Studies in Religious and Cultural History in Honor of Carlos M. N. Eire*. Emily Michelson, Scott K. Taylor, and Mary Noll Venables, eds. Burlington, VT: Ashgate, 2012, pp. 205–18.

Roberts, Jennifer. *Transporting Visions: The Movement of Images in Early America*. Berkeley: University of California Press, 2014.

Robie, Harry W. "Kiotsaeton's Three Rivers Address: An Example of 'Effective' Iroquois Oratory." *American Indian Quarterly* 6: 3/4 (Autumn–Winter 1982), pp. 238–53.

Ronda, James P. "The Sillery Experiment: A Jesuit-Indian Village in New France, 1637–1663." *American Indian Culture and Research Journal* 3: 1 (1979), pp. 1–18.

Rosenzweig, Roy. "Can History Be Open Source? *Wikipedia* and the Future of the Past." *Journal of American History* 93: 1 (June 2006), pp. 117–46.

Rothenberg, Gunther E. "Venice and the Uskoks of Senj: 1537–1618." *Journal of Modern History* 33: 2 (June 1961), pp. 148–56.

Ruiz, Teofilio. *From Heaven to Earth: The Reordering of Castilian Society, 1150–1350*. Princeton, NJ: Princeton University Press, 2004.

Rushing, Janice Hocker. "Ronald Reagan's 'Star Wars' Address: Mythic Containment of Technical Reasoning." *Quarterly Journal of Speech* 72: 4 (1986), pp. 415–33.

Ryan, Salvador. "The Persuasive Power of a Mother's Breast: The Most Desperate Act of the Virgin Mary's Advocacy." *Studia Hibernica* 32 (2002–3), pp. 59–74.

Saler, Michael. *As If: Modern Enchantment and the Literary Prehistory of Virtual Reality*. New York: Oxford University Press, 2012.

Salles-Reese, Veronica. *From Viracocha to the Virgin of Copacabana: Representations of the Sacred at Lake Titicaca*. Austin: University of Texas Press, 1997.

Sánchez Pérez, José Augusto. *El Culto Mariano en España: Tradiciones, Leyendas y Noticias Relativas a Algunas Imágenes de la Santísima Virgen*. Madrid: Instituto Antonio Nebrija, 1943.

Sanfaçon, André. "'A New Loreto in New France': Pierre-Joseph-Marie Chaumonot, S.J., and the Holy House of Loreto." *Decentring the Renaissance: Europe in Multidisciplinary Perspective, 1500–1700*. Germaine Warkentin and Carolyn Podruchny, eds. Toronto: University of Toronto Press, 2001, pp. 200–220.

Santarelli, Giuseppe. "Gli Ordini Religiosi al servizio della Santa Casa." *Il Santuario di Loreto: Sette secoli di storia, arte, devozione*. Floriano Grimaldi, ed. Rome: Autostrade, 1994, pp. 204–11.

———. *Indicazioni documentali inedite sulla traslazione della Santa Casa di Loreto*, Loreto: Congregazione Universale della Santa Casa, 1985.

———. *Loreto: Guía histórico-artística*. Angel Echeverria, trans. Ancona: Edizioni Aniballi, 1997.

———. *Tradizione e Leggende Lauretane*. Loreto, Italy: Congregazione Universale della Santa Casa, 1990.

———. *La traslazione della Santa Casa di Loreto: Tradizione e Ipotesi*. Loreto: Congregazione Universale della S. Casa, 1980.

Scheer, Monique. "From Majesty to Mystery: Change in the Meanings of Black Madonnas from the Sixteenth to Nineteenth Centuries." *American Historical Review* 107: 5 (2002): pp. 1412–40.

Schilbrack, Kevin. "Religion, Models of, and Reality: Are We Through with Geertz?" *Journal of the American Academy of Religion* 73: 2 (June 2005), pp. 429–52.

Schwartz, Stuart. *All Can Be Saved: Religious Tolerance and Salvation in the Iberian Atlantic*. New Haven, CT: Yale University Press, 2008.

Schweitzer, Albert. *The Quest of the Historical Jesus* [1911]. W. Montgomery, trans. Mineola, NY: Dover, 2005.

Seed, Patricia. *Ceremonies of Possession in Europe's Conquest of the New World, 1492–1640*. New York: Cambridge University Press, 1995.

Segal, Robert A. "The Myth-Ritualist Theory of Religion." *Journal for the Scientific Study of Religion* 19: 2 (June 1980), pp. 173–85.

Sered, Susan Starr. "Rachel's Tomb and the Milk Grotto of the Virgin Mary: Two Women's Shrines in Bethlehem." *Journal of Feminist Studies in Religion* 2: 2 (Fall 1986), pp. 7–22.

Servants of the Pierced Hearts of Joseph and Mary. "The Virgin Mary and the Holy House of Loreto." 2006–14. http://www.piercedhearts.org/treasures/holy_sites/loreto.htm. Accessed 31 May 2015.

Shalev, Zur. "The Death of Pilgrimage?" "Geographia Sacra: Cartography, Religion, and Scholarship in the Sixteenth and Seventeenth Centuries." Doctoral diss., Princeton University, 2004, pp. 82–111.

Shefrin, Elana. "*Lord of the Rings*, *Star Wars*, and Participatory Fandom: Mapping New Congruencies between the Internet and Media Entertainment Culture." *Critical Studies in Media Communication* 21: 3 (September 2004), pp. 261–81.

Simpson, Patricia. *Marguerite Bourgeoys and Montreal, 1640–1665*. Montreal: McGill-Queen's University Press, 1997.

Skendi, Stavro. "Crypto-Christianity in the Balkan Area under the Ottomans." *Slavic Review* 26: 2 (June 1967), pp. 227–46.

Smith, E. Baldwin. *Architectural Symbolism of Imperial Rome and the Middle Ages*. New York: Hacker Art Books, 1978.

Smith, Jeffrey Chipps. *Sensuous Worship: Jesuits and the Art of the Early Catholic Reformation in Germany*. Princeton, NJ: Princeton University Press, 2002.

Smith, Jonathan Z. *To Take Place: Toward Theory in Ritual*. Chicago: University of Chicago Press, 1987.

Snow, Dean R. "Iroquois-Huron Warfare." *North American Indigenous Warfare and Ritual Violence*. Richard J. Chacón and Rubén G. Mendoza, eds. Tucson: University of Arizona Press, 2007, pp. 149–59.

Soergel, Philip M. *Wondrous in His Saints: Counter-Reformation Propaganda in Bavaria*. Berkeley: University of California Press, 1993.

Sommervogel, Carlos, S.J. *Bibliothèque de la Compagnie de Jésus*. Première partie, *Bibliographie*, par Augustin et Aloys Debacker. Deuxième partie, *Histoire*, par Carlos Sommervogel, S.J. Paris: Alphonse Picard, 1890.

South China in the Sixteenth Century. C. R. Boxer, ed. London: Hakluyt Society, 1953.

Spence, Jonathan. *The Memory Palace of Matteo Ricci*. New York: Elisabeth Sifton Books, 1984.

Spitta, Silvia. *Between Two Waters: Narratives of Transculturation in Latin America*. Houston: Rice University Press, 1995.

Sronek, Michal. "The Veil of the Virgin Mary: Relics in the Conflict between Roman Catholics and Utraquists in Bohemia in the 14th and 15th Centuries." *Art* 57: 2 (2009), pp. 118–39.

Stanfield-Mazzi, Maya. *Object and Apparition: Envisioning the Christian Divine in the Colonial Andes*. Tucson: University of Arizona Press, 2013.

Stannek, Antje. "Al cospetto della Vergine." *Il Santuario di Loreto: Sette Secoli di storia arte devozione*. Rome: Autostrade, 1994, pp. 231–42.

Stefanic, Vjekoslav. "Two Frankopan Glagolitic Charters to the Paulicians." *Zbornik Historijskog Instituta Jugoslavenske Akademije*. Vol. 1. Zagreb, Yugoslavia: Historical Institute of the Yugoslav Academy of Sciences and Arts, 1954, pp. 137–48.

Stone, J. C. "Origins and Sources of the Blaeu Atlas of Scotland with Particular Reference to 'Extima Scotia' (Atlas Novus, 1654)." *Imago Mundi* 26 (1972), pp. 17–26.

Stratton, Suzanne L. *The Immaculate Conception in Spanish Art*. Cambridge, MA: Cambridge University Press, 1994.

Strelan, Rick. *Paul, Artemis and the Jews in Ephesus*. Beihefte zur Zeitschrift fur die neutestamentliche Wissenschaft (BZNW Series), vol. 80. Berlin: W. De Gruyter, 1996.

Studnicki-Gizbert, Daviken. *A Nation upon the Ocean Sea: Portugal's Atlantic Diaspora and the Crisis of the Spanish Empire, 1492–1640*. New York: Oxford University Press, 2007.

Tacchi Venturi, Pietro, S.J. *Storia della Compagnia di Gesù in Italia*. Vols. 1 and 2. Rome: Edizioni "La Civiltà Cattolica," 1950–74.

Tavard, George H. *The Thousand Faces of the Virgin Mary*. Collegeville, MN: Liturgical, 1996, pp. 146–47.

Taylor, William B. "Our Lady of Guadalupe and Friends: The Virgin Mary in Colonial Mexico City." Morrison Library Inaugural Address Series. Berkeley, CA: University of California Press, 1999.

———. "Two Shrines of the Cristo Renovado: Religion and Peasant Politics in Late Colonial Mexico." *American Historical Review* 110: 4 (October 2005), pp. 945–74.

Tilmans, Karin. "*Sancta Mater versus Sanctus Doctus?* Saint Anne and the Humanists." *Sanctity and Motherhood: Essays on Holy Mothers in the Middle Ages*. Anneke B. Mulder-Bakker, ed. New York: Garland, 1995, pp. 331–51.

Timberlake, Marie. "The Painted Colonial Image: Jesuit and Andean Fabrication of History in *Matrimonio de Garcia de Loyola con Ñusta Beatriz*." *Journal of Medieval and Early Modern Studies* 29: 3 (Fall 1999), pp. 563–98.

Triff, Kristin A. "Rhetoric and Romanitas in Thirteenth-Century Rome: Nicholas III and the Sancta Sanctorum." *Artibus et Historiae* 30: 60 (2009), pp. 71–106.

Trigger, Bruce G. *The Children of Aataentsic: A History of the Huron People to 1660*. Carleton Library Series 195. Montreal: McGill-Queen's University Press, 2000.

"Trsat and Our Lady Sanctuary." Rijeka, Croatia: Grad Rijeka, 2015. http://www.rijeka.hr/Default.aspx?sec=428. Accessed 16 May 2008.

Turner, Victor W., and Edith L. B. Turner. "Religious Celebrations." *Celebration: Studies in Festivity and Ritual*, V. W. Turner, ed., Washington, DC: Smithsonian Institution Press, 1982, pp. 201–19.

Tweed, Thomas A. *Crossing and Dwelling: A Theory of Religion*. Cambridge, MA: Harvard University Press, 2006.

Tylenda, Joseph N., S.J. "Introduction." *A Pilgrim's Journey: The Autobiography of St. Ignatius of Loyola*. San Francisco, CA: Ignatius, 2001, pp. 7–28.

Umberger, Emily. "Bac on the Border." *Anales del Instituto de Investigaciones Estéticas* 29: 91 (2007). http://dx.doi.org/10.22201/iie.18703062e.2007.91.2250. Accessed 13 April 2018.

Urton, Gary. *The History of a Myth: Pacariqtambo and the Origin of the Inkas*. Austin: University of Texas Press, 1990.

———. *Inca Myths*. London: British Museum Press, 1999.

Vallance, Edward. *Revolutionary England and the National Covenant: State Oaths, Protestantism and the Political Nation, 1553–1682*. Rochester, NY: Boydell, 2005.

Valone, Carolyn. "Women on the Quirinal Hill: Patronage in Rome, 1560–1630." *Art Bulletin* 76: 1 (March 1994), pp. 129–46.

Varela Hernández, César Iván, and Jaime Gil Jaramillo. "Dermatology from the Discovery of America to the Colony: The Influence of the Conquest and the New Diseases [in Colombia]." *History of Latin American Dermatology*. Ricardo Galimberti, Adrián Martín Pierini, and Andrea Bettina Cervini, eds. Toulouse: Éditions Prevat, 2007, pp. 115–16.

Vélez, Karin. "Catholic Missions to the Americas." *The Ashgate Research Companion to the Counter-Reformation*. Alexandra Bamji, Geert Janssen, and Mary Laven, eds. Burlington, VT: Ashgate, 2013, pp. 147–62.

———. "'Do Not Suppose That Those Tears Proceed from Weakness': Jesuit Weeping on Mission Frontiers, 1560–1760." *Frontiers of Mission: Perspectives on Early Modern Missionary Catholicism*. Alison Forrestal and Séan Alexander Smith, eds. Boston: Brill, 2016, pp. 22–41.

———. "'A Sign That We Are Related to You': The Transatlantic Gifts of the Hurons of the Jesuit Mission of Lorette, 1650–1750." *French Colonial History* 12 (2011), pp. 31–44.

———. "Stones and Bones: Catholic Responses to the 1812 Collapse of the Mission Church of Capistrano." *Material Religion: The Journal of Objects, Art and Belief*, 2017. http://dx.doi.org/10.1080/17432200.2017.1379375. Accessed 13 April 2018.

———. "Urban Driftwood: Mobile Catholic Markers and the Extension of the Seventeenth-Century Atlantic Public Sphere." *Urban Identity and the Atlantic*

World. Elizabeth Fay and Leonard von Morzé, eds. Palgrave-MacMillan, 2013, pp. 61–76.

———. "Les Voyages outre-mer d'un nom: De Loreto en Italie à la Jeune-Lorette au Canada" / "The Overseas Travels of a Name: From Italy's Loreto to Canada's Jeune Lorette." *Revue d'histoire de l'Amérique française* 64: 3–4 (March 2013), número thématique, "Nouvelle-France et le monde Atlantique français," Thomas Wien and Catherine Desbarats, eds., pp. 119–44.

Verástique, Bernardino. *Michoacán and Eden: Vasco de Quiroga and the Evangelization of Western Mexico*. Austin: University of Texas Press, 2000.

Vernon, Edward W. *Las Misiones Antiguas: The Spanish Missions of Baja California, 1683–1855*. Santa Barbara, CA: Viejo, 2002.

Vigneras, Louis-André. "Saint Thomas, Apostle of America." *Hispanic American Historical Review* 57: 1 (February 1977), pp. 82–90.

Villaseñor Black, Charlene. "St. Anne Imagery and Maternal Archetypes in Spain and Mexico." *Colonial Saints: Discovering the Holy in the Americas, 1500–1800*. Allan Greer and Jodi Bilinkoff, eds. New York: Routledge, 2003, pp. 3–29.

The Virgin, Saints and Angels: South American Paintings 1600–1825 from the Thoma Collection. Suzanne Stratton-Pruitt, ed. Stanford, CA: Skira, 2006.

Vucinich, Wayne S. "Review: *Radovi Staroslavenskog Instituta*." *Speculum* 32: 1 (January 1957), pp. 202–7.

Waller, Gary. *Walsingham and the English Imagination*. Burlington, VT: Ashgate, 2011.

Ward, Haruko Nawata. "Jesuits, Too: Jesuits, Women Catechists, and Jezebels in Christian-Century Japan." *The Jesuits II: Cultures, Sciences and the Arts, 1540–1773*. John O'Malley, S.J., Gauvin Alexander Bailey, Steven J. Harris, and T. Frank Kennedy, S.J., eds. Toronto: University of Toronto Press, 2006, pp. 637–57.

Warner, Marina. "Mater Dolorosa." *Alone of All Her Sex: The Myth and the Cult of the Virgin Mary*. New York: Random House, 1983, pp. 206–23.

Watkins, Carl S. *History and the Supernatural in Medieval England*. New York: Cambridge University Press, 2007.

Webb, Diana. *Patrons and Defenders: The Saints in the Italian City States*. New York: I. B. Tauris, 1996.

Wessels, C. *Early Jesuit Travellers in Central Asia, 1603–1721*. New Delhi, India: Asian Educational Services, 1997.

Winston-Allen, Anne. *Stories of the Rose: The Making of the Rosary in the Middle Ages*. University Park: Penn State University Press, 1997.

Witcombe, Christopher L. C. E. "Sixtus V and the Scala Santa." *Journal of the Society of Architectural Historians* 44: 4 (December 1985), pp. 368–79.

Wolff, Larry. *Venice and the Slavs: The Discovery of Dalmatia in the Age of Enlightenment*. Stanford, CA: Stanford University Press, 2001.

Wonderly, Anthony. *Oneida Iroquois Folklore, Myth and History: New York Oral Narrative from the Notes of H. E. Allen and Others*. Syracuse, NY: Syracuse University Press, 2004.

Worcester, Thomas, S.J. "Anti-Jesuit Polemic." *The Cambridge Encyclopedia of the Jesuits*. Thomas Worcester, ed. New York: Cambridge University Press, 2017, pp. 30–35.

Wright, Jonathan. *God's Soldiers: Adventure, Politics, Intrigue and Power—a History of the Jesuits*. New York: Doubleday, 2004.

Zarandona, Juan Miguel. "The Biography of Vasco de Quiroga (1470–1565), Bishop of Utopia, by Benjamin Jarnés (1881–1949)." *Spaces of Utopia: An Electronic Journal*, no. 3 (Autumn/Winter 2006), pp. 69–83. http://ler.letras.up.pt. Accessed 13 April 2018.

Zarri, Gabriella. "From Prophecy to Discipline, 1450–1650." Keith Bosford, trans. *Women and Faith: Catholic Religious Life in Italy from Late Antiquity to the Present*. Cambridge, MA: Harvard University Press, 1999, pp. 83–112.

Zupanov, Ines G. "Aristocratic Analogies and Demotic Descriptions in the Seventeenth-Century Madurai Mission." *Representations* 41 (Winter, 1993), pp. 123–48.

INDEX

A NOTE ON THE TYPE

THIS BOOK has been composed in Miller, a Scotch Roman typeface designed by Matthew Carter and first released by Font Bureau in 1997. It resembles Monticello, the typeface developed for The Papers of Thomas Jefferson in the 1940s by C. H. Griffith and P. J. Conkwright and reinterpreted in digital form by Carter in 2003.

Pleasant Jefferson ("P. J.") Conkwright (1905–1986) was Typographer at Princeton University Press from 1939 to 1970. He was an acclaimed book designer and AIGA Medalist.

The ornament used throughout this book was designed by Pierre Simon Fournier (1712–1768) and was a favorite of Conkwright's, used in his design of the *Princeton University Library Chronicle*.